a special gift

presented to:

_____

from:

_____

date:

_____

The Women's Devotional Series

Among Friends
The Listening Heart
A Gift of Love
A Moment of Peace
Close to Home
From the Heart
This Quiet Place
In God's Garden
Fabric of Faith
Alone With God
Bouquets of Hope
Colors of Grace
Beautiful in God's Eyes
A Word From Home
Morning Praise
Heaven's Whisper
Grace Notes
Sanctuary
Love Out Loud
Renew
Blessed
Breathe
Altogether Lovely
Living His Love
Love You More
Notes of Joy
In His Presence
I Am Loved
Color My World With Love
Covered and Carried
New Every Morning
He Knows My Name

Almost Home

Karen Pearson
EDITOR

Pacific Press®
Publishing Association
Nampa, Idaho | www.pacificpress.com

Cover design: Erika Mike
Cover image: ©Freezmanstudio | Dreamstime.com
Interior design: Aaron Troia

Copyright © 2025 by General Conference of Seventh-day Adventists
Printed in the United States of America
All rights reserved

The authors assume full responsibility for the accuracy of all facts and quotations as cited in this book.

Scripture quotations marked ESV are from The Holy Bible, English Standard Version® (ESV®), copyright © 2001 by Crossway, a publishing ministry of Good News Publishers. Used by permission. All rights reserved.
Scripture quotations marked KJV are from the King James Version.
Scripture quotations marked TLB are from *The Living Bible,* copyright © 1971 by Tyndale House Foundation. Used by permission of Tyndale House Publishers Inc., Carol Stream, Illinois 60188. All rights reserved.
Scripture quotations marked *The Message* are from *The Message,* copyright © 1993, 2002, 2018 by Eugene H. Peterson. Used by permission of NavPress Publishing Group. Represented by Tyndale House Publishers, Inc.
Scripture quotations marked NASB are from the New American Standard Bible®, Copyright © 1960, 1971, 1977, 1995, 2020 by The Lockman Foundation. All rights reserved.
Scripture quotations marked NIV are from THE HOLY BIBLE, NEW INTERNATIONAL VERSION®. Copyright © 1973, 1978, 1984, 2011 by Biblica, Inc.® Used by permission. All rights reserved worldwide.
Scripture quotations marked NKJV are from the New King James Version®. Copyright © 1982 by Thomas Nelson. Used by permission. All rights reserved.
Scripture quotations marked NLT are from the Holy Bible, New Living Translation, copyright © 1996, 2004, 2007, 2013, 2015 by Tyndale House Foundation. Used by permission of Tyndale House Publishers, Inc., Carol Stream, Illinois 60188. All rights reserved.
Scripture quotations marked NLV are from the New Life Version copyright © 1969 and 2003. Used by permission of Barbour Publishing, Inc., Uhrichsville, Ohio, 44683. All rights reserved.
Scripture quotations marked RSV are from the Revised Standard Version of the Bible, copyright © 1946, 1952, 1971 by the Division of Christian Education of the National Council of the Churches of Christ in the U.S.A. Used by permission.

To order additional copies of this book, call toll-free 1-800-765-6955, or visit AdventistBookCenter.com.

Library of Congress Cataloging-in-Publication Data
Names: Pearson, Karen (Editor), editor.
Title: Almost home / Karen Pearson, editor.
Description: Nampa, Idaho : Pacific Press, Publishing Association, [2025] | Summary: "A collection of 365 devotional thoughts for women to encourage and strengthen faith"— Provided by publisher.
Identifiers: LCCN 2025002437 (print) | LCCN 2025002438 (ebook) |
  ISBN 9780816370733 (trade paperback) | ISBN 9780816370740 (ebook)
Subjects: LCSH: Christian women—Prayers and devotions. | Christian women—Religious life. | Devotional calendars.
Classification: LCC BV4844 .A338 2025 (print) | LCC BV4844 (ebook) |
  DDC 242/.643—dc23/eng/20250312
LC record available at https://lccn.loc.gov/2025002437
LC ebook record available at https://lccn.loc.gov/2025002438

May 2025

Dear Reader,

One of the achievements of Rose Otis, the first General Conference director of Women's Ministries, was beginning a scholarship fund for college women who need a little financial help. Her dream of a women's devotional book written by women for women with proceeds channeled into the scholarship fund became a reality in 1992. The edition you hold in your hands, *Almost Home*, is the thirty-fourth book. To date, we have awarded nearly $1.5 million for 2,838 scholarships to Adventist women attending college or university in 147 countries. The newest countries represented are Gabon Equatorial Guinea and Gambia.

The devotional book is an international Women's Ministries project. Meet our Women's Ministries (WM) leaders in the world field:

Debbie Maloba, East-Central Africa Division WM director
Akseniya Liberanskaya, Euro-Asia Division WM director
Edith Ruiz-Espinoza, Inter-American Division WM director
Dagmar Dorn, Inter-European Division WM director
DeeAnn Bragaw, North American Division WM director
Raquel Arrais, Northern Asia-Pacific Division WM director
Jeanete Lima de Souza Pinto, South American Division WM director
Eva Ing, South Pacific Division WM supervisor
Margery Herinirina, Southern Africa-Indian Ocean Division WM director
Krupa Victor, Southern Asia Division WM director
Virginia Baloyo, Southern Asia-Pacific Division WM director
Karen Holford, Trans-European Division WM director
Omobonike Adeola Sessou, West-Central Africa Division WM director
Nickey Shum, Chinese Union Mission WM director
Amal Fawzy, Middle East and North Africa Union Mission, WM liaison
Irina Begas, Ukrainian Union Conference WM director
Ross Ann Krishner, Israel Field WM director

It is our hope that this edition will connect you day by day with women who live, love, and grow in faith in different corners of our global home. And that proceeds from the sales of 2026 WM devotional book will enable more women to finish their education and serve their families, churches, and communities more effectively.

Best wishes,
Galina Stele
Women's Ministries Director
General Conference of Seventh-day Adventists

Dear Reader,

You are part of something beautiful! In your hands, you hold more than just stories of God working in the lives of women around the world—you hold opportunity, promise, and hope.

The stories in this book are more than words on a page. Through the purchase of this devotional, you are helping provide scholarships for undergraduate women in the North American Division. These young women represent the hope of future generations as they prepare to serve Jesus in their chosen fields. We encourage you to pause and pray for these women in whose lives you have a part. And as you read, we also invite you to reflect on and share your own story of God's work in your life. Because He is working—right here, right now, through you.

With gratitude and hope,
DeeAnn Bragaw
Erica Smith
Women's Ministries
North American Division

Women Helping Women

There is an aspect of this book that is unique
None of the contributors have been paid—each has shared freely so that all profits may go to scholarships for women. Recipients of the Women's Ministries scholarships are talented women who are committed to serving the mission of the Seventh-day Adventist Church.

General Conference Women's Ministries scholarship fund in the North American Division
All profits from sales of the Women's Ministries devotional book in the North American Division support women's higher education in Seventh-day Adventist colleges and universities in the United States and Canada.

Purpose of the women's devotional book
Among Friends, published in 1992, was the first annual women's devotional book. Since then, the proceeds from these devotional books have funded scholarships for Adventist women seeking to obtain higher education. But as tuition costs have soared in North America and more women have applied for assistance, funding has not kept pace with the need. Many worthy women who apply must be turned down.

Recognizing the importance of educating women—to build stronger families, stronger communities, and a stronger church—each of us can help. Together we can change lives!

There are many ways to support our sisters
- Pray for women worldwide who are struggling to get an education.
- Tell others about the Women's Ministries scholarship program.
- Write for the women's devotional book (guidelines are available).
- Support women's education with a financial gift or a pledge.

To make a gift or receive materials, send us the following information:

Name _____

Street _____

City _____ State/Province _____

Postal Code _____ Country _____

Email _____

To contact us:
Women's Ministries Department   Phone: 443-391-7265
9705 Patuxent Woods Drive   Email: ericajones@nadadventist.org
Columbia, MD 21046   Website: https://www.nadwm.org/

The scholarship application and devotional book writers' guidelines are available on our website.

January 1

The Mountains Between Here and Home

Seek those things which are above, where Christ is, sitting at the right hand of God. Set your mind on things above, not on things on the earth.
—Colossians 3:1, 2, NKJV

Our camping trip had been a success, and as we packed up, my husband suggested climbing Mount Princeton, a nearby "fourteener" (a peak above fourteen thousand feet elevation). It was nearly noon, long past the typical early-morning start of such a climb, but the clear skies and perfect weather beckoned us.

Our two young sons eagerly agreed to the idea, so instead of heading home, we drove toward the trailhead. Suddenly pulling off the steep road, my mountaineer husband pointed out a faint trail leading toward the peak.

"Let's take this way instead of the main route! It'll save us time."

Rugged beauty surrounded us, and our spirits were high as we climbed. After reaching the summit late in the afternoon, we paused to snap a family photo before deciding to hike back down the well-traveled main trail. Tired legs and only one headlamp slowed our descent. The boys cheered when we reached the trailhead sign, but we all knew we still had far to go to where we had parked farther down the steep road. After a long time, our youngest grew anxious and voiced a question we all shared.

"Shouldn't we be back at the truck by now, Dad? What if something happened to it? How will we get home?"

My husband reassured him that angels were watching over us, we were together, and Jesus would take care of us. Praying aloud and singing together boosted our spirits as we hiked on in the dark. At last, we rounded another steep curve, and the same son let out a happy shout! We found the truck right where we had left it. All was well as we headed home.

On the journey to our ultimate home, we will face daunting mountains. Even on sunny days the path can be long and steep, and weariness may set in. The darkness of fear and discouragement may threaten to overwhelm us, and we might begin to wonder whether something has happened that could prevent us from reaching home. But together, let us keep going, singing songs of hope and courage, knowing Jesus has promised His presence to light the way.

Together, let us keep our eyes on Jesus, the One who started and will finish our faith journey. We are almost home!

DeeAnn Bragaw

January 2

A New Thing

"Forget the former things;
do not dwell on the past.
See, I am doing a new thing!
Now it springs up; do you not perceive it?
I am making a way in the wilderness
and streams in the wasteland."
—Isaiah 43:18, 19, NIV

It was a brand-new year, the beginning of a new month, a new day, and a new start, all on the same day. Awakening early that morning, as my habit, I looked out the window. My eyes were captivated by a spectacular scenic moment. The bright yellow moon setting in the vibrant blue sky was as clear as crystal. Its brilliance lit up the atmosphere and everything nearby. I was stunned. It was a special moment God had prepared just for me, and I felt incredibly blessed to be the recipient.

The scripture that tells of God doing a new thing resonated in my mind.

"Forget the former things;
do not dwell on the past.
See, I am doing a new thing!
Now it springs up; do you not perceive it?
I am making a way in the wilderness
and streams in the wasteland" (Isaiah 43:18, 19, NIV).

As I stood savoring the moment, I sensed the nearness of God's presence with me. A profound feeling of gratitude flowed through me, compelling me to express a prayer of thanksgiving to Him for this moment. I thanked Him for His extraordinary favor in carrying my family and me safely through all the ups and downs of the previous year and for granting us the honor of seeing the beginning of another new year.

At eighty-two years old, I do not have a clue of God's plans for me or how He wants to use me this year, but I humbly surrender myself to Him and pray He will do a new thing in me. I want Him to fill me with the desire to faithfully follow Him and help me to serve Him willingly in whatever capacity He chooses.

His words through King David encourage me to trust Him as I press onward. "I will instruct you and teach you in the way you should go; I will counsel you with my loving eye on you" (Psalm 32:8, NIV).

Dear heavenly Father, thank You for forgiving all my sins and giving me incredible glimpses of Your unshakable love for me.

Shirley C. Iheanacho

January 3

Hide-and-Seek

Be still, and know.
—Psalm 46:10, KJV

Have you played hide-and-seek lately? If you have little ones, chances are good you have. Their precious giggles usually give away their hiding spot. It is so hard to keep very still when you are excited!

I will never forget the time I hid in the closet in my house when I was growing up. I had discovered the perfect spot. It was hard to get tucked in behind all the card tables and chairs without making any noise, but I did it. I could hear the joyful screams as each hider was found, and I was basking in my hiding prowess. But after a while, I realized I had been hiding for a long time. Eventually, all the happy voices were gone, and it was dark. I was alone and scared.

Isn't this like life at times? Everything is going great, and then something awful or unexpected happens. That is why Scripture reminds us to "fear not" more than three hundred times throughout the Word. But fear, anxiety, and depression are hard to deal with on your own. God tells us in Psalm 46:10, "Be still, and know that I am God" (KJV). He knows our situation. He sees where we are hiding. He knows we are scared. *Trust Me*, He says—*I am God!*

He does not forget about us and move on to someone or something more important. He is right there in the dark with us, and He asks us to cry out to Him. "I sought the Lord," wrote the psalmist, "and he heard me, and delivered me from all my fears" (Psalm 34:4, KJV).

Last year, I was getting ready for elective surgery to replace my right knee with a "bionic" one. Woo-hoo! I admit I was a bit frightened at the prospects of what could happen. As I lay on the uncomfortable table with a big X marked on my good knee and the doctor's initials on the bad knee, I felt so alone. Then the thought came to mind, *"Be still, and know"* (Psalm 46:10, KJV). God had this! I did not need to fear.

How are things with you? It seems every family has something scary going on these days. Now, my deal was not life-threatening, but yours might be. I do not know what I would have done without Jesus and His promises. God has so many texts that remind us He is there and that He cares. He wants to still the storm in your heart. Seek Him. Wait for Him. He will deliver you.

Cheri Gatton

January 4

Today

Oh that men would praise the Lord for his goodness,
and for his wonderful works to the children of men!
—Psalm 107:8, KJV

Today is not just another day. Today, God reveals more of the myriad ways He communicates with me and the opportunities He gives me to praise Him and emulate His love. Am I prepared for today? Maybe not. But I trust Him, and each day He prepares for me is never just another day.

Today, I roll out of bed and trudge to the kitchen to make breakfast for my three roommates. I linger a little longer by the large kitchen window, taking in the beauty of the untamed country yard. The neighbor's rottweilers are barking more than usual at three little boys who are rummaging through a garbage bin in the nearby park. The two older ones watch while the youngest stands on tippy toes to reach for something inside the bin.

One of my roommates calls out to them, "What are you searching for?"

"Bottles!" one of the older boys shouts.

How did we not notice them before today? I wondered. *Is this how they spend their Sundays? Going through the garbage in our neighborhood in search of scraps the residents had thrown out after their Saturday night parties?*

Today, we notice them and call them over to our house. We learn their names and find out they are related—two brothers and one cousin from the same children's home. Their mission is to find bottles to sell so they can buy food for themselves. They are hungry. The youngest one reaches into his backpack for the one hard-boiled egg they must share between them. We notice it has cracked open during their foraging. They are wearing grubby clothes. Their feet are dirty. Their toenails poke through the holes in the dilapidated shoes they wear.

Today, we feed them breakfast and send them off with food to share with the others at the children's home. Today is not just another day. It is the day that God gives me to live for Him. Today, He shows me how rich I am in His love. Today, I forget about student loans and other financial woes. Today, God has shown me that He is faithful. Today, I thank Him for my family and roommates and for opportunities like these—to glorify Him through serving others. Today, I praise the Lord for His goodness and His wonderful works to the children of men!

Joan Dougherty-Mornan

January 5

Embracing God's Gift of Time

*For everything there is a season,
a time for every activity under heaven.
A time to be born and a time to die. . . .
A time to cry and a time to laugh.
A time to grieve and a time to dance.*
—Ecclesiastes 3:1–4, NLT

The most important time in life does not lie in the future nor in the past. It is right now. That might sound strange to those of us who have our sights set on the future. We have lots of plans, things we want to do, castles to build, and goals to reach. We live for the success that will surely come to us. The most important time in life is still ahead.

For others, our greatest moments lie behind us. We remember the battles we have fought and won, the glamour and recognition that crowned our career. We think of ourselves as the person who did this or that. We believe the most important time in life is behind us. Yet, today is the only slice of time that we really own.

An old story revolves around a group of men who are arguing over the best time to cut an ash stick. One argued it was in the spring when the sap was rising.

Another said, "No, summer is the best time because the wood is at its best."

The third disagreed entirely. He said, "The fall is the best time to cut the ash stick because the sap has matured and seasoned the wood."

The fourth argued, "Winter is the best time because the sap is gone and the wood can be cut smoothly."

Finally, the men decided to seek out the local agricultural expert and ask him. The expert listened to the arguments of the four, and then the four men pressed their question, "When do you say is the best time to cut an ash stick?"

The expert thought for a moment and then replied, "The best time to cut it, gentlemen, is when you see one, because it may not be there the next time you pass by."

God puts great emphasis on the present. "Today, if you will hear His voice, do not harden your hearts" (Hebrews 4:7, NKJV), and "Today is the day of salvation" (2 Corinthians 6:2, NLT). Now is the only time we own, the only time to do His precious will. Do not wait until tomorrow, for the clock may then be still. Today is at hand. Time stops for no man. All we hold in our hands is this moment—now. The time to do something about life eternal can only be done today. Tomorrow is yet to come, though it is not guaranteed. Yesterday is history. But we have today! Let us embrace God's gift of time and not waste a moment.

Mary Ranjan

January 6

Praise Ye the Lord

I will praise you, Lord my God, with all my heart;
I will glorify your name forever.
—Psalm 86:12, NIV

I turn to God for everything. Everything! That is the problem. I have found that my communication with God has become one of ask! Ask! Ask! Life is filled with so many issues, so many circumstances, cares, burdens. I am not able to fix many of them on my own.

Jesus told me to cast all my cares on Him, for He cares for me (1 Peter 5:7, my paraphrase). He also said I should bring all my burdens to Him, and He will give me rest (Matthew 11:28, my paraphrase). I take Him up on this offer. Constantly.

The problem is that I forget to praise God. I forget to give thanks as often as I ask things of God. For example, I get on an airplane, and I pray and ask God for a safe journey. After the plane lands, with all the activity involved in disembarking, I forget to give thanks for the safe journey. I take God's care for granted.

In Psalm 50:23, God says, "Whoso offereth praise glorifieth me" (KJV). My connection and communication with God need to be one of worship and praise. He has answered my prayers; He has blessed me. His handiwork is all around me. He makes so much possible. He cares about the little things in my life. Even when I think something is too small to ask God to intervene, He cares. His presence surrounds me. I must praise Him.

It is easy to call on God when things are bad, but when things work out, we often forget God is the reason they worked out. It is easy to think things work out because of our own effort. While hard work and effort are essential, it is because of God's hand in everything that we accomplish what would not be possible without His intervention.

I praise God because of my relationship with Him—a relationship that will be reflected in all I do. Then, the world will see Jesus in me and want to know more. I will be a witness to the love of God. It all starts with praising God and giving glory to Him. The challenge is to remember not to take God for granted. So let us say with David, "I will praise you, Lord my God, with all my heart; I will glorify your name forever" (Psalm 86:12, NIV).

Jean Arthur

January 7

Surrounded, Yet Still Singing

They began to sing and praise.
—2 Chronicles 20:22, NKJV

It was a crazy time to start singing. Dressed up in battle gear, they were headed out to battle a bunch of enemies who had come together to destroy them. They were outnumbered and no match for the armies coming toward them. Yet they geared up and headed out to meet them—with the singers in front of the soldiers. Picture the awkward seventh-grader with a squeaky voice and lanky body headed out to fight the senior football team. And he is singing.

Then something crazy happens.

The enemy hears them singing about how big and great their God is and becomes confused. They start to fight each other. By the time the small army gets to a break in the trees where they can see down onto the battlefield (they are not there yet), the enemy is dead. They have killed each other. There is no one to fight. That is hard to believe! They head down to check it out, their courage building. They get there and not only find it is true but also spend the next three days gathering treasures from a battle they never had to fight.

I think God shares this story in 2 Chronicles 20 to give us a battle plan. When life is hard and we do not know what to do, when one thing right after another seems to hit us and we are ready to give up, when hope and courage are hard to find, when we just want to hide under the covers or eat a quart of mint chocolate chip ice cream or focus on a screen instead of the problems or buy something new or do whatever you do to hide and cope—this story challenges us to turn to God. I'm not saying just pray a quick prayer and then get back to hiding or fighting the "whatever" on our own. I'm saying stay focused on the God who is bigger. Start singing praises. Look the battle in the eye and believe God has a plan.

And when we start to sing and trust God instead of hiding or trying to fight it on our own, our enemy will be confused. Our confidence that God has us will make him afraid.

It is not an easy game plan. We tend to want to do something. Fix it. We want to whine and complain and vent, not sing. We would rather run and hide in something that brings comfort instead of facing conflict. But in those moments, cue the singing. Give it a try the next time you feel overwhelmed and defeated. You have nothing to lose but fear and discouragement.

Tamyra Horst

January 8

Heaven, the Happy City

This is the Lord *for whom we have waited;*
Let us rejoice and be glad in His salvation.
—Isaiah 25:9, NASB

Even if you run your finger down a list of fun cities to visit, no two cities appeal to every traveler. Some cities are proud of their parks, outdoor concerts, or historical sites. Tourists who like to gamble go to towns and hope to win at the gaming tables. Adventurous skiers drawn to rustic settings seek snowy slopes and cozy lodges. Some cities famously tempt visitors to indulge in the decadence readily available on their streets.

The Old Testament reveals much about the future City of God. In His newly created earth, God promises to lay low arrogant man-made cities (see Isaiah 26:5). Throughout Isaiah, the prophet describes heaven by repeatedly using the words *rejoice, joy,* and *gladness*. Compared to our earthly existence, the New Jerusalem will be branded a happy city.

Besides the golden streets and sparkling gates, the veil will be gone—the separation between God and man will be eradicated. We will see God as He is. His peace and justice will be established, and the earth's beauty will be restored. Isaiah adds that the voice of weeping will not be heard (see Isaiah 65:19). Ultimately, for the people who love the Lord, there will be no more tears (see Revelation 21:4).

The biggest difference in the city, I think, is that death will be swallowed up—in victory (see 1 Corinthians 15:54). When you consider human life, death remains the main source of our sorrow on this side of heaven. It is beyond our capacity to prevent death. While tears may be cathartic, the weeping that arises from the sting of death springs from a primal cry deep within our hearts. Isaiah reminded his readers of the pain experienced at the death of the innocent, and David bemoaned the death of the righteous.

Thank God that one day soon the sting will be gone forever as Christ conquers sin and suffering eternally. When God unites with His people, the Righteous Judge Himself will wipe away our tears and bring healing in His wings (see Malachi 4:2). The righteous dead will live again: "You who dwell in the dust, awake and sing for joy!" (Isaiah 26:19, ESV).

Courage, friends. We are almost home!

Elinor Harvin Burks

January 9

Focus

"Stop striving and know that I am God; I will be exalted among the nations, I will be exalted on the earth."
—Psalm 46:10, NASB

Strive: "to devote serious effort or energy."*
Know: "to perceive directly, have direct cognition of. . . . **Synonyms**: comprehend, grasp, understand."†
Exalted: "held in high estimation: glorified or praised."‡ **Synonyms**: glorious, honored, celebrated.§

Here is my version of Psalm 46:10: "Stop working so hard to save yourself and grasp that I am God; I will be honored among the nations, I will be celebrated on the earth."

Why do we put so much effort into attempting something that is not our job? *Our* job consists of honoring God with our thoughts, deeds, and actions. We honor God by spending time with Him; loving those He loves; serving those He would serve; doing right, loving mercy, and keeping Him uppermost in our thoughts.

We celebrate Him, who He is, and what He does. We celebrate Him as the guest of honor each moment of our lives.

How? you ask. We cannot stop whispers of doubt, birds of depression, moths of insecurities, and glimmers of addictions from lingering around us. We can bolt the door of our minds and slam shut the windows to keep out the whispering, depressive, and insecure thoughts. We can snip the addictions in the early stages before they become deeply rooted in our lives. But how? Through His power, not ours. By lifting our thoughts to Him moment by moment.

When my daughter was three years old, I took her to gymnastics lessons. The activity provided an extra hour of mommy-daughter bonding after a long day of teaching for me, and an outlet for her creative, boundless energy. She loved falling into the foam pit. She did her best to tumble, roll, and walk the long balance beam. I watched her from the bleachers. Eyes fixed a few inches from her feet, she wobbled her way across the beam until she fell into the pit. In the car, on the way home, we discussed the challenge.

"Focus on the end of the beam," I encouraged. "Look as far down the beam as you can. Your feet will follow the beam."

Now, those words echo in my head. Focus on Jesus. Look at His life, His words, His actions. Follow Him while walking the balance beam of life. It will lead us home.

Faith Ann Laughlin

---

* *Merriam Webster*, s.v. "strive," accessed Nov. 11, 2024, https://unabridged.merriam-webster.com/collegiate/strive.
† *Merriam Webster*, s.v. "know," accessed Nov. 11, 2024, https://unabridged.merriam-webster.com/collegiate/know.
‡ *Merriam Webster*, s.v. "exalted," accessed Nov. 11, 2024, https://www.merriam-webster.com/dictionary/exalted.
§ *Merriam Webster Thesaurus*, s.v. "exalted," accessed Nov. 11, 2024, https://www.merriam-webster.com/thesaurus/exalted.

January 10

Waiting for Tammy

"Watch therefore, for you do not know what hour your Lord is coming."
—Matthew 24:42, NKJV

The tropical storm watch was elevated to a hurricane warning when Hurricane Tammy metamorphosed into a Category 1 storm. All weather and governmental advisories pled with residents to prepare for the storm. For some, that meant grocery shopping, stocking up on food and other essentials, or filling their vehicles with fuel. For others, it meant relocating to a safe shelter. Hurricane shutters were activated, and we battened down. We had experienced the wrath of previous hurricanes. We knew what to expect. Then we waited.

The rain started on Friday and fell spasmodically as the day transitioned into night, but there were no wind gusts. Sabbath was the same. We wondered if the hurricane had changed its course but learned it had slowed down and was scheduled to reach the Leeward Islands in the northeastern Caribbean Sea by Saturday night. We waited, listening for the wind, but none came.

It occurred to me that there were many similarities between waiting for the hurricane and waiting for Jesus' second coming. The meteorologists gave the coordinates, informed us of Tammy's movements, and predicted possible times it would make landfall. We expected the hurricane, and we prepared for it. Jesus' second coming has been prophesied. We know that the gospel must be preached in all the world, and then Jesus will come. Like the hurricane, we know the conditions that will signal His return, but unlike the hurricane, we do not know the date or time. So we must prepare and be ready.

Preparation for Jesus' return does not require hurricane shutters or shelters or grocery shopping. Our preparation is an internal surrender to Jesus and our commitment to follow His guidance, which will be manifested externally. Jesus is the Way. We follow Him, surrender daily to Him, and grow in our faith.

When hurricanes change course and weaken or fizzle out, do we regret the time and effort we gave to prepare for the storm? Never! So let us prepare for His return and stay ready, busily engaged in our Master's business. Let Jesus find us ready when He comes to take His children home. We are almost there!

Valerie Knowles Combie

January 11

Random Acts of Kindness

"Thus says the Lord of hosts, '. . . Show kindness and mercy to one another.'"
—Zechariah 7:9, ESV

For many years I have been practicing random acts of kindness. It is a lot of fun and so rewarding to know you have made a difference in someone's life—no matter how small.

Recently, I was in a dollar store, standing in line to pay for my few purchases. Behind me stood a teenage boy with three bottles of beverage. He had three dollars and change out, waiting for his turn to pay the cashier. I could tell he had an attitude going on and thought to myself, *This could be interesting.* I told the cashier I had yet to do my random act of kindness for the day, so I wanted to pay for the young man behind me. When his turn came, he was told his purchases had been paid for. He thanked the cashier and then looked daggers at me. The cashier told him not to thank her but to thank me, which he very grudgingly did before he walked out the door.

Kindness, even when it is not appreciated or reciprocated, is always appropriate and never wasted. Mother Teresa is credited with the counsel, "Be the living expression of God's kindness: kindness in your face, kindness in your eyes, kindness in your smile." Kindness, even when rebuffed, will eventually start a seed growing, and the result will be magnificent. Won't we have a wonderful time when we eventually get to heaven and find out that some of the seeds we have planted have grown into delightful fruit for the spiritual life?

Before Jesus comes, we all need an attitude adjustment. This boy was a minority, and I consider myself to be one too—just being old puts me in that category. Those of you who are older might know what I am talking about. Maybe he has never heard that Jesus loves every one of us the same. Maybe he has never heard about the saving grace of a Savior who came and died for him. Whatever the case, it appeared that this boy, in his short life, had learned to dislike certain people. How sad, because these feelings are taught or come from unpleasant experiences. Whatever the case, I saw this as an opportunity to pray for this young man, to ask Jesus to help him in his walk through life, and I have not stopped remembering him. Can Jesus work a miracle? Yes, He can.

Jesus invites us to "show kindness and mercy." Let us fervently pray for one another and show kindness every day. Jesus is coming soon.

Grace A. Keene

January 12

Seeds of Kindness

Whatsoever a man soweth, that shall he also reap.
—Galatians 6:7, KJV

The Bible often uses metaphors to convey wisdom and truth. One example of this is sowing seeds of love and righteousness that will blossom into beautiful things later in life.

On Sunday mornings, I normally go for a run, then to the gym for a swim. One week, as I completed my swim and headed for the sauna to relax, I passed a young lady with her two daughters.

She asked, "Are you Deborah?"

When I responded "Yes," she told me she recognized me from Bethel College, in Butterworth, South Africa, from more than twenty-five years ago. I was pleasantly surprised and asked if she had been a student of mine at the primary school. She said she remembered me all these years because of one particular day in church when I was asked to pray and how I had appealed to God for help, as a people, to accept things we cannot change and to grant us the ability to make a difference.

"That prayer," she said, "has stayed with me my entire life."

I was stunned someone would remember a prayer I had long forgotten but grateful my words had left a positive impact on this lady.

As I drove home, I gave glory to God for using me to make a difference in one person's life. Then I wondered, *If I had said or done something harmful to her, how would I have felt on meeting up with her again?*

It is important for us to be intentional in how we engage with people. We live in a world where people who hold opposing views choose to break each other down and cut people from their lives. How can we keep from falling prey to this disease?

I believe as we pursue inner peace, we should balance it by making this world a better place through planting seeds of kindness to all we meet. A kind word, a prayer, and an act of love can go a long way. People are struggling with personal challenges, making it all the more important to be wise with our words and ensure we plant seeds that bear fruit for eternity.

Kindness is a seed that when cultivated will grow. Kindness is knowing the right thing to do and possessing the courage to do it. Kindness gives hope to those who feel all alone in this world. Dear sisters, it is my prayer we will continue to sow seeds of kindness and that we will reap a rich harvest throughout eternity.

Deborah Matshaya

January 13

My Turn

Give, and it shall be given unto you; good measure, pressed down, and shaken together, and running over, shall men give into your bosom. For with the same measure that ye mete withal it shall be measured to you again.
—Luke 6:38, KJV

One Friday I hurried to run some errands in preparation for the fast-approaching Sabbath. While at a local grocery store, I exchanged pleasant words with a woman in a produce aisle. After I had all I needed in my shopping cart, I headed for the check-out line and noticed the same lady standing directly behind me. As I prepared to pay for my groceries, I felt impressed to pay for her things in addition to mine. I have been praying for more strength to follow divine instructions when they are given. I have found it helps me avoid rationalizing myself out of doing what I have been asked to do and thereby missing the opportunity to stand for Jesus. So I quickly told her I would pay for both of our purchases. When she realized what was happening, she protested, then soon began to thank me.

Perhaps only she and God knew what was happening in her life that day and knew her needs. I smiled, feeling warm inside during the exchange and over the next few days whenever it crossed my mind. I felt I had been more blessed than she. What a privilege it was on that day to touch a life for Christ and pass His blessings along. I wondered about His thoughts while on the cross, yielding His dear life for me and all those who mocked Him that day. Oh, the gratitude that rests in my heart for the marvelous gift of His blood that covers my life day by day.

Later that same day I went to fill my car with gas. After several unsuccessful attempts to use my card, which I knew was good, I asked the attendant for help. He encountered the same problem, so he tried his card to make sure the device was working properly. It was. He paid for my gas. When I asked how I could reimburse him, he said, "You're good!" as he walked away smiling. Within hours Christ returned to me that which I had given.

My trust in our Savior continues to grow as I watch Him at work around me, time and again. I pray I will be faithful when it is my turn to give again. I can hardly wait to thank Him personally for His many gifts to me. I am learning more and more that it truly is "more blessed to give than to receive" (Acts 20:35, KJV).

Cherryl A. Galley

January 14

Never Too Busy

He who watches over Israel
Will neither slumber nor sleep.

The L*ord* *is your protector;*
The L*ord* *is your shade on your right hand.*
—Psalm 121:4, 5, NASB

A few years ago, a Christian influencer told me she was "in a busy season," so we would have to connect later—when her life was not so busy.

Since I have experienced busy seasons of my own and have seen others around me in busy seasons, I understood what she meant and agreed to reach out a few months later. This led me to think of a spiritual parallel. We may be too busy to spend quality time with our friends and family, but God is never too busy to spend any amount of time with us. He is available to us literally 24/7, 365 days a year, and He is ready to help at any moment.

Think about this: The God who made the heavens, the earth, the galaxies, and all the universe always has time for us, no matter the day or night, no matter what we are going through or where we are physically located in the world. Among the more than eight billion people populating this planet, He sees you and me. Despite the ever-increasing population explosion, God treats each of us as if we were the only person on earth. He cares about every single detail of our lives. He wants us to come to Him in prayer and pour out our hearts to Him. He cares about everything that concerns us.

God loves to hear us praise His name, and He is open to hearing our requests. Most of all, God loves to answer our prayers and delights in tending to every detail of our lives as only He can. Sometimes we may feel like God is running late. We do not understand why He makes us wait or why He seems to delay His response to our prayer requests. When that happens, we need to remember that God's timing is perfect. His answers always arrive right on time. He is never too busy for us. We need to trust Him and keep drawing near to Him. As we draw near to Him, He promises He will draw near to us (see James 4:8). We are His children. His unconditional love for us endures forever (see Psalm 136). God will never fail us.

May we take heart in knowing that though God is busier than we will ever be, He is never too busy for us. He always has time for us. Let us make time for God every day—for He always makes time for us.

Alexis A. Goring

January 15

Share a Smile

Therefore encourage one another and build each other up, just as in fact you are doing.
—1 Thessalonians 5:11, NIV

Walking in my neighborhood early one morning, I met some students walking to school. Realizing "strangers could be danger," I quick-prayed for wisdom, and out of my mouth came the words, "Enjoy a wonderful Wednesday at school today!" They looked at me with a blank expression and kept walking. Several days passed. When I encountered the same group of kids again, I smiled and said, "Enjoy a fantastic Friday at school today." This time, smiles cracked their faces, our eyes met, and we all kept walking.

The following week, we had a similar exchange. I said, "Enjoy a terrific Tuesday at school today." This time their smiles were wide, their eyes, bright, and I saw them whisper something to each other and smile some more. While I do not know their thoughts or words, I do know many kids head out to school without a happy, optimistic send-off. So why not give them—or whomever we meet—a bit of heaven's encouragement with a smile and a few thoughtful, meaningful words?

Greeting each person I see with some sort of verbal positivity has become a fun habit. Anticipating how my Best Friend may actually encourage others through me has revitalized my interactions. I must admit, there have been a few sour experiences, but they are minimal and so far have not kept me quiet. Most often the response is, "You too," followed by a wide smile and a nod of the head.

I used to watch my mom talk to people on our small city streets and wonder how she could speak so easily with strangers. She glowed with heaven's goodness. I also have a great living example with my husband, one of the most creative verbal cheerleaders I know. It is exciting to share our experiences at the end of our day. It is fun to watch God put smiles on faces. It only takes a moment, but it can have an impact for good that may last a lifetime.

We could all do with a word of encouragement from time to time. Job understood that more than most and told his friends, "My mouth would encourage you" (Job 16:5, NIV). So how do you share heaven's encouragement with others? Share a smile with someone today and make their day a little brighter!

Lynn Ortel

January 16

Was It Coincidence?

For we are God's handiwork, created in Christ Jesus to do good works, which God prepared in advance for us to do.
—Ephesians 2:10, NIV

I found my cul-de-sac to be the perfect place to walk for exercise while listening to meditative music through my headphones. Several neighbors mentioned I would enjoy joining a walking group, the Nature Gurlz.

"No, thank you," I replied. "I'm retired and being somewhere at eight-thirty in the morning is too much like going to work." However, after being isolated for over two years, the companionship of walking with the Nature Gurlz sounded appealing.

So I set my alarm in time to have worship, dress, eat a snack, and drive to the location. "Lord, please give me a new testimony," I prayed. When I arrived, forty-one ladies stood in a circle, meeting and greeting, ready to stretch, pray, take a group photo, and sing the Nature Gurlz song. How wonderful! We walked at our own pace for two miles through the scenic nature preserve.

I chatted with many delightful ladies, including a retired university chaplain. The forty-second chaplain of the United States Senate, Barry Black, was scheduled to speak at my church, and I shared this news with her. She was excited! We exchanged phone numbers, and I mentioned that I worshiped on Saturday. No problem. She had a close friend who attended church on Sabbath in Nashville, Tennessee, USA, so she was familiar with my denomination. For the next two weeks, we enjoyed walking together and often shared the blessings of the Lord.

My family and friends prayed with me that she would come to church and be blessed by the service. Both prayers were answered. Thank You, Jesus! Since then, she has read one of Chaplain Black's books, enjoyed a Sabbath afternoon meal, and watched several Sabbath services online, including the Breath of Life Ministries. She has not hesitated to ask questions about our beliefs.

When I think about stories in the Bible like Esther and Joseph and the events of their lives that seemed to be coincidences, I am reminded that the Lord can orchestrate anything, anytime, and anywhere for His glory. If we are willing to be used by Him, even when we cannot see the end from the beginning, just imagine what He could do in seemingly ordinary moments of our lives! The question to ask ourselves is this: Are we willing?

Shirley Sain Fordham

January 17

With Eagle's Wings

*But they that wait upon the LORD shall renew their strength;
they shall mount up with wings as eagles.*
—Isaiah 40:31, KJV

Fear is not foreign to this life. We experience it when we are seconds away from a car accident, face a potentially life-threatening illness, or get a pink slip. The fear I felt many years ago had nothing to do with any of these events. Quite to the contrary, I was about to embark on an adventure I had been looking forward to since I was nine years old. It scared me half to death.

That same year, I watched video clips of Susan Boyle and witnessed her metamorphic journey as an unknown forty-seven-year-old Scottish singer who became an overnight sensation. Total strangers around the world were pulling for her to win the *Britain's Got Talent* contest. Two years prior, Paul Potts experienced the same phenomenon with his brilliant performance on the same show. Yet, just days before their auditions, they were just two ordinary people with a dormant talent that exploded at the right moment in each of their lives.

The fear I was experiencing as I drew nearer to the big day took me by surprise. Nerves of steel were an essential part of my daily armor after raising six children practically on my own, combined with over twenty years of teaching. So what generated this unexpected reaction in the pit of my stomach? After many years of setbacks and detours, I was about to try my wings as a full-time writer. With my home paid for and no debts to cloud the horizon, I announced my resignation from my position as teacher and principal. The unexpected fear as I stepped outside that zone of security into the unknown and envisioned myself teetering at the edge of a high mountain made my pulse race and my throat go dry. Would I fall or fly?

While I have no illusions that I will storm the world as Susan Boyle or Paul Potts did, I do believe my talent is specifically geared toward the person God created me to be. As the moment of transition drew nearer, I slowly began to believe He was the strength that would empower me to mount up with wings like eagles. Knowing He is there continues to transform fear into anticipation. Though the butterflies never totally vanished, they were no longer quite as frantic.

God wants each of us to trust that where He leads, we can safely follow and leave the outcome to Him. So spread your wings, and see where He will take you.

Sharon (Clark) Mills

January 18

You Prepared a Table

"Look at the birds of the air: they neither sow nor reap nor gather into barns, and yet your heavenly Father feeds them. Are you not of more value than they?"
—Matthew 6:26, ESV

My husband and I stepped out into the refreshingly crisp, dew-filled morning air. A light breeze caressed my face. It felt so good to be walking. This had become our favorite time of the day. Walking two miles each morning set an invigorating start for the rest of the day, and we felt stronger. Exercise is stimulating and is known for many benefits to the body and mind. It increases circulation, which results in an increased heart rate, strengthens the lungs, stimulates the immune system, and lifts the mood, to name just a few benefits.

Walking up the first slope caused me to slow down a little to catch my breath, and that's when I noticed a bird. We saw it was flying with something in its bill.

"Breakfast," I said to my husband.

"Well, you know the saying," he said. "The early bird catches the worm."

This was not a worm but a chunk of food. We thought it might be taking food to a nest to feed its babies. As we followed the bird in flight, we observed it perch on a sawn-off tree trunk and place whatever it had in its beak on the stump.

"Look," I said, "he even has a table."

The bird continued to eat his food off the stump.

My husband and I marveled as the scene unfolded in front of us. The bird was using the tree stump as its table. God had provided the bird with food and even a table on which to comfortably perch and eat.

We simultaneously began to quote Psalm 23, "The LORD is my shepherd; I shall not want. . . . Thou preparest a table before me in the presence of mine enemies: thou anointest my head with oil; my cup runneth over" (verses 1–5, KJV).

How comforting! The God who provides for the sparrows can certainly provide for me. Today, I am counting the many ways God has supplied everything I need. I invite you to join me in doing the same. How many blessings can we number? What amazing things has He done in supplying our daily necessities? How will we praise Him today?

Gloria Barnes-Gregory

January 19

Why Do We Fall?

You keep him in perfect peace whose mind is stayed on you, because he trusts in you.
—Isaiah 26:3, ESV

Peter saw Jesus walking on the water and wanted to do the same. So he asked Jesus to call him. Jesus called, and Peter stepped out onto the water. We know the story well.

As long as his eyes were fixed on Jesus, Peter did fine. But soon pride entered his heart, and he began to think, *Oh! I'm walking on the water! Are my friends seeing this?*

When he turned and lost his focus, Peter started to sink. "Lord! Save me!" he shouted, and immediately Jesus took hold of his hand and lifted him to his feet.

In taking his eyes off Jesus, Peter saw the wild waves. What if one of them should knock him over? What if he could not keep his footing? He forgot the only reason he was able to walk on water was because of Jesus' power.

> Looking unto Jesus, Peter walks securely; but as in self-satisfaction he glances back toward his companions in the boat, his eyes are turned from the Saviour. The wind is boisterous. The waves roll high, and come directly between him and the Master; and he is afraid. For a moment Christ is hidden from his view, and his faith gives way. He begins to sink. But while the billows talk with death, Peter lifts his eyes from the angry waters, and fixing them upon Jesus, cries, "Lord, save me." Immediately Jesus grasps the outstretched hand, saying, "O thou of little faith, wherefore didst thou doubt?"
>
> Walking side by side, Peter's hand in that of his Master, they stepped into the boat together. But Peter was now subdued and silent. He had no reason to boast over his fellows, for through unbelief and self-exaltation he had very nearly lost his life. When he turned his eyes from Jesus, his footing was lost, and he sank amid the waves.*

How often have we become proud, forgetting the grace and power of Jesus who has blessed us? How many times have we become successful because of our close fellowship with the Lord and the power He provides? When we lose focus—we fall. May we remember that Christ is always beside us, and He alone can rescue us. *Lord, help me keep my faith, focus, and trust in You alone. Amen.*

Betty Lyngdoh

---

* Ellen G. White, *The Desire of Ages* (Mountain View, CA: Pacific Press®, 1940), 381.

January 20

Sheltered in His Hands

*Surely God is my salvation;
I will trust and not be afraid.
The LORD, the LORD himself, is my strength and my defense;
he has become my salvation.*
—Isaiah 12:2, NIV

I arrived at the park for my usual morning walk. The wind began to blow, causing my hair to whip across my face. The usually calm waters alongside the jetty began to ripple. The wind seemed to start with a whisper, then it grew into more like a gentle swish, and then it slapped at the water as it began to pick up speed. Though it looked like rain was in the forecast, I did not feel particularly concerned at that point. I thought the strong winds would blow the dark clouds, heavy with rain, far away. As I reached the hilltop, I glanced toward my right and noticed the sky had begun to pour its contents onto the other side of the shore. I broke out into a jog, not wanting to be caught in a heavy downpour. Still, I knew I had time to reach the parking lot where I had left my car.

On the last leg of the route to the parking lot, I noticed an elderly man walking ahead of me. He strolled unhurriedly. Walking slowly and steadily, he occasionally looked at the newspaper in his hand. He was not at all concerned about the impending rain nor bothered by the dark clouds which loomed above him. On closer inspection, I noticed an umbrella hooked over his arm. I realized that because he was prepared for the incoming rain, he had no reason to feel perturbed by the weather—unlike myself and many others who were scrambling to reach the safety of our cars, away from the incoming downpour. We had been caught unprepared.

Experience tells us that being ready for the unexpected gives us confidence. However, even our best preparation provides no guarantee that we will sail smoothly through life's challenges. How encouraging to realize that while we may not know what the future holds, we know Someone greater than ourselves who knows everything about us. We can trust God in whatever lies ahead, for we are assured that we are in good hands. We do not need to scramble or run for shelter in the storms of life because we know we can walk safely in the shelter of God's hands. We can walk in confidence knowing that God is our protector, strength, and salvation. The Lord Himself is our strength and defense.

Be blessed today as you walk in the shelter of God's hand.

Debbie Saul-Chan

January 21

Postponed Prayer Can Be Deadly

Pray without ceasing.
—1 Thessalonians 5:17, KJV

Prayer is the best gift God has given to humanity. It connects us to heaven and, specifically, to the throne of our heavenly Father, who loves to send the help and blessings we need each moment. Without prayer, we would be like orphans, with no one to take care of us. The Bible encourages us, "Praying always with all prayer and supplication in the Spirit, being watchful to this end with all perseverance and supplication for all the saints" (Ephesians 6:18, NKJV). God invites us to pray without ceasing, and we should be careful not to postpone our prayers. This lesson has been engraved on my heart by God's grace after the following experience.

In my office, my secretary and I fast and pray each Wednesday. We spend time in the morning interceding for others, and we present our departmental projects and our challenges to God. One Wednesday my secretary had some errands to run, so I prayed alone. When she returned to the office in the afternoon, I let her know I had already prayed so we should probably focus on getting our work done for the day.

I had a feeling we should pray for our colleagues, particularly the staff who had gone out to do some evaluations. Though I knew we ought to pray, we had too much work to attend to, so I reasoned that we could pray about it later, after we had finished the day's work.

Though I tried to work, I could find no peace. Finally, I invited my secretary to join me in prayer, and we knelt to pray for the colleagues who were at work in the field. We asked God for protection and success in their endeavors. Friends, little did we know that these colleagues were on the plane at that exact moment and that their plane was not able to land. For whatever reason, they had to remain in the air for an extra thirty minutes before they were finally permitted to land. Interestingly, my husband was on the same plane, and he was the one who told me about their ordeal. It had occurred at the exact moment the Holy Spirit impressed our minds to pray.

How I would have regretted it if I had postponed praying until the end of the day. When the Holy Spirit prompts us to pray, when God seeks for an intercessor, let us respond immediately. He will act in response to the prayer of faith. Postponed prayer could be deadly.

Omobonike Adeola Sessou

January 22

"Small" Prayers

Casting all your care upon him; for he careth for you.
—1 Peter 5:7, KJV

In the third grade, I learned that God truly cares about every aspect of my life. I was learning a difficult piece on the piano, "Hawaiian Warriors Dance," arranged by John W. Schaum. I prayed as I walked to my piano teacher's house that God would help me play through the song correctly. And He did! I felt so relieved that I just kept thanking Him.

During school worship, sometime in the fifth grade, the pastor asked for prayer requests. Students raised their hands and mentioned concerns for the sick, traveling mercies, and unspoken requests. I had a favorite cassette tape that was missing, and I wanted it brought before the Lord in prayer. When we prayed, the pastor mentioned the other kids' prayer requests by name, and then toward the end of his prayer, he thanked God for caring about the "little things" in our lives. At first I felt slighted. He had failed to mention my prayer request to find the missing cassette tape. He must consider it a "little thing." But then I remembered how God cared about the "little things" in my life. I thought of how He had seen me through playing the "Hawaiian Warriors Dance." And of course, in time, God helped me to find my missing tape.

Years later, in my twenties, I tried to open a jar of peach jam. I was really struggling that day, physically and spiritually. I cried to the Lord, "If You truly care, please help me open this jar!" When I tried again I was shocked at how easily it opened. It was almost as if an angel had opened it for me. I did not have to keep trying in my own strength. The Lord fought my little battle for me.

Then, in my thirties, I accidentally put my iPod in the washing machine. I felt so sad and certain I would never be able to use it to listen to music while on my walks anymore. I said a prayer and turned it on. Can you believe it? It worked!

Remember, "nothing is too great for Him to bear, for He holds up worlds, He rules over all the affairs of the universe. Nothing that in any way concerns our peace is too small for Him to notice."*

Is there something you think is "too small" to bring to the Lord in prayer today? Go ahead and ask. He cares about every aspect of your life!

Mary C. D. Johnson

---

* Ellen G. White, *A Call to Stand Apart* (Hagerstown, MD: Review and Herald®, 2002), 27.

January 23

Quiet Time With God

My sheep hear my voice, and I know them, and they follow me.
—John 10:27, KJV

I like quiet time. Time when I can be alone to study a passage of Scripture and pray. It is a special time when I am alone with God. Unfortunately I have not always valued this time with the Father. Too often I have rushed through worship, said a quick prayer, and dashed off to start my day.

But then, while I was still a young woman, adversity hit. Divorce. Death. Single parenthood. Financial challenges. Job insecurity. All of which sent me to my knees. Sometimes I would cry out, "Where are You, God?" Other times, I would rant, "Have you forgotten me?"

On one of those occasions, my dear mother pulled me aside and reminded me of the need to spend quality time with God.

"But I pray every day," I told her.

She gave me a devotional book and a newly purchased New Century Version Bible. She suggested I start a daily plan for reading and studying both. Then she said something I have never forgotten. "Yvonne, do not be so quick to get up from your knees when you talk to God." She had my attention as she continued, "Linger a while and allow Him to speak to you. Listen for His direction. Give Him your concerns and see how He answers."

I listened to Mom's advice and began to read the devotional book and study God's Word each day. But taking the time to listen for God's direction took many years of conscious effort. And now that I am much older, I have come to appreciate my quiet time with the Master. As I linger, listening for His guidance, I sense the Holy Spirit nudging me to stretch beyond myself. He calls me to become involved in reaching out to my community. To tell someone every day about His love. Most importantly, to share the news He is coming back soon.

Sisters, it is so sweet to have quiet time with God. Every day my heavenly Father and I have a designated appointment that I do not miss. Thanking Him for His love toward me is the first order of business, and at our closing, I listen for His direction. Later in the evening, before falling asleep, I remind Him that I love Him and cannot wait till we talk again in the morning.

Father, as much as I enjoy my time with You, I look forward to the day when we will be able to talk face-to-face. Lord Jesus, please come quickly!

Yvonne Curry Smallwood

January 24

Delightful Devotions

"Before they call I will answer; while they are yet speaking I will hear."
—Isaiah 65:24, ESV

You made an intentional choice today to read this devotional. You want to discover the message God has wrapped in these few words, just for you. I have found that being intentional in our morning devotions is the most delightful way to start the day. That is one reason why I suggested some years ago to my husband, who is the priest of our home, that we include our favorite Bible verses as a part of each morning's worship because they remind us of how Jesus leads and comforts us.

Some people find that having a pattern for devotional time makes the experience more rewarding. Memorizing Scripture is definitely a good and intentional pattern. We have found these verses have become more precious to us. They give us a jump start for our day. I will share some of our favorites. They are probably some of your favorites.

No matter whether you enter into your morning devotions alone, with a mate, or with others, read whichever Bible version you choose. We usually offer our prayer after the priestly blessing of Numbers 6:24–26.

Call on God for His will to be done for the petitions you offer: Psalm 119:154.

Ask Jesus to dress you in His armor for the new day: Ephesians 6:14–17.

Trust in God's plans for the day, and for your future: Jeremiah 29:11.

Claim God's strength as you grow older day by day: Isaiah 46:4.

Ask that He be with you, and for you not to cause anyone unhappiness: 1 Chronicles 4:10, NKJV.

Ask for His blessing, with His smile, and His provision of peace: Numbers 6:24–26.

Express your delight for today, another day of life with Him: Psalm 118:24.

Renew your belief in the fact that you will see Jesus face-to-face: Revelation 22:4.

Be confident in your faithfulness, for all things will work for your good: Romans 8:28.

By the way, my husband, Johnny, always reads from the women's devotional book as a part of our morning devotions. He feels that Christian women are practical and intentional about their relationship with God our Father, our Lord Jesus, and the sweet Spirit—all of whom we invite into our morning circle of worship and devotion.

Betty Kossick (deceased)

January 25

God's Word in Your Heart

Your word I have hidden in my heart, that I might not sin against You.
—Psalm 119:11, NKJV

Years ago, I decided to memorize as many of God's promises as I could. It turned out to be one of the best decisions I have ever made.

Whenever trials assail me, David reminds me, "The LORD is my rock and my fortress and my deliverer; my God, my strength, in whom I will trust" (Psalm 18:2, NKJV). James challenges me to consider a heavenly perspective when he states, "Count it all joy when you fall into various trials, knowing that the testing of your faith produces patience" (James 1:2, 3, NKJV). And when I am feeling completely overwhelmed by the challenges of life, God promises, "When you pass through the waters, I will be with you; and through the rivers, they shall not overflow you. When you walk through the fire, you shall not be burned" (Isaiah 43:2, NKJV).

Making a major decision can be difficult. I am grateful for the reminder found in Philippians that assures me, "Be anxious for nothing, but in everything by prayer and supplication, with thanksgiving, let your requests be made known to God; and the peace of God, which surpasses all understanding, will guard your hearts and your minds through Christ Jesus" (Philippians 4:6, 7, NKJV). We do not have to feel intimidated by the future. "For I know the thoughts that I think toward you, says the LORD, thoughts of peace and not of evil, to give you a future and a hope" (Jeremiah 29:11, NKJV).

When house repairs or other unexpected expenses loom, I do not panic, for "my God shall supply all your need according to His riches in glory by Christ Jesus" (Philippians 4:19, NKJV). Moreover, He has promised, "Before they call, I will answer; and while they are still speaking, I will hear" (Isaiah 65:24, NKJV).

Jesus walked on the earth and was tempted—just like us. But, praise God, "no temptation has overtaken you except such as is common to man; but God is faithful, who will not allow you to be tempted beyond what you are able, but with the temptation will also make the way of escape, that you may be able to bear it" (1 Corinthians 10:13, NKJV).

These are some of the promises I regularly claim. I am sure you have a similar list. My friends, let us memorize God's Word while we are privileged to have our Bibles with us.

Cecelia Grant

January 26

When Going Slower Is Better

It is good to wait quietly for salvation from the LORD.
—Lamentations 3:26, NLT

You may have heard the saying, "If at first you do not succeed, try, try again." My version of the expression is more like, "If at first you do not succeed, go faster next time." I try to think of myself as an efficient person and pride myself on reaching the bottom of my to-do list with time to spare. While I do get many things done well, trying to go fast has a few side effects. One is that I am a bit of a klutz. Things tend to spill, topple over, or drop around me. Another side effect is frustration at those things that refuse to be done quickly, like the preparation of some meals or drying my hair before work.

I thought about this recently while trying to remove a sticky label from my debit card. I started by peeling it off from one corner, but the label started to split, leaving a sticky residue behind. I stopped and switched to another corner. I did not want to be stuck scraping off sticker gunk with my fingernail. The same thing happened. I changed corners once more, going very slowly, and this time it worked. As I slowly peeled, the entire sticker began to come off and left no residue behind. Encouraged, I worked even slower, and it not only peeled off the side of the sticker I was working on but also the sticky part of the paper that had split and stuck on the other corners. It seemed like the slower I went, the better the result.

This past year, I have been dealing with a traumatic event that happened to me. As usual, I have been trying to get over this thing quickly, certain that I could push past the pain and the anxiety it has caused me and get back to being the person I was before. I felt tired of being sad, scared, and hopeless. I wanted it to be over. But that is not how life works. Slowly I have been learning, through the patience of God and the help of therapy, that some things take time. There are some things God wants to do in us and for us, but for them to be done well, we need to allow God time to accomplish His work. It is probably more time than we want to give.

But I am beginning to learn. As I practice going slower and waiting on God, I discover that His timing is always better. It is exactly what I need. It turns out that going at God's pace, even if it is slower, is always better.

"It is good to wait quietly for . . . the LORD" (Lamentations 3:26, NLT).

Rhonda Bowen

January 27

Stay on the Wall

"You shall not fear them, for it is the LORD your God who fights for you."
—Deuteronomy 3:22, ESV

The book of Nehemiah tells the story of the rebuilding of the wall around Jerusalem by the returning exiles. One thing that stands out for me is how Nehemiah focused on completing the task God had sent him to do.

The second he started to work on the wall, his enemies attacked. First, they tried derision. Sanballat, Tobiah, and Geshem laughed at Nehemiah when they learned of his plans to rebuild (Nehemiah 2:19). Then they became angry and mocked his efforts (Nehemiah 4:1–3). When that did not work, they turned to threats (verses 7, 8). As the story unfolds, Sanballat and company become increasingly more menacing. This story is a metaphor for how the enemy works in our lives—especially when we are determined to do God's work.

It is easy to focus on the actions of our enemies. It is easy to become inactive, paralyzed by fear. We may be tempted to stop the work for fear of reprisals or further attacks. However, rather than focus on the dissenters, I want to highlight Nehemiah's response and the lessons we can learn from him.

Every time his enemies came at him, Nehemiah prayed. Every time they tried to prevent him from working, he made another plan, one that enabled him to keep working. When his enemies tried to discourage him, Nehemiah spoke life and encouragement over himself and those helping him.

Maybe your courage is failing because you have been in the battle for a long time. Or you do not have the words to speak life over your situation. Perhaps you are worn out and exhausted from all your battle scars. I understand, sweet friend, so let me be the encouraging Nehemiah to you. The Lord has entrusted you with that task because He knows you can do it with His help. He wants you to call on Him so He can strengthen you. He wants you to come to Him for wisdom and to depend on Him for resources. The enemy comes to kill, steal, and destroy, but Jesus came to give you an abundant life.

Keep your focus on Jesus. You are doing fantastic work. Stay on the wall! Do not come down—for it is the Lord your God who fights for you.

Aminata Coote

January 28

Be God's Voice

Have you not known?
Have you not heard?
The everlasting God, the L{\small ORD}*,*
The Creator of the ends of the earth,
Neither faints nor is weary.
His understanding is unsearchable.
—Isaiah 40:28, NKJV

The world is crying out for help! Due to the presence of evil, there are wars literally around the world. Somehow, we have become immune to the pain and horror, and we regard them as common everyday occurrences. Today, more than ever, God needs us to be His voice, His tender touch in a world that simply does not know how to heal. God's people are the voice of calm in a chaotic world. But sometimes God's people need to calm their own souls. We need healing. Even Christians go through storms, disappointments, and heartbreak. So how do we become God's voice to a hurting world?

We need a daily walk with the Lord in the power of the Spirit. Without this divine connection, the flesh kicks in. We lose patience, vision, and hope. Ultimately, we lose our direction. It is a daily thing, my friends. It takes discipline to stay connected to God. We must determine daily to take time to read His Word and listen for His voice. Then we will "go from strength to strength" (Psalm 84:7, KJV). Power is promised to us.

Though we tire and grow weary, though our hearts are crushed, our God does not leave us to suffer alone. He never tires and never becomes exhausted. He is always here for us. We can be the salt of the earth when we find our strength and power from His Spirit. We can bring light and hope to others, even when we are struggling. If we remain connected to God daily, we can walk with joy. Not because our lives are perfect but because we are connected to the Source of power. He perfects His power within us. What an amazing assurance.

We are His children, and we are promised eternal life when Jesus returns. Let us live like we know the Father. Let us not be afraid to come to Him with everything that troubles us, with anything that has a hold on our lives. He is strong enough to carry us through any trial. And one day soon, He will welcome us into His arms.

While we wait for that day, let us stay connected to Him and, through His Spirit, be His voice to a troubled world. We belong to God's kingdom. Let us bring as many with us as we can!

Elena Flores

January 29

Grafted In

If some of the branches have been broken off, and you, though a wild olive shoot, have been grafted in among the others and now share in the nourishing sap from the olive root, do not consider yourself to be superior to those other branches. If you do, consider this: You do not support the root, but the root supports you.
—Romans 11:17, 18, NIV

I love apples. They are my favorite fruit, and I almost missed out on them. I once had the opportunity to spend five years in Rochester, New York, USA. When the first fall came, my sister took me to an apple orchard. Now, I grew up in the South, and we had no apple orchards there. The apples that were available to us were transported across the country from the apple-producing states. I found them to be soft and sometimes on the sour side. I never developed a taste for those apples. But on that crisp fall day, standing in an orchard full of apples, I pulled one from a tree and took my first bite of absolute deliciousness. Oh! What wonderful flavors I discovered that fall. I was hooked. When an apple is fresh, it is crunchy and juicy, not at all like the apples I had been eating from those bagged varieties in the grocery stores.

It was during these wonderful apple-picking seasons that I began to study apples. I learned apple seeds do not grow the same wonderful apples as the parent trees, but instead they become a hybrid apple. In fact, they need to be cross-pollinated, and grafting is the process that ensures the desired characteristics are maintained in the new apples.*

Come on now. Talk about nature shouting the goodness of God! Adam was made in God's image, and yet, as we have grown our families in this sinful world, our fruit has become a hybrid of all kinds of things that no longer represent our Creator. Selfishness, greed, unkindness, and dishonesty are a few of the traits found in mankind that come from the enemy and not the Creator. This means we must be grafted into Jesus in order to bear the fruits that are pleasing to Him and come of the Holy Spirit. God takes the unpleasant, sour parts of our natures and transforms them into a fresh sweetness that only He can give.

This is not anything for us to brag about. We are not bringing anything to the graft. It is the parent stock that gives us everything. Like the olives in Romans 11. Like freshly picked apples.

Faye Wadlington

---

* "Why Do We Graft?," accessed Oct. 30, 2023, https://www.colorado.edu/cumuseum/sites/default/files/attached-files/why_do_we_graft.pdf.

January 30

Seasonal Plums

O taste and see that the L*ORD* *is good: blessed is the man that trusteth in him.*
—Psalm 34:8, KJV

Jesus Christ the same yesterday, and to day, and for ever.
—Hebrews 13:8, KJV

A couple of years ago, my sister-in-law and I were shopping at one of the wholesale clubs for snack items for church. She picked up some plums as one of the items to place in the snack bags that Sabbath.

At church, after she passed out the bags, she handed me a plum and told me I had to try one, as they were delicious. She was right. They were so good that I made a trip to the wholesale club to buy a bag for myself. These particular plums were only available, per the label, for about two to three weeks each year. I made a mental note to be sure to buy some the next year.

Fast-forward, and my, how a year does fly by, to mid-August, when I went on "plum watch." After adding it to my calendar, I started to check the store for the plums. I had told others about these plums, so they were waiting too. I stopped by the store a couple of times and noted they were not yet in stock. Then, in early September, I was so excited to see they had arrived! While still in the store, I texted everyone to let them know the plums had arrived. I could hardly wait to get home and enjoy a delicious treat.

Once home, I washed a plum and bit into it. Yuck! That was not what I had enjoyed the previous year. The skin was bitter, and the flesh had no taste. Since there were two varieties, I concluded we must have bought the other variety last year, so I returned to the store the next day to try that one. Oh, how disappointed I was to discover that those were not good either.

I had waited a whole year to enjoy those delicious plums, only to be badly let down. I refused to spend any more money looking for the sweet plums I had previously enjoyed. Nothing was wasted, though, as I shared the fruit with my family and my church family.

Reflecting on my "plum watch," I felt thankful to know that Jesus is always the same—yesterday, today, and forever. He never changes. He is always available. He invites us to taste and see how good He is, and He will never disappoint.

I look forward to heaven, where the fruit will be unlike anything I have experienced on earth. It will be available throughout eternity and will taste the same each time I enjoy it. I cannot wait!

Angèle Peterson

January 31

A Basketful of Sour Lemons

Though I have fallen, I will rise. Though I sit in darkness, the Lord will be my light.
—Micah 7:8, NIV

They say that when life gives you lemons, you should make lemonade, but that is easier said than done. Life is hard, and change is not always understood and processed easily. Up until a number of years ago, I did not know what depression really was. But this changed quickly when I found myself trapped in a low-paying, pointless job. My employer had promised that I could continue to work while they sponsored me to study. But things changed, and it became impossible for me to study and continue with my existing job. I was offered a different job, but it was not suitable for me.

Each day I would drive to work crying and praying. It was hell. But God visited me! One day, I noticed a pigeon that seemed to be following me while I was stuck in traffic. It swept down in front of my car and onto my windshield. It continued to hover above my car until I reached my workplace, where I saw it rest on a lamppost. It then turned and looked in my direction for a moment. I felt God was telling me, "I feel your pain. I care for you deeply."

I decided to resign and take time off to look after myself. My son was going through a difficult time in school, too, and was at home sometimes. So I thought it would do him good to have me around the house. I wanted to look after both of us. It was indeed a painful time, and I felt surrounded by darkness and all alone. I would wake up in the middle of the night and talk to God. I took time to pray, fast, read, and meditate. Singing and praise became part of my every moment. My days and nights were merged into a long conversation with God. He became my only trusted friend!

Micah 7:8 brought me such comfort and light. Despite the darkness, God showered me with His grace, and I saw a glimpse of His beautiful character of love. Then, in a miraculous manner, I found a better job. Looking back, I recognize how this experience strengthened my faith and renewed my courage in the Lord.

If you are going through difficult times today, I would like to say to you, walk closely with the Lord. He will not let you down. He will turn your basket of sour lemons into sweet and refreshing lemonade you can share with others!

Anna Karatzidou-Papaioannou

February 1

Faithfulness in Little Things

The Lord is my strength and my shield; my heart trusted in him, and I am helped: therefore my heart greatly rejoiceth; and with my song will I praise him.
—Psalm 28:7, KJV

God is faithful and unchanging and expects the same in return. Regardless of the life one leads, God remains constant, forever faithful to His nature. Faithfulness carries with it a promise. The Lord promises to give much if we are faithful in the little things (see Matthew 25:21). God does not seek grand, expensive, or extraordinary gestures. He delights in the small things done well. God will take those small acts and make them significant.

God values the purposeful efforts of His children. This principle is exemplified in the life of Booker T. Washington, an American educator, author, and orator. Known for his significant work in Atlanta, Georgia, USA, Washington's efforts gained the attention of both politicians and the public. His influence was substantial in black politics, earning him support from both the black community and the white population. But beyond his public accomplishments, Washington knew God personally and lived by the biblical foundation of focusing on small things. He was the first president of the Tuskegee Institute in Alabama and attributed his success to his belief in the importance of the little things.

God Himself orders our steps and assigns our daily tasks, guiding us in actions that connect us to heaven. The small things in life, such as visiting the sick, helping the needy, and showing kindness and compassion, call heaven's attention. These small acts lead to a purposeful, happy, and fulfilled life. They bring joy to others and also to us.

Our loving God uses the seemingly insignificant aspects of our lives to reveal our commitment and love for Him. Small things can be difficult and tedious and may even feel trivial, but God sees the faithfulness in the doer of these routine tasks. He rewards this faithfulness with greater responsibilities and bigger opportunities. Little becomes much in God's hands.

While it may be challenging to remain faithful and committed to God through small routines, God is attentive to every small task accomplished. As Jesus reminds us, "He who is faithful in what is least is faithful also in much" (Luke 16:10, NKJV). Faithfulness in small things is the secure preparation for more significant responsibilities.

Julie Williams

February 2

What God Will Do

He will also keep you firm to the end, so that you will be blameless on the day of our Lord Jesus Christ. God is faithful, who has called you into fellowship with his Son, Jesus Christ our Lord.
—1 Corinthians 1:8, 9, NIV

As Christian women, we are called to look to the Lord in faith while looking forward with anticipation of what He will yet accomplish.

To find the greatest evidence of looking upward in faith, just look at the faith chapter, Hebrews 11. The chapter starts with the definition of faith: "Now faith is confidence in what we hope for and assurance about what we do not see" (Hebrews 11:1, NIV). From there, the author goes on to mention several heroes of faith: Noah, Abraham, Joseph, Moses, Gideon, David, and Samuel. Even Rahab is mentioned. Though they were all just weak, sinful humans, as are we, they had faith. Where did they get it, and where can we get it?

God gives each of us a measure of faith, according to Romans 12:3. Faith is God's gift to us, and once we have that gift, we are called upon to grow it. James tells us that growth comes through trials and challenges that test our faith (James 1:2, 3), but we can be assured that through it all our Lord is with us and will never leave us or forsake us. We can have faith in Him because He is faithful.

As we consider God's faithfulness, our hearts will fill with gratitude. David, in Psalm 103, provides a wonderful list of things for which to be grateful. He writes, "Bless the LORD, O my soul, and forget not all his benefits" (verse 2, KJV). Our Lord forgives our sins, heals our diseases, redeems our lives, crowns us with love and compassion, satisfies our desires with good things, renews our youth, and works righteousness and justice (see verses 3–6). He has not failed us, and He never will.

In addition to all these blessings, Jesus outlined our greatest hope and expectation for the future when He promised, "Do not let your hearts be troubled. You believe in God; believe also in me. My Father's house has many rooms; if that were not so, would I have told you that I am going there to prepare a place for you? And if I go and prepare a place for you, I will come back and take you to be with me that you also may be where I am" (John 14:1–3, NIV).

Blessings are ours as we trust in God's promises for the future.

Myrna L. Hanna

February 3

Unyielding Triumph

No weapon formed against you shall prosper, and every tongue which rises against you in judgment you shall condemn.
—Isaiah 54:17, NKJV

Almost twenty years ago, at the Lord's leading, we established a humble social school project in Windhoek, Namibia, that continues to serve as a beacon of hope and light, grounded on the solid foundation of the Lord. From the very outset, the hand of God was evident, guiding the miraculous growth of our efforts. Yet, as so often happens when we step out in faith, with every stride forward, the enemy sought to tear down what God had so lovingly ordained.

There came a time when the attacks intensified to such an extent that it felt as though everything we had built was on the brink of collapse. Satan's intent was unmistakable: to seize and obliterate the project and to destroy what had been built in faith.

During one of the most challenging periods, a deceptive business investment threatened to undermine everything. It was a plot orchestrated by the one whose primary purpose is "only to steal and kill and destroy" (John 10:10, NIV). But God, in His infinite mercy, intervened. The truth came to light, and once again we were reminded that what God has blessed, no man with evil intent can take away.

As the psalmist reminds us,

> He saved them from the hand of the foe;
>   from the hand of the enemy he redeemed them.
> The waters covered their adversaries;
>   not one of them survived.
> Then they believed his promises
>   and sang his praise (Psalm 106:10–12, NIV).

God shattered the chains that sought to bind us, breaking through every barrier the enemy tried to erect.

Today, I give thanks to God for His unfailing love, for His wonderful deeds, and for the victories He has secured on our behalf. Trust in the Lord with all your heart, for He will never leave you nor forsake you. He is faithful, and His mercy endures forever.

To those enduring trials, remember this: God sees you, He is with you, and He is fighting for you. Though the battle may be fierce, victory belongs to the Lord. Stand firm in your faith, for He who promised is faithful. Hold on, for your deliverance is near, and your praise will resound as a testament to His glory.

Emma Nangula Kakona

February 4

But!

Jesus looked at them and said, "With man this is impossible, but with God all things are possible."
—Matthew 19:26, NIV

The word *but* can be used for multiple purposes. It can work as a conjunction, a preposition, an adverb, a noun, or a coordinating conjunction* to connect contrasting ideas. Have you ever noticed how that little word is used in the Bible to pivot a story and introduce God's intervention?

That small word is used effectively in 2 Kings 5:1–26, the story of Naaman, captain of the army of the king of Syria. Naaman was a great man, honorable, and a mighty man in valor, *but* he was afflicted with leprosy. Notice how *but* is used here. All his bravery, when compared to the devastation of his illness, was of little use. He was a courageous man, *but* he had a deadly disease. The word adds additional information and changes the impression and impact given by what precedes it. His situation seemed hopeless—that is, until a little servant girl told him she knew where he could go to find the healing he desperately needed.

Sooner or later, we all face conflicting, contrasting situations in life—you know, those upside-down moments that leave us confused or overwhelmed. Sometimes they are annoying. At other times they can derail our plans and dreams. We work hard for a family vacation and finally have enough saved, *but* the car breaks down and must be repaired. Or we take years to get a degree in an area we expect will be our lifework, *but* after doing the job, we discover it is not what we expected, and we hate it.

If, like Naaman, you are faced with that little word that has you feeling like life's turned upside down and you are not sure where to turn, I want to encourage you. I know Someone who knows exactly what to do for you. So pick yourself up, open God's Word, and find the promise He wants to give you right now. One of my favorite go-to verses is found in 1 Corinthians 15: "But thanks be to God! He gives us the victory through our Lord Jesus Christ" (verse 57, NIV).

Would you allow Him to change your life? If it seems impossible, remember, "with God all things are possible" (Matthew 19:26, NIV). Give it to Jesus. He is more than able!

Juliet L. Lucas Languedoc

---

* Henry Lawrence, answer posted to question "Is but a preposition or conjunction?," Quora, accessed Nov. 12, 2024, https://www.quora.com/Is-but-a-preposition-or-conjunction.

February 5

My Crucibles

There hath no temptation taken you but such as is common to man: but God is faithful, who will not suffer you to be tempted above that ye are able; but will with the temptation also make a way to escape, that ye may be able to bear it.
—1 Corinthians 10:13, KJV

All of us experience crucibles in our lives, both big and small. They often come when we least expect them. I recently experienced several crucibles, one after another. They brought me so much stress and affected my health. My husband and I have no children of our own, but God placed love and a burden on my heart to take care of our family members in the Philippines. My brother had five children but no permanent work. After he passed away, I needed to take over his responsibilities, especially the financial ones. We sent the children to a Christian school to finish their college education.

On another island we took care of the education of my sister's four children. We have used almost all our savings; however, our enemy, Satan, knows exactly what to do to harm God's children. He is using my nephews and nieces to deeply wound my heart. Almost the whole family has become involved. I have been living in Germany for more than thirty years and have helped to provide for my family from the start. Since Satan started to use my family to discourage me, I realize, in part, what Jesus went through in order to give His love to us.

Jesus healed the sick, fed the hungry, and gave them hope and happiness, often without receiving any thanks. Later those same mouths who sang "Hallelujah to the King!" and shouted praises to His name cried "Crucify Him!" Roman soldiers slapped His face, put thorns on His head, and made Him carry the heavy cross. When the soldiers poked a spear in His side, no one stepped forward to help Him. Sinless and innocent, Jesus died for you and for me. He endured the crucible from which He chose not to escape. Oh, praise the Lord—He overcame the world.

He is our example and strength. Through Him, we can give thanks for whatever crucible comes our way. When we do so, we share a little bit in the suffering of Jesus, knowing that we can overcome in His strength. We need to fix our eyes on Him and stay connected to Him every day, for we shall see Him soon. No matter what crucible you are experiencing, hold on to your faith, dear sisters, until Jesus comes.

Loida Gulaja Lehmann

February 6

Do Not Be Afraid

"Do not be afraid, Abram. I am your shield, your exceedingly great reward."
—Genesis 15:1, NKJV

Fear. We have all experienced it. To a greater or lesser degree, we know how fear can stun and numb us, leaving us feeling crippled. But fear is not always a bad thing. Sometimes it can help protect us from something that could put life or integrity in danger. Even with this realization, however, it is still true that fear never feels good or pleasant.

Fear haunted Abram and Sarai as they became elderly and had no children to leave their fortunes to. Their lack of legitimate heirs weighed on their hearts every day. Sarai was now old and had been barren even as a young bride. In her old age, she knew beyond any doubt she would never conceive. Abram, too, had lost hope of becoming a father. Who would carry on their lineage? To whom would they leave their wealth? They were bitterly disappointed.

Even though he had nephews and faithful servants who were like sons, Abram longed to have a son of his own. Had God not promised to make him the father of many nations? But time passed, age advanced, and still, the promised blessing did not come. Abram learned to come to terms with his disappointment and fear.

However, he served the God of the impossible, and for Him, no barriers are too difficult to overcome. God knows no haste or delay. He who promised is faithful. The Lord blessed Sarai, and she became pregnant at the age of ninety and gave birth to a beautiful little boy whom they named Isaac. Can you imagine how they must have glowed with joy? The promise had been fulfilled. God changed their names to Abraham and Sarah and turned their disillusion into joy and laughter. Abraham and Sarah experienced the good and perfect will of God.

In this world, we still feel the losses and consequences of being part of a creation that has been degenerated by evil. But Jesus continues to lead His children. He defends and protects His people and will do so until He comes to take us home. When we allow the Lord to be our shield, we never need to fear. Remember, God is faithful! He is all-powerful. We have nothing to fear with God on our side.

Sueli da Silva Pereira

February 7

Late or on Time?

Hear my cry, O God; attend unto my prayer.
—Psalm 61:1, KJV

Many women dream of having a baby, particularly when they are in love and happily married. My husband and I got married almost ten years ago and decided to start a family soon after. The sight of two lines on the pregnancy stick shortly after that was one of the greatest feelings. The joy and hope in our hearts were unlike anything we had experienced before.

Six weeks later, I started to spot, and my doctor referred me for an ultrasound. I begged God to save my baby. During the ultrasound, the tech informed me there was no cardiac activity but that it would be confirmed at a one-week follow-up. I felt brokenhearted and spent the week pleading with God for a miracle. My go-to verses reminded me, "From the end of the earth will I cry unto thee, when my heart is overwhelmed: lead me to the rock that is higher than I" (Psalm 61:2, KJV). I remained confident God would answer my prayers.

At the follow-up scan, I heard the daunting news, "Fetal demise." Why did He fail me? What had I done to deserve this? I thought God no longer cared about me.

In my pain, I turned to the Word and studied how Hannah dealt with her infertility. I brought my petition before God and, like Hannah, promised to dedicate my child to His service if He would grant my request. Shortly after my miscarriage, I conceived again. Surely God had answered my prayer, just like Hannah.

Eight weeks later I started to spot and miscarried again. The questions came flooding back. During this time I came across a fertility center that specialized in finding the root cause of infertility. Ultimately I fell pregnant again and carried my baby to full term. During my pregnancy, I prayed daily, dedicating my child's life to God—and what a blessing she is.

With hindsight, I see that God's timing is perfect. Though we may feel like Martha after her brother Lazarus had died, thinking God's answer has come too late (see John 11), we can trust Him even when He does not give us what we want when we want it. "When Jesus received the message, he said, 'This sickness is not unto death, but for the glory of God, that the Son of God might be glorified thereby.' "*

As hard as it is to see in our moments of anguish, God knows what is best for each of us. We can safely trust His love, no matter how He chooses to be glorified in our lives.

Jerylyn Richards

---
* Ellen G. White, *The Spirit of Prophecy*, vol. 2 (Battle Creek, MI: Seventh-day Adventist Publishing, 1877), 360.

February 8

Holding On to Faith in the Storm

He heals the brokenhearted and binds up their wounds.
—Psalm 147:3, NIV

My world upended when my six-month-old baby, usually full of energy and joy, suddenly became gravely ill. No matter what I tried, I could not soothe his cries of pain. After I rushed him to the Adventist Medical Center in Manila, Philippines, the doctors delivered a horrifying diagnosis: ileocolic intussusception. This means that part of his intestine had folded into itself, causing a life-threatening blockage. They informed us he needed immediate surgery. The overwhelming fear and helplessness I felt at that moment were indescribable. My heart was crushed with excruciating pain. As my husband and I watched our little boy being wheeled into surgery, the gravity of the situation hit us hard. All we could do was pray—we had no other choice. I vividly remember holding my husband's hand as we knelt and prayed desperately, pleading with God to guide the surgeons and heal our son. At that moment I felt an urgent need to place all my trust in God.

This experience profoundly deepened my faith and allowed me to connect with the promise in Psalm 147:3 that God heals the brokenhearted and binds up their wounds. As we waited anxiously during the two-and-a-half-hour surgery, that promise resonated within me like never before. Our Christian faith teaches us to cling to God during difficult times, believing He sees our pain and is working out everything for our good. This experience reinforced my belief in the power of prayer, especially during times of crisis. We believe God is not distant but actively involved in our lives. As I prayed for my son's recovery, this conviction served as my anchor. It was no longer just about asking for a miracle; it was about surrendering to God's will, trusting that His plan is perfect even when we cannot understand it.

Miraculously, my son's surgery was successful, and he began to recover. Today he is healthy and strong, a testament to God's mercy. This experience strengthened my belief that God is always with us, even in our darkest moments. He hears our prayers and is faithful to bring healing and comfort in His perfect time. Reflecting on that difficult time reminds me that faith is crucial, especially during life's storms. No matter how intense the storm is, we can find peace and strength by holding on to God's promises—regardless of the outcome.

Ardie Diaz

February 9

When All Seems Lost

He who planted the ear, does he not hear? He who formed the eye, does he not see?
He who disciplines the nations, does he not rebuke?
—Psalm 94:9, 10, ESV

It truly seems like the world is going from bad to worse. With the pandemic, new diseases, wars in various areas, and unrest in many places, we are all affected and suffering in some way. But even in difficult times, the psalmist reminds us that God is all-powerful. He is always there when we need him. "He who formed the eye, does he not see? He who disciplines the nations, does he not rebuke?" (Psalm 94:9, 10, ESV). How could the One who created everything not have the power to help us if we ask Him? What is more, He already knows what we need before we ask Him—even before we know we need it.

Often the connotation for the word *discipline* is negative, but sometimes what we think is a punishment is actually a situation that God uses to teach us, one that will strengthen us for the days ahead. Even in these moments of difficulty and sadness, God promises, "The Lord will not forsake his people; he will not abandon his heritage" (verse 14, ESV). He never abandons us, even though sometimes we feel He may have. And that gives me great peace and tranquility.

> If the Lord had not been my help,
>   my soul would soon have lived in the land of silence.
> When I thought, "My foot slips,"
>   your steadfast love, O Lord, held me up.
> When the cares of my heart are many,
>   your consolations cheer my soul (verses 17–19, ESV).

So even in moments where we feel tempted, tired, and about to slip, God is there to help us; we only have to ask. Even in our worries, those that steal our peace of mind, God is there to comfort us and cheer our spirits. If we remember what God has done for us in the past, we will be reassured of His help in the future.

"But the Lord has become my stronghold, and my God the rock of my refuge" (verse 22, ESV). We all go through difficult times, and if you are struggling through one today, take a moment to stop and think back on how the Lord has helped you in the past. No matter how hard the situation or how awful the pain, God is always close to His children.

Cecilia Nanni

February 10

Learning to Live by Faith

So then faith comes by hearing, and hearing by the word of God.
—Romans 10:17, NKJV

In my twenties, I suffered from migraines almost daily. Though I did not know it at the time, they were caused by food allergies. My face would break out in boils, and the pain in my head left me incapacitated. The migraines sapped my energy, and I felt a hundred years old.

As a member of the Norwalk Seventh-day Adventist Church in California, USA, I loved being involved in its thriving city ministry that included a bakery, a bookstore, and a daycare, among other things. Members took turns cooking lunch for about thirty people each weekday for the volunteers who worked in those various ministries.

One day, when it was my turn to prepare lunch, I had a terrible migraine once again. While I knew everyone would be depending on me for lunch, I felt powerless and unequal to the task required of me. I prayed, "Lord, You know how I feel today and the task I must accomplish. You have promised that to those who have no might, You will increase their strength [Isaiah 40:29]. I claim Your assurance that 'I can do all things through Christ which strengtheneth me' [Philippians 4:13, KJV]. I trust You to fulfill these promises for me today. Lord, I choose to trust in Your Word."

Leaning all my weight on God and pressing hard into these beautiful promises, I left the house, walked over to the kitchen, and began to prepare the meal. Amazingly the energy was there for the task. The pain left, and I was able to fix the meal. I even had the strength to clean up the dishes afterward and pack everything away.

Two hours later I walked back home, and as soon as I entered my house, the pain returned, and my energy drained from me. It happened so suddenly, so intensely, that I was left in no doubt that God had supernaturally sustained me for the task of the day. Oh! How I praised His Holy name!

The Lord taught me an invaluable lesson that day, and from this experience, I have learned how to lean hard into God's promises for the help I need. When I ask according to His Word, He always comes through for me. The Bible is filled with so many wonderful promises that He begs us to claim and ask—so we may receive.

My friends, please join me today in taking God at His Word. He who promised is faithful!

Sarah Burt

February 11

Find Your Happy Place

You will show me the path of life; in Your presence is fullness of joy; at Your right hand are pleasures forevermore.
—Psalm 16:11, NKJV

As I navigate the various roles and responsibilities in my life, from family to career and everything in between, finding true happiness can sometimes feel like an unattainable goal. In a world filled with life's uncertainties and complexities, why does the pursuit of happiness seem so elusive? As a child I experienced challenging times, but I clung to the hope found in the Bible, specifically the verse in James that states, "Count it all joy when you fall into various trials, knowing that the testing of your faith produces patience" (James 1:2, 3, NKJV). My childhood experience taught me that true happiness does not depend on external conditions but is cultivated from within through a deeply grounded faith.

Have you experienced the happiness that transcends the ups and downs of life, or are you still searching? I find that I am truly happy when I serve others. As women we can find happiness in serving others within our family, church, and community or in the workplace. When I give of myself, I enjoy a profound sense of fulfillment and purpose. So you may still be wondering, How do we find genuine happiness? "She is clothed with strength and dignity; she can laugh at the days to come" (Proverbs 31:25, NIV). Think about all the challenges you have faced and where you are now. I find that strength, resilience, and grace have led me to a deeper sense of happiness. "The joy of the Lord is your strength" (Nehemiah 8:10, NKJV).

Trust God's plan for you even amid uncertainty, cultivate a heart of gratitude, and focus on the blessings in your life. Surrender to God's will and trust in His promises. " 'For I know the plans I have for you,' declares the Lord, 'plans to prosper you and not to harm you, plans to give you hope and a future' " (Jeremiah 29:11, NIV).

I am learning that happiness is found in a deep and abiding relationship with God. Embracing principles of contentment, service, and gratitude helps me experience a profound sense of happiness. As I seek to anchor my life in faith and align my heart with God's truth, true happiness is a daily choice and not a destination; it is truly a transformative journey. My prayer is that we all experience the joy God grants us day by day.

Eleasia Charles

February 12

Growing in Jesus

So then, just as you received Christ Jesus as Lord, continue to live your lives in him, rooted and built up in him, strengthened in the faith as you were taught, and overflowing with thankfulness.
—Colossians 2:6, 7, NIV

Do you remember the first time you experienced Jesus? What were your feelings? Were you overwhelmed with joy and peace? Was your heart filled with thankfulness for His grace and mercy? Oh! I know it must have been a beautiful experience. Even now, as I think about my own experience, my heart is stirred with emotion.

When David was going through a difficult time, the Bible says that he "found strength in the Lord his God" (1 Samuel 30:6, NIV). When others were seeking to take his life, David turned to his God. He had seen the Lord's leading in his life. In fact, God says of him, "I have found David the son of Jesse, a man after mine own heart, which shall fulfil all my will" (Acts 13:22, KJV).

When we read the Scriptures, we see that David's walk with God was not an easy one. He had many ups and downs spiritually. He experienced great highs and deep lows, but through it all David never gave up his faith in God. When he was confronted with his sin, David humbled himself before God. He continued to walk with God in humility, learning each day more and more from God. He was like a "tree planted by water . . . [that] does not cease to bear fruit" (Jeremiah 17:8, ESV).

What can we learn from David's example? It is simple to say but difficult to live out. But it is not impossible, for as Paul says, "I can do all things through Christ who strengthens me" (Philippians 4:13, NKJV). We are to grow daily in Christ. As we read the Scriptures and root ourselves in them, as we drink the living waters and quench our thirst for righteousness, we grow in Christ. As we practice our faith daily, our hearts will be filled with thankfulness, for we will see God's mercy and grace at work in our lives, transforming and strengthening us in ways that will honor Him and encourage others.

Dear Father, thank You so much for the mercy You show us daily. We want to grow daily in Your ways. We long to be rooted in our faith and for our hearts to overflow with thankfulness and praise. Amen.

Priscila Kandane

February 13

Friendship

A woman of Samaria came to draw water. Jesus said to her, "Give Me a drink."
—John 4:7, NASB

I have a beautiful friend. I love her. I am filled with admiration for her. I consider her a true sister of my heart—my friend Zvonka. We are of the same age, my friend and I. Although dissimilar in many ways, we share a love for God that is vital. Anyway, I have found these dissimilarities only enhance our connection. Her perspectives contrast to mine, and I see God and the world in fresh, new ways through her. She builds me up, and God uses her in my life to refresh my heart.

But I have failed even this beautiful person whom I love. I let the business of my life, the pressures of my "now," cause me to let her slip from my mind and to the edges of my community. "Woulda, coulda, shoulda"—the saddest cliched saying because it is so often true. If I had followed through on my fleeting urgings from our God to reach out to her instead of trying to push the responsibility of supporting her onto others, if I had been a better and more constant friend . . . But I was not.

My friend is generous and kind. She loves me well, and in my sad realization and heart repentance, I know that God will continue to fill our friendship with joy, laughter, shared vistas, love, and beautiful days of swimming in cool, refreshing water: our shared pleasure.

If you feel overwhelmed in the "now" of life—your friendships strained, your inner life parched and dry—perhaps you feel like the woman Jesus met beside Jacob's well. Listen to what He shared with her: "Jesus answered and said to her, 'Everyone who drinks of this water will be thirsty again; but whoever drinks of the water that I will give him shall never be thirsty; but the water that I will give him will become in him a fountain of water springing up to eternal life'" (John 4:13, 14 NASB).

God is so good and generous. He says to us, "If you knew the gift of God, and who it is who is saying to you, 'Give Me a drink,' you would have asked Him, and He would have given you living water" (verse 10, NASB). With Him at the center of our lives, our friendship with Him and others will overflow with the fresh, living water of God's present paradise. Praise be to God!*

Gail Wettstein

---

* Adapted from *familytexts* (blog), Aug. 12, 2024, https://familytexts.wordpress.com/2024/08/12/august-12-2024/. Used with permission.

February 14

Sharing His Love

"Love each other. Just as I have loved you, you should love each other. Your love for one another will prove . . . that you are my disciples."
—John 13:34, 35, NLT

For the past ten years, at the beginning of each year, I have chosen a word on which to focus for the new year. In my journal I write out my commitment to concentrate on this word. I write a list of songs that use the word and find Bible texts that reflect it. One year, while looking for a new word, I read Galatians 5:22, 23 and was surprised I had never chosen the first fruit of the Spirit: love!

As February approached I started to think about how I could share God's love with others on Valentine's Day. I decided to make cookies. My husband, Ron, loves oatmeal-raisin cookies, so I determined to bake these for him and share them with others.

The day before Valentine's Day, I mixed up the dough and began to bake the cookies. I made them large, and for fun I shaped them into hearts. They turned out quite nicely. The next day, I met with a group of ladies, and we celebrated our love for each other with Valentine's Day cards and special treats. We had a wonderful time together. The ladies loved my heart-shaped cookies. A couple of ladies from our group were not at the meeting. I had cookies left over and felt impressed to share them with the missing members.

I drove to one lady's house, and she was delighted with the special treat and card. Next I drove to Debbie's house. Debbie was alone on this day. He husband had recently died, and she missed him terribly. She was so happy to receive a Valentine's Day gift from our group and the card, which we had all signed for her. It meant a lot to her to be remembered. As we sat together, I listened to her tell wonderful stories about her husband and their special times together. I told her how much we all loved her and that we were praying for her. Then I asked if we could pray together. She bowed her head, and we held hands as we prayed. We hugged each other, and I went on my way, rejoicing. It was a wonderful way to give love to her.

I am so thankful that God gives us opportunities to share our love and God's love with others each day. Let us look for every chance to do so. Opportunities are all around us. "Dear friends, since God loved us that much, we surely ought to love each other" (1 John 4:11, NLT).

Sharon Follett

February 15

How Do You Define Love?

Love is patient, love is kind.
—1 Corinthians 13:4, NIV

As a high school senior, I experienced the sweetest definition of love. Lois and Bob Pratt, my principal at Adelphian Academy in Holly, Michigan, USA, took me into their home and changed my life forever. They loved me and gave my life stability.

I learned many elementary things, such as removing the doily on a table and dusting the entire tabletop, not just around the doily. Bob allowed me to be a reader for the Bible Doctrines class he taught. I was amazed he trusted me to grade my own paper. As a reader I was able to contribute toward the cost of my education. Mom Pratt took me shopping and outfitted me from head to toe for graduation weekend. With great wisdom they shipped me off to Emmanuel Missionary College (now Andrews University) the day I graduated from academy. I sent them a thirty-page letter the first week. I missed them so desperately.

They officiated at my wedding in 1958 and brought me back into their home while my husband served in the army and I was expecting my second child. Mom Pratt took a leave from her nursing job and assisted in the delivery of Steven at the hospital where she had previously worked as head of Labor and Delivery. Their daughters babysat my five-year-old daughter Sharilyn during that time. When marriage turned to divorce, they never gave up on me.

Throughout my life, I yearned for the maternal love my mother, who suffered from her own losses, had been unable to provide. I kept trying to win her love, but it never happened. I missed the love of my father, who had abandoned me. My parents divorced when I was four, and I never saw him again until I was seventeen.

I chose to define love by becoming a hospital chaplain assistant, where I mirrored God's love for me in my volunteer pastoral assignments. Love meant sharing supper with a friend, giving her a respite from the bedside of her dying grandson. Love meant using my meager talents to counsel others in need. Love meant buying a new dress for an academy student and giving her phone cards, snacks, and bedding for her dorm room at Cedar Lake Academy.

Thank You, God, for the people who defined love for me in practical ways and filled my life with demonstrations of Your care and comfort. May we all define love in this manner.

Patricia Hook Rhyndress Bodi

February 16

Blessed Are the Meek

Take my yoke upon you, and learn of me; for I am meek and lowly in heart: and ye shall find rest unto your souls.
—Matthew 11:29, KJV

The first verse I learned by heart is Matthew 5:5, "Blessed are the meek: for they shall inherit the earth" (KJV). But this verse bothered me my whole life. What did it mean to be meek? I did not know anyone I could describe as meek, as a real-life example. That is, until very recently.

At the end of last year, I received a devotional book in the mail. I did not order it, so I wondered how I had come to receive it. At the school where I work, the teachers sometimes receive books as gifts. I thought it might be a gift from the school. But when I asked other teachers, they had not received the book. I mentioned it to my good friend, who was as puzzled as I was until a few weeks later when she excitedly enlightened me.

"You received this book because your story is published in it!" She continued, "I was checking the authors who are all listed at the back and found your name. Apparently the publisher sends a copy of the book to all the authors, and since you're an author, they sent it to you."

When I opened the book to the back page, sure enough, I saw my name listed. I felt ecstatic. I opened to the story and showed my husband, my colleagues, and my children, and excitedly announced, "I have a story published in this book!" I was so proud of myself and this wonderful accomplishment. It was the first time in my life that I had my story and my name published in a book. So, so exciting!

Then I thought of the friend who had shown it to me. She was the one who helped me write and submit the story in the first place. Two of her stories were published in the same book. Not only that, but she has already published several books, one containing more than fifty stories and another one that is currently with the publisher. Yet she never brags about it. She is not proud, haughty, or full of herself. Rather, she is down-to-earth, humble, and so helpful. She is my best friend.

At that moment I realized that I now knew what it meant to be meek, for I had seen a living example. Thank You, Jesus, for Your meekness and for giving me a living example of what it means.

Durdica Kukolja

February 17

In His Time

He has made everything beautiful in its time.
—Ecclesiastes 3:11, NIV

My church has learned from our Ghanaian culture that "everyone is everyone's keeper." This makes it look and feel like we are all from one family. Of course, we are from the "family of God," and, as such, are closely knitted together. We love to make every occasion special for anyone celebrating a birthday, marriage, or baby dedication. We want them to feel seen, loved, and happy. We also come together when someone experiences a bereavement.

In typical Ghanaian fashion, we go to the person celebrating or mourning to perform all the traditional norms and top it off with joyous music, dancing, and eating until daybreak. This is a time to laugh, chat, and, yes, even weep if we need. How often laughter and tears combine in our lives! I wish you could witness one of these occasions so you would understand what a wonderful time we have when we come together.

Last year, both a wedding and a birthday were announced in church. A double celebration! I felt happy but also a little disturbed. Why? The reason was that the most important part of these celebrations is to give something special, a gift, or money to the celebrant at the end of the event. I did not know what to take, nor did I have any money to give. I started to worry a bit because all gifts are recorded so that the recipient can call you later to show appreciation. If you give nothing, the records will show that you came empty-handed. While no one will criticize or question you, the feeling of having fallen short will follow you all the time. So my lack of resources weighed heavy on my mind. I kept my worries from my husband, Adjei, knowing that our heavenly Father, who cares for all the details of our lives, would deal with it.

The moment came. We had to leave for the celebration, and I still had nothing to give. As we were dressing for the wedding, Adjei handed me an envelope that a brother had given to him in church. I opened it and inside found enough money to give to both the wedding and birthday. Though I was not surprised, I was dumbfounded. God had done it again! He took my anxious situation and "made everything beautiful in His time."

Who is this God, so perfect and kind? This Savior who knows all our thoughts, all our cares? Do you know today? He wants to make all things beautiful for you. Draw close. You will find Him.

Mabel Kwei

February 18

A Beautiful Collection

"The Father himself loves you dearly."
—John 16:27, NLT

It was not the rocks crying out; it was my bottle collection whispering a beautiful new thought to me. My collection began when I brought a few brightly colored bottles to my otherwise boring office and arranged them on the wide windowsills. People noticed the bottles and began to bring me more. There is the tall, sleek purple one from my son and the soft pink one, with flowers embedded in the shape, from my daughter. There is the bright blue one with the Golden Gate Bridge etched in the side, and a maroon one shaped like a string base. Another is a sister's perfume bottle, and still another looks like a watermelon and reminds me of the camping trips I enjoyed with my family as a kid.

A student brought me an antique orange one as an apology for speaking disrespectfully to me the week before. Another student, who had been cleaning a historic cemetery on her community service project, brought me broken pieces of a purple bottle. I immediately found a place of honor for those pieces, cemetery dirt and all!

"Something is missing!" a campus consultant said after he observed my collection. "You don't have a red one!" During this conversation, we recognized each other. He had been one of my work supervisors when I was in academy—many years before. The next time he was on campus, he brought me a stately red bottle.

"Mrs. Corder, we found something that made us think of you!" the young sisters burst into my office, not even trying to contain their excitement. "We found this on the dumpster in our trailer park!" It was, honestly, a very ugly brown bottle still fragrant with whiskey, but they were so delighted to give it to me—I found a special place for it on one of the windowsills.

These are just a few of the stories I could tell you about my bottles. If I were to show them to you, I would be compelled to exclaim, "Aren't they beautiful? I treasure each one."

God has a collection, too, but not of bottles. He collects people. Some are sleek and impressive. Others are broken and dirty. Others feel like they have been left on a dumpster. God is willing to take them all into His collection. He delights in how unique they all are, He knows every story, and He treasures each one.

Cheri Corder

February 19

In the Good Shepherd's Care

*For He is our God, and we are the people of His pasture,
and the sheep of His hand.*
—Psalm 95:7, NKJV

Sheep are mentioned more than five hundred times in the Bible. In Genesis 4, we learn that Abel was a keeper of sheep. Further on we read of the large flocks of Abram and Lot. Abram's grandson Jacob was a skilled shepherd whose flocks must have also been large because ten of his sons tended their father's sheep. King David was first a shepherd boy and wrote the well-loved Shepherd's Psalm.

The duties of the ancient shepherds included keeping their flocks intact, protecting them from predators, and guiding them to market areas in time of shearing. Shepherds would graze their sheep, guiding them to areas of good forage, always sure to keep a watchful eye out for poisonous plants.

We see sheep as meek and gentle creatures, but they are also quite fearful and timid. Sheep have an intensely companionable social instinct that allows them to bond closely with one another. They are a prey species, and their only defense is to flee. Separation from the flock can cause stress and panic; however, the sound of their shepherd's voice quickly calms them. When I understand the role of a good shepherd, I am glad that Jesus is my shepherd, for He assures me in John 10:14, "I am the good shepherd; and I know My sheep, and am known by My own" (NKJV).

Driving through the southeastern part of the state of South Australia, we saw thousands of sheep grazing on pastureland. There had been heavy rain, and large pools of water lay in the depressions of the land. On two occasions we saw sheep waterlogged and unable to move because of the heaviness of their rain-drenched wool. Another time, I saw a sheep bogged in mud. Where was their shepherd?

Shepherding has changed since Bible times—but the Shepherd who leads us never changes. His name is Jesus, the One who gave His life for me—one of His wandering sheep.

The LORD is my shepherd;
I shall not want.
He makes me to lie down in green pastures;
He leads me beside the still waters. . . .

I will fear no evil;
For You are with me (Psalm 23:1–4, NKJV).

The Good Shepherd is also your Shepherd.

Lyn Welk-Sandy

February 20

Lost and Found

"For the Son of Man came to seek and to save the lost."
—Luke 19:10, NIV

My husband, Jerry, and I were living in Lamar, Colorado, USA, in our first pastoral district after leaving the seminary. Jerry was gone for the day, making some visits. I stayed home with our two children and another little boy, the son of some of our church members, who had come to play with our son. The two little boys, aged four and five, were playing on a vacant lot directly across the street from our house, happily digging in some dirt piles. We lived on a dead-end street with no traffic.

I did my best to keep a close eye on them while also taking care of our baby. After a while, I glanced out the window and did not see them in the vacant lot. I searched for them in the yard and the neighborhood. We were a one-car family, and this was long before cell phones, so I had to wait for Jerry to come home before we could finally drive around and search further for the two little boys. We called the visiting boy's mother, who also started to search, and eventually we notified the police. They, too, began to search. As evening approached and a predicted storm started to move in, the police put out an announcement on the radio.

A pastor from another denomination heard the radio announcement and decided to join the search. Before too long he spotted two little boys that fit the description he had heard on the radio. They were happily playing in a churchyard. He brought them home to some very relieved parents! Their explanation? They needed a shovel in the other little boy's garage. Never mind that they had to walk nearly a mile and cross a busy highway to get there. And, of course, talking to me about their plan would have been a really good idea!

Thinking of this story reminds me of the story Jesus told about the shepherd searching for his one lost sheep (Luke 15:1–7) and these words: "The darker and more tempestuous the night and the more perilous the way, the greater is the shepherd's anxiety and the more earnest his search."* Nothing else mattered until the one little lamb was safely back in the fold. Knowing how I felt at the sight of those two boys safe and sound helps me understand a little about how Jesus, the Good Shepherd, must feel when His sheep return safely to the fold. He says, "Rejoice with me; I have found my lost sheep" Luke 15:6 (NIV).

Sharon Oster

---

* Ellen G. White, *Christ's Object Lessons* (Washington, DC: Review and Herald®, 1900), 187.

February 21

The Need of Him

But I trust in your unfailing love. I will rejoice because you have rescued me.
—Psalm 13:5, NLT

Throughout time and space, men have always looked for God. Men tend to look for an encounter with God in the grandiose and awesome, equating their experience with the adrenaline of a conquest. Men tend to think big in monumental, huge, and spectacular ways. And they migrate that form of thinking to their devotional life and walk with God. They need the thunder; they need the imposing presence of the Almighty to shake them.

But as every daughter of Eve through generations has known and learned, God most often displays His grandiose presence as He accompanies us in the daily chores and seemingly mundane tasks of our everyday lives. God meets His daughters at the kitchen sink; He waits by the ironing board, the washing machine, and even the toilet bowl and bathroom sink to encounter us where we are. He knows we are busy and can often feel unseen. God knows we need His presence and His tender care as we are exhausted from caring for others in addition to the responsibilities we carry outside the home.

We do not need the grandiose; we need the tender Shepherd who loves and cares for His sheep and those who are with young. We need the love of our Master who has no prejudice or arrogance. We need the teachings of our Savior that apply to our lives and deliver the strength we need as we make our way through our daily to-do list. We need His watching eyes over us and warm reminders that even if nobody else notices, He does.

We long for our Savior's coming. We long for a break from the stress of this world. We yearn to be in the presence of the One who lifts us out of the dust and tenderly raises our chins in gentle dignity. We need Jesus; there is no doubt about it. And as much as we hear about the awesomeness and miracles, I am so glad that He who can calm the storm stands alongside me, doing the dishes with me as I sing hymns in gratitude for the strength to keep going forward.

What about you, my friend? Do you need Him? Then ask God to show you His care and guidance in every moment of the day—and hold fast to Him. We need to cling to Him above all else. Maranatha!

Yvita Antonette Villalona Bacchus

February 22

The Gem Cutter

*The Lord their God will save his people on that day
as a shepherd saves his flock.
They will sparkle in his land
like jewels in a crown.*
—Zechariah 9:16, NIV

Have you ever seen a gem cutter at work? I have a friend who is a gem cutter. Once, I had the opportunity to visit his workshop and admire his artwork. When I entered his showroom, a new world opened for me. I saw showcases beautifully decorated with precious stones, gemstones such as jasper, sapphire, topaz, amethyst, lapis lazuli, and many more. They were different shapes and sizes, and some had very costly settings of gold, platinum, or other precious metals. The light in the showcase made the stones shine at their best. It was incredible.

We talked about the unique characteristics of the gems, where they could be found, and how they are brought to light. Then I asked him to show me what an unprocessed gemstone looked like. We went to his workshop, and I noticed an immediate difference between the two rooms. The workshop was nothing special, just a normal workshop full of dust and dirt. Here, everything looked so common. There were shelves with lots of boxes filled with stones and rough pieces of rock. They were gray, angular, ugly, without any beauty. I was a bit disappointed.

He took a stone out of a box. I still did not see anything special in the stone. Then he began to work on it. Carefully, he cut the stone, carved from one side, polished another, and cut some more here and there. It seemed to me as if there was no plan whatsoever in his actions. But as I watched, the ugly, irregular rock transformed into a beautiful gemstone. It was amazing!

And then it suddenly dawned on me: God, the master artist and gem cutter, cuts, shapes, and polishes. He does not see the ugly rock, the stone without any value. No! He sees the perfect gemstone He is gently cutting and polishing. He sees that one day I will be in the showcase. We look at our shortcomings, blind spots, weaknesses, anxieties, and unholiness, but God sees the gem transformed by His touch.

We are still living in the gem cutter's dusty workshop, waiting for the day when Jesus returns, "in that day when I make up my jewels" (Malachi 3:17, KJV). Then, in His glorious showroom, we will shine as His precious jewels forever!

Dagmar Dorn

February 23

Precious Pearls

"The kingdom of heaven is like a merchant seeking beautiful pearls, who, when he had found one pearl of great price, went and sold all that he had and bought it."
—Matthew 13:45, 46, NKJV

Pearls fascinate me. It is amazing how an oyster can turn a piece of grit into a beautiful white pearl. It covers the ugly and unwanted irritant in layers and layers of mother-of-pearl until a perfect pearl is formed.

So it is poignant that Jesus tells a parable of a merchant who finds the most precious pearl he has ever seen and sells everything he has to buy this one beautiful gem. Pearls are different from many of the other gems, which come from stones. Pearls are born in the heart of the oyster, and they are formed to soothe the oyster's pain and discomfort.

I have seen how the challenges and tragedies of my life have been wrapped in layers and layers of God's incredible love so that now I have come to see them as precious and beautiful pearls in my life. A miscarriage, five years of a life-limiting illness, a horrendous tragedy, and the loss of a job when my husband was unexpectedly relocated to pastor in Scotland. Over time all the things that felt like broken glass in my soul have been transformed into gifts that are incredibly precious to me. Out of them have come some of my books, empathy, a degree in family therapy, and the preparation needed to turn the once shyest girl in the school into a division Family Ministries director.

God sees each of us as precious pearls. Jesus gave up everything He had to come and save us. He took a long diversion to find an outcast Samaritan woman with a life full of complexities, brokenness, and pain. The Messiah was looking for the pearl of a wounded woman who could be transformed only by His loving grace. And though she came to the well looking for water, her deeper longing was for the Pearl of great price.

And this is what the kingdom of God looks like—a merchant seeking a pearl. Jesus is still the Pearl of great price. He is *our* Pearl, and we are His pearls of great price. He pours His love and mercy over us time and time again, covering our pain layer by layer and transforming us into His precious gems that show His loving and gracious character.

Karen Holford

February 24

God's Got My Back

Be anxious for nothing, but in everything by prayer and supplication, with thanksgiving, let your requests be known to God; and the peace of God . . . will guard your hearts and minds through Christ Jesus.
—Philippians 4:6, 7, NKJV

One Sunday last winter, I awoke and thanked God for being alive, but honestly, I felt overwhelmed and frustrated. Things were not going well at all, and to add insult to injury, both vehicles were acting up, the washing machine was giving problems . . . the list went on and on.

I decided to put all the issues before God, including the fact that, except for our son, the rest of my family members were unemployed. I decided to pray every hour from nine o'clock to whenever the answer would come. And that I did.

When it was approaching three o'clock, the Spirit said, "Pray now." I obeyed, and after praying I sat for a few minutes meditating. At 3:02 P.M. the phone rang. I hesitated a bit, then answered. To my surprise, it was a friend whom I had been thinking about the week before. We chatted a little, and then she said, "Would you be interested in going back to do legal work? A friend of mine is looking for a senior person. If you're interested, please email your info to me so I can recommend you."

Without hesitation, I blurted out, "Yes!"

Sisters, that was God who answered for me because I had told myself I would not work with another lawyer ever again. I had worked for thirty-three years at my last job and thought it was enough time spent in that profession.

I sent my friend the information, and the next day, a Monday, before 6:30 A.M., I received a call for an interview. The person who interviewed me asked a few questions and then said, "I don't need to ask any more questions because my heart is telling me that you are the one for the job." That person is now my boss.

Today, a little more than a year later, I am still employed, managing the office, receiving almost the same salary as when I left my former job six years ago. I am enjoying the blessings of the Lord. My prayer is that this testimony helps someone who is waiting in line for their blessing. God has our best interest at heart and is more than willing to bless us. Keep trusting—the blessings are on their way. God is an on-time God, and He has our back.

Brenda Browne-Ashe

February 25

Made Redundant Twice

It was good for me to be afflicted so that I might learn your decrees.
—Psalm 119:71, NIV

Almost five years ago, my position in church administration was made redundant midway through my term. It was a very difficult time. The position had been challenging, and I had done my best with only minimal help from the team with which I worked. All these years later, the pain can still sometimes resurface.

To make matters worse, three years after that experience, my position in departmental leadership was also made redundant. Can you imagine how that made me feel? With the wounds from my first redundancy still not fully healed, the second redundancy reopened everything and left me emotionally bleeding once more.

I felt hurt, angry, and disappointed. Though I tried to understand why it was happening, I was left feeling sad and confused. Just when I thought I knew what I was doing in that position and where I was going, just when I felt confident in having found my voice—now I felt crushed. I cried a lot. I walked a lot. I prayed a lot.

Fast-forward to today. I have the benefit of seeing things from hindsight and can better understand what David meant in Psalm 119:71. It was good for me to be afflicted. It was not pleasant, but it was good. God allowed me to be afflicted so that I might learn the deeper lessons of His love, patience, and understanding. This helped me learn some important things about myself and what it means to be a leader. I learned lessons in humility, teachability, leadership, forgiveness, and how to make difficult decisions.

It seems we cannot learn certain vital lessons unless we are afflicted in some way. How else would I be able to understand what another person may be going through unless I had experienced something similar? I am grateful for the decision I made the first day after my redundancy. While walking and crying out loud, and with tears streaming down my face, I said, "I choose to forgive those who made this decision. I am willing to walk this valley with God, knowing He will work it out for my good." Though it took a long time to heal and for my head and heart to sing the same song, looking back, I recognize that it was good for me to be afflicted.

Are you facing afflictions? Trust God. He will work it out for your good. He did it for me.

Danijela Schubert

February 26

Welcome Home, Children

The LORD is near to the brokenhearted and saves those who are crushed in spirit.
—Psalm 34:18, NASB

The year my mother turned ninety-three was a challenging year for my siblings and me. Two weeks after her birthday celebration, Mother complained of severe abdominal pain. A CT scan revealed a malignant tumor at the base of the ascending colon. Coherent and alert, she made all the decisions for her care and signed the consent for surgery. Mother made it through the procedure, but complications with her lungs took her life three weeks later.

My siblings and I had been able to Facetime with our mother while she was in the hospital, and as we monitored her progress, we booked a flight for her scheduled release date. We were devastated by her loss before we could fly home. The loss of a mother cannot be adequately explained. She was the reason for family reunions. We had planned a special celebration for her ninety-fifth birthday, and children, spouses, grandchildren, and great-grandchildren were preparing for an event that would not happen.

After her death I found myself silent with grief. When the Sabbath School teacher asked me to comment on the lesson, I refrained from speaking, which was unusual. The only outside commitment I accepted was to continue teaching nursing students. This became my solace and comfort as I battled depression. Sharing clinical scenarios of my mother's case was my way of expressing my grief and loss, and the students learned how to make sense of evidenced clinical situations.

Elizabeth Kübler-Ross identified the five stages of grief as denial, anger, bargaining, depression, and acceptance.* By God's grace and mercy, I accepted the loss but desperately missed talking with my mother. Paul writes that "the peace of God, which transcends all understanding, will guard your hearts and your minds in Christ Jesus" (Philippians 4:7, NIV).

I am so grateful for all the good things God has given: faithful parents who now rest in Jesus and the glorious hope in the resurrection morning when Jesus shall welcome all His children home. Then we will say, "I have fought the good fight, I have finished the race, I have kept the faith" of Jesus (2 Timothy 4:7, NIV). On that day there will be no more sorrow, no more tears (see Revelation 21:4). Maranatha!

Edna Bacate Domingo

---

* Elisabeth Kübler-Ross, *On Death and Dying: What the Dying Have to Teach Doctors, Nurses, Clergy, and Their Own Families* (New York: Macmillan, 1969).

February 27

Just Like That

Why, you do not even know what will happen tomorrow. What is your life? You are a mist that appears for a little while and then vanishes.
—James 4:14, NIV

It was the first Android phone gifted to me by a girlfriend. How I cherished it—for two years. One night I put it on the charger, and the next morning it would not power on. Finally a technician explained that the battery had stopped working. The phone, which had seemed fine and in good working order the night before, had now died. Just like that.

It reminded me of a WhatsApp chat with a friend.

"Hey, how is your stomach doing?" I asked.

A little while later, a message notification popped up, and I reopened the chat and received the shock of my life.

"Hi, this is his nephew. Sadly, he died suddenly yesterday afternoon."

Immediately I was plunged into waves of grief, denial, anger, and depression. My heart sank to such a depth of sadness. My friend was gone. Just like that.

He was a very good friend, one to whom I could speak about anything under the sun. We loved to exchange funny videos and jokes. In reviewing our chat history, I noticed the last message he sent me was just the day before. I struggled to believe that someone I had literally just spoken to and joked with was gone. Just like that.

We never get used to the suddenness with which life can change or be taken away. Even news of the unexpected deaths of people we do not know closely shocks and saddens us. James 4:14 reminds us that life is like a vapor, and in his play *Hamlet*, Shakespeare describes man as "the quintessence of dust."* Nothing in life is guaranteed. Like my phone, many people seem fine but go to bed and never wake up. The battery of their heart dies. Just like that. This is why we must make the very best of each day and live our lives for God. Psalm 90:12 cautions us to "number our days," consider the brevity of life, and live wisely.

As I reviewed further conversations I had with my friend, I noticed where he advised me "to enjoy every moment. Never live with rage, anger, hatred, regret, or anything that interferes with enjoying every moment granted to you by the Good Lord. Life is best lived by the enjoyment of every moment."

I will apply my heart to this wisdom: Life is but a mist, so I will choose to live for God and enjoy every moment. My prayer is for all of us to do the same.

Judelia Medard-Santiesteban

---

* William Shakespeare, *Hamlet, Prince of Denmark* (London: Blackie and Son, 1902), 60, act 2, scene 2, line 308.

February 28

The Hopeful: Lessons on Grief

Brothers and sisters, we do not want you to be uninformed about those who sleep in death, so that you do not grieve like the rest of mankind, who have no hope.
—1 Thessalonians 4:13, NIV

Not too long ago, one of my students passed away unexpectedly. He was a fun young man, a go-getter who communicated his needs and wants openly. I have vivid memories of him walking around the building, searching for solo cups because he was thirsty, or passing out chips and popcorn for a quick snack. He had the best smile and would often ask me to help him with assignments or join my small group with a cheerful, "Dr. Williams, can I come with you?" I will definitely miss him.

The day after his passing, I arrived at school and found out the news. I was devastated—it was one of the hardest days of my professional life. There was not a dry eye in the building, and students flocked in and out of counseling sessions all day. Having experienced recent loss myself, I dreaded the days ahead, anticipating the difficulty of helping our students navigate their grief. However, what I witnessed was the exact opposite.

The next day, students flooded in wearing red, actively debating whether or not red was his favorite color. They painted their faces with his sports numbers and acronyms in his memory, signed posters throughout the halls, and made homemade condolence cards for his family. They also planned weekly fun days to help get through the last few weeks of school.

Since his passing, I have seen resilience and community like never before, and I am thankful to God for that.

A few weeks later, I attended his funeral. It was a difficult but beautiful celebration of his life. It was heartening to see coworkers and students, along with their families, come together in support of his grieving family. At the end of the service, four young people gave their lives to Jesus. What a testimony!

Through this moment God whispered to me that while life brings heartaches we cannot fathom, He has a way of working all things out for good. We can experience hope in the face of immeasurable loss. Through community and faith, even the darkest times can be transformed into moments of growth and unity. How blessed are we to have this hope? I am beyond grateful.

LaKeisha Williams

March 1

The ABCs for Women

She opens her mouth in wisdom,
And the teaching of kindness is on her tongue.
—Proverbs 31:26, NASB

Women are designed with unique and amazing qualities—just look at Proverbs 31. Let us examine how we can discover our value, worth, and purpose by listing some ABCs for women.

A—Acknowledge and accept who we are. Jesus created us, and we are worthy. We have great value, and as we acknowledge Him, "He shall direct [our] paths" (Proverbs 3:6, NKJV). Let us put our whole heart, mind, and spirit into trusting God and learn anew to bring all our decisions, concerns, and works of service to God in prayer, always listening for His still, small voice.

B—Beauty. In Ecclesiastes 3:11 we read, "He has made everything beautiful in its time. Also He has put eternity in their hearts" (NKJV). God has made us beautiful. Let us go forth, humbly acknowledging our beauty. He has set eternity in our hearts, so let us set eternal goals daily. He wants our lives to count and for us to be productive, effective, and impactful. We can go outside our comfort zones and explore various ministries—or create our own as God leads. We can allow God to show us His purpose. We will be amazed as our trust in God empowers us to share the good news of Jesus Christ—with beauty. He wants to expand our territory.

C—Courage. In Esther 4:14, Mordecai says to Esther, "For if you remain completely silent at this time, relief and deliverance will arise . . . from another place. . . . Yet who knows whether you have come . . . for such a time as this?" (NKJV). Demonstrating courage means we will always choose to trust God, knowing He is faithful. He wants us to be copartners with Him in ministry. This world is not our home. We are just passing through it, and we have been called to participate with the Lord to complete the divine assignments He has given. We are here to make known the blessed hope that we hold so dear. Let us lay aside our fears and boldly establish a loving commitment to serving others, trusting that what we lack, God will provide. My friends, let us take action with God-given courage and be like Esther.

We do not have to stop at ABC. I encourage you to complete the additional twenty-three letters of the alphabet in your study time. God will give you the Scripture and words that will further define your value, worth, and purpose in Him.

Ella Clark-Tolliver

March 2

Admirable Women of the Bible

*Charm is deceptive, and beauty is fleeting;
but a woman who fears the LORD is to be praised.
Honor her for all that her hands have done,
and let her works bring her praise at the city gate.*
—Proverbs 31:30, 31, NIV

Sarah might be my favorite woman in the Bible, perhaps because I see so much of who I am in her. Yet God answered her deepest desire, and she made it into the hall of faith in Hebrews 11. Sarah was by no means perfect. She doubted when God told her something, and when He seemed slow to deliver on His promise, she reasoned it away and took matters into her own hands. How I resonate with Sarah.

I have been there. I have grown tired of waiting on God and have taken matters into my own hands. The outcome was not pleasant. Friends, please tell me I am not the only one.

But God! But God, in His infinite grace and mercy, still gives what He has promised, and Sarah is thus considered a woman of faith.

Another woman in the Bible who is not typically spoken of much is Queen Vashti, the reigning queen before Esther became queen. Vashti's husband acted foolishly after becoming drunk and demanded she perform for him and his friends. Queen Vashti said no. She stood up for what she believed to be right. As I contemplate my own life, I pray that I will have Vashti's courage when I am asked to do something that goes against my beliefs. I want to be able to say no as she did—no matter the consequences.

Then there is Queen Esther. When I read her story, I just have to say, "God had a plan!" God placed Queen Esther in the palace specifically so that through her He could save His children, the Israelites, from total annihilation. He blessed her, and she found favor with the king, demonstrating great wisdom, grace, and reliance on God as she approached the king on behalf of her people. Before going in to see the king, she called on her people to fast, humbling themselves before the King of heaven, and their petitions were answered.

I have not even begun to scratch the surface of all the stories of the incredible women in the Bible. But I want to share Proverbs 31:30, 31, which states,

> Charm is deceptive, and beauty is fleeting;
>   but a woman who fears the LORD is to be praised.
> Honor her for all that her hands have done,
>   and let her works bring her praise at the city gate (NIV).

Kaysian C. Gordon

March 3

Hannah's Third Height

"I am the woman who stood by you here, praying to the Lord. *For this child I prayed, and the* Lord *has granted me my petition which I asked of Him."*
—1 Samuel 1:26, 27, NKJV

Many have heard Hannah's story, but is it relevant to us? Let us see. Hannah's family lived in the city Ramathoim Zophim, which means "two heights." In this story, we meet several sets of two, sets of two contrasts. Hannah and her husband Elkanah were childless, but he was from the country of Ephraim, which means "fruitful." To solve the problem, he took a second wife. Then one wife was childless; the other was fruitful. Their names were also in contrast: Hannah means "grace," and Peninnah means "ruby/red precious stone." An inner beauty versus an outward beauty. A divine characteristic versus a material one. Other contrasts are also in the story: meekness and jealousy, feast and fasting, joy and sorrow, a husband's love and his misapprehension, an apparent victory by Peninnah and real victory by Hannah, and something impossible for men to accomplish but possible for God.

Hannah's city, which had double heights, stands as a symbol of our lives, where good and bad are often found side by side. Today we have joy—tomorrow, sorrow. However, Hannah found the third height, the height where God lives. She brought her problem to Him. In her prayer she expressed her faith in *Elohim Sabaoth*, "the Lord of hosts," who can do the impossible. She did not receive an immediate answer, but she gained the peace that only God can give. This was a time when the word of God was rare among the people of Israel. God was looking for an upright family in which to raise up a prophet.

Hannah's family was imperfect, but God used it to fulfill His plan. Though Hannah had previously prayed earnestly for a child, now she not only prayed but also was ready to return His gift to Him to be used for His glory. Hannah's life continued, filled with other contrasts. She asked for a child; God gave her children. The Lord of hosts also became the Lord of her little boy. She gave Samuel to God, and God made him a prophet. God's plans for us and our children are always much bigger than we can imagine. Will we allow Him to use us and our imperfect family for His perfect plans? For His glory? Are we willing to discover the third height, as Hannah did, and meet our God, who is able to do the impossible?

Galina Stele

March 4

What Is Salvation?

Neither is there salvation in any other: for there is none other name under heaven given among men, whereby we must be saved.
—Acts 4:12, KJV

I am part of a global digital missionary group that meets weekly via Zoom for training, reports, and worship led by Adventist World Radio personnel. It is always a blessing, but little did I imagine how the Lord would use it to profoundly redirect the way I live and work for Him.

For the last five years, a relative has been staying in my home. With some trepidation, I agreed to help him as he promised, "It is for a short time. Just until I get on my feet." I never dreamed it would become a nightmare. As time passed, his drinking and smoking came to light. I tried different strategies to help him get rid of these habits, but nothing worked. I asked every prayer group to pray for him. I prayed for him, I talked with him, I counseled him, I fussed at him, I offered him professional resources, and I gave him all the facts surrounding his negative habits. I ignored him, elders visited with him, relatives spoke to him, and his healthcare workers spoke to him. We had daily devotions and prayed together, but still, nothing worked.

On that life-changing Zoom call, the theme of the worship segment was titled "Salvation Is Not an Event: It Is a Person." As we were assigned to our breakout rooms to pray, we were charged to ask Jesus to change us—not to repair us, not to mend or fix us, but to give us new hearts. In addition, we were asked to present Jesus to our contacts, whether they were in our homes, our local communities, or our digital communities.

The worship leader said, "If someone is smoking and/or drinking around you, remember this: Salvation is not an event; it is a Person."

How that statement resonated with me. It grabbed and held my attention. And as we prayed together, each one echoed the same sentiment. We had never heard it stated in such clear language, even though we thought the love of God was something we knew about.

It does not matter how hard we try, how much good we think we are doing, or how much effort we put forth to try to transform the unbeliever; let us first endeavor to have the Person of Jesus make us anew each day. This is the Person we need to introduce to others. Only when this principle is lived out in our own lives will our testimony have power. My relative is slowly accepting this Jesus. Amen!

Pauline A. Dwyer-Kerr

March 5

A Time to Witness

"You are my witnesses," declares the Lord.
—Isaiah 43:12, NIV

One of the valuable lessons I have learned from my long career as a nurse is how not to be a bad patient. Several pointers include not asking your nurse to do something you can do for yourself, not expecting instant service unless it is an emergency (nurses are typically overextended), being cheerful even if you do not feel your best, and always saying thank you. Most people do not realize that good patients get better service.

Recently I found myself a patient in a large teaching hospital after complications from an emergency colon resection at my home hospital. My surgeon felt it unwise to attempt further surgery there, so he referred me to a university hospital. In the operating room, I asked and was permitted to say a prayer for God's presence and care during surgery.

After a lengthy surgery by three specialists, I awoke with a large incision, colostomy, catheter, NG tube, and an IV. My daughter, Julie, was there to lovingly support me. I determined to be a good patient. I used my call light with discretion, helped bathe myself, walked in the hall several times a day, and was cheerful and grateful. Each morning before the doctor's rounds, I got up early, sponged off, brushed my teeth, and put a smile on my face. Whenever they made a positive comment about my condition, I said, "Praise the Lord."

One morning after rounds, one of the residents returned to my room and asked to pray with me. Another day, a medical student returned to my room and stated, "I feel the Holy Spirit in this room." Occasionally, a nurse would come by just to visit for a minute.

While there, I frequently played soft religious music, which gave me peace. One morning, the song "Give Me Jesus" came on. I just could not help myself and enthusiastically sang, "In the morning when I rise, give me Jesus."

My door abruptly opened, and a nurse said with a smile, "We heard you singing."

My stay there was lengthy and not without challenges, but I did my best to be an encouragement and a blessing each day. My recovery progressed nicely, and discharge day arrived. My surgeon sat on the foot of the bed and told me I had been a very good patient.

I felt blessed to have been given a precious opportunity to be a witness to all my caregivers. We can be a witness of God's goodness everywhere. May we not waste a single opportunity.

Rose Neff Sikora

March 6

Let's Play Tag

The Lord GOD hath given me the tongue of the learned, that I should know how to speak a word in season to him that is weary: he wakeneth morning by morning, he wakeneth mine ear to hear as the learned.
—Isaiah 50:4, KJV

I remember playing outside with my friends as a child. We had lots of energy to burn and plenty of time on our hands. We played countless games, but one of my favorites was tag. The idea of the game was to choose one player to be "it." Whoever was "it" had to run after the other children, attempting to tag one of them, who would then become "it." How we loved to chase each other around the trees.

Now, many years later, I am a minibus tour guide in Bermuda, and I pray every day, "Lord, help me to reach someone within my sphere of influence so I can touch someone for You." What God really wants is someone willing to speak for Him, and He will do the connecting.

On one particular day I had a wonderful family of eight who were happy and excited to be on tour. They enjoyed swimming at the beach and exploring our beautiful island. However, one member of the group did not join us due to an emergency. As the tour neared its end, one of the family members received a call and learned that her father was being kept at the hospital and her mother needed to get back to the ship.

As the mother entered the van, she was crying in distress. She thanked me for the ride, and I asked her if there was anything I could do to help. I shared that I had a pastoral pass and would be allowed to visit her husband in the hospital.

She surprised me by responding, "Yes, I know you do. I looked you up before I came on tour this morning."

Later that day I "tagged" my pastor because my tour schedule was full for the next few days, and I was unable to get to the hospital. Because of the sensitivity of her husband's condition, we agreed the pastor was the best one to visit the hospital. They had a meaningful, encouraging visit. I was also able to connect and pray with his wife when she returned home.

As I considered the turn of events, the game from my childhood popped into my head. God, in His divine foresight, uses us to reach others. Many years before, God used my husband to "tag" me with the gospel so that I could "tag" others. So I encourage you today, "Let's play tag!"

Julie Richardson

March 7

Growing Through Prayer

Never stop praying.
—1 Thessalonians 5:17, NLT

I once heard someone say, "Prayer is like the air we breathe; without it, we are spiritually dead."

For Christians, prayer is one of the most essential aspects of our lives.

Luke records that "Jesus often withdrew to the wilderness for prayer" (Luke 5:16, NLT). He needed to take a break from the demands of His busy life to recharge and connect with His Father. His life serves as an example, demonstrating what we should aspire to as His followers. Even though Jesus was God incarnate, He did not rely on His divine powers to navigate life's challenges. Instead, when He faced exhaustion, burdens, or spiritual dryness, He would slip away to pray, drawing strength, vision, and clarity from God's presence.

In Luke 23:46 we find Jesus speaking with great reverence and recognition of His Father's supremacy, saying, "Father, 'into Your hands I commit My spirit' " (NKJV). He was willing to obey even during His great suffering on the cross, realizing that God was the author of His life on earth. He clung tightly to hope, and as a result, He could fully claim God's blessings through a powerful spiritual connection with His Father, deepening His divine purpose.

However, our prayers can sometimes feel repetitive and mundane. Sometimes they even seem stale, which can lead to a sense of ineffectiveness. When we rush into prayer without preparing our hearts and minds, we fail to be receptive enough to hear His voice.

One powerful prayer we can use to kick-start our day is, "O Lord, be gracious unto us; we have waited for thee: be thou their arm every morning, our salvation also in the time of trouble" (Isaiah 33:2, KJV). Isaiah's words, spoken from an earnest and sincere heart, can help us move forward each day. I truly believe the Holy Spirit directed Isaiah's prayer, as He can direct our prayers.

Prayer is our most powerful weapon as we engage daily in spiritual warfare. The key to a vibrant prayer life lies in recognizing our need to submit to Christ's authority, even as He submitted to His Father's authority. Additionally, it is essential to cultivate a love for Scripture and deepen our relationship with God through prayer. Time spent in the Word and in prayer will strengthen and empower our lives. May God bless us as we grow in Him through prayer.

Orathai Chureson

March 8

So Many Women

"Sing to the Lord, *for he has triumphed gloriously; the horse and his rider he has thrown into the sea."*
—Exodus 15:21, ESV

Moses is certainly the hero of the biblical Exodus story, but have you ever thought about how many women were important in making this story what it is? See Exodus chapters 1–15.

First, there are the midwives: Shiphrah and Puah. I have read that an Egyptian inscription lists the name Shiphrah. While there is no indication that it referred to a midwife, it was certainly a known name. They saved many babies by claiming that the Hebrew women delivered their babies before the midwife could arrive, thereby negating Pharaoh's death order.

It seems it was Jochebed's idea as to how to save her third child, baby Moses, by building a little floating cradle and putting it among the bulrushes. Miriam was important in this plan and played her part perfectly, offering to find a Hebrew woman to nurse the baby without revealing she would call the baby's mother, although the princess may well have guessed. The princess is an important part of the story too. She easily could have followed the rules and had the baby killed, but she adopted, educated, and protected Moses until he was forty years old. It is believed that this princess may have been the famous eighteenth-dynasty princess who later became Queen Hatshepsut. There is still an impressive temple of Hatshepsut in the Valley of the Kings south of Cairo, in Egypt. Her name has been almost completely chipped out, indicating that she may have fallen out of favor. Maybe for having adopted the Hebrew who became a murderer?

Next, there is Zipporah, the daughter of the priest of Median whom Moses married. She bore him two sons. But it is on the way back to Egypt with Moses that she becomes important, saving Moses' life. This story has always puzzled me, but I have read that by circumcising her son and touching it to Moses's feet (genitals), it functions as an expiation for the guilt Moses still carried for committing murder—there was a myth that circumcision could quell divine wrath.

Miriam shows up again, leading the women to dance with timbrels as they sing their song of victory. I have read that Old Testament women were the ones who led the singing and maybe writing the songs of victory, as only women are seen with timbrels in ancient inscriptions.

We thank God for using women to accomplish His will, then and now.

Ardis Dick Stenbakken

March 9

Fix It, Lord

*And he said unto me, My grace is sufficient for thee:
for my strength is made perfect in weakness.*
—2 Corinthians 12:9, KJV

I struggled with infertility. I prayed, fasted, ate well, and exercised. I followed "old wives tales" and took medication. Finally I surrendered. My prayer was, *Three more months, Lord. If this is not Your will for me, keep me from falling pregnant, and let me have peace.*

The first month, nothing. I cried. The second month, still nothing. I was sad. The third month, I was OK. I accepted it and was not angry. I was simply ready to move on with my life. As I cleaned out my fertility cupboard, I looked at the last two pregnancy tests in my now diminishing pile. *Well, that's the end of that. Might as well use them up.* So I did. The test read positive.

Fast-forward thirteen years: My daughter had been sick on and off for a year and kept growing worse. The doctor said surgery was her best option. While it would not fix the problem, it would stop it from worsening, though she could possibly experience some pain. With her situation growing severe, she needed surgery immediately. She would then be home-schooled for about a year and would have to relearn how to walk. Did I mention she might still have pain? How was this a solution? No! I could not believe this was happening. *God, You have to fix this!*

Many times, this is how we feel. God blesses us, only for life to turn things upside down and leave us feeling our life is cursed. The dream job is stressing you so much your hair is falling out. That handsome dude you married has morphed into an object of abject misery. The post you prayed you would get at church has become a burden. Things change, people change, and now you are in a dungeon of dread, demanding deliverance from God. *Fix it, Lord!* is your ongoing cry. *I cannot do this!*

Then God opens His arms and comforts us. "It's OK, daughter. My grace is sufficient. I've got you. My strength is made perfect in your weakness. I am here for you and always will be. It's going to be OK."

Life is hard, but we can take comfort in the fact that we are never alone, for God has promised He would never leave or forsake us. You do not have to carry your burdens all by yourself. As life threatens to overwhelm you, turn to Jesus, rely on Him, and allow Him to carry you through the trials in your life.

Kathy-ann Best

March 10

Barren and Desperate

Is anything too hard for the LORD?
—Genesis 18:14, KJV

Sarai was a prestigious woman, wife to a wealthy, influential husband, but something was missing. She was childless. To complicate matters, Sarai and her husband, Abram, were past childbearing age. Decades earlier God had promised He would bless them with a child, but the years passed, and the promise remained unfulfilled. Sarai became desperate and devised her solution to the problem. Unfortunately when we go outside God's plan and fail to trust and obey, we suffer the consequences.

Sarai convinced Abram to take Hagar, her Egyptian maid, as a second wife and surrogate mother through whom they could have children. After Hagar became pregnant, she began acting superior to Sarai, looking at her with disdain. When she persuaded Abram to take Hagar, little did Sarai think she was opening the floodgates for rivalry and hatred that still exists today.

Sarai was distressed and blamed Abram for Hagar's attitude toward her. Abram told Sarai, "Hagar is still your maid, so do whatever you think is best with her."

Then Sarai exerted her authority as Abram's wife, but Hagar refused to submit. Instead she ran away with no specific destination in mind. In the desert she encountered the God who sees and knows everything. He admonished her to return and submit to her mistress. He also made her a promise of hope and a future for her and her unborn son.

In His forgiving love and mercy, God appeared to Abram when he was ninety-nine years old and assured him that his long-barren wife, although now ninety years old, would conceive. To confirm His promise, God changed Abram's name to Abraham and Sarai's to Sarah (Genesis 17:5, 15). The aged pair laughed at the announcement, both for different reasons. Abraham's laughter was the joy of a man of faith. Sarah's was that of doubt. But God assured her, "Is anything too hard for the LORD?" (Genesis 18:14, KJV).

At the time appointed, God fulfilled His promise to Sarah and Abraham. Sarah conceived and gave birth to a son, whom they named Isaac. Sarah now had good reason to laugh—for joy. As Christians may we always remember that God keeps His promises and that our intervention is unnecessary.

E. May Clarke

March 11

In God's Appointed Time

It was you who opened up springs and streams;
you dried up the ever-flowing rivers.
The day is yours, and yours also the night;
you established the sun and moon.
It was you who set all the boundaries of the earth;
you made both summer and winter.
—Psalm 74:15–17, NIV

The morning light stretched long shadows across the desolate winter garden. Tangled shrubs stripped of their leaves and tree branches weighed down by freshly fallen snow looked weary and ghostly. The garden seemed to echo the discontent I felt. "Pitiful," I muttered, clutching my coat tightly as I trudged through the snow-covered landscape. Suddenly a sharp tug on my hair brought me to an abrupt halt. Someone was pulling my hair!

Turning, I realized I had been ensnared by the thorny New Dawn climbing rose that adorned one of the arches at the garden's entrance. The tug had felt deliberate, as if nature itself was scolding me, demanding my attention to its silent resilience. The rose bush, now stripped bare of its summer glories, stood as a stark reminder of the passage of time. Though devoid of blooms, buds, or petals, its gnarled branches harbored a quiet promise of renewal and beauty yet to come.

As I struggled to free my hair from the rose's thorny grasp, a flood of memories rushed in, transporting me back to the spring and summer flower gardens. Underneath the expansive sky, this same arching rose had burst into a breathtaking display of pink blossoms, teaching me that in the natural world, everything adheres to its own timeline, patiently awaiting the right moment to emerge and reveal its splendor.

The psalmist's wisdom reminds me that every season has its purpose. See Psalm 74:15–17. In the ebb and flow of life, where uncertainty and longing often grip our hearts, the steadfastness of God's promises sustains us. The wisdom of the Scriptures reminds us there is a time for everything, a season for every activity under the heavens. This profound truth reveals that each moment of our lives is divinely orchestrated to serve a greater purpose. As we navigate the various seasons of our lives, God's promises serve as an anchor for our hope. His assurance of eternal life and redemption remain unshakable, providing a comfort that transcends our immediate struggles. Let us hold fast to the unchanging promises of God. They are the steady foundation on which we build our faith. His promises will hold us fast until the end.

Olga Valdivia

March 12

God's Plan Is Always the Best

Man proposes, but God disposes.
—Proverbs 19:21, TLB

Looking back, I did not make many plans for my life, but I wanted to be a counselor. My mother wanted me to be a nurse and enrolled me in a high school where I could graduate as a practical nurse. Starting clinicals, I acknowledged that nursing was my mother's dream, not mine. While studying psychology in college, God placed me in a job that started my career in information technology.

God also gave me a desire to serve Him full-time. Shortly after the tragedy of 9/11 in the United States of America, I sought to be a missionary but ended up joining the Peace Corps. Through that organization I helped provide aid in West Africa while representing the United States. I taught computers at a college and worked for the church while there. On my return home after two years, I wanted to start a nonprofit to train women on welfare how to use computers and qualify for better jobs. Without the financial support to get this going, I had to find work, and God blessed me financially once again.

Still, I had the desire to work more directly for Him and thought of working as a literature evangelist, though I was unsure I could support myself in that work. I wondered how God would get me from where I was with a good government job to working full-time for Him.

Then the time came when my mother could no longer live by herself. I dropped everything and moved a thousand miles to live with her. After five years her dementia meant she could not be left alone; however, I needed to work to survive. My sister suggested we move in with her and her husband as their children no longer lived at home. That way I would not have to work and could stay home with my mother.

I marvel at God's design in giving me the flexibility to work for Him. I serve my church as a Bible worker and lead my church's web team and family life ministry. I assist a local Christian college with their online Missionary Training School, and recently I started a weekly Bible study in our apartment building. I see this as God's plan from the beginning. I also believe this is just the beginning. He is preparing me for a greater work, leading others to Him.

God has a work for each of us to do. As we follow Him, He will lead us to it.

Mirlene André

March 13

Our Unshakable Foundation

These things I have written to you who believe in the name of the Son of God, that you may know that you have eternal life, and that you may continue to believe in the name of the Son of God.
—1 John 5:13, NKJV

The strength of the foundation on which a house is built determines its ability to stand firm. The same applies to our Christian faith. Our faith in God depends on the truths that have been settled in our hearts and minds forever—truths that have been tested in the storms, trials, and challenges of our human experiences. Every precious promise in the Word of God is grounded in the merits of Christ Jesus. In moments when you are tempted to doubt, question how God feels about you, or wonder what your future holds, three truths will help you stand unshakable:

Truth 1: God loves you, and nothing you do can change His love for you. "I have loved you with an everlasting love; therefore with lovingkindness I have drawn you" (Jeremiah 31:3, NKJV). Romans 8 settles forever that nothing shall ever separate us from the love of God. Our love for God may waver, but His love for us will never change.

Truth 2: Sin has damaged everything in us. "But we are all like an unclean thing, and all our righteousnesses are like filthy rags" (Isaiah 64:6, NKJV). This truth will keep us from trying in our own strength to be what only Jesus can make us through the power of the Holy Spirit. Our part each day is to yield, abide, and surrender every sin and brokenness that sin has created in our lives so that Christ can heal and restore us.

Truth 3: We can live confidently in the assurance of our salvation. "These things I have written to you who believe in the name of the Son of God, that you may know that you have eternal life" (1 John 5:13, NKJV).

We may doubt our salvation, but as we look at Jesus hanging on the cross for us, all doubts vanish. Our salvation has never and will never be based on our merits but on the merits of Jesus. Therefore, live each day with the assurance of your salvation: "Being confident of this very thing, that He who has begun a good work in you will complete it until the day of Jesus Christ" (Philippians 1:6, NKJV).

Lillian Torres

March 14

It Is a Process—Not a Product

And I am certain that God, who began the good work within you, will continue his work until it is finally finished on the day when Christ Jesus returns.
—Philippians 1:6, NLT

Every day we are bombarded with information that encourages us to change, to become the best version of ourselves—better than we have ever been. I am sure you have seen some version of this message.

When I determined it was time for me to change, I began to listen to all the voices. Some told me to journal. I tried it but found I could not keep it up on a daily basis. Others suggested meditation. I was not comfortable with the "Eastern thought" meditation.

Finally I began to understand that I could not change myself without outside help. So I turned to the Lord, and He reminded me that I was first His. He created me as a person with free choice, and He had just been waiting for me to ask for His help.

Now, let me make this admission—I am the person who needs to be in control. Yet the Lord reminded me that if I really wanted to change, I could not do it on my own. I would definitely have to let go and allow Him to be in control. It was freeing to know I did not have to work this out on my own. He would handle everything I was willing to put in His hands.

> For the LORD God is our sun and our shield.
> He gives us grace and glory.
> The LORD will withhold no good thing
> from those who do what is right (Psalm 84:11, NLT).

Here is another admission—even though I know this to be true, it is still a daily challenge to allow Him to be God.

I find encouragement in the fact the Lord does not change me all at once. I do not think I could handle that. He walks with me every day, and He allows me to be me, and sometimes that means He rescues me from myself. I love that He never says, "I told you so!" In fact, in our quiet moments, He asks if I learned anything from my experience.

Since He has not yet returned, I look forward to the day when He has finished His work in me. I will spend the ceaseless ages of eternity praising Him and thanking Him for His lovingkindness and patience toward me and the place He has prepared with me in mind. One day soon, friends. It is not long now.

I look forward to seeing you there.

Wilma Kirk Lee

March 15

God's Transforming Love

"I have loved you with an everlasting love; therefore I have continued my faithfulness to you."
—Jeremiah 31:3, ESV

I stood in front of the dresser and glanced at the red stickers with the white letters. They read, "I AM LOVED." I had seen them before, but this time God got my attention. I sensed His pure, true love. It was so gentle and light, it took away a heaviness I did not even know existed. The gentle presence of His love caused me to give my complete devotion to God. I never wanted to serve the world again. In that moment I felt as if I had never been loved before, as if this were the first time the sweet tendrils of love had wrapped around my heart. I knew God had created me for a relationship with Him. I wanted to stay wrapped up in His love forever, but the feeling dissipated.

I remember the day I received the stickers. As my thirteen-year-old daughter and I walked past the carousel in the mall, a middle-aged man introduced himself and asked if he could pray for us. I thought of all the times I had been told to beware of strangers, but I smiled and said, "Yes." We bowed our heads, and he prayed. After he said "Amen," he reached into a bag and pulled out a couple of pins and stickers, red with white letters spelling out "I AM LOVED." I tucked them into a small zippered pocket in my purse and forgot about them. Years later I noticed the purse hanging unused in the back of my closet. I decided to clean out all the old receipts, dried-up pens, and the other junk that collects in a purse. When I found the stickers, I smiled at the memory and put them on my dresser to remind me of God's love.

I long to reexperience the power of that moment in time when God's love showed up so clearly—with noise-canceling headphones and strong glasses. But it did provide me with a true north to the compass of my life. Now, when I am tempted to sin, I try to remember to ask for the sweetness of the power of God's love to protect me. I picture it like the wings of protection He promises to cover us with.

"He will cover you with his feathers, and under his wings you will find refuge; his faithfulness will be your shield and rampart" (Psalm 91:4, NIV). Feathers may not seem to provide much protection in the whole scheme of things, but when we hide under God's love, His faithfulness changes us. We are transformed by His love.

Miranda Hadley

March 16

God's Look Alike

*So God created human beings in his own image. In the image
of God he created them; male and female he created them.*
—Genesis 1:27, NLT

Some years ago my older sister shared with us, her siblings, an experience she had while riding along on the bus to the city to run some errands. As she reached the neighborhood where our mother grew up, an older woman boarded the bus and sat close to her. As they traveled along, my sister said that, after a few minutes, the woman looked over at her and began to speak. She asked a very simple question, "Are you Myrtle's daughter? You look just like her."

My sister was shocked that the woman had been able to recognize her mother in her features. She responded by affirming that Myrtle was indeed her mother's name. The woman then went on to talk about how much my sister looked like our mom when she was younger, even in the way she spoke. She mentioned that even her gestures were so similar, and she just could not get over it.

My sister's experience got me thinking about how we, as children of God, should look like our heavenly Father. We often profess that God is our heavenly Father, and we should be like Him—but are we like Him? Do we reflect God in the things we do and say? What do people see in us as they board the bus of life or when they meet us on the street? At the moment we come into a person's presence, will they be able to ask us the question, "Are you a child of God?"

When the world looks at us, they should be able to call out and say, "You look just like Him; everything about you reminds me of Him." When my family members look at photos of my mom as a teenager or even as a young adult, we can all clearly see how much my sister looks just like her.

It is my prayer for us to be a reflection of the God we claim as our heavenly Father to such an extent that the world around us will be fascinated by our resemblance. We read, "But we all, with unveiled face, beholding as in a mirror the glory of the Lord, are being transformed into the same image from glory to glory, just as by the Spirit of the Lord" (2 Corinthians 3:18, NKJV).

It does not take much effort. The more time we spend with the Lord, the more we will reflect Him. It is by beholding that we surely will become changed and be God's look-alike.

Candy Monique Springer-Blackman

March 17

A Moment-by-Moment Thing

Do not imitate what is evil, but what is good. The one who does what is good is of God; the one who does evil has not seen God.
—3 John 1:11, NASB

Salvation is a gift from God. Our actions and behaviors do not earn us salvation. There is no gold star chart in heaven to track our good habits. The scales of justice with weights of good versus evil is not how God's system works.

I visited a friend and his family not long ago. His six-year-old son reminded me of him at that age. Have you noticed how we often mirror our parents and relatives unconsciously? The more time we spend with them, the more alike we become.

Likewise, as we grow closer to Jesus, we desire to know and imitate Him. It does not happen in the blink of an eye or the snap of a finger. Day by day, moment by moment, we decide: choose Jesus or not Jesus?

A few years ago I accepted a new job. After twenty-eight years of teaching everything from kindergarten-age children to adults, I would begin teaching at a university. I looked forward to the privilege of teaching teachers how to teach. I arrived at the university two years before my daughter entered as a student. After a few weeks of freshman classes, she told me this story.

"One day in my PE class, I was chatting with a new friend. As we talked, a strange look came over her face. I stopped in mid-sentence.

" 'Are you OK?' I asked.

" 'What's your last name? Wait, don't tell me. You're Dr. Laughlin's daughter.' "

My Kaiti Ann smiled. " 'Yes, yes, I am. Guilty as charged.' "

She did not become like me in an instant. I believe it happened over time, unconsciously, as we lived and worked together. Nature and nurture blended together. It is a moment-by-moment thing.

What will it take for people to stop us mid-sentence to ask if we are a child of God? Can they see our Father in us? Is there a family resemblance? In word, in deed, in action? Do we need to spend more time with Him? Talk to Him on the way to run errands?

Hey, Jesus, want to ride along while I get the oil changed? Next week I am driving over to see my daughter, Lord. Would You like to ride shotgun?

Faith Ann Laughlin

March 18

Pull Out the Plank

"How can you say to your brother, 'Let me take the speck out of your eye,' when all the time there is a plank in your own eye?"
—Matthew 7:4, NIV

"Thank heavens, it's finally Friday!" Melissa exclaimed, setting down her book bag. "On Monday, Jesika got mad at another student's comment. Today she was still playing that same whiny off-key string, and it's been so-o-o *unmitigatedly* wearing. She can't change what happened and just wasted energy all week for nothing. It makes me mad just thinking about it."

"It is wearing, undeniably and unequivocally," I replied. *I can use big words too.*

"I guess you can't fix stupid." Melissa sighed heavily.

"Right again," I said, "if by 'stupid' you mean exhibiting behaviors that do no one any good and result in negative outcomes. Only the person displaying the behaviors can change them—can 'fix stupid,' as you put it. About your getting mad, what's the difference between Jesika getting mad and then you getting mad at Jesika for her getting mad at another student?"

"Yikes. When you put it that way, it's *blatantly ridiculous*, that's what," Melissa exclaimed. "Doing the same thing—just for a different reason." Pause. "You never do *that*."

"I wish!" I said, grimacing. "We all do *that*, at least sometimes. Fortunately I do it much less frequently than I used to. Unfortunately I did it just the other day."

"Do tell!" Melissa said, assuming a cross-legged "I'm-listening, keep-talking" position.

"I got upset at some news I heard over the car radio. Caught myself. Realized what I was doing. Pulled the plank out of my eye and was grateful I was by myself." I chuckled ruefully.

"Then what did you do?" Melissa asked, readjusting her position on the carpet.

"I told the Lord, 'Thank You for bringing this to my attention and for giving me the desire and energy to change my thoughts'—to 'fix stupid,' as you put it. Jesika wasted energy all week for nothing. How much have you wasted, also for nothing?"

"A lot!" Melissa acknowledged, turning on her iPad. In a moment she read aloud, " 'You hypocrite. First pull the plank out of your own eye,' . . . hmm-m-m. Guess this was a problem in Bible times too. Well, I'm pulling out my plank. Jesika can handle her own speck."

"Good decision," I said. "For both of us."

Arlene R. Taylor

March 19

Fix Your Thoughts

Fix your thoughts on what is true, and honorable, and right, and pure, and lovely, and admirable. Think about things that are excellent and worthy of praise.
—Philippians 4:8, NLT

Philippians 4:8 is the text I read on the daily calendar my sister gave me many years ago. The pages show evidence of how much it has been used. Many times, my damp hands have flipped the pages where the calendar sits in my kitchen window above the sink. It is not only helpful to keep track of the date but also filled with encouragement. Printed below the verse are the words, "When counting my blessings, I hardly know where to begin! Give me a thankful heart this day. Amen."

I liked it so much that I took a picture of it yesterday and thought I would send it to my sister. After my morning worship today, I walked into the kitchen, and when I saw the calendar, I remembered I had not sent the picture to Margie. Immediately I got my phone out and sent it to her. A few minutes later my sister called to say she had received the picture, but it was too small for her to read. She recognized it was the calendar she had given to me, and after I read the verse to her, we shared several blessings we had experienced during the week and so many things for which we were thankful.

Throughout the day I noticed even more things for which to be thankful. In the evening, I received a phone call from her daughter. She said that my sister had fallen and they were on the way to the emergency room. Before we prayed we recounted again everything we were grateful for—including the circumstances of the fall.

Time passes slowly while you wait for news. I wondered how serious the injury was and whether or not Margie would be admitted to the hospital. I remembered how it had slipped my mind to send her the picture the day before, and I was so glad I had sent it earlier in the day. Would we have remembered all the things we were thankful for as they were driving to the hospital if we had not? I do not know. David reminds us,

> Whenever I am afraid,
> I will trust in You.
> In God (I will praise his word),
> In God I have put my trust (Psalm 56:3, 4, NKJV).

Eleven hours later, after a peaceful night's sleep, I received a text: "Sorry we were so wrapped up I forgot to text. She's pretty banged up. No broken bones or ribs! She's a lucky lady."

May we be mindful of His presence each day and praise Him for all His blessings.

Rita Kay Stevens

March 20

Hard of Hearing

"Whoever has ears, let them hear."
—Matthew 13:9, NIV

Many years ago, when I had problems understanding everything that was said in a noisy room, my children would say, "Go and see an otologist. Get a hearing aid." Finally I made an appointment.
The doctor asked, "Why have you come to see me?"
"My children say my hearing is bad. I don't hear everything."
He replied, "Why do you want to hear everything?" and we laughed.
After the examination the ear specialist told me that though my hearing was reduced, it was not yet necessary to get hearing aids. But eventually, after a couple of bouts with acute hearing loss, I finally asked my ear doctor to prescribe hearing aids. He now felt happy to do so and said it would be good for me to learn how to cope with those little gadgets sooner rather than later. It has taken some time to get used to them, but they do help in most situations.

I understand why many people avoid getting hearing aids, but now that I wear them, I realize I am not alone. Suddenly I notice how many others wear hearing aids. It is nothing to be ashamed of.

During the 2023 French Open Tennis Grand Slam Tournament in Paris, France, I watched Yannick Hanfmann defeat his first-round opponent in a five-set match that lasted almost five hours. Hanfmann was born with a hearing defect and normally wears hearing aids, but while on court with a crowd cheering loudly, he prefers to play without them. He finds the noise distracting. Without his hearing aids, he can concentrate much better. Perhaps that was the reason he won in the end.

We have ears so that we can hear. My doctor's question, "Why do you want to hear everything?" is a good question. Maybe we do not need to hear everything. "Whoever has ears, let them hear!" Jesus challenged his listeners repeatedly. He wanted them to hear and understand what *He* had to say. Like Hanfmann, we need to tune out all the distracting messages. Then we will hear and understand the real message of salvation. We do not need to hear everything—only what matters. May we listen only for what is essential.

Hannele Ottschofski

March 21

Noisy Streets and Answered Prayers

"Truly I say to you, if you have faith and do not doubt, you will not only do what was done to the fig tree, but even if you say to this mountain, 'Be taken up and cast into the sea,' it will happen. And all things you ask in prayer, believing, you will receive."
—Matthew 21:21, 22, NASB

My family lives on a junction of streets that are incredibly noisy. So noisy, in fact, that it is enough to awaken you as early as four o'clock in the morning. We really struggled to adjust to it when we first moved, but with time, we are beginning to get used to it.

One way I am learning to cope amid the rush of traffic and the frantic pace around me is by turning to the Lord. As I lie on my bed, I let my thoughts focus on Him through prayer and meditation. During this time of communion with God, I am learning so many things. I find joy in praying for the people I hear on the streets—those hurrying by and those whose loud arguing fills the air. As the scream of a nearby ambulance announces an incoming hospital emergency, I pray for the safety of those involved and for wisdom to be granted to the healthcare workers.

As I talk with God, I sense Him speaking to my heart. He has answered my prayers many times, and I would like to actually pray on the streets one day.

Recently I needed to travel to another state for an important appointment, so I planned to leave early. I reached the bus stop near the junction around six o'clock that morning. Surprisingly no buses stopped. As the minutes dragged on, I became anxious. At seven o'clock I prayed to God, "Lord, please provide a ride for me so I can make it in time for my appointment." No sooner had I opened my eyes than someone helped me to the next bus stop, where it would be easier for me to catch a ride to my destination. Little did I realize that God had more blessings for me. As I spoke with the driver, I discovered he was headed for the same destination!

Oh! How good is our God? He provided a way for me to get to my appointment on time. He literally made a way for me that would take me to the precise spot I needed without having to navigate bus stops and busy streets.

When the Bible says we can ask for anything, it is true. It does not matter if it is a large or small, simple or complex request. God hears and answers the prayers of His children.

Taiwo Adenekan

March 22

The Fly

No weapon formed against you shall prosper.
—Isaiah 54:17, NKJV

One night, I was not sleepy, so I took out my Bible, pen, and study guide and began to read. A fly started buzzing loudly around my head. After a few moments I got up from my seat and searched for a flyswatter. I found it, and the chase was on!

I repeatedly flailed my instrument of destruction but kept missing the fly. It would not rest on a solid object long enough for a good aim. I swatted and swatted but still could not hit the fly. Finally I thought, *The main reason I came here was to study my lesson, so that is what I am going to do.* I laid down the flyswatter, sat in my chair, picked up my lesson, and began to read.

"Oh, no!" I shouted a little later. Two annoying insects were singing and buzzing around me. "That does it." I went and got the bug spray. I sprayed and caught the first singing insect, a mosquito. Now for the second intruder, the fly. It was so fast. The more I sprayed the air, the faster it flew.

After a few minutes of attempting to gas the fly, the thought hit me. *If I spray anymore, I might poison myself!* Disgusted, I set the can down and returned to my chair. Then I prayed, "God, if You want me to study my Sabbath School lesson, then You get the fly."

I settled down in my chair, determined to study my Sabbath School lesson. All of a sudden something flew toward me and hit me in the face. It fell between my eye and my eyeglasses. I swiped it away from my face, and it fell onto the floor and under a chair. I just knew it had to be that fly. I started to investigate the black spot under the chair but decided I had spent enough time on it already.

Satan had sent the fly to distract me. I had tried to handle the matter myself, but when I finally asked for His help, God quickly took care of it.

I have found that the best way to study my Bible is to find a quiet area and reduce all distractions. Purge your study area. Remove distracting magazines and electronic devices. Remove annoyances, like pesky flies. Then you can get really serious.

Pray for the Holy Spirit to give you wisdom and understanding, and then praise God for the time well spent.

Ruth Cantrell

March 23

Lessons From an Earthworm

Praise the L*ORD*, *my soul;*
all my inmost being, praise his holy name.
Praise the L*ORD*, *my soul,*
and forget not all his benefits.
—Psalm 103:1, 2, NIV

I rescued two large earthworms today. They were trying to get across the path I walk each morning. To most this is probably an insignificant event, but to me it is quite the opposite.

Few realize how important the lowly earthworms are to us. They aerate the soil and provide access to the earth for rain, air, and other small creatures. If you walk in the forest, you will find mounds of fallen leaves in the autumn but very few in the spring. This is thanks to earthworms.

An earthworm basically takes in vegetation and processes it into humus.

One year, my young son Steve adopted an earthworm. Herman was moved into one of my flowerpots. Periodically Steve would dump out the contents of the pot and admire Herman. In the spring, I insisted that Herman be set free. Steve and I discovered several little casings that turned out to be mini Hermans. One large worm went into the pot and exited along with many little wormlets. We learned that baby worms are released as tiny eggs into the soil. Eventually they hatch and grow into large earthworms.

I read about a man who bought a piece of worthless ground. People told him how foolish he was, but he paid no attention. He dug up the ground, buried vegetable scraps in it, and added earthworms. After a year or two, he had a garden that produced more food than he could use. He set up a market stand and quickly recovered the cost of his project. Suddenly people took notice of his methods, and he became recognized as a gardening expert.

This story makes me consider our thoughts. One thought can often "hatch" into little thoughts that, if nurtured, will grow into grand new ideas. My gardener friend certainly used his one thought to profit many.

While I do not think Solomon wrote about the value of earthworms, he certainly could have. Proverbs and Ecclesiastes are filled with many valuable life lessons that can be learned from nature. Solomon did notice ants. When he says, "Go to the ant . . . observe its ways and be wise" (Proverbs 6:6, NASB), we should pay attention.

And now, perhaps we can add "consider the earthworm" to Solomon's list.

Patricia Cove

March 24

My Teacher and Comforter

"If you are pleased with me, teach me your ways."
—Exodus 33:13, NIV

Recently I woke up in a reflective mood as I considered the coping skills the Lord had taught me. These skills helped carry me through some mind-numbing challenges in my life, some of which were so bad that I contemplated suicide. The Holy Spirit intervened, however, and taught me how to create quiet spaces in my mind where I could sit with the Lord and be revived. I want to share one of those quiet places with you today.

I had a small wooden house in a rural setting. This clapboard house was perched on a hill. At the foot of the hill was a river. The riverbed was covered with stones of varied sizes, and crystal-clear water rippled over them while the golden sun twinkled in the rolling waters. From the house a path went down to the river, and where the path ended sat a huge stone.

Sometimes I would sit on the porch in a rocking chair, slowly rocking, rocking, rocking. Two or three children would be in the yard playing, and I would watch them as I rocked. There were days when the children did not come to play. On those days the Lord Himself would come. I would get up from my rocking chair and walk down the path to the river. I would sense Him walking slowly ahead of me as I followed. Once at the river, I would picture Him sitting on the huge stone with His feet dangling down as the crystal water bubbled over His feet.

I would sit down then and imagine myself leaning against His back, my feet in the water. And there we would sit, held in a sweet silence as I observed the cool water washing over my feet. Time stood still during those golden moments.

I am not sure how I came upon creating this life-saving scene. I can only say that it helped me develop crucial coping skills and survive that awful portion of my life. As I remember those days, Exodus 33:13, 14 comes to mind,

> "If you are pleased with me, teach me your ways so I may know you and continue to find favor with you. . . ."
> The LORD replied, "My Presence will go with you, and I will give you rest" (NIV).

Yes, My Lord and Master has been teaching me His ways, and His presence has been with me. I have learned to place my issues at His feet and leave them there. His peace, like a diamond, is most precious, and He gives it to all who draw near to Him.

Jasmine E. Grant

March 25

For All

"Come to me, all who are weary and burdened, and I will give you rest."
—Matthew 11:28, NASB

Cycles and seasons are part of life. Seasons are the times when we struggle, preserve, thrive, and revive—again and again. In these seasons we can find ourselves overwhelmed, weary, and burdened by the challenges we face. Whether it is the pressures of work, relationships, or personal struggles, it can feel as though we are carrying a load too heavy to bear. Yet it is in these moments that Jesus invites us to come to Him for rest. Matthew records this beautiful promise from Jesus, "Come to Me, all who are weary and burdened, and I will give you rest" (Matthew 11:28, NASB). This promise of relief does not comes as a result of withdrawing from life; it comes as a result of drawing closer to the One who can sustain us through every trial.

As I write to you, my body is tired, my soul is tired, and even my mind feels tired today. For a moment I feel guilty about not being able to move faster. To do more. To accomplish more. But as I pause and breathe, my mind focuses on God's grace and compassion, and I know that He understands, He feels, and He knows my limits. Through my weaknesses, He is repurposing my circumstances to accomplish His plan in my life.

So if you are in this season today, remember that God, our Creator, is also our Sustainer. Our *rest*. When life demands more than we think we can give, it is tempting to look for relief in things that promise temporary comfort. Yet these worldly solutions often leave us feeling even more empty and drained. Instead of checking out through distractions, addictions, or unhealthy coping mechanisms, we are called to check in with God. He is the source of true peace and strength, and His arms are always open to receive us.

Philippians reminds us of God's faithful provision, "And my God will supply all your needs according to His riches in glory in Christ Jesus" (Philippians 4:19, NASB). God is fully capable of providing for us—not just materially but spiritually and emotionally as well. Yet for Him to meet our needs, we must turn to Him.

God is ready to pour His grace and strength into us. If you cannot see the possibility of a ray of light, remember that the strength of your faith does not change the power of God. Just turn to Him and trust in His promises: "Come to me *all* . . ." You are included! His rest is for all.

Raquel Queiroz da Costa Arrais

March 26

GRACE

Where sin increased, grace increased all the more.
—Romans 5:20, NIV

"Mom, Don's had a stroke!"

I began to tremble at these words, and as I gripped the phone in my hands, an icy cold sweat enveloped my body. Grateful that I had not passed out at the news, I waited until I was finally able to speak. I asked my daughter, "How bad is it?"

She replied, "He is paralyzed on the entire right side of his body."

As the details began to unfold, I recognized all the miracles that had surrounded my son—a self-proclaimed agnostic. He usually visits his daughter each Sunday to have dinner with her family, but this time he went a day early to help watch the children while his daughter and son-in-law held a garage sale. Because he went a day early, he had immediate access to medical attention after the stroke. As he likes to remind us, the stroke could have taken place as he drove over to his daughter's house at seventy miles per hour.

Another miracle was that the stroke could have happened while he was home alone. No one would have known it had happened until it was too late to help. But the greatest miracle of all, as he says, "God forbid, it had occurred during any of the sixty-nine years before that Saturday, while I lived outside the realm of God's protective power!"

Julia H. Johnston wrote the beautiful hymn "Marvelous Grace." The last verse says,

> Marvelous, infinite, matchless grace
> Freely bestowed on all who believe!
> You that are longing to see His face
> Will you this moment His grace receive?*

Each miracle listed above is a manifestation of God's grace on my son's behalf. Each one pointed him to the cross and his Savior.

Following weeks of intensive therapy and rehab, my son is no longer paralyzed. He can walk, drive, and travel alone. He volunteers with an organization that advocates for abused children. He loves to tell his family and friends of his decision to faithfully walk in the path of God's commands. Don's undying love and gratitude to the omniscient, omnipresent, omnipotent God is a testimony of God's GRACE: God's Redemption At Christ's Expense.

Do you have a loved one who has not yet responded to God's grace? Pray for it on their behalf—it is there for the asking—and then watch and see God work in their life.

Helen O. Byoune

---

* Julia H. Johnston, "Marvelous Grace" (1910).

March 27

The Beauty of Kindness

The desire of a man is his kindness.
—Proverbs 19:22, KJV

As I left work after a busy day, I received a phone call from a lady who had been given my number by a mutual acquaintance. She asked if I would be willing to do speech therapy with her mother, who had suffered a stroke and was having difficulty speaking. As she told me the details about her mother, I realized I knew who her mother was. She had been admitted to the hospital and placed in the intensive care ward where I work before being moved to another ward. I remembered she was a very strong-willed person yet well-liked by the nurses.

I started to work with her, first with the alphabet, then with words and pictures on cards. Little by little, she began to speak more fluently. I loved to listen to her share the stories of her remarkable life. She had battled cancer of the lymph nodes; she carried the scars from her surgery, but the cancer was long gone. She had worked for many years as a cook, and even though she now had to move around with the help of a walker, she still enjoyed making food, baking cakes, and preparing delicious fruit ice creams.

But what impressed me most was whom she cooked for. It was the lady who had first contacted me. I had assumed she was the daughter, but, in fact, she was a former daughter-in-law. She had been married to the older woman's only son, who had worked in the ambulance services. He had died as a young man in a traffic accident while on duty. Her former daughter-in-law had been remarried for many years, and together they had a daughter who came almost every day to see her grandmother. Although she was not the daughter's biological grandmother, she still called her Grandma. The little girl did her homework at Grandma's house and enjoyed the goodies she prepared.

As part of her speech therapy, we read from the children's Bible together, and I encouraged her to read the full Bible story. I think that is why we met, to read from the Bible together.

When Jesus was on earth, He showed kindness to people every day. He was concerned for their good; He healed their sickness, taught them, and revealed the kingdom of God. Solomon wrote, "He who pursues righteousness and kindness will find life" (Proverbs 21:21, RSV). May we follow our Savior's example and pursue kindness today.

Magdalena Alina Lupu

March 28

Divine Interventions in Unexpected Moments

For my thoughts are not your thoughts, neither are your ways my ways, saith the Lord. *For as the heavens are higher than the earth, so are my ways higher than your ways, and my thoughts than your thoughts.*
—Isaiah 55:8, 9, KJV

I boarded the plane, put my carry-on in the bin above my head, and settled into my seat. As the flight attendant closed the overhead bins, she noticed my bag extending slightly over the edge and said I would need to check it in. My heart sank.

Then she asked, "Do you have a connecting flight?"

"To Reno," I replied. Then, to my surprise, she rolled my bag to the front of the plane, where she found an empty bin in the last row of first class and smoothly stowed away my bag. Returning, she provided me with the seat number below which my bag was stored.

This simple act of kindness echoed how God's favor often works in our lives, weaving it into a larger, divine narrative. It whispers to us amid life's unpredictability—a delay that protects, a closed door that redirects, or an unexpected solution that surpasses our original plans.

It is easy to feel disheartened when things do not go as expected. Yet these moments often reveal God intricately working His plan for our good, as Romans 8:28 reminds us. We may not fully realize the blessings of God's favor until we look back and see how the pieces of our life have come together. Joseph's story in Genesis exemplifies this—amid tribulations, God orchestrated a greater plan.

God's favor often works behind the scenes, turning our trials into triumphs. What may seem like a setback could very well be a setup for a greater blessing. The challenge lies in trusting His goodness and timing, even when we cannot see the full picture.

So how do we embrace God's favor in our daily lives? It begins with a heart of gratitude and trust. Proverbs 3:5, 6 encourages us to trust in the Lord with all our hearts and not lean on our own understanding. If we submit our ways to Him, He will direct our paths. By trusting in God's sovereignty, we open ourselves to countless ways He wants to bless us.

Father, even when life's circumstances seem to take detours, may we know that Your favor is upon us and trust You are always working in our best interest at every step of our journey.

Florence E. Callender

March 29

Showing Gratitude

But do not forget to do good and to share, for with such sacrifices God is well pleased.
—Hebrews 13:16, NKJV

My husband, Morris, and I traveled to Nigeria to attend the ninetieth birthday celebration of his only remaining uncle, as well as his uncle's wife's eightieth birthday, their sixty-two years of marriage, and his seventeen-year reign as king of his village.

It was a delightful experience to commemorate this momentous occasion with family and friends. Although it rained throughout the night and most of the big day, it did not dampen our spirits. I was amazed to see hundreds of well-wishers who had braved the inclement weather to be present. The event was held under huge tents in the yard, and it was impressive to listen as celebrants lavished their love and gratitude on this beloved couple.

The next day I accompanied my husband and visited friends who had impacted his life as a young man. We traveled over flooded roads, rugged terrain, deep potholes, and unnamed streets to find people in four villages. It was a very difficult journey, but his presence brought them so much joy. They expressed their gratitude to him for coming such a long distance under such difficult conditions. He thanked them for impacting his life and shared gifts with them. Among the people we visited were widows of dear friends as well as a childhood friend. Morris recalled how they had played together as children.

While in college, Morris traveled to northern Nigeria to canvass to help pay for his tuition. He stayed at the home of a man who was a telecommunications officer for the government. Through the kindness of this friend, Morris did not have to pay rent or purchase food. When it was time to return to college, his friend contributed money to help with his tuition. Now, many years later, this man had retired, suffered a stroke, and was bedridden. Morris had the privilege of thanking this kindhearted couple for their thoughtfulness. What a joy to bring a smile to their faces.

My heart was profoundly touched as I witnessed my husband's determination to brave the horrible weather and the long bumpy journey into the interior of the country to reach each village to express his gratitude. Showing gratitude is a blessing to both those who give it and those who receive it. Let us each bless someone with our gratitude today.

Shirley C. Iheanacho

March 30

An Attitude of Gratitude

Rejoice in the Lord always. Again I will say, rejoice! . . .
Be anxious for nothing, but in everything by prayer and supplication, with
thanksgiving, let your requests be made known to God; and the peace of God, which
surpasses all understanding, will guard your hearts and minds through Christ Jesus.
—Philippians 4:4–7, NKJV

Some time ago I heard this story, which I would like to share with you today. Bill was a Christian construction worker who had a very positive attitude, and he always praised God for everything that happened to him. His coworkers made fun of him for his constant optimism and gratefulness to God under any circumstances.

One day while the construction crew was taking their lunch break, Bill sat under a shady tree, opened his lunch bag, and closed his eyes to say a blessing for his food. Before he could finish his prayer, a stray dog snatched his lunch bag and ran off with it. Bill chased after the dog. He wanted his lunch back. After he had run quite a distance, he suddenly heard a loud blast behind him. When he looked back, he saw a huge cloud of smoke at the construction site. Apparently there had been an enormous explosion of some sort that left most of the workers who had been nearby badly injured.

Bill was very sorry and sad to see his coworkers badly hurt. He immediately prayed for his them and thanked God for protecting him from getting hurt in the explosion. If the stray dog had not run away with his lunch bag, and if he had not chased after it, he, too, would have been hurt in the detonation and suffered much pain.

Friends, please remember that when we put our faith and trust in the Lord, no matter what happens in our lives, we can trust God with the outcome. No matter how it may look in the moment, we can be assured that in the end God will work it out for our good. God knows the future, and He cares for His children.

"Oh, give thanks to the Lord, for He is good! For His mercy endures forever" (1 Chronicles 16:34, NKJV). What a wonderful promise.

My challenge for all of us today is to always live with an attitude of gratitude to our heavenly Father, who loves us more than we can ever know.

Stella Thomas

March 31

Follow the Leader

These are the ones who follow the Lamb wherever He goes.
—Revelation 14:4, NKJV

I have two dogs, a pit bull named Frankie and a German shepherd named Tillie. My husband and I often joke that I am unable to go anywhere in the house without them following me. If I close a door before they can go in with me, they feel dejected and sad until I come back into the room and they can be close to me once more. If I must leave, they have to have treats, and then they watch for me until I get back home. At bedtime they have to have their "nigh-nigh" treats and dance about until they get them. They have even influenced our older cat, Pogo, who thinks he is a dog, and now he insists on his own "nigh-nigh" treats.

Having them follow me everywhere, though comical, can sometimes be annoying, especially when I make a sudden change in direction and trip over one of them. Pogo wants to be close to me anytime I sit down. Right now, he is lying on my lapboard and against my left arm as I try to type. These animals love me, and they know I love them; that is why they follow me everywhere.

Revelation tells of God's people following the Lamb wherever He goes. The reason is that they love Him and want to be as close to Him as possible. When Jesus asked the disciples to follow Him, they did not hesitate. They left jobs and families to follow Jesus wherever He led. Their love grew so deep and strong, even when they suffered terrible persecution for following Him. Their love was unselfish, and they worked hard to draw others into the circle of Jesus' love.

I am drawn toward admiring those who have the gift of leadership, especially when I believe they are honest, sincere, and going in the direction where I want to go. There is no better leader in the universe than Jesus. He will never lead His followers in the wrong direction. He will never become annoyed because you or I follow too closely. We need to remain close. He never promised His followers a trouble-free life. Rather, He said the opposite. "These things I have spoken to you, that in Me you may have peace. In the world you will have tribulation; but be of good cheer, I have overcome the world" (John 16:33, NKJV).

Let us be faithful in keeping our eyes on Jesus and follow wherever He leads. He will never lead us astray, and one day soon He will lead us home.

Mona Fellows

April 1

Rescued

I wait for the Lord, my whole being waits, and in his word I put my hope.
—Psalm 130:5, NIV

While studying the story of Rahab, I keep thinking of Lot's wife. Both live in cities about to receive the full judgment of God, and each woman is given the opportunity by two witnesses (angels and spies) to be rescued from certain destruction. Comparing and contrasting similar stories is a thought-provoking way to study biblical narratives. Let's look at these two stories.

Mrs. Lot cannot influence any of her extended family to head for safety. It takes angels to rescue her immediate family, dragging them out of town by their hands. Rahab, on the other hand, somehow convinces her extended family that her home (on the wall, first in the line of danger) is the only means of safety and rescue. I imagine her clinging to their hands, preventing their departure when the march around Jericho had ended and nothing happened—for seven days.

Mrs. Lot's children do not seem to respect the warning from the angels, perhaps reflecting inconsistency or lack of integrity in spiritual matters of the parents, children, or both. Rahab's family, one assumes, begins to respect her message because of her regenerated heart, the result of encountering the men of God sent by Joshua to spy out the territory.

Mrs. Lot leaves her home with no enthusiasm and without her possessions. She looks back on her old life and loses not only her present life but also the promise of eternal life. Rahab is spared in her home with all that she has. She looks forward to a restored life and gains the promise of eternal life through her descendant Jesus, our Savior.

Rahab is passed over in judgment and rescued because of the scarlet thread—an image reminiscent of the blood dripping from the doorposts in Egypt at the Passover and of the blood dripping from the body of Jesus on the cross. Because of her faith, her entire family escapes the crashing walls of Jericho's judgment. They live in the Promised Land as God's people.

Today, like Rahab and Lot's wife, I live in a city facing the full judgment of God and imminent destruction. I believe salvation comes only to those under the protection of the scarlet cord—but is my belief as visible and palpable as the cord? Will my family be gathered in our ark of safety, expecting rescue by True Joshua? I pray we are all found worshiping Jesus and waiting with longing hearts to begin a new life as God's people in the Promised Land of eternity.

Rebecca Turner

April 2

Our Hearts, Your Home

By this time they were nearing Emmaus and the end of their journey. Jesus acted as if he were going on, but they begged him, "Stay the night with us, since it is getting late." So he went home with them.
—Luke 24:28, 29, NLT

Because we know the story well, our familiarity with it can lead us to miss the power it holds. Whenever we find ourselves skimming over the Word, we need to remember to slow down. To read with intention. Savor the beauty. Be amazed by its power. David writes of God's Word as being "sweeter than honey, even honey dripping from the comb" (Psalm 19:10, NLT). So slow down with me and take a closer look at what happened that night as the two disciples journeyed home from Jerusalem to Emmaus.

They found themselves deeply confused. Troubled. Their Savior had been crucified, leaving their hearts and hopes shattered. Adding to the distress, some of the women had testified that Jesus had risen from the tomb. As they grappled with this mind-blowing news, trying to grasp the meaning of it all, another traveler joined them on the road. He was a stranger to them, but they welcomed the company. Good conversations can shorten a long journey.

"What are you discussing so intently?" He asked. In response to their answer, the Stranger began to take "them through the writings of Moses and all the prophets, explaining from all the Scriptures the things concerning himself" (Luke 24:27, NLT). As they near home, their hearts, so recently frozen in fear, are now on fire with a holy hope. They turn to enter their home, and the Stranger walks onward. They could let Him continue—He had given them much to ponder. Instead they beg Him to come home with them and stay the night. He turns to follow them, and there, under their roof, they discover the risen Savior. Seated at their table, breaking bread, He looks completely at home—within their home.

What of us, His modern-day disciples? When life has our hearts caught in an icy grip, when we struggle to breathe through the fog of overwhelming distress, and worst of all, when we feel isolated within our pain—we have a choice. We can ask Jesus to come and abide in our home, to make His home within our hearts. He longs to set our hearts on fire. May our prayer be, "Make our hearts Your home, Lord!"

Karen Pearson

April 3

Tetelestai: It Is Finished

When Jesus therefore had received the vinegar, he said,
It is finished: and he bowed his head, and gave up the ghost.
—John 19:30, KJV

Summertime is among the favorite seasons of the year. For many it is stress-free, relaxing, and fun. The warmer weather makes it a time for the beach, traveling, and other recreational activities. The flip side to summer often includes catching up on the projects we have shoved to the back burner for days, weeks, months, and sometimes years. Regardless, the best projects are those that get done.

One summer my husband, Michael, and I decided to make a workbench for our carport. We were excited to work on building something together. Michael is very methodical and strategically planned the design. He utilized wood that had been discarded on the roadside. Michael purchased the necessary screws, paint, and extra wood to get it done. Then the hard work began. He sanded the rough edges and imperfections to reveal almost brand-new material. It was not as easy as I had imagined. I needed a lot of muscles, which I lacked. But my husband, who is a skilled workman, assured me I would get a handle on things.

He taught me how to use a handsaw, an electric saw, an electric drill, and sandpaper to smooth away the bumps and how to correctly hammer a nail. A week later, when the task was over, we felt a rush of exhilaration. We did it! We had accomplished our task, and despite the minor glitches, we had finished what we had started.

In like manner Jesus accomplished the task He came to do. He gave up His kingship, kingdom, and crown. He lived, was crucified, and was resurrected just for you and me. Though He encountered multiple obstacles, threats, scorn, and rejection, He did not quit. He worked hard as He taught, healed, and fed the people; He even restored life while on His mission. He kept the faith, stayed on course, and followed in His Father's footsteps.

As He hung on the cross, His last words were, "*Tetelestai!*" meaning, "It is finished!" (John 19:30, KJV). He did it. He completed His task. He finished His assignment so we can have life—abundant life (John 10:10). So now, as we race toward the finish line, my friends, let us run, strong in the faith, armed with truth and light. And by God's grace, may we be found faithful as we finish the race.

Corletta Aretha Barbar

April 4

The Woman in the Middle

Then the scribes and Pharisees brought to Him a woman caught in adultery. And . . . they . . . set her in the midst.
—John 8:3, NKJV

The woman is in the middle. All eyes are on her. How often are women placed in the middle, exhibited, put on display, under the spotlight, and objectified in advertising and media? It is no different for the woman in this story.

Everyone stands around staring, pointing an accusing finger at her. She is on display as they monitor every detail and observe the smallest feature in her appearance. What she has done is outrageous. It must be punished. There is no other way. Where would we end up if we allowed her to go? They continued to pass judgment on the terrified woman in the middle. Moses was right to regulate things like this. Now, we only have to convince this Jesus. If He is the Messiah, He cannot let this pass. Adultery is the worst sin. The bystanders did not address the woman. They spoke about her without speaking to her. She felt ostracized, excluded, and condemned.

Can you identify with the woman in the middle? Or have you placed someone in the middle? Talked about them instead of with them? Have you found yourself passing judgment without knowing the whole story? We are no different from the Pharisees and scribes when we act in this manner.

But look at Jesus. He is completely different. In response to the insistent questions and the demands to deal with the sinner, Jesus simply bends down and begins to write in the sand. Then He says, "He who is without sin among you, let him throw a stone at her first" (John 8:7, NKJV). How outrageous! Why is He defending her? As the angry bystanders read Jesus' words, one after the other, they walk away until the woman is left standing alone. No longer surrounded by her accusers, she can now see Jesus face-to-face, and what a change. He treats her with respect and dignity. He absolves her of the death penalty, for although He alone is without sin, He forgives and does not condemn her.

A little later He will stand in the middle, surrounded by a mob of people who mock and spit. He will be scourged and condemned, crowned with a ring of thorns, and finally nailed to a cross in the middle—for her and us. Our Savior took our place and stood in the middle to save us all.

Dagmar Dorn

April 5

The Cross

But God forbid that I should boast except in the cross of our Lord Jesus Christ, by whom the world has been crucified to me, and I to the world.
—Galatians 6:14, NKJV

One spring, my husband and I decided to prepare a piece of land and grow potatoes. We live in a mountainous area, so I hired a bulldozer to prepare the land. I am always grateful to the Lord for creating brilliant minds who can imagine and create things that make our lives easier. The bulldozer started to scoop deeply into the earth when suddenly I heard a crunch of stone. The man operating the machine gently placed the load on the ground, and we all moved closer to identify the object that lay in the excavator bucket. To our amazement we discovered a heavy stone cross, slightly broken on one side.

We cleared it with great excitement and wondered what a cross was doing in our garden. My husband remembered that there was a time when every family buried their dead on their property, but he did not remember who might have been buried there. When I was able to identify the name on the cross, my husband recalled family stories about a woman who bore the name on the beautifully carved stone cross. It was dated 1830.

I put the cross in the garden where I can look at it when I go out to weed my field. It reminds me of another cross and the One who was crucified for me. I have not been able to learn much about our great-great-grandmother in the garden. I do not know what kind of person she was, what she loved, or even how long she lived, but I do know so much about my Savior. He has compassion for human suffering. When my Savior lived on earth, He healed the sick, raised the dead, and loved much. He hated sin and hypocrisy, forgave much, and saved all who came to Him for eternal life.

We had discovered a cross that remained hidden for more than seventy years. No one remembered it or even knew it was there. What about the cross of our Savior? Is it buried under the clutter in our lives? Hiding behind habits we need to let go? Can anyone see the resurrected, living Christ within us? What do we do with Jesus?

It seems to me that this old stone cross was all I needed to remind me anew of Jesus' cross and all He has done for me. He promises, "I will put My law in their minds, and write it on their hearts, and I will be their God, and they shall be my people" (Jeremiah 31:33, NKJV). Let us honor His sacrifice today and share His love with others.

Florentina Coman

April 6

Abide in the Vine

"Abide in me and I in you. As the branch cannot bear fruit by itself, unless it abides in the vine, neither can you, unless you abide in me."
—John 15:4, ESV

I love to have fresh-cut flowers in a vase in my home. They seem to just brighten a space and provide a little glimpse of Eden. There are so many types of blooms to enjoy, and many are fragrant with sweet nectar. Placed in a lovely vase and displayed in a sunny spot, they are nature's mood lifter. There is only one problem with fresh-cut flowers—they do not last forever. They die.

When we snip the flowers from our garden and bring them in for our enjoyment, we cut them off from their life source. Their leaves begin to shrivel, and their petals become brittle. The colors fade, and they wilt in defeat. It is a sad sight to behold, and yet we continue to bring in fresh-cut blooms.

Just as blossoms need life-giving nourishment to survive, we need the life-giving nourishment that comes from being connected to Jesus. If we cut ourselves off from Him, we begin to shrivel and die spiritually. It may not happen right away, but it will eventually happen. How do we cut ourselves off from Him? We may begin to pull back from things like attending church, small groups, Bible study, or even personal prayer. We grab the occasional verse of the day to keep the proverbial water in our vase, but that is not enough to keep us alive spiritually. We must be attached to the Vine to bear more fruit and stay alive spiritually. We must remain in the Vine to produce fruit. A branch cannot grow new fruit if it is cut off from the vine, just as we cannot grow any new spiritual fruit unless we abide in, or remain connected to, the Vine.

Do you know what you will never see? A flower stem that has been cut off and removed from its life source growing new blooms. It must have continual nourishment to thrive. The nourishment we need comes from Jesus. He is the Vine, and we are the branches (see John 15:5). Keep connected to the vine and be fruitful. Grow continuously and thrive in Jesus. He is the Life-Giver, the Source of life.

The next time you enjoy having fresh-cut flowers in your home, see it as a reminder to stay connected to the heavenly Vine.

Cyndi Woods

April 7

Connected to the Vine

"I am the vine, you are the branches; the one who remains in Me, and I in him bears much fruit, for apart from Me you can do nothing."
—John 15:5, NASB

My life has been somewhat disorganized over the last few years. In the fall of 2020, my husband and I contracted COVID-19, and while my case was fairly mild, my husband ended up in the hospital for eleven days, three of which were in the intensive care unit. The accompanying isolation, shutdowns, and canceled trips became our new norm.

In August of the following year, my husband was diagnosed with cancer. Life changed dramatically with multiple procedures, appointments, tests, radiation, and chemo. It felt like we were on a roller coaster and could not get off.

In the spring of 2022, we decided to start a raised bed garden using animal troughs we purchased. My husband did all he could, and I did most of the heavy work. We placed heavy stepping stones under the corner of each trough, and after we had placed a few, I became very tired. With only two to go, he placed one in front of me, and I put the one in my hands on top and moved to take both to the other side of the trough. As I did, I heard a loud pop, and pain instantly flooded my lower back. After an X-ray and MRI, I learned I had broken my lumbar spine in three places. At that point we were both in bad physical shape, but God has seen us through the worst. My fractures have healed, and my pain has greatly diminished. My husband is off his chemo and feels better.

Today I went out to water and trim a few plants in the yard and garden. Some of the extra cantaloupe vines needed to be cut back to allow the fruit-bearing vines a better chance to mature. The vines had become tangled, and in pruning them, I accidentally cut off the largest fruit from the vine. I felt sick. I had been checking faithfully each day on its progress. Now it was gone due to my carelessness.

As I spoke to God about it, He gently reminded me that if a plant is not connected to the vine it will fail to grow. Instantly I realized the lesson He was trying to get across to me. With all the changes in my life, I had let my study and prayer life slip. I needed to reconnect to the Vine if I wanted to grow and be fruitful in the Lord. How well are you connected to the Vine, my friend?

Sue Anderson

April 8

Answered Prayer

"Then you will call upon Me and go and pray to Me, and I will listen to you."
—Jeremiah 29:12, NKJV

I once heard the Christian life described as one either being in the middle of the storm or coming out of the storm. Well, I was in the middle of the storm. We had planned a family vacation my two young boys were excited about. Yet the enemy was destroying my marriage and my family, and the vacation no longer seemed a reality.

Despite the difficulties, I decided to take the boys to the amusement park they had so excitedly begged for. My older son wanted to build a special sword at an amusement park, and I had made the reservation many months in advance. We arrived at the theme park, trying to put the stressful months behind us, only to find out I had made a mistake. I had made the reservation for the wrong day! My son was crushed.

"Let's pray," I said. "No matter what, God is always listening to us." My son wanted to believe, but disappointment rocked his nine-year-old world. I prayed for God to make a way for us so my son could experience God in a personal way. I added a plea for a dinner reservation. We were number thirty-one on the waitlist for building a sword and were told by the staff that no one ever canceled, so we were unlikely to get in. There was no way we would get a reservation.

Well, my God is an awesome God! All we need to do is call upon His name. Nothing is too trivial or small, no matter what. God knows our hearts, and He hears our concerns. As soon as we finished dinner, I got a text. Someone had canceled, and our reservation to build the special sword was waiting! My son was speechless. He jumped up and down with joy. As I watched him, I told him, "Jonathan, God heard our prayer! He is a God of possibilities, a God of love, and He attends to His children."

Through the difficult challenges we faced, my boys learned that God is good. He is a loving God who listens to our prayers and knows our hearts. God became real in the hearts of two little boys that summer day. There is so much more for them to learn as they walk with Jesus, but on that day, they learned to trust. Jesus had heard the prayer of our hearts and had answered exactly as we had requested. What an awesome God!

Elena Flores

April 9

A Delightful Answer to Prayer

"You can pray for anything, and if you have faith, you will receive it."
—Matthew 21:22, NLT

I felt the sting at the tip of my nose. You may also have experienced it—the sting that signals "I am about to cry!"

During and after my divorce, I relocated from my home in Maryland, USA, and found myself living in Cody, Wyoming, USA. On this particular day some years later, I felt so incredibly lonely. All I wanted to do was hop on a plane and return to Maryland. How I longed to reunite with the family and friends I felt so comfortable with. I wanted to be with those who knew me best. The tears came, and I begged, through prayer, for God to find a way to get me to Maryland before my birthday. Even as I asked, I wondered how it would be possible. My work commitments and finances made it impossible for me to arrange on my own. Despite that, I continued to pray and left the planning to Him.

A week before my birthday, I went out to my makeshift pottery studio, which takes up one corner of my garage. There, under my slab roller, sat a box my ex-husband had brought me the last time he visited. I had not opened it yet—even though it had been a few years. I opened the garage door to let in more light, sat down, and decided I should finally open the box and take a look inside. And there it was—my trip to Maryland!

The box was filled with photos from my life on the East Coast. I spent several hours poring over all the pictures in the box. They spanned the years and took me back in time to all the vacations, family get-togethers, pets, events, and holidays I had so enjoyed. You name it, it was captured in the photographs I held. I laughed, I cried, and I found myself saying things like, "Oh, I had forgotten all about this!" Or "Wow! I can't believe such and such," and "Oh! This was so fun!" The memories filled my heart to overflowing.

God had heard my pleas and had graciously provided a way to get me home to Maryland. Not in the conventional way, by boarding a plane and flying across the country. Yet my heart was comforted. I felt satisfied, fulfilled, seen and heard, and incredibly thankful for the memories I had been able to enjoy. *Thank You, God, for a creative answer to my prayer!*

My friend, how will God answer the longing of your heart today?

Gayle Cochran Wright

April 10

Now!

"We do not know what to do, but our eyes are on you."
—2 Chronicles 20:12, ESV

As the seasons change, I am reminded of the change beginning to take place in my own heart. Six months ago, my husband and I left a rental house, confident God would immediately provide another home. Yet here we are still cramped together in a two-hundred-square-foot tiny house, dependent on the kindness of my in-laws.

The week prior to our rental exit, I had been reading the story of Abraham. Everything in his faith journey struck a chord of relatability. As I read about God's promise and faithfulness to Abraham, I felt God was using his story to promise me a house. The part I neglected to focus on was God's timeline. A timeline that made space for waiting while growing Abraham's trust in God.

Abraham and his wife, Sarah, had to wait so long that when God reminded Sarah of His promise, she literally laughed out loud. How impossible it sounded to be pregnant at her age. But sure enough, Sarah fell pregnant, and at ninety she gave birth to Isaac.

Maybe I have not waited for a home as long as Abraham and Sarah did for a child, but no matter. It has felt overwhelming and filled with despair. Thankfully a dear friend gifted me a book, *Now and Not Yet: Pressing in When You're Waiting, Wanting, and Restless for More*, by Ruth Chou Simons. This book has both encouraged and challenged me. I have learned that my hope has been placed more in the deliverance from my problems rather than in the Deliverer Himself. Such a slight change in wording but a huge difference in the heart. It is sad how much time and energy I put into wishing away the "now" for the "not yet." My longing for what is yet to come blinded me from the precious treasures found only in the present. How easy to get caught in the trap of thinking, "Life will be better when . . ."

I look through photos and videos from the summer and am blown away by the precious life I am experiencing now! God has given me so much for which to be grateful in the here and now. While I cannot wish a house into existence, I can choose to find joy even in the waiting. So in the face of uncertainty, my heart cries out to the Lord, "We do not know what to do, but our eyes are on You" (2 Chronicles 20:12, ESV).

Alyssa Morauske

April 11

The God of Perfect Timing

It is God who arms me with strength and keeps my way secure.
—Psalm 18:32, NIV

Our God is a miracle-working God. He leads His children in the way that is best and right for them at all times. Sometimes we do not understand the way He leads. We think He is making a mistake in taking us through certain paths in life, and we try to help Him or to counsel Him. Sometimes we ignore Him and go in the way we consider best for ourselves. In the end, we realize we have made a mistake and have only ourselves to blame for not allowing the all-knowing God to plan our steps for us.

Through personal experience I have learned it is better to wait for God to lead the way. He alone is able to arm me with strength and make my way perfect. But sometimes I still grow impatient as I wait for the Lord to handle my situation. Talk about the folly of human nature, indeed. Recently God performed another miracle to remind me to allow Him to take charge.

I needed a few different visas for the trips on my work itinerary. I applied for them one by one, including a visa to Israel, but the consulate did not respond. Additionally, I needed to renew my American visa, and I prayed that the Israeli Consulate would call for an interview as soon as possible. When they did not, I had to drop off my passport in order to receive my American visa. At the time, my husband was traveling, making the issue all the more complicated.

The day for departure on the trip to Israel drew closer. I still had no visa, and my passport was at the American embassy. I prayed again, and it seemed God was too silent. So I decided to leave the Lord to sort it out Himself while I occupied myself with the work at hand.

One morning I received a call from my husband, who told me he had just heard from the Israeli Consulate. They said we should come and pick up our visa on June 7. I shouted for joy to see how perfectly the Lord had timed everything. My husband was due to return home by June 5, I could collect my American visa by June 6, and we would be ready to travel to Israel by June 11. What a God of perfect timing. He made the best plans for us concerning these trips.

Dear friends, do not worry yourself out of God's perfect plan for you. Trust His timing—He is a faithful God. Wait for Him, and He will arm you with strength and make your way perfect. What a wonderful God we serve!

Omobonike Adeola Sessou

April 12

Stop! Look! Listen!

Lift up your eyes on high, and see who has created these things.
—Isaiah 40:26, NKJV

God, Master Designer and Artist, created many beautiful things, and He did so for our benefit and enjoyment. We often hear the phrase, "Beauty is in the eye of the beholder," so I want to ask you, my dear sisters, to stop and look at the roses. Not only are they beautiful—they also perfume the air.

During my years of active involvement in the Adventurer Club, I learned many lessons about different trees and leaves. A close examination of a mulberry leaf, for example, will reveal a delicate and intricate pattern. Our God is truly incredible.

There is nothing more delightful than to see a squirrel scamper along a fence or run up and down a tree. As soon as it hears the slightest sound, the squirrel stands upright—like a soldier in the army. Try to approach it, and the squirrel will flee at lightning speed.

My fellow dog lovers can relate to the joy found in seeing a dog lie flat on its back, just waiting for a belly rub. Dogs speak their own language when they bark, whimper, or growl.

Beauty is also in the ear of the listener. There is no sweeter melody than birdsong.

God is interested in how we relate to all the beautiful things He created for us. Do we take them for granted, hardly noticing them, or do we stop, look, and appreciate the beautiful roses, majestic trees, or scampering squirrels? Do we pause to listen to the singing birds?

God formed us in His image, and He wants us to see one another through His eyes. Every one of us is beautiful in our unique way. The psalmist David penned these words: "I will praise thee: for I am fearfully and wonderfully made" (Psalm 139:14, KJV). Let us take the time to really "look" at one another and "see" the beauty within—then speak an encouraging word. Kind words are a healing balm for a hurting soul.

God has given us a precious gift: our shared sisterhood in Christ. He provides opportunities for us to pause from our busy lives, to really see one another, and to lend an ear to a sister in need. Sabbath provides the perfect time and place for us to connect with one another.

We demonstrate our love for God whenever we embrace one another with love, compassion, and grace.

Winsome Joy Grant

April 13

Count It All Joy

Consider it pure joy, my brothers and sisters, whenever you face trials of many kinds, because you know that the testing of your faith produces perseverance.
—James 1:2, 3, NIV

For my entire life I have believed the lie that it is important to stay busy, and have viewed rest as laziness. I believed the lie that rest is weakness, but last week I experienced a torn ligament in my foot. I looked at the doctor in complete frustration because this was the third injury to my right foot in five months. I knew the treatment: the splint, the ice, elevation, and the forced rest. God physically sat me down to rest.

When life slows down, especially due to something unexpected like a ligament injury, it can feel frustrating, especially if you are someone who loves to move and stay active. Suddenly the pace you are used to is replaced by stillness, and you are faced with the challenge of waiting. Yet it is often in these very moments that God performs some of His deepest work in us.

Rest and recovery may feel like limitations, but they are also opportunities for growth. Through this pause God can teach us valuable lessons in patience and endurance. These qualities are not easy to develop when life is always moving quickly, but they are essential for spiritual maturity. As much as we resist waiting, there is something profound about surrendering to God's timing and trusting that He knows what is best for us, even when we cannot see it.

If you are nursing an injury right now or struggling with something else, it may just be a reminder that not everything is within your control. But it is also a wonderful opportunity to rest in the knowledge that God is in control. Paul tells us that "suffering produces perseverance; perseverance, character; and character, hope" (Romans 5:3, 4, NIV). In your waiting, God is shaping your character, making you stronger on the inside as you heal on the outside. Your roots are growing.

This season of rest, though not easy, is a time for reflection, prayer, and learning to fully lean on God. Trust that He is preparing you for what is coming next and that, in His perfect time, you will be able to move forward stronger and more grounded in faith than ever before.

Though we may not see it at the time, God is fitting all the pieces together for our good and the good of everyone involved—so we can trust Him and count it all *joy*!

Raquel Queiroz da Costa Arrais

April 14

Travel Light

"If you really know me, you will know my Father as well. From now on, you do know him and have seen him."
—John 14:7, NIV

We all have traveled from one place to another, and when it comes to travel, there is a funny, often repeated belief that women carry more luggage than men. I am not sure about that. What I do know is that we all need to feel relaxed, have good food or snacks, wear comfortable clothes, and have good music or books to kill time, depending on how long the journey will last.

In John 14 Jesus reminds us how much He loves us. It was time for Him to die on Calvary, and He knew how sad and uncertain His disciples felt. They loved Him, and He loved them. He reassured them that He was going to prepare a place for them, and He promised He would come back to take them to a wonderful place where they would live with Him. In fact, He would be preparing places specifically for them to live for eternity.

It is never a good feeling to separate from loved ones; the moment is often bittersweet. It was not easy for Jesus to leave His followers, but it was time for Him to do what He needed to for our salvation. He comforted them by saying, "Do not let your hearts be troubled. You believe in God; believe also in me" (verse 1, NIV). The disciples just needed to believe Him and continue following Him. Jesus promised that if they knew Him, they would know the Father (see verse 7).

Though we have lost loved ones, let us not be troubled but believe that Jesus is coming and will restore what we have lost when the dead in Christ are raised. He left us with the Holy Spirit to be our Comforter and Guide whenever we feel troubled.

I love the hymn "Jordan's Stormy Banks," especially the chorus:

> We will rest in the fair and happy land, by and by
> Just across on the evergreen shore.
> Sing the song of Moses and the Lamb, by and by,
> And dwell with Jesus evermore.*

In the meantime, my friends, let us travel light. Jesus has our backs, and soon He will come and take us home where we will live in the mansions He has prepared for us—forevermore.

Nokukhanya Ncube

---

* Samuel Stennett, "Jordan's Stormy Banks" (1908).

April 15

Angels Protect Us

For he shall give his angels charge over thee, to keep thee in all thy ways.
—Psalm 91:11, KJV

It was a hectic day. My daughter, Sharon, and I had traveled hundreds of kilometers from our hometown to the capital for Sharon to register after having finished her nursing degree. After hours of waiting, we finished our work and started the journey home. We purchased our tickets for the local train just as I saw a train arriving at the next platform. Without thinking it through, I foolishly urged my daughter to jump onto the train track and climb the platform to board the train. She hesitated, but I jumped, and she followed. Because she was a lot younger, she easily climbed up onto the platform, but I could not. Though I tried and tried, I could not pull myself up and out of danger.

Suddenly I heard a train racing toward the station. When I looked, I saw it was heading toward me on the tracks where I was standing. The people on the opposite platform shouted at me, warning me of the oncoming train. Even with all the adrenaline flooding my body, I still could not climb onto the platform. At the very last second, two men jumped down from the opposite side and pulled me up. Grasping my arms tightly, they hauled me to safety as the train shot past. It was all over in a fraction of a second. I was so shocked that I stood shivering from head to foot. I did not see the faces of the two men who saved me while risking their own lives. They disappeared into the crowd.

When I came to my senses, I realized that God must have sent His angels and saved me despite my careless decision. I pray that I will see them in heaven one day, whether they are angels or men. I would like to thank them.

Yes, my dear sisters, how true it is that God sends His angels to guard and keep us safe in all our ways. He has promised, "He shall call upon me, and I will answer him: I will be with him in trouble; I will deliver him, and honour him" (Psalm 91:15, KJV). God is faithful in His promises. Though we may fumble and take some unwise steps, God, the keeper of Israel, who neither sleeps nor slumbers, watches over us and protects us. I can testify to the truth of this promise: "I have been young, and now am old; yet have I not seen the righteous forsaken" (Psalm 37:25, KJV).

So do not worry. Place your trust in Him. He is a caring, loving Savior.

Jeyarani Sundarsingh

April 16

Wanting

That which is crooked cannot be made straight: and that which is wanting cannot be numbered.
—Ecclesiastes 1:15, KJV

Early Thursday morning turned out to be rather musical while I walked my usual route. The air was fresh and clean, the sun lifting its covers to give generous amounts of warmth and golden beauty. As I basked in nature with very little interruption from vehicles, my ears noticed a distant sputtering and clanging. The clanks grew closer and closer, and an object came into view, traveling in the opposite direction. Still uttering the strange noises, it crept and crawled, dancing and twisting as it jumped about, displaying its reggae-style dance moves.

As the old burgundy passenger van faltered, now directly in my view, I could see the culprit—the left rear wheel. The rubber tire was in shambles. The rim, now dismantled, crooked, and bent, rocked along, providing the heavy metal music as it hit the asphalt. Old Faithful's body, patched, dented, scraped, and bruised, danced and pranced as it moved along, sometimes bouncing six inches above the road.

The driver continued to steer his van as safely as he could. I assumed he was trying to reach a tire shop. The closest one lay about a mile away. I watched the battered and worn-out rim yell and yell in agony as it left its marks on the road. Only three wheels were carrying the load on this poor lopsided vehicle. One member of the wheel family was completely gone. The rim could not be straightened; there was no wheel, no tire, and no air. It needed life support immediately—cardiopulmonary resuscitation to its left rear wheel.

As the driver continued down the road in search of a wheel, tire, rim, and help, I reflected on the object lesson in front of me. Are any members of our body, family, or church missing or bent out of shape? What are we doing to reclaim our missing friends? And what about us? Are our lives without air? Are we filled with scratches and bruises? Are we in agony? What marks are we leaving? What marks have we left? We all need the One who restores and makes all things new. He gives us purpose. If we try to continue with missing parts, we will not function optimally. Do we recognize where we are wanting? Jesus can fully restore today. He wants to because He knows that no one can replace you or me. Let us come to Jesus. Only He can supply all we need.

Pauline A. Dwyer-Kerr

April 17

Rescue the Perishing

The Lord is not slow in keeping his promise, as some understand slowness. Instead he is patient with you, not wanting anyone to perish, but everyone to come to repentance.
—2 Peter 3:9, NIV

When I taught at a physical therapy college, I would encourage my students to come to my cabin every day if they did not understand something we had covered in the classroom. After classes many of them would stand in line to ask their questions.

One evening I met with a student who patiently waited until everyone left. She wanted to talk but hesitated. I broke the silence and asked how her studies were going. Tears rolled down her cheeks. She could not answer. I gave her a loving hug. She held me tight and started to cry bitterly. She was from a wealthy family, but her busy parents never gave her attention. She longed for love and went looking for it in a twisted relationship with a married man. She knew it was wrong, and she desperately needed help to end it. She asked if I would pray for her. I felt very empathetic toward this young woman and started counseling her. As I spent time with her and continued to pray for her, she responded well and was so receptive to the truth. It was such a blissful moment when she showed signs of change. And I rediscovered the fullness of the mission Jesus has given me. God is very interested in the salvation of every individual living in this world.

He tells us, "Before I formed you in the womb, I knew you, before you were born I set you apart" (Jeremiah 1:5, NIV). God has never ceased to work on our behalf. He invites us to be witnesses to the perishing who do not know Him. He longs to use us. When we witness and pray with a burden for the lost, something always happens. People who do not know the truth matter so much to God that when they are found, all heaven rejoices and throws a party! There is more joy over one sinner coming to Jesus than over the ninety-nine people who are already in the fold. If lost people matter this much to God, they should matter just as much to us. Are we willing to give everything needed to reach the lost?

My friends, let us keep the faith, keep sharing, and keep praying. There are people around us in bondage to sin, drowning in desperation and longing for rescue. Please pray with me, "Here am I. Send me, oh Lord."

Esther Synthia Murali

April 18

How God Is Changing Our Community

Go ye therefore, and teach all nations, baptizing them in the name of the Father, and of the Son, and of the Holy Ghost: Teaching them to observe all things whatsoever I have commanded you: and, lo, I am with you always, even unto the end of the world.
—Matthew 28:19, 20, KJV

A few years ago my husband and I began to intentionally pray for our community. We started a new church fifteen minutes from our home. I invited my neighbor Kelly,* who asked her friend Ann, who invited her twin siblings. We now had four new young people from our neighborhood attending church with us.

As we studied with them, they were hungry for the Word of God. One of the twins asked, "Ms. Jazmin, when will we be baptized?"

We worked with them and set a date for the following year. It was an extraordinary day, and their parents participated in the reading of the scriptures. The following year, Kelly's sister started attending church and was baptized. These children consistently attended church. One of my neighbors saw the changes in the children and asked if her three children could attend church with us. We found ourselves needing two cars to get everyone to church.

Each Sabbath, seven young people attended church with us. When the COVID-19 pandemic hit and we could not attend church in person, our neighbor asked, "Ms. Jazmin, why don't we have church in my house?"

We began to think and plan how we could worship together. My husband suggested streaming live on Facebook. I was hesitant at first, but it has truly blessed many people. At one point about twenty people worshiped in the house church during the pandemic. In August 2020 two more teens were baptized in the pool behind the house.

One woman attended our baby dedication and was impressed with the performance of the children who participated in the service. She asked if her two children could attend church with us. We studied with the new children, and they and another young person were soon baptized. Today all but those who moved are still attending church. God has done great things due to our prayers and inviting people to worship with us!

Jazmin Wildman

---

* Names have been changed.

April 19

The Power of Hope

And now these three remain: faith, hope and love. But the greatest of these is love.
—1 Corinthians 13:13, NIV

Uncertainty is an unwelcome companion that often shows up uninvited. It leaves me feeling lost in a dense fog, unsure of my next step. In these moments I remember the power of hope. Hope is the anchor that holds us fast, a beacon that shines brightly in the darkness.

The Bible showcases the power of hope through the lives of Ruth and the woman with the bleeding disorder. After Ruth had lost her husband, home, and sense of security, she clung to hope, trusting that God had a better plan for her. Even in her emptiness, she believed that God would restore and redeem her story. And He did.

Similarly the woman with the bleeding disorder had tried every medical option and had exhausted all her resources without finding relief. Yet in her darkest moment, hope remained. With a glimmer of faith she reached out to touch the hem of Jesus' garment, believing that He could do what medical science could not. Her story teaches us that even when all else fails, hope in God's power and love can lead us to miraculous breakthroughs. These two women, from different walks of life, demonstrate the power of hope in the face of uncertainty. They show us that hope can lead us out of the darkest places and into a brighter future. May we, like Ruth and the woman with the bleeding disorder, hold on to hope, especially when our circumstances seem uncertain.

So how do we cultivate hope amid uncertainty? First, we pray, pouring out our hearts to God. Second, we practice gratitude and focus on the blessings in our lives. Third, we surround ourselves with a supportive community and help each other in our walk with God. As we navigate uncertain times, let us determine to cling to hope, trusting in God's love and care. May we trust that God has a better plan and that His power and love can lead us to miraculous breakthroughs.

Dear God, fill us with hope amid uncertainty. Help us to trust in Your love and care, even when the path ahead is unclear. May our hope be the anchor that holds us fast, the beacon that shines brightly in the darkness. Amen.

Vanessa T. Mutambara

April 20

Who Can Find a Virtuous Woman?

Who can find a virtuous woman? for her price is far above rubies.
—Proverbs 31:10, KJV

I believe the Holy Spirit inspired the description of womanhood in Proverbs 31:10–31 not only as a magnificent poem but to provide us with instruction and inspiration. Let us take a closer look at what the Lord wants us to learn through the counsel given to King Lemuel by his mother.

This longest scriptural statement on womanhood begins with a question and suggests that the one who discovers a woman like this will have really struck it rich. Rubies are among the most valuable and costly of precious stones—and the virtuous woman's value is listed as being far above rubies. Only wisdom is accorded equal value in the Scriptures, leading us to infer that this woman was also wise.

Virtue is not a commonly used word, so what does it mean? It is defined as "a trait of excellence. . . . A disposition to choose actions that succeed in showing high moral standards. . . . When someone takes pleasure in doing what is right, even when it is difficult or initially unpleasant, they can establish virtue as a habit."* A virtuous woman is wise, kind, clothed with dignity and strength. She is a comfort and encouragement to those around her. She loves God and her fellow men and is a blessing to many.

Every woman who has walked with God has a story to tell. From Sarah we learn that nothing is too difficult for God. Hagar teaches us that even in the desert, God is there. Rahab shows us that God can use anyone for any purpose. Ruth tells us that it is not over until God says it is over. Esther shares that God can transform an unworthy person into a queen. The woman with the issue of blood teaches that when all has failed, God never fails. Mary and Martha tell us that death can be changed into life. And from Dorcas we learn that God never forgets what we do for others.

My dear sisters, it is our privilege to walk with God and become virtuous women. When we walk with the Lord, we, too, will have a story to share with others. We are living in the last days. We do not know when our mighty God will come to this world to take us to our heavenly home. We must be ready and invite others to be ready to meet Him in the clouds of heaven. May God bless you, your families, and your churches.

Krupa Victor

---

* *Wikipedia*, s.v. "Virtue," accessed Sep. 2, 2024, https://en.wikipedia.org/wiki/Virtue.

April 21

Tell It to Jesus Alone

"Call to me and I will answer you and tell you great and unsearchable things you do not know."
—Jeremiah 33:3, NIV

I am not very good at sharing my heart with others, but when it comes to telling God how I feel and sharing my thoughts with Him, I am an open book. I went to camp in Choiseul, Saint Lucia, at the secondary school in La Fargue for a weekend in July. It was one of the most adventurous times I have ever enjoyed. Though I had initially been very reluctant to go and only decided to attend at the last moment, I was glad to be there.

The countryside scenery is always beautiful and serene, and we all need to take the opportunity to enjoy nature at its finest. David reminds us in the Psalms, "The heavens declare the glory of God; the skies proclaim the work of his hands" (Psalm 19:1, NIV). My time away gave me a chance to reflect on the goodness of God and to open my heart in communion with the Lord.

Recently I made a covenant with God that I would be faithful to Him in everything that He directs me to do. On Sabbath morning I poured out my heart to Him. For some time I had been battling over a decision I needed to make. I had a sense that He was calling me to build a home, but I struggled with a desire to return to school. Whichever choice I made would impact my life, and I wanted to be sure I was honoring God in making my decision.

As I looked out at Gros Piton Peak from my balcony, God revealed His will to me. There, in the beauty and stillness of His creation, I heard His voice whisper to me, "It is time to move to the country." I knew what it would demand of me, and with painstaking effort, as I gasped for breath, I responded, "Yes, Lord, I will."

I thank God for always revealing His will for my life. At that moment I realized, more than ever, that He alone was the One with whom I could share the longings of my heart. He knew the obstacles I was confronted with and the challenges I faced. He answered my silent petitions and gave me peace. He assured me that He would guide me along my journey.

My friends, you can pour out your heart to Him today. He loves you. He hears you, and He will answer when you call.

Rosemary Kasandra Lucien

April 22

Enough!

And except those days should be shortened, there should no flesh be saved: but for the elect's sake those days shall be shortened.
—Matthew 24:22, KJV

It rained last night. After more than sixty days with no rain and scorching temperatures, it was a welcome relief. All around us wildfires burned, people evacuated with only minutes to outrun the flames, homes and animals were lost, and now, finally, it rained. I have to wonder, with the weather we are experiencing, is God trying to get our attention? Do we need a wake-up call?

God could send the proper amount of snow in winter and rain in summer and also protect us from all the forces of nature, but if He did, we would be living in a "heaven on earth." We would have no desire or need to seek His will, to know Him more, to share the gospel with others, and to be ready to meet Him. Everything on earth would be just peachy.

Summer is a season everyone usually loves, with its vacations, beach time, hiking, warm days, and cool breezy evenings. But in recent years on the western side of North America, summer has become a fearsome time—fear that lighting may spark a fire or a careless human may unintentionally start one. Fear the next big fire will be chasing me!

Though God sent a worldwide flood to destroy humankind in Genesis, most of the natural disasters today are the works of the enemy. As with Job, God may allow Satan to trouble us, and in those troubles God intends to awaken us to the fact of how much we need Him. And how much we need Him! Though our current fire season could have gone on unabated through September and into October, last night, God said, "OK, this is enough. I will reach down and send the rain. I will help My people."

In Matthew 24, Jesus speaks about the days of tribulation being shortened or no one would survive. It felt that way this summer. God shortened the fire season and blessed us with rain. In Daniel 10, the angel says to Daniel, "Don't be afraid, Daniel. Since the first day you began to pray for understanding . . . your request has been heard in heaven. I have come in answer to your prayer. But for twenty-one days the spirit prince of the kingdom of Persia blocked my way" (Daniel 10:12, 13, NLT). Today, all these years after Daniel's time, Jesus is still fighting for us. This time He sent rain and cooler weather, and we praise His name!

Elizabeth Versteegh Odiyar

April 23

Eternity With Jesus

And this is what He promised us—eternal life. . . .
And now, dear children, continue in him, so that when he appears
we may be confident and unashamed before him at his coming.
—1 John 2:25–28, NIV

Do you have something you really love to do? Walking out in nature is the "something" I love to do. This "something" became even more meaningful, needed, and precious to me back in March 2020 when COVID-19 shut down the world. Spending time outside allowed me to spread my wings, so to speak. It gave me time to shed the feelings of isolation and confinement, even if momentarily, that seemed to blanket our lives.

The day dawned bright—warm sunshine and blue skies, with spring flowers and cherry trees in full bloom. Yes, the world may have shut down, but God's creation continued to be on full display. It is on days like this, after coming out of a cold, wet West Coast winter, that I truly understand why I live in beautiful British Columbia, Canada.

Walking time equals communion time with my best friend, Jesus. It is a time to pour out from deep within my heart my deepest desires, fears, and longings, a time to talk openly and candidly, with no boundaries. I can tell my best Friend everything. Nothing is withheld.

It is also a time when I love to sing. The old hymns are among my favorites. The words speak to the depths of my soul as I praise Him in song. I see and find God in the words. Each hymn tells a story. "How Great Thou Art," "Nearer, My God to Thee," "I Come to the Garden Alone," "What a Friend We Have in Jesus," "The Old Rugged Cross," and "Amazing Grace." Each one is precious! On one of my walks, these words filled my heart:

> When we've been there ten thousand years,
> Bright shining as the sun,
> We've no less days to sing God's praise,
> Than when we'd first begun.*

Wow! I literally stopped dead in my tracks on the trail. My eyes filled with tears, and my heart overflowed with joy as I stood and looked upward into the blue heavens.

My friends, we really will be with Him for eternity, which will never end. Hold on! We are almost home! As the writer of Hebrews so eloquently says, "Let us hold unswervingly to the hope we profess, for he who promised is faithful" (Hebrews 10:23, NIV). Thank You, Jesus!

Dorian Honey

---

* John Newton, "Amazing Grace" (1779).

April 24

Psalm 25

In you, LORD my God, I put my trust.
—Psalm 25:1, NIV

The golden hour always captivates me, especially as it graces the tranquil confines of my gardens. As the sun gently sinks, its warm rays paint the world in a rich tapestry of gold and crimson, casting a soft glow that enhances every detail with depth and splendor. Yet the golden hour is more than just a visual delight to the senses. It symbolizes the transition between day and night, representing the potential for transformation and new beginnings.

The king of Israel, David, faced his share of transformation and new beginnings. He experienced periods of doubts and challenges and had to navigate through uncertain times. Despite every difficulty, he drew strength from his faith in God, trusting His divine purpose to guide him through each transition. His courage and unwavering belief allowed him to overcome obstacles and leave a lasting legacy as one of Israel's most revered and best-loved kings.

David's life stands as a timeless testament to resilience and hope, offering enduring lessons on how to confront change with courage and embrace new beginnings with conviction. David was acutely aware of his flaws and limitations, yet he never lost sight of his commitment to God. His ability to maintain integrity and pursue righteousness, even in the face of personal failings, underscores the importance of remaining true to one's values and purpose.

"David was beloved of God, not because he was a perfect man, but because he did not cherish stubborn resistance to God's expressed will. His spirit did not rise up in rebellion against reproof. . . . David erred greatly, but he was just as greatly humbled, and his contrition was as profound as his guilt. . . . He never lost his confidence in God. . . . He was beloved, also, because he relied upon the mercy of a God whom he had loved and served and honored."*

David's story encourages us to approach our challenges with the same courage, humility, and faith that characterized his journey. By reflecting on David's life, we are reminded that we, too, can navigate through life's transitions with a resolute spirit and a hopeful heart. His life serves as a powerful reminder that resilience and hope are attainable through faith and determination, inspiring us to face change with courage and embrace new beginnings with conviction.

Olga Valdivia

---

* Ellen G. White, *Elder Daniels and the Fresno Church*, pamphlet 28, 1890.

April 25

Emptying

In humility value others.
—Philippians 2:3, NIV

Have you ever experienced encouragement, loving consolation, Spirit-led guidance, affection, and mercy from Jesus? Paul suggests these are the primary inducements to live a Christ-minded life (Philippians 2:1–3). Such a life exhibits humility, consideration of others, letting go of preconceived notions, and letting self be replaced with obedience (verses 4–8).

Some time back, a pastor requested I arrange for "my" long-time music group to facilitate a bluegrass gospel event at my former church—as part of an annual, largely secular, ten-day music festival. My late husband, Jim, and I had previously worked together on this event for five years running, before the COVID-19 pandemic. God had blessed. Community and local musician attendance had swelled to three hundred! But at this point I was a widow and had moved to a neighboring state. Reluctantly I agreed, feeling "one more time" would serve, in part, as a tribute to Jim's memory.

For nine months our music group collaborated, planned, and practiced. Then, just days before the scheduled event, I learned of a family group (whom I had never met) from another state that was interested in joining us! The pastor strongly urged collaboration, though he had never heard their music either. Who were they? Would our musical styles even be compatible? Finding out on a performance stage before hundreds of spectators is not the place to experiment! Should I let go of a tried-and-true formula—for an . . . experiment? Either success or failure would reflect on the sponsoring church. I was so torn! Especially when I learned that the leader of the family group might be interested in becoming a member of my denomination! "In humility value others" (Philippians 2:3, NIV). God, help me! I fasted, camping in Philippians 2:1–11, and prayed for the attitude and leading of Christ. Finally I received the humility to "let go." Providence acted with lightning speed.

Two days before the event, half of "my" group could not make it due to medical challenges. The family group joining with our "remnant" made up a complete band with energy, youth, and drive. Our final song was "Will the Circle Be Unbroken?" Abruptly the audience—different ethnicities, denominations, and age groups (some in wheelchairs)—rose to their feet as one, joining hands in a large circle. Smiling. Singing. Weeping. I almost trembled. What if I had declined humility? Not valued others? The outcome could have been so sadly different!

Carolyn Rathbun Sutton

April 26

Share Your Blessings

"Then you will call upon Me and go and pray to Me, and I will listen to you."
—Jeremiah 29:12, NKJV

Growing up in a small southern town afforded me limited exposure to the real world. I enjoyed reading about faraway places. One of the places that intrigued me and I frequently longed to see was New York City. But I had no hope that this desire would ever become a reality. God, however, had a plan already in place that included not only New York City but also the ability to visit four other continents.

My first adventure was an invitation to live with a relative in Pennsylvania who was not a Seventh-day Adventist, with the understanding that I would be able to work and save for school. That proved to be a great disappointment. I ended up being the babysitter and housekeeper. God was there with me in the midst of my pain and disappointment.

One Sabbath at church a Bible worker reached out to me and later invited me to go with her to visit her sister, who lived in Massachusetts. What a wonderful experience. She then encouraged me to go to Massachusetts, live with her sister, and work at the local hospital. This became one of the most enjoyable and rewarding opportunities in my educational journey. I began calling her sister Aunt Roseva. She was a friend to all the youth and provided Christian counseling and guidance. I was blessed with a job as a nursing assistant at the hospital. Aunt Roseva's friend from Jamaica, New York, visited her often. When I shared my desired goal with her, she immediately invited me to go to New York and work for better pay. Aunt Roseva approved the plan. What a blessing! I got a job at the state hospital and was able to enroll in the school of nursing and receive a biweekly stipend. Once I had completed the diploma program, I was motivated to achieve a bachelor of science in nursing and then a master's degree.

When I count God's goodness toward me, I am moved to share His blessings and help provide financial assistance to students on their educational journey. I know I will never amass wealth with so many students in need, but God has poured out His blessings on me, so how can I do anything less than show my thankfulness and gratitude to Him by helping others? When we share our blessings, God delights to bless us even more!

Mary Head Brooks

April 27

The Silent Listener

*"It shall come to pass
That before they call, I will answer;
And while they are still speaking, I will hear."*
—Isaiah 65:24, NKJV

Many days during my time as a professional graduate student, I saw God's hand at work in my schedule and assignments. During registration I joined the waiting list for two sections of a course. The registrar's office notified me of the section I was placed in, but I believe it was Abba who chose the right section for me. During the first week of classes, the instructor informed us that our evaluation for certification was scheduled for the first Sunday of our spring break. He admonished us to mark our calendars because attendance was mandatory if we wanted to be certified as mediators.

On the Sunday of our certification session, I overheard one classmate explaining to another that the other section of the course had their evaluations the day before, and they did not complete the process until 2:30 P.M. It was then I realized that Abba had orchestrated my schedule so that I was in the section that was evaluated on Sunday instead of the section evaluated on Sabbath.

One Friday evening I was rushing home, eager to begin Sabbath preparations. I stopped to help a friend who needed to complete an assignment before sunset. I forgot that I needed to send two emails to my mentors, letting them know of my availability to do observations the following week. A few minutes before sunset, one of the mentors emailed me to ask if I was interested and available to do an observation at 8:30 A.M. on Monday morning. I responded in the affirmative, and during the observation, he offered me three additional observations for the same week.

One of the observation sessions had to be canceled as a participant did not show up. However, the information gleaned while waiting was exactly what I needed to make an informed decision about which course I should register for during summer school.

These three incidents reminded me of the value of praying instead of worrying. When we place our trust in God, He can listen to our prayers and the desires of our hearts. Our faith and trust in Him then permit Him to work all things together for our good.

Desrene L. Vernon

April 28

Listen and Obey

We ought to obey God rather than men.
—Acts 5:29, KJV

Dr. Walter Pearson was the featured speaker for the North American Division's Net 2004 satellite evangelistic initiative by the Seventh-day Adventist Church. The theme was "Experience the Power," and it was hosted at the Miracle Temple Seventh-day Adventist Church in Baltimore, Maryland, USA. On the last Sabbath of the event, I was at my home church, Sligo, in Takoma Park, Maryland. After I greeted my friend Joy, she suggested we drive to Baltimore to attend the Net 2004 meetings. We hastily left after Sabbath School.

Thankfully, after we had parked the car, we quickly found seats in the packed congregation. After the inspiring sermon ended, it was announced that the afternoon program would begin at three o'clock. It suddenly dawned on me it would be impossible to go home for lunch and return in time for the program. Neither of us wanted to miss it—but we had brought no lunch.

Once outside we walked by open car trunks and picnic blankets filled with tantalizing food, filling the air with the fragrance of savory patties, creamy salads, and caramelized delights. I turned to Joy and said, "All these people are Adventists. We all enjoy the same food. I am going to ask one of them if they would be willing to share their lunch."

I walked over to a sister in Christ and expressed our predicament. She invited us to help ourselves to ginger beer, sorrel juice, vegetable Pelau, callaloo, fried fish, macaroni pie, and salads. The meal was so delicious that Joy went back for seconds.

Once finished I distinctly sensed the Holy Spirit urging me, "Get up! Hurry back to the church!"

Turning to Joy, I said, "We need to leave right away." We thanked our kind host and began to help clean up after the meal.

Again the voice commanded, "Hurry! Leave now!"

Joy was still eating, but I headed for the church. When I got to the door, security allowed me in, but Joy was not with me. I pled with him to wait a minute because I could see her hurrying toward us. She barely made it. We got the last two available seats and sat down as the cameras started to roll. Joy was unusually silent, then quietly asked, "How did you know we needed to leave?"

I told her I had heard the Holy Spirit and chosen to listen and obey. May we always be sensitive to listening to the Lord and prompt to obey.

C. Marion Hudson

April 29

The God Who Answers

"Ask, and it will be given to you; seek, and you will find; knock, and it will be opened to you."
—Matthew 7:7, ESV

Today one of my neighbors had an emergency and called 911. The ambulance arrived shortly afterward and administered help as needed. However, she needed to be transported to the hospital. One of the emergency medical services team members stayed in the home with her while two others went outside to get the stretcher from the ambulance. Though they tried and tried, they could not retrieve the stretcher. It would not budge. Finally they turned the engine on and were able to successfully get it onto the ground. However, it was still connected somehow to the back of the ambulance, and they could not move it until their team member came out of the house to help them. What should have taken a few minutes took over thirty to accomplish.

They went into the home and brought my neighbor out on the stretcher after what seemed like forever. They tried to place her into the ambulance, but they could not do it, though they tried and tried. Two of them wheeled her back into her home and waited with her there. Eventually another ambulance arrived on the scene. They were able to easily remove their stretcher, and soon my neighbor was wheeled toward the second vehicle without further delay. It took only about five minutes before she was on her way to the hospital.

Meanwhile the first ambulance and the three men who arrived in it had more trouble trying to get the stretcher back into it. They eventually succeeded—without the patient who had originally placed the call. As I looked on I prayed they would get her to the hospital before it was too late. I hoped it was not a life-or-death situation.

Think how good our heavenly Father is: when we call Him, He is always there. Do you remember the story of Elijah telling King Ahab it would not rain for three years? At the end of the drought, when all the people had gathered to watch which God would answer with fire, the prophets of Baal prayed all day without their gods answering them. When Elijah called on God to accept his sacrifice and so prove who was the true God, the Lord responded without any hesitation.

Our God hears the prayers of His people. He alone is the true God, and He is so good!

Bessie Russell Haynes

April 30

The Rickety Old Bridge

Now faith is the substance.
—Hebrews 11:1, NKJV

Now that it had finally arrived, spring was showing off. Warm breezes collected and spread the fragrances from budding trees. Daffodils, daisies, impatiens, and irises smiled an invitation to enjoy the beauty of the outdoors! So inspired, I decided to visit the next township.

At first I was so enthralled with the playful lambs and calves in the pastures that while following the GPS, I was not paying close attention to where I was actually going on the twisting, turning, sloping, one-lane country road. Ahead of me was a rickety old bridge without guardrails. There was no "bridge weight limit" sign. It did not look like much with its wooden slats of a sickly, washed-out gray—lending credence to my belief that there was no way this bridge could support the weight of my vehicle. There was simply not enough substance to the seemingly haphazardly constructed bridge. I paused. Surely the township would not allow an unsafe structure to remain open. Would they?

Cautiously I proceeded forward, flinching at every creak and groan of those wooden boards. When I had successfully crossed the bridge, a sobering thought crossed my mind. Though I had never encountered this particular bridge before, and it certainly appeared structurally unsound, I had shown enough faith in the township's ability to care for its roads to move forward. Did I show as much faith in God, who has proven He can be trusted over and over again? Sometimes we can look at a situation and proclaim it too dangerous, too hopeless, too impossible, or too big for our God to handle, and so we stand still. We do not move forward.

Although the Lord had told Joshua He would go before the children of Israel and drive out the Canaanites and the Hittites (Joshua 3:10), they had never encountered a situation like the one they faced at the Jordan River. When they had faced the Red Sea years earlier, it parted before they crossed over. But this time the priests had to wade into the fast-flowing waters before the waters would part. We place our faith in many man-made objects like airplanes, boats, and, yes, bridges without much thought. But let us pray that, like Joshua, we will demonstrate the most important kind of faith—faith in God, who can use even rickety old bridges to teach us a lesson while guiding us safely to the other side.

Charmaine Houston

May 1

A Sense of Place

"I will come back and take you to be with me that you also may be where I am."
—John 14:3, NIV

I have been contemplating John 14:1–3. The New International Version reads, "Do not let your hearts be troubled. You believe in God; believe also in me. My Father's house has many rooms; if that were not so, would I have told you that I am going there to prepare a place for you? And if I go and prepare a place for you, I will come back and take you to be with me that you also may be where I am."

I am intrigued by the phrases *many rooms* and *prepare a place*. I grew up on the King James Version, which says "many mansions" instead of "many rooms." But I have learned that the King James Version phrasing, which can lead to a materialistic interpretation of the verse, is not an accurate one.

The Greek word translated as "rooms" in the NIV has a vague concept of "a space for you." The idea is similar to the way Bedouins enlarge their tents to provide sleeping space for more and more guests and family members. It is a relational term more than a spatial expression.

Jesus' going to provide a place for us after His resurrection is the action of His reconnecting us with the Father and cementing our right to be in the Father's heart and home forever, despite the great rebellion that removed us in the first place.

More and more, the phrase "a sense of place" is used here in this world in political and lifestyle discussions. It can refer to the setting in which one grew up—in the city or the countryside. It can refer to the region of the world from which one's ancestors most recently came rather than one's current country of residence. It can also be used concerning where one feels "at home." Bars and pubs have long been that place for a segment of society, and in some areas of the world, coffee houses and, now, nonalcoholic bars are available to provide "a sense of place."

I am overjoyed that because of the resurrection, my "sense of place" is in the Father's heart and home. I can claim that space right now, to a limited degree, whether or not I have a happy niche in which I belong here on this earth. But even more, someday, in heaven or the earth made new or anywhere else in the universe for that matter, the place Jesus has prepared for me by His death and resurrection is secure, forever and ever.

Kathy Beagles Coneff

May 2

Trusting God in the Hard Times

In all your ways acknowledge Him, and He shall direct your paths.
—Proverbs 3:6, NKJV

Retirement was approaching, and my husband and I began considering what that transition would look like. We longed to leave the fast-growing, congested city where we lived and move to a smaller, not-too-distant town that was closer to nature and provided some breathing space. So we began looking in nearby rural settings for a small home with land.

Unfortunately many others had similar ideas. Homes were being snatched up quickly, and the price tags were out of our reach. After much prayer we changed course. We extended our search a little farther from the city and started looking for land, putting it into God's hands.

We found a piece of land located less than an hour from the city, not far from a small Adventist church. In time, we located a reputable, affordable builder, sold our home in town, and began the process of building a house. But then the dream and reality converged.

Things began as expected. We finalized house plans, excavators began their work, and the search for a well driller commenced. Who knew that it could take up to two years to schedule a well-driller in our state? Not us! After months of frustration and delays, we finally acquired an excellent well-driller. We praised the Lord! But that was only the beginning of difficulties, which eventually included our builder declaring bankruptcy. The whole ordeal became a nightmare.

We—and others—began questioning our experience. Had we followed our own will and not the Lord's? Was God trying to teach us something? Even though we believed that God was leading, we had to wonder whether we had gotten it wrong.

We are finally living in our new home and are truly grateful to God, but I must admit to still not having the answers to my questions. What I have come to realize, however, is that when we make mistakes, God does not leave us. He helps us to grow through the tough times and come out of them realizing our total need of Him even more fully. Also, making the "right" decisions does not mean that things will go smoothly. Even though the way is hard and rocky, it could still be God's plan that we travel that road for reasons we will come to understand only in heaven.

Do we love and trust God even when all things appear to be against us? That is the question we must answer if we want to one day enter our new home in heaven and be with Jesus forever.

Sandra Blackmer

May 3

In His Time

And I, if I be lifted up from the earth, will draw all men unto me.
—John 12:32, KJV

Sometimes in one's golden years, the tendency is to sit back, relax, and count our blessings.

I purchased a recliner lift chair for my husband after he became very ill. It made a big difference and helped ease some of the challenges that come with growing older. A few years later we needed to move in with our oldest daughter. One evening I noticed that everyone was relaxing, enjoying a chance to put their feet up. Yet here I was, sitting in a less-than-comfortable captain's chair. My son-in-law encouraged me to purchase a recliner, and by the grace of God, I was able to make that purchase. Now I could join the rest of the family in relaxing.

After four months of enjoyment, my chair started to make loud noises every time I tried to recline it. I asked my son-in-law to take a look, and he found the problem. Armed with this information, I called the manufacturers. Now, I am usually adamant about keeping the instruction manuals of everything I purchase. After making a note of the date of purchase, I typically put them away safely. But now, I could not find it anywhere. How frustrating!

When I made the call, the first thing they asked for was the reference number. I explained my dilemma and was told they could not help without the date and number. Once again, I searched but found nothing. I called the company back, and they repeated their instructions. But this time I had prayed before calling.

The customer service representative said, "Mrs. Johnson, if you can take a video with your phone and send it to us, we will be able to hear the noises and may be able to help." I am not a videographer, but I made a video and sent it. A little later I called to make sure they had received my video. They confirmed they had, and then I heard no more from them.

One day I received a package. I was not expecting anything, so imagine how happy I felt to open the package and find a replacement part for my chair. God had answered my prayer. I was overjoyed.

My friends, God cares about the little things in our lives. He loves us unconditionally with an agape love that can never be duplicated. If you are waiting for an answer, be patient. Our time is not His time, but in time He will show Himself faithful.

Elaine J. Johnson

May 4

The Black Tulip

"He will wipe every tear from their eyes."
—Revelation 21:4, NIV

Tulips are supposed to be bright and colorful. After the long, dark winter months, many people look forward to the yellow daffodils and red tulips—a splash of color to cheer them up. A few weeks ago I took a photo of the tulips and daffodils in our garden. They were beautiful, radiant in red and white. But the other day, I saw some black tulips. Well, they were almost black. Black tulips are relatively rare and are considered something special.

The 1850 novel *The Black Tulip*, by Alexandre Dumas, was inspired by the myth of the existence of a black tulip. It is a story of a challenge to produce a pure black tulip. The first person to do so would win a valuable prize. The story influenced generations of Dutch growers who wanted to create a black tulip. A few almost succeeded. In 1891, a well-known breeder produced a tulip that he called La Tulipe Noire in allusion to the book by Dumas, claiming that he had won. However, the color was not truly black but more of a dark purple.

We can now find a yet darker tulip created by the horticulturist Geert Hageman in his greenhouse in a small Dutch village. He had planted thousands of tulip seeds, hoping to be able to get a perfect cross of dark varieties. As the plants grew, Hageman checked on them regularly. On a cold winter night on February 18, 1986, he spotted a small plant just starting to show a bit of color. Could this be the flower of his dreams?

The next day he presented his black tulip at a flower show, where it was received with amazement. After eleven more years, he had created enough stock to start marketing the black tulip he named Paul Scherer. Today, black tulip bulbs are available everywhere. And yet it is not perfectly black; it still has a faint purple hue.*

Today is my friend's birthday. It should be a joyous occasion, but the bright flowers she loves were replaced by white lilies when her beloved son passed away a few weeks ago. And now, it does not seem to be the right time for colorful flowers. Maybe it is time for black tulips.

Mourning a beloved son is a challenging time. Perhaps, right now, the beauty of black tulips is more fitting. And just as the black tulip is not a true black, even the darkest days can hold a trace of color, a promise of better days to come.

Hannele Ottschofski

---

* "The Black Tulip," Amsterdam Tulip Museum, accessed Nov. 14, 2024, https://amsterdamtulipmuseum.com/pages/the-black-tulip.

May 5

The Florist's Mistake

We are . . . Christ's ambassadors, as though God were making his appeal through us.
—2 Corinthians 5:20, NIV

When my sister Diana called and asked, "How are you?" I did not say, "Fine." I blurted out the whole truth. I told her all about the stresses I was having as I prepared for an event at work, and feeling like quite the martyr, I exclaimed, "Someone should give me a plaque!"

On the day of my event, when I saw a man walk by my office window carrying a gorgeous floral arrangement, I knew instantly that it was for me from Diana. I was right, except that the card was not just signed "Diana." She had included my mother, my other five siblings, two of my nephews, and a niece.

It was amazing! There was just one thing: The card read, "You never seem to admire us." I read it again. "There must be some mistake," I reasoned. However, I had carried on at length about myself in that last phone call. Maybe I should have asked more questions and been more interested in the others.

"The flowers came, and they're just gorgeous!" I told Diana's voicemail. "It's just like you to be so thoughtful! But, umm, the card says I never seem to admire you, and I really do; I admire all of you, and I will try to do better at expressing that in the future."

Before long, she called back. "The card was supposed to say, 'You never cease to amaze us'!"

"Ohhh!" I laughed, but she was not amused.

"I'm going to call them and have them do it over!" she exclaimed.

"Don't worry about it," I assured her. "This will make a great story!"

"I wasn't trying to send you a story. I was trying to send you words of affirmation!"

A few days later I received a large, beautiful card from the florist. This time, and I am not kidding, it read, "You never seem to amaze us!" It took a while for Diana to see the humor in all of this, but we have laughed about it often. We have also noted how destructive the experience would have been if I had not checked with her about the message to know her real intentions.

God has called me to be His florist, to pass on His message to the world. In both how I live and what I say, am I getting it straight?

Cheri Corder

May 6

Why Does the Gardener Prune?

"Every branch in Me that does not bear fruit He takes away; and every branch that bears fruit He prunes, that it may bear more fruit. You are already clean because of the word which I have spoken to you."
—John 15:2, 3, NKJV

One of my favorite descriptions of what it means to be in Christ is the analogy of Christ as the Vine and us as the branches. This describes a special connection. I have always wanted to be a fruit-bearing branch, not one that will end up being tossed into the fire.

Flowers outside my window are a joy for me. When I open my blinds in the morning, I am always overjoyed to see their colorful blooms. Yet, to keep them abundant with bloom, I must either deadhead the spent blooms or prune the nonbearing plants. I know that this must be done, but it is always an emotional struggle for me. I have wondered if I hurt my plants. I freely confess that I talk to my plants. For me it is like when I corrected my children's misbehaviors in the past. "This is more painful for me than it is for you," I would tell them. I loved them and did not want to cause them any discomfort. Reprimands never feel good, but sometimes they are exactly what is needed.

Pruned plants grow more abundantly with their blooms or fruit after pruning. Why is that? It is because pruning is a cleansing process, preparing the plant for sweeter fruit or more beautiful blooms.

I had read John 15 for seventy years before I applied it to myself in a physical way. I had always taken it only as a spiritual cleaning. But I see it now as physical too. For many years I have endured pain 24/7. I am a writer and am unable to take medication or do many of the prescribed protocols that help some people deal with pain. I have never asked God, "Why?" But I ask Him for relief.

John 15 now helps me to understand that the Husbandman, God, is pruning me so I can continue to minister. He has allowed me to reach an advanced age and to cope with the constant pain because I must write. It diverts my mind from the pain, and when I minister through my writing, I am producing better blooms and sweeter fruit that blesses others—far more in my old age than in earlier years. As He prunes me, I rejoice in the privilege of blooming for His glory.

Betty Kossick (deceased)

May 7

Parable of the Sower

"And because lawlessness will abound, the love of many will grow cold."
—Matthew 24:12, NKJV

Spring came, and my husband and I cleared a field because we wanted to grow some vegetables. We prepared the soil, removed the stones, leveled it to conserve water, added manure to ensure a rich crop, and then planted our seeds: rows and rows of potatoes, beans, corn, red beets, and zucchini. We waited with confidence, anticipated with pleasure, and watched with joy for the first signs of a rich crop to appear. We weeded and protected each plant and watched them grow. They were beautiful! I imagined the rich harvest we would enjoy and looked forward to the healthy food our field would produce.

June passed. July came with high temperatures, and my plants had already reached maturity.

Imagine my disappointment when I realized the maize had aged before its time, and the beans had blossomed but did not bud. The pumpkins had lost their fruit after reaching only a few centimeters in size. And the potatoes dried up before they could bloom. I felt very sad and wondered, *What could have gone wrong? Was it the drought or the soil? Too little manure? What can I do so it does not happen again in the next growing season?*

I remembered the parable of the sower. *I must find the answer in that story*, I thought to myself. It took me a few days to understand the message God had for me in His Word. I realized that the soil in our garden did not have enough nutrients to bring the plants to maturity, despite our best efforts to fertilize it, because it is clay soil and not naturally nourishing to plants. Though they had developed and flourished and looked beautiful, they did not bud. So close—but not close enough.

What about my heart? I wondered. What kind of soil is present? How many nutrients does it receive daily? Does it bud and bloom, producing fruit? Do I receive the Word that enriches me in bearing love, forgiveness, and patience? Do I still love, even while living in a world where love grows cold and lawlessness multiplies?

Help us, God, to gather Your Word into our hearts so that we do not sin against You. Help us to bear a rich harvest and rejoice in joy, love, patience, peace, and kindness. May people all around us see Your loveliness in our lives and turn to You.

Florentina Coman

May 8

POP for a Cause

Accept the way God does things,
for who can straighten what he has made crooked?
Enjoy prosperity while you can,
but when hard times strike, realize that both come from God.
Remember that nothing is certain in this life.
—Ecclesiastes 7:13, 14, NLT

The second Friday in May each year is celebrated as POP Day—Put on Purple. It is to raise awareness of lupus, an autoimmune condition that affects 1.5 million Americans and 5 million worldwide.*

I have been passionate about supporting other causes in the past, but this one recently became personal. A few years ago I started to experience extreme fatigue. Sleep was very comforting, but I would wake up feeling tired again. It was a very strange phenomenon to explain to someone, but it aptly described how I felt. You probably know someone who feels the same way. I was ill and did not know it.

My condition began to reveal itself slowly when one day I looked in the mirror, and there they were: quarter-sized bald patches on my head. I was terrified. My hair was gone without a moment's notice. After years of trying to find the cause, strange bouts of illness, and many visits to different medical professionals, I received a lupus diagnosis, and later another autoimmune condition was added to my record.

To date, I continue to fight the battle against autoimmunity, and while it has not been easy, I am comforted when I read today's text because it reminds me that God is with me in the good times and in the bad times. Max Lucado writes, "God is plotting for our good. In all the setbacks and slipups, He is ordaining the best for our future. Every event of our days is designed to draw us toward our God and our destiny."† So if you are facing a difficult situation, do not be dismayed; God will make a way.

When I learned of the efforts of others to raise awareness, I joined the cause. Won't you POP with me about a condition that mainly affects women? You can be a tower of strength, a prayer partner, or a friend to a lupus patient. Ecclesiastes 4:9 says that "two people are better off than one, for they can help each other succeed" (NLT). Will you help someone today?

Taniesha K. Robertson-Brown

---

* "Put on Purple for World Lupus Day," Lupus Foundation of America, accessed Nov. 14, 2024, https://www.lupus.org/lupus-awareness-month/put-on-purple.
† Max Lucado, *You'll Get Through This* (HarperCollins Christian, 2015), 127.

May 9

The Exam

But my God shall supply all your need according to his riches in glory by Christ Jesus.
—Philippians 4:19, KJV

I had taken the Psychiatric Mental Health course and finished it in less than a year. This was unheard of, especially for someone working full-time with a second part-time job in the evening. Additionally, I voluntarily served as the president of an association, which required more time than two full-time jobs. I knew it was only by God's grace that I made it through the program successfully—with my sanity intact.

During this time, I became very anxious and overwhelmed with my day-to-day responsibilities and demanding schedule. The pace was relentless. The load was almost unbearable. At times, I felt I did not have the mental capability to speak to God clearly, even to state my needs, as I attempted to have my daily devotions in the morning. I forgot where my source and strength came from and tried to accomplish everything on my own, but to no avail.

I had scheduled a date for my exam but changed it because I knew I was not prepared to take the proctored exam on the scheduled date and time. The new date was soon approaching, and yet I knew I had not given myself enough time to study and retain the necessary information. I had no other option but to take the exam I had rescheduled because it was too late to make any further schedule changes.

I realized I only had a few days left to study and determined to make the most of every minute. Sabbath was approaching. Should I use it as a study day? I remembered that God promised in Philippians 4:19 to supply all our needs and decided that studying was not an option on the Sabbath. The other days would have to be sufficient. I followed God's commandment and kept the Sabbath day holy. I began to study on the Sunday before the exam.

My sisters, we can take God at His word. We can trust Him even when we cannot see Him at work. The Bible is filled with powerful promises He invites us to claim. A favorite of mine is "My God shall supply all your need according to his riches in glory by Christ Jesus" (Philippians 4:19, KJV). If we are faithful to God, He will be faithful to us.

I was successful in the exam. We serve a living God; all we have to do is trust and obey.

Christie Simon-Waterman

May 10

Raised to Be Brave

*Train up a child in the way he should go,
and when he is old he will not depart from it.*
—Proverbs 22:6, NKJV

One night, as my mother and I sat together on the bed, we found ourselves in one of our usual candid, laughter-filled conversations. When she teased me, I would laugh and say, "But I'm like this because of you. I got it from my momma." Then we would both laugh. When I asked, "What about my personality frightened you as a mother?" she took a deep breath before responding.

"You're a risk-taker, my darling," she said, her voice tinged with concern.

"Why does that frighten you?"

"Because the world is often unkind to women who forge their own paths."

"Well," I said, "I guess we should be grateful you raised me to be brave."

We both laughed, comforted by our shared understanding. My mother had instilled in me confidence, tenacity, and unshakable faith, knowing I would need these traits for the road ahead.

In primary school I was bullied terribly and often came home in tears, where I would be reminded, "You know the truth of who you are. Never let anyone drown out that truth." As a teenager in high school, I struggled with a negative self-image, believing I was fat and ugly and that no one would love me. My mother told me how beautiful I was, to which I responded, "Of course, you would say that—you're my mom." But she did not stop there. She reinforced how talented and smart I was, never allowing me to wallow in self-pity but guiding me to focus on my God-given traits.

At university I was not easily swayed by newfound freedom or my peers. I had been taught to think for myself and to put God first. My university years were filled with service to God, surrounded by wholesome friends. I never drank, smoked, or was mesmerized by bad boys—not because I lived a sheltered life but because I knew none of these things served me. I had been trained to "put on the whole armor of God" (Ephesians 6:11, NKJV).

The world has not always been kind to me, yet here I stand by God's grace, a young woman who is God-fearing, self-assured, purpose-driven, and accomplished. I am not perfect. I make mistakes, stumble, and fail, yet I know whose I am. I am also my mother's daughter. *I am brave.*

Sibongile Tshabalala

May 11

Different Kinds of Quilters

Even so you, since you are zealous for spiritual gifts, let it be for the edification of the church that you seek to excel.
—1 Corinthians 14:12, NKJV

My mother, Rose, was an amazing homemaker. She not only cooked nutritious meals, made bread and noodles, canned, gardened, cleaned, and did laundry but also was very gifted at sewing and quilting. My twin sister and I were fortunate to be the recipients of the outfits she created for us. When she finished a dress, coat, blouse, or skirt, she always kept the remnant fabric. With these, she pieced together a memory quilt by hand with a flower garden pattern. We could look at this quilt and remember each beautiful outfit and the occasion for which she had made it. She shared her gift with us and others.

As I contemplated my mother's gift of quilting, I realized that we are all "quilters" of some sort. A writer pieces together words to express ideas. A doctor or nurse may take specimens to gather healing information. A cook likes to take scraps of ingredients here and there to create a new recipe. A pharmacist mixes a prescription of compounds to produce a new drug. A teacher puts together a lesson plan to present a concept to the students. A meteorologist gathers information from the atmosphere and its phenomena to predict the upcoming weather.

God has given all of us gifts. The Bible states, "But to each one of us grace was given according to the measure of Christ's gift" (Ephesians 4:7, NKJV). Some are called to be apostles, prophets, evangelists, pastors, or teachers. These are not all-encompassing titles. God can use our gifts, be what they may, in many ways to stitch and bind His message to those around us.

As Christians the Bible tells us to be "zealous for spiritual gifts" and to use them to edify, teach, and build up one another (1 Corinthians 14:12, NKJV). I may not be able to quilt as my mother did, but I enjoy "quilting words together" to express to others what amazing things the Lord has done in my life.

What kind of quilter are you? How could you use your gifts to help create unity, knowledge, and a loving spirit in those around you? If you are unsure, ask the Lord to show you the gifts He has given you, and then use them to His glory.

Karen M. Phillips

May 12

His Mother's Name

I am reminded of your sincere faith, a faith that dwelt first in your grandmother Lois and your mother Eunice and now . . . dwells in you as well.
—2 Timothy 1:5, ESV

As part of our daily family devotions, my husband and I read a chapter of the Bible together with our daughters. We want to encourage them to read the Word of God every day. As we read through 1 and 2 Kings, I noticed again that in introducing each king, details of their fathers, how old they were, and when they began their reign were included. Much less often the names of their mothers were included. So in a heavily patriarchal society, why did God see it important to add details about the mothers of the kings?

In the days of the kings, many of the monarchs mentioned could fall into one of two groups: those who did what was right in the sight of the Lord and those who did what was evil. I was fascinated to discover that a king as evil as Ahaz (2 Kings 16:1–4) could have a good son like Hezekiah. But Hezekiah ended up with the evil Manasseh (2 Kings 21:1–9) as his son. You would think that if the king was evil, he would produce an evil child. Or a good king would produce a good child. Though it did happen for some, it did not always occur.

Could the mothers have made a lasting impact on how the kings turned out? While the kings were busy ruling or going to war, who was raising their children? The mothers likely had a lot of help, but at the end of the day, they spent more time with their children than the kings did. Most likely, if the mother was good, she passed along those traits to the young princes.

As women, God has called each of us to be a mother figure to someone in our sphere of influence—wherever He has placed us. The question is, What kind of influence do we exert? Think of the examples of Mary, the mother of Jesus; Elizabeth, the mother of John the Baptist; Lois and Eunice, grandmother and mother of Timothy. And the unnamed mothers of Daniel, Elijah, and Deborah. Their influence was felt for generations. Could it be that the Lord has positioned us specifically to raise this generation through whom He can impact the world for eternity? Today He asks us to let Him change us so that the influence we exert on this generation will be for good. Are we willing? By His grace may we all, like Deborah, arise as faithful mothers in Israel.

Lynn Mfuru Lukwaro

May 13

Those Pesky Fleas

Thy word have I hid in mine heart, that I might not sin against thee.
—Psalm 119:11, KJV

My son has a cat. My son visits me. His cat wanders in the woods. Not all fleas are annihilated by flea poison. Conclusion: I occasionally have unwelcome invaders.

A few days ago I saw a tiny black spot on my leg, and sure enough, I found a flea! I was quick enough to pinch it between my thumb and forefinger before it could jump. Now, how to get rid of it? Aha! A bowl of water sat in my kitchen sink. The perfect solution—or so I thought. I put my thumb and forefinger deep into the water, opened them up, released the flea, and walked away, feeling smug. Then a thought hit me—can fleas survive in water?

I went to the internet, where I learned that, yes, surprisingly, fleas can survive in water for hours. They have an oily covering that protects them and, at times, even enables them to jump out of water. I rushed back to the sink and found the flea floating, so I turned the water on, dumped the contents of the bowl and the flea down the drain, and ran the water long enough that I felt it surely had to be gone for good.

How like the flea are the "little" sins in our lives? We think we have dealt with them for good, only to have them pop up again. We begin to question ourselves and wonder, *Am I just being legalistic, or is this really a sin?* Have you ever found yourself looking for a loophole? My friends, our salvation does not depend on our good or bad habits; it depends on our dependence on Jesus. We need to be aware of anything that makes the things of the world look more attractive to us. Those are the things that pull us away from our Savior rather than help us be ready for His return.

Why can sin appear to be so attractive? Why are bad habits so hard to break? Because they reward us with a good feeling—for a while. Every time we choose to repeat an action, the pathways in our brain become stronger until it becomes easier and easier to continue. Jesus can help us if we ask. Is it worth the struggle? We each have a choice to make. Jesus wants us to be the best that we can be. He is preparing a home for us where we will live with Him for eternity. Is it worth it? Oh yes! A thousand times, yes!

Lila Farrell Morgan

May 14

Psalm 118

This is the day which the Lord *hath made; we will rejoice and be glad in it.*
—Psalm 118:24, KJV

The jangle of the alarm suddenly jolted me out of a deep sleep. *I am so tired,* I thought. *It cannot be that time already.* Yet it was—time to emerge from the soft, warm comfort of my cocoon. I rolled out of bed into the chilliness of the morning air, quickly pulled up the blanket, smoothed out the wrinkles, and jumped into the shower. Moments later, dressed and ready, I headed out the door to greet the world.

A light mist covered the windshield of Nessie, my SUV, as I drove down the street. *Spring showers are upon us,* I mused. Earlier showers had watered the desert throughout the winter months, and the wildflower display, already in process, promised to be stellar. My eye caught sight of the ocotillos' buds, set on the tops of their branches, waiting to erupt into reddish-orange flowers like firebrands across the desert.

I love it here! I said to myself. The mountain behind me now wore a veil of white snow after the night's rain. The sky, a mixture of dark clouds, swirled with streams of light and splotched with occasional patches of blue.

Another day stretched before me, filled with errands, doctor appointments, and more. "Dear God," I prayed, "thank You for life, for another ordinary day. Thank You for all my blessings: a comfortable home, a loving husband, my family, and for Jesus, my Savior. Use me to bless others and to do good in my world today." Peace and contentment filled me. My decision to enjoy life today gave me an appreciation for the rain and clouds, the beauty around me, and another ordinary day with its blessings, which could so easily be taken for granted.

Most of life is made up of the ordinary. It is the little things, the habits, attitude, attention to detail, and mindfulness in making healthy choices that build character—the only thing we will take with us to heaven. Rather than the mad quest for materialism, the competition to be first, to value the things that do not last, let us rather give our attention to thinking of others, being honest, and having integrity. When life invites us to snuggle up in comfort, it is time to stretch ourselves and reach beyond ourselves, to engage in another ordinary day and help others to see beauty amid the showers and swirling clouds of life.

Martha J. Feldbush

May 15

The Path of Providence

"For I know the plans I have for you," declares the Lord, *"plans to prosper you and not to harm you, plans to give you hope and a future."*
—Jeremiah 29:11, NIV

God often calls us to step out of our comfort zones and trust Him completely. My husband and I faced a crucial decision: Should we attend the university by taking online classes or wait until the doors open for in-person instruction? We decided to travel to the United States and volunteer while waiting for in-person classes at Andrews University to resume.

In His providence, God placed us as volunteer missionaries in the field of agriculture at Blue Mountain Academy in Pennsylvania. This time of service taught us that true growth occurs when we follow the greater purpose God has for us and that every experience, no matter how small, can be a lesson in faith and gratitude. The journey was not easy, but at every step, we saw God's hand guiding us and providing for our needs.

After serving for six months, we received an invitation to continue in more specific roles, marking a significant milestone in our adventure. During that year, we experienced total immersion in an environment where English was the primary language. This learning process was not only academic but also deeply spiritual. Facing the language barrier and adapting to a new environment made us realize that every challenge offered an opportunity to rely more on God and experience His guidance and provision in unexpected ways.

The transformative power of serving others became evident in our daily lives. Through every task and interaction, we discovered that our service was not only impacting those around us but also shaping our character and faith. We learned to view each challenge as an opportunity to grow and improve, recognizing that true strength comes from a spirit of love and self-discipline, not from comfort and security.

Today, consider in what areas of your life God might be calling you to step out of your comfort zone. Reflect on the challenges you face—they may be opportunities for personal and spiritual growth. Remember He has plans for you to give you hope and a future. Accept God's invitation to serve with a spirit of courage and trust, and open your heart to the transformation He has prepared for you.

Nadia Trossero

May 16

Freedom Through Captivity

We demolish arguments and every pretension that sets itself up against the knowledge of God, and we take captive every thought to make it obedient to Christ.
—2 Corinthians 10:5, NIV

A client came to me in distress. They felt God had given them clear instructions, but they had chosen their own way. "I think God forgives me, but I'm still a disappointment to Him. Now it's almost impossible to connect with God," they moaned.

I listened empathetically to this all-too-familiar story. The truth is that our thoughts inform our feelings, and our feelings often inform our behaviors. My client's belief that they were a sore disappointment to God led to feelings of shame, anxiety, and unworthiness. With that uncomfortable mix of thoughts and emotions, they muddled through their devotional time. In shame they started to isolate themselves from God, and agony sank in.

Sometimes it is hard to believe how a single thought can have the power to shape how we feel, how we show up for ourselves, how we interact with the world, and even how we approach God's presence. But that is why I believe 2 Corinthians 10:5 gives us actionable counsel on what to do about our thoughts.

Here is a simple tool rooted in biblical principles that helps us take charge of our thought life and, in turn, our feelings and behaviors. This can shape our character, our relationships, and our healing journey for the better: Find. Argue. Replace.

Find: The first step in taking a thought captive is to identify it. What thought are we holding on to that is causing distress?

Argue: Next, use your God-given authority to argue against that thought with the Word of God. We are taking our thoughts to court. If it does not align with God's Word, we throw it out. But we cannot stop there.

Replace: Replacing that thought with truth means having something living and powerful ready to fill that space. Take action and walk in it.

My client experienced relief over the next few weeks as God spoke truth into their heart and they allowed the truth to shape their understanding of God's heart toward them instead of shame. It changed everything. The same can be true for you. Make time to take your thoughts captive.

Sarah Casper

May 17

Hidden Jewels

May He send you help from the sanctuary and grant you support from Zion.
—Psalm 20:2, NIV

Do you sometimes need support from those around you, especially when you are in the midst of the storm? Most of us receive great comfort from knowing we are seen and understood. Emotional support gives us the strength to go on and, most importantly, to thrive in life.

A few years ago I found myself traveling by car on a journey I was not keen to take. It was a gloomy and miserable day, and I had unfortunately been dragged into an argument. Upset and frustrated, I could not hold back my tears. As I looked at the sky and raised a silent prayer, something caught my attention. A small patch of rainbow stared back at me, reminding me that God could see me and that He cared deeply for me.

God wants us to know that our tears mean a lot to Him. We might think they are insignificant, but they are not. Our emotional tears are not just saline. They have a similar structure to saliva and contain enzymes, lipids, metabolites, and electrolytes. Moreover, each tear has three layers. Rose-Lynn Fisher, an award-winning photographer, has captured images of her tears and compiled them in her book, *The Topography of Tears*. When she was going through a difficult time and grieving, she decided to look at her tears under the microscope. What she discovered was mind-blowing. Her tears had beautiful patterns, some simple, some complex, depending on the reason for them! Our tears may exist for a few seconds, but to God they are precious. Like snowflakes they are beautifully hidden jewels, and God collects them in special bottles. David wrote: "You keep track of all my sorrows. You have collected all my tears in your bottle. You have recorded each one in your book" (Psalm 56:8, NLT).

What a loving Father! He is *El Roi*, "the God who sees me." He sees and takes note. He acts. His love is so deep that He even sends help from above and support from the heavenly sanctuary when we are in distress. It might not be a host of armies, but a glimpse of the rainbow might be all that is needed.

As rain is to the flower, so is the knowledge of a caring heavenly Father to us—One who takes note of our tears, the Creator who designed our bodies with beauty and perfection, even down to the minutest detail of a teardrop.

Anna Karatizidou-Papaioannou

May 18

From Pain to Joy

"Blessed are you when people insult you, persecute you and falsely say all kinds of evil against you because of me."
—Matthew 5:11, NIV

I grew up in a small village called Hong in Arunachal Pradesh, India, where the majority of people practice *Donyi Polo*, the worship of the sun and moon. There are very few Christians in this area, and I am blessed to belong to one of the Christian communities.

Several years ago an Adventist family came to live in my village, and we became friends. I worshiped with them every Sabbath for nearly one year. When an evangelistic meeting was held in my village, I attended with my younger sister. We learned more about the Sabbath and the Ten Commandments from the Bible. After having Bible studies, we decided we would be baptized. My family strongly opposed us. My husband beat me, separated me from our two-year-old son, and chased me away. During this time I remembered Jesus' words, "He that loveth father or mother more than me is not worthy of me" (Matthew 10:37, KJV).

After I became a Seventh-day Adventist, I faced many problems. I was all alone, but the good Lord never left me. Later, with the encouragement of several pastors, I left my hometown with just a few clothes and was given a safe place to stay. I continued to learn about God's love and prayed He would allow me to get my son back so I could teach him about God. My prayers were answered, and I now have my son.

After seeing what God has done for me and how my faith has grown, my mother and a few of my friends have joined the Adventist Church through baptism. A plot of land has been purchased in my village to build a church.

Right now I am a teacher at the Itanagar Adventist School, and my son is studying in class 1 and is learning about the true God and true worship. We have a good place to stay. In fact, everything I need has been restored to me. I lack nothing. I have learned that no matter how big our problems are, when we believe and have faith in God's promises, He is always there to help us.

All my sufferings have been turned into blessings. My pain has been turned to joy. I praise the all-powerful God for healing my broken heart and supplying all my needs. Whatever your needs are today, remember this: We serve a mighty God. He is faithful to all who follow Him.

Punyo Moni

May 19

Answered Prayer

In the morning will I direct my prayer unto thee, and will look up.
—Psalm 5:3, KJV

I inserted my card into the ATM, and a notice popped up to inform me the machine was not working at the moment and to please try again later. I tried again, but the result was the same. I did not leave, but others who tried it met with the same failure. A lady waiting behind me stepped forward after I had withdrawn my card. Being quite close to her, I noticed that she had inserted it the wrong way. I approached and showed her how to correct the error, but because the same notice popped up, she turned to leave in a huff. I quickly pulled out a favorite book about Christ and offered it to her, along with some words of encouragement.

She looked at it and smiled, noting the author's name. "You're an Adventist!" she exclaimed. I confirmed that I was, and she continued, "If you only knew how long I have been praying that God would bring an Adventist into my path so I could talk to her and get her to clarify various problems for me."

We moved aside from the ATM, and she told me she was from a nearby country town. Her family had a house fire that left her and her husband struggling to repair the damage. As she shared her story, the Holy Spirit reminded me of a story I had recently read from my daily devotional, and I related it to her.

The story went like this: One day, a storm destroyed a farmer's entire harvest. Together with his son, who was a little boy at the time, he began to sing a song of praise without arguing with God about the damage done by the storm. God helped them, and they were able to meet the family's needs. Years went by. The farmer's son became a pastor, and one day, while the farmer listened to his son preach, a thought flashed through his mind. The year he had lost his harvest, the real harvest was his son! The powerful influence of the father's attitude in the face of suffering and calamity marked his son and impacted his life choices forever.

This lady listened with teary eyes. I directed her to prayerfully study the Scriptures and urged her to go to the baptismal class, where all her questions would be answered. I ask you to intercede for her and her family, for their salvation, that they may become jewels in Christ's kingdom through eternity.

Magdalena Toma

May 20

A Test of Obedience

"Now if you obey me fully . . . you will be my treasured possession."
—Exodus 19:5, NIV

I spend my summers in northern Michigan, USA, up near Lake Superior, where beautiful agates can be found. I love searching for them, and I find some almost every time I go looking. One day I found a beautiful, bright white-on-white agate! I scooped it up. It was the best one I had found all summer. Then the thought came to me: *You need to give this one away.* I argued with myself, *But surely not!* but could not get rid of the thought. Then another thought: *Do you ever want to find another agate?* That stopped me in my tracks.

I remembered a recent conversation with the Lord. I had assured Him I was not idolizing the agates. I just loved finding them because He had made them, and they were beautiful, and each one was unique. I believed He was testing me now. But who should I give it to? Several people came to mind, but none seemed right.

Then I noticed a couple on the beach, looking for stones. She sat on the seat of her walker, and I knew immediately it was for her. When I asked if they were looking for agates, the man said, "Yes, but we haven't found any yet."

I handed the white agate to the woman and told her the Lord had invited me to give it to her. She looked surprised as she took it. She said it was beautiful and thanked me. She shared that she was having back problems, and they had come to the beach just to get out and have some fun.

As I walked away, an overwhelming sense of joy flooded my soul, and tears filled my eyes. How incredible to think that God had used me to give a message of encouragement to a stranger. To let her know that He was thinking of her in her pain. He saw her—and loved her.

I continued to look for stones, my eyes scanning the beach. It had become a habit by now. Then I saw it: an exquisite stone patterned with swirls that wound around little holes. A special gift from God, it reminded me instantly of Van Gogh's *Starry Night.*

It may not seem like much to most people, but giving away the white agate was a big thing, even though I have many. The biggest thing of all, though, was being used by God to bless one of His children. I am so glad I listened. The blessing of obedience is greater than any agate. Besides, when we get to heaven, I will receive a white stone from the hand of Jesus Himself!

Susan Erickson

May 21

The Stones Will Cry Out

"I tell you," he replied, "if they keep quiet, the stones will cry out."
—Luke 19:40, NIV

My morning walks with my friend Thelma take me through an affluent neighborhood to a trail we enjoy walking. I appreciate the beauty of the landscaped yards we pass by, and several years ago I thought of a way to give back. Being an artist, I had collected stones I intended to paint for fun. Soon I was painting bugs and encouraging words on each stone.

One early spring I decided to slip a stone or two into my pocket before our walk. Then I looked for the right yard to place it in. I wondered when the owners would notice it and whether they would read and keep it or just throw it away. As the months passed I watched for each stone as we walked past the homes. Sometimes the painted stone would get moved to a different spot, and other times they disappeared altogether.

A year and a half later, my walking friend took another friend and her six-year-old granddaughter, Lilly, on our walk. Soon Lilly began to get weary of walking up the hill. Thelma thought of a game for Lilly. Knowing where I had placed the stones, she first told Lilly to look for a stone painted like a mouse and then one with a bumble bee. As they came around the corner, she asked her to find a ladybug in the next yard. Lilly quickly found the ladybug and picked it up to show her grandma. Just then the lady of the house glanced out her window and saw her holding the stone. She came running out and asked them a question.

"Do you know where this stone came from?" she asked.

Thelma told her that a friend had painted it and placed it there. The homeowner's eyes teared up, and she asked, "Can I give you a hug?"

She shared that on the day she first noticed the stone, she had received a cancer diagnosis and felt terribly discouraged. When she picked up the ladybug stone and read, "Keep hope and have peace," she felt like a special message had been sent just to her! She asked her neighbors if they knew where the stone had come from, but no one did.

"I treasure my ladybug," she said, "and keep it in a special place in my flower bed to remind me to hold on to hope."

Thelma could hardly wait to tell me the story. If Lilly had not gotten tired and Thelma had not come up with the game, we never would have discovered the impact of that stone. I guess stones truly can speak!

Judith Woodruff Williamson

May 22

Give It to God

Cast your burden on the LORD, *and he will sustain you.*
—Psalm 55:22, ESV

Have you ever attended church only to have the sermon begin with an apology? And then been told that the prepared message would not be given because you were in the congregation? That recently happened to my husband and me. Let me explain.

It had been almost nine years since we had been at that church. The speaker, our friend David, went on to say that the last time he had seen us was at the airport the day after my husband had retired, and we were flying to Florida, USA. David suffered from heart disease, and his only hope for life was a heart transplant. He was on his way to Boston, Massachusetts, USA. for a second opinion. My husband prayed for him while I silently asked God to give me something encouraging to share with our friend.

I told him I had recently been informed that the heart murmur I had lived with since my teen years had now cleared up. It was gone. David shared how our prayers and encouragement had given him hope. He was no longer afraid of his death-sentence diagnosis. He knew God would heal him. He testified he was able to give it completely to God and wanted us to know what had transpired in the intervening years.

The report from Boston confirmed the original diagnosis, and though he did not understand, he trusted that somehow God would work it out. He and his wife prayed for guidance, and through a series of amazing events, he was scheduled for a heart transplant in less than six months—not the typical two-year wait. After the surgery he was able to communicate with the surgical staff and asked them to extubate him because the machines were causing damage to the healing process his body was trying to do. Perhaps because he is a doctor, they did what he asked. Only five days late he was discharged with his new, God-given heart.

David read the following quote: "The same compassionate Saviour lives today, and He is as willing to listen to the prayer of faith as when He walked visibly among men. . . . It is a part of God's plan to grant us, in answer to the prayer of faith, that which He would not bestow did we not thus ask."* You may be the one who needs hope or encouragement today—or you may be the one to offer encouragement. Whatever the situation, look for the door God wants to open for you.

Rita Kay Stevens

---

* Ellen G. White, *The Great Controversy* (Mountain View, CA: Pacific Press®, 1911), 525.

May 23

Shining Lights

"Let your light shine before others, so that they may see your good works and give glory to your Father who is in heaven."
—Matthew 5:16, ESV

"My life is falling apart. Nothing is going right today!" Anna screamed.

"I am so sorry. Is there something I can do to help?" Ezzy asked.

"My dad just sold his parents' property and told my relatives he has given the money to me for my cancer treatment. I don't have cancer! How could a father lie about his own child? It hurts so much!"

Anna continued, her voice filled with anguish, "Furthermore, to add to my misery, a friend just lied about me to my church family. It feels like she is trying to get the pastor and the church to hate me. And on top of that, my coworker just lied about me to my boss. Everything is falling apart!"

"Have you heard the song 'This Little Light of Mine'?"* Ezzy asked. "It is a gospel song that Harry Dixon Loes wrote a popular adaptation to in the 1940s. I think it applies to your situation. Remember what the verse says: 'Don't let Satan blow it out.' What does this mean?"

Ezzy explained, "Satan is the biggest liar. He lied about Jesus. He made multitudes go against Jesus; he made one disciple to betray him, another to doubt him, and yet another to deny him, not just once but thrice. Satan is always trying to blow out your candle. Don't let him do it! He doesn't try to blow out your candle only through your enemies but also through your family, your friends, your church members, and your colleagues."

Friends, do you remember the verse that goes, "Hide it under a bushel? No!" When Satan tries to blow out our candles, we tend to want to hide them under a bushel. But that is when God invites us to shine even brighter by showing a caring spirit, loving heart, and acts of compassion. So let us determine to hold fast, be strong, be brave, and let God shine His light through us.

Matthew reminds us, "Let your light shine before others, that they may see your good deeds and glorify your Father in heaven" (Matthew 5:16, NIV). Let us be diligent in allowing God to work in and through our lives, shining His light and helping others find their way home.

Suhana Chikatla

---

* Harry Dixon Loes never copyrighted or claimed credit for writing the original, which remains of unknown origin.

May 24

Lights On

In Him was life, and the life was the light of men. And the light shines in the darkness, and the darkness did not comprehend it.
—John 1:4, 5, NKJV

A guest speaker at church used an analogy of the electrical grid in the United States to make the point for his sermon of trusting God. He spoke of the trust we place whenever we flip a light switch. We do not doubt the lights will go on. The same is true for the many different ways we use electricity, such as heat and cooking. He told of how fragile the system is and how vulnerable the population has become due to our dependence on electricity. What would happen if all the electrical grids in the whole country went out? It was a good sermon and gave me much to think about.

Jesus said He is the light of the world (John 8:12; 9:5), and He called on us to be lights. Matthew records His words, "You are the light of the world. A town built on a hill cannot be hidden. Neither do people light a lamp and put it under a bowl. Instead they put it on its stand, and it gives light to everyone in the house" (Matthew 5:14, 15, NIV).

Using the analogy of the electrical grid, I picture Jesus as the source of the electricity. We, as His children, plug in to Him and become His lights, spreading His love, compassion, and mercy to a world filled with darkness and pain. That sounds good, right? But I have to make sure that my light switch is in the "on" position. When I was growing up, my dad often yelled at us children to turn off the lights. I found myself saying the same thing to my children, and you may have had a similar experience. As I ponder this, I recognize that, often, my light switch is turned off.

Jesus' power is unlimited. It will never run out. He is more than able to provide an unending current to His lights. His power grid's vulnerability and fragility are His people. So then it becomes vitally important for us to stay connected to the power source. We will never have any light of our own. Maybe that is why we are counseled to "pray without ceasing" (1 Thessalonians 5:17, NKJV). Prayer and Bible study keep us plugged in to Jesus. When we are connected with our power source, we can spread His light wherever we go throughout the day.

May we all be plugged in with the switch in the "on" position 24 hours a day, for all 365 days each year, so our world is lit up with the glory and light of our Savior.

Mona Fellers

May 25

Wrecked for Good

And we know that all things work together for good to those who love God, to those who are the called according to His purpose.
—Romans 8:28, NKJV

Early one morning I drove the familiar interstate on my way to work, along with other commuters and what seemed like an unusual number of freight trucks. A drizzling rain began to fall, and I shivered, wishing the heat in my little Dodge Dart worked consistently. *At least I have a car, and at least I'm dry,* I thought. With several payments left on the Dart, I would not be able to afford another car for a long time. I did not look forward to another summer without air conditioning.

I noticed an SUV a few car lengths ahead of me, and then, without warning, its brake lights lit up as the driver spotted a traffic jam around the curve up ahead. I hit my brakes just in time, but my eyes flew to my rearview mirror. There was no time to react. The giant headlights were too close and growing bigger and brighter. *Smash!* My airbag deployed. My face plowed into it, and I tasted salty metal. Then I heard and felt a second *smash* as the front of my car slammed into the back of the SUV. My glasses were flung off my face. The key ring, with the key in the ignition, snapped, and keys flew through the air. The back of my head hit the headrest, and everything grew still.

A commercial semi-truck had hit me and totaled my car, smashing it like an accordion between the truck and the SUV. Apart from some minor cuts and bruises, I made it out of the wreck with my life—a walking testimony of God's protection.

To my surprise, when I received a check from the truck's insurance, it was enough for me to get a much more reliable used car without the need for financing—a car with working heat and air conditioning. To this day I still experience a moment of gratitude each time I turn the dial and the air starts to blow without a hitch.

The wreck will forever be a reminder to me of God's grace and protection. He can use the most terrifying experiences for the good of those who love and trust Him. Have you ever looked back on a terrible experience only to be amazed at how God used that experience for good? Though we sometimes struggle to see God's hand amid trauma, these experiences are often the gateway to great blessings. We can trust God to work all things for our good.

Kristin Beaven

May 26

Uh-Oh!

Where sin increased, grace increased all the more.
—Romans 5:20, NIV

"Uh-oh, there's the police. Does he want me to pull over? Was I speeding?" he asked.

"I don't know. I wasn't paying attention," I responded.

Steve pulled over. We had been on our way to the home improvement store to buy supplies for my latest bright idea. The flashing blue and red lights followed us into the parking lot.

"Get my registration and insurance from the dash," Steve directed. I handed him the documents as the officer approached our open window.

"State trooper Krause," he said.

"What's the problem?" Steve asked.

"Your registration has expired," he pointed to the document.

"You've got to be kidding me!" Steve looked closely at our proof of registration. "You're right!" Steve was honestly shocked.

"How did that happen?" I asked. Steve is always very careful about taking care of all the paperwork.

The trooper smiled.

"I'll tell you what: if you have a smartphone, you can sit here and renew the registration. Just be careful pulling out. Enjoy the rest of your day."

While we sat in the parking lot taking care of business, we wondered how this important detail could have slipped through the cracks. We felt so grateful the trooper realized our honest mistake, even though our registration was five months overdue.

This, folks, is grace—undeserved favor. This, too, is mercy. He could have fined us. It was something we should have taken care of, but the trooper recognized that, given the chance, we would make it right. I came away from this experience determined that the next time I find a glaring error someone has made, I will give them a chance to fix it.

Do you know someone who needs you to extend grace and forgiveness? Sometimes what looks like an offense could just be an honest mistake. Let us determine to be gracious to others. And hopefully there will be no police involved!

Ann Trout

May 27

Saved

They hit me when I was down, but GOD stuck by me.
... I stood there saved—surprised to be loved!
—Psalm 18:17–19, *The Message*

Struck by a Cadillac and thrown into the air! That was the scene in Boston, Massachusetts, USA. Our six-year-old daughter, June, lay at the center of the drama. She was returning from the local swimming pool one summer day with her older sister and some friends. They had gone with our permission. It would be their last swim before we left Boston. There had been many lasts—the last church service, the last day of school, and now the last swim. How could we refuse? But now June lay sprawled on the road, bringing traffic to a standstill. Her terrified sister and friends screaming, and the Cadillac driver was very worried.

At the hospital she was thoroughly checked out, given a lollipop, and sent home. Home to tears of relief and feelings of guilt. For, you see, neither parent was there initially. We had been completing some lasts of our own—the last meeting with college classes, the last box of books to pack. June was unhurt, but we were riddled with guilt. We should have been there. We could not even find words to discuss the incident.

Quietly we finished packing and left Boston in a fog after almost losing our middle child. Our fashion-conscious, outspoken, loveable June. That incident was a defining moment in her life—and our lives, the day we almost lost her. Whenever I see accidents like this on the news, most end badly. Why was she saved without a scratch? What plans does God have for her life?

We had almost lost her before when, after an uncomplicated birth, she developed stomach problems as an infant. Could her great aunt, a pediatric nurse, help her? We had to do something, so we took her to her aunt, who lived on a neighboring island. June returned to us seven months later, round as an orange, and seldom got sick again.

I tell these stories so she, now June Egypt, wife, mother of two, and clinical social worker, will know how much she is loved, not by her father, mother, and family alone but by her heavenly Father. May she pass on these stories to her children and her children's children.

Child of God, you, too, are loved by God. When life knocks us down, He will save us!

Annette Walwyn Michael

May 28

My Story—Part 1

*O LORD, You brought my soul up from the grave;
You have kept Me alive, that I should not go down to the pit.*
—Psalm 30:3, NKJV

I first learned about Seventh-day Adventists in my mid-twenties. I diligently read and completed Bible studies through the mail and learned about the Sabbath, tithing, clean and unclean meat, and many other things that I embraced as truth. But the one area I was very weak in was having a relationship with Jesus Christ. I found an Adventist church and faithfully attended, but again, I did not know the Lord in a real personal way or of His power to help me conquer my fear and sin.

I would pray in my bedroom, but I struggled. Inside I was locked in fear, doubt, low self-esteem, and a host of other sins. Eventually a day came, while struggling again in prayer, that I just gave up and accepted the thought that God could not save me. That belief put me into the darkest, scariest pit of my life. I thought I was in bad shape before, but this was an unbearable mental torture. I was filled with fear because I had lost hope. The consuming fear, with no relief in sight, filled me with self-hatred.

It is unbelievable, but God extended only love and mercy toward me. My hatred was real. I felt it enter my arms like an electrical current. Like a fish caught in a net or a bird trapped in a snare, I, too, was caught. Although my mind and heart were alienated from God, the one thought that penetrated my faculties was that I had nowhere else to go for help but to the church.

The pastor knew of my intense battle and prayed for me. At this point I could not talk. His prayers were unable to break through my darkness, and realizing he could do no more, he phoned a great woman of prayer. She came to the pastor's home and tried to communicate with me, but my mouth was shut. As she prayed she spoke a message of hope from the Lord: "Yes, she loves Me; she just doesn't know it yet."

She invited me for counseling, and at our first session she remarked on how I was able to respond and talk. She prayed and asked God to show me something. It took just a moment, but I saw in my mind's eye a rushing, gushing stream of pure white water. God was penetrating the dark, the fear, and the hatred with His love. He had not given up on me!

Rosemarie Clardy

May 29

My Story—Part 2

*For I know the thoughts that I think toward you, says the L*ORD*,*
thoughts of peace and not of evil, to give you a future and a hope.
—Jeremiah 29:11, NKJV

For God has not given us a spirit of fear,
but of power and of love and of a sound mind.
—2 Timothy 1:7, NKJV

Every week I attended church, even though the fear and hatred inside remained constant companions. Each day was a struggle. I had no hope for the future, making my life a mere existence. At work there was a person who did not understand why those in my church were not praying for me to be delivered. She would ask me if I was saved. This became torturous in its own way. I could not answer yes to her question because I had no confidence I was saved, and I could not answer no either because that would reflect a failure on my part. I wanted relief but did not want God. Yet I still went to church.

Through this awful time God put a special man in my life—someone I met at church. This man listened to all my troubles. I needed a friend, someone who would consistently be there for me, and he became that friend. After three years he asked me to marry him. Marriage was far from my mind. Months went by, and he asked me again. This time I said yes. God had a plan and a future for me, even though I did not have one for myself. The Lord blessed us with three children. This gave me another purpose to live. My children needed me, so I could not give up.

My mind took years and years to heal. The cursing, hate, and fear that were once inside me have now subsided. Now I can feel love and compassion in my heart. I can pray to God with trust and hope. This change did not happen quickly but has taken a lifetime. Each day the Lord has given me has been a gift to help in the healing process.

If you are struggling with pain inside and feel like you are not making it and are unsure things will change for the better, please know that God has graciously given you this day to let you know He does care and is working on your behalf. God is the Lord of time. He works through time to help us and to bring us to the place where we can say, "Yes, Lord, You love me. You always have and always will. And yes, Lord, I love You too."

Amen for His faithfulness. Where would we be without it?

Rosemarie Clardy

May 30

The Miraculous Meeting

Sing to the LORD, *praise His name; proclaim his salvation day after day.*
—Psalm 96:2, NIV

One chilly morning I hummed a hymn as I carefully poured water into the flower pots out front. When I reached the flowers by the shed, a gentleman working on the fence of the neighbor's house respectfully greeted me.

"Are you a Christian?"

"Yes," I replied. "Why do you ask?"

"I really like that song you're singing. It's lovely."

I looked at the neatly dressed man in front of me and noticed his immaculate white shirt, the first three buttons unbuttoned, under which shone a thick gold necklace. Without thinking, I asked him, "But how do you know this song?"

"Well, I'm Orthodox, but I've visited several Protestant churches. I liked it a lot, especially the music, and when I heard you humming, I recognized the tune. Which one do you belong to?"

"I'm a Seventh-day Adventist. That is, I worship God on Saturday."

"Yeah, I know. I like that you Adventists talk a lot about Jesus and faith in God."

That evening, I told my husband about our conversation, and with his practical turn of mind, he asked if I had given the man any literature. I had not thought of it, even though I frequently buy books to hand out to people. I selected a book and prayed he had not finished working in my neighbor's yard.

I also found a Bible and went to the neighbor's fence. He was still at work.

"It's good to see you again. I'd like to give you a book. It contains many aspects of my faith. Do you have a Bible?"

"No, I don't, though I would very much like one."

I gave him the Bible and said, "I hope it will bring you joy and light." He thanked me and promised to read it and visit our church. He clutched the books to his chest and looked so happy.

My dear sister, let us share the joy of salvation with someone today. It could change their lives, and we will be so blessed!

Elena Petrescu

May 31

Are You Ashamed?

For I am not ashamed of the gospel, for it is the power of God for salvation to everyone who believes, to the Jew first and also to the Greek.
—Romans 1:16, ESV

We are living in an interesting era of history. Thanks to technology, we can know what a person half a world away had for dinner. We get intimate glimpses into the lives of people we do not know—and sometimes even people we do not want to know. Social media encourages people to embrace their inner everything. We are told to say whatever we please, regardless of whether it is true or how it may make another person feel.

Do you know what is not encouraged in our society? Pursuing God with our whole hearts. We are not influenced to become the men and women God created us to be. We are not inspired to develop characters God can be proud of. In fact, depending on the group you find yourself in, they may try to convince you God does not exist.

The apostle Paul found himself in a similar climate. While the Jews believed in God and looked forward to the coming of the promised Messiah, they did not accept Jesus as the Son of God. They rejected and abused Him and, ultimately, murdered Him on a cross (John 18:28–19:42). When Jesus rose from the dead, they spread lies, saying His disciples had stolen the body (Matthew 28:13).

When Paul taught the good news of Jesus' death and resurrection, some mistreated him. They beat him, stoned him, and threw him in prison. They tried to cancel him. But Paul was having none of that. Just look at his bold declaration: "I am not ashamed of the gospel" (Romans 1:16). Paul had experienced the power of the gospel firsthand and knew what Christ could do. He also knew the God he served and was proud to let people know he believed in Jesus. He went from persecuting the saints to leading the early church. Talk about the transformative power of the gospel!

My friends, Jesus loved us enough to die for you and me. He left heaven's glory to live a life of poverty and humiliation—for us. Jesus has done marvelous things for us! How hard can it be for us to acknowledge Him as Lord and Savior? As we spend time with our heavenly Father, we will boldly proclaim with Paul that we are not ashamed of the gospel. May the transforming power of Christ within be at work within our lives today!

Aminata Coote

June 1

Almost Home

"The eternal God is your dwelling place, and underneath are the everlasting arms."
—Deuteronomy 33:27, ESV

Home. Just say the word, and memories, images, and emotions flood the heart, mind, and soul. What does *home* mean to you? What does it look like? A safe space? Or a place you long to leave?

In our early ministry years, my husband, Michael, and I experienced homelessness. We felt led to step away from pastoral ministry to enter a ministry in music—a step of faith. We exchanged our house for a secondhand sixteen-foot camper and hit the road with some good friends to share Jesus with the world. And though they did not say it, I know we left our parents scratching their heads and wondering, *What in the world?*

Oh! The stories we could tell! In the winter we would wake up in the morning to find a glass of water frozen on the nightstand. At church an envelope slipped into a pocket, and it contained enough money to fill our gas tank. Bags of groceries were left anonymously at the door of our camper when our cupboards were bare. So many stories!

When we stepped away from music ministry, we had nowhere to go. Literally. We sold our camper, and a friend opened her door to let us in. We stayed in her guest room for months as we tried to find our footing. We were homeless. Alone. And lonely. We had stepped out in faith, for goodness sake; surely our story should contain the words *and they lived happily ever after*. But it did not. We were poor, homeless newlyweds with no pathway back home.

One night, while fighting discouragement and tears, I slipped into the circle of Michael's arms. As I lay my head against his chest, I knew this much was true.

"This is my home," I whispered. "Right here in your arms."

For the first time I realized home is more than bricks and mortar, picket fences, and window boxes filled with flowers. Home could be found within the arms of the one I loved—the one who loved me.

If you are facing homelessness, my friend, whether literal or spiritual, know this: "The eternal God is your dwelling place, and underneath are [His] everlasting arms" (Deuteronomy 33:27, ESV). Home is found within the arms of the One who loves you. Lean into Him, and know that all will be well. As we remain in Him, our stories will ultimately testify, "and they lived happily ever after." Hold on! We are almost home!

Karen Pearson

June 2

The Promise of Dawn

"But I say to all of you: From now on you will see the Son of Man sitting at the right hand of the Mighty One and coming on the clouds of heaven."
—Matthew 26:64, NIV

In the quiet predawn hours, my husband and I embarked on a journey toward Point Udal, the pinnacle of Saint Croix, in the United States Virgin Islands, and the most easterly point of the United States of America. It was a pilgrimage of sorts, a gathering for morning devotions amid nature's grandeur.

As we traversed the winding roads, the world lay still, shrouded in darkness save for the symphony of nocturnal creatures. Yet as we drew closer to our destination, a gentle transformation began. The darkness yielded to the faintest glimmer of light, and dawn tiptoed in like a silent sentinel.

Arriving at the towering landmark, we were met with a multitude of fellow seekers, for Point Udal is a famous tourist attraction. Thus, while a few of us came to seek solace in the quiet majesty of the dawn, the masses came armed with chairs and cameras to behold and capture the spectacle of sunrise.

And then it happened. Slowly, somewhat hesitantly at first, the sun emerged from behind the clouds, casting its golden rays upon the waiting earth. The sky became a canvas painted with orange, pink, and golden hues, a masterpiece unfolding before our eyes.

At that moment I could not help but think of the return of Jesus as described by Ellen White. "Soon our eyes were drawn to the east, for a small black cloud had appeared, about half as large as a man's hand, which we all knew was the sign of the Son of man. We all in solemn silence gazed on the cloud as it drew nearer and became lighter, glorious, and still more glorious, till it was a great white cloud. The bottom appeared like fire; a rainbow was over the cloud, while around it were ten thousand angels, singing a most lovely song; and upon it sat the Son of man."*

As certain as the sunrise is the promised return of Jesus. Let us eagerly await that glorious day when we shall behold our Savior in all His splendor. And in His coming we will find hope, redemption, and eternal joy!

Gerene I. Joseph

---

* Ellen G. White, *Early Writings* (Washington, DC: Review and Herald®, 1882), 15.

June 3

God Delivers—Praise His Name!

The Lord is my rock, and my fortress, and my deliverer; the God of my rock; in him will I trust: he is my shield, and the horn of my salvation, my high tower, and my refuge, my saviour.
—2 Samuel 22:2, 3, KJV

Not a day goes by without some trouble or care pressing in upon us. Our homes, schools, workplaces, and even our churches are filled with care. It often seems they crowd in around us, over and above us. And they come in many forms: sickness, sorrow, distress, loss, financial woes, and broken relationships. Frequently women are the ones who carry the brunt of the load. As the backbone of the family, wives, mothers, aunties, and grandmothers often become the burden bearers for many, carrying cares for which they do not have answers nor the power to fix.

Where do we go for help when the heaviness of this life becomes too much for us to bear? Whom do we turn to for deliverance, not only for ourselves but also for those who depend on us? And sometimes even for those who may not know us but for whom our heart aches.

My courage comes from knowing we have an advocate in our Savior, Jesus Christ, whom I like to refer to as our Care Manager. He pleads our case to the heavenly Father. In fact He ever lives to make intercession for us, and as Captain of the heavenly host, He has never lost a battle. He always hears when we call. He always answers our prayers, even when He knows the outcome is not what we hope for or expect.

Yes, our God is the same yesterday, today, and forever, and when we turn to Him in prayer, He has the power to deliver us. He is our strong Deliverer, our mighty fortress. But now that we know that—what do we do next? We praise His name! Because of the "multitude of [His] tender mercies" (Psalm 69:16, KJV), we will always have a reason to praise Him.

May our heartfelt response be, "I will sing unto the Lord as long as I live: I will sing praise to my God while I have my being. My meditation of him shall be sweet: I will be glad in the Lord. . . . Bless thou the Lord, O my soul. Praise ye the Lord" (Psalm 104:33–35, KJV). Surely, "I will sing of the mercies of the Lord for ever: with my mouth will I make known thy faithfulness to all generations" (Psalm 89:1). "Blessed is the people that know the joyful sound: they shall walk, O Lord, in the light of thy countenance" (verse 15, KJV).

Elizabeth Ida Cain

June 4

Hold My Hand and Walk Beside Me

*"For I am the L*ORD *your God*
who takes hold of your right hand
and says to you, Do not fear;
I will help you."
—Isaiah 41:13, NIV

It was only the eighth day of the new school year, and I was walking back to my office after visiting a fourth-grade classroom to lead a math activity. As I passed the kindergarten rooms, the sound of a fire alarm pierced the air and the hallway lights began to flash, signaling an evacuation. I paused and waited for the kindergarteners to exit their classroom and continue to the outside door. It was obvious their teacher had prepared them for this event, the first drill of the year. The children came out quietly and in an orderly manner as I waited for them to file out of the classroom.

The next child out the door caught my eye. Tears were streaming down her face, which showed the anguish she felt. The noise, lights, and threat of a possible fire had caused a stress reaction in the little girl, even though she remained quiet and kept moving in the direction the class had been instructed to take.

Instinctively I reached down and took her hand in mine. I walked beside her down the hall, out the door, and to the assigned spot in the parking lot where the class was to assemble. When we got there, I looked down at the small child. She was no longer crying. In fact she seemed to be fine now. I smiled at her and gave her hand a little squeeze before releasing it, and she smiled back. I could not stay with her because I had assigned duties to perform, but I was glad that she was no longer afraid.

I was pleased that my presence had brought comfort to this little one. I had not spoken a word to her. All I had done was hold her hand and walk beside her. I can certainly relate to that little girl. There have been times when I have struggled with fear and anxiety. How reassuring to know our God is always available to comfort and guide. His hands are strong enough that nothing can snatch us away from Him (see John 10:27, 28).

He promises, "There is no fear in love. But perfect love drives out fear" (1 John 4:18, NIV). His peace will sustain us now and for eternity. And as we remain in His presence, His love will drive away all fear.

Marsha Hammond-Brummel

June 5

One of the Smallest Muscles

*The words of the reckless pierce like swords,
but the tongue of the wise brings healing.
Truthful lips endure forever,
but a lying tongue lasts only a moment.*
—Proverbs 12:18, 19, NIV

Have you ever said something without thinking and ended up offending someone? Or completely embarrassed yourself by saying something tactless? Looking back at a particular incident, I still cringe with embarrassment.

Part of my role as a specialty nurse is to care for patients with stomas such as colostomy, ileostomy, and urinary diversion—usually as a result of cancer or another underlying disease. Before surgery I review the patient records, undertake an assessment, provide education to prepare the patient for the possibility of a stoma, and explain what life will be like afterward. Because of the sensitive nature of these conversations, it is important to establish a rapport with patients within the first five minutes.

On this particular day I received a call to work with a gentleman in his mid-fifties who had recently been diagnosed with bowel cancer. There was a strong possibility he would need a stoma formed during his surgical procedure. In the Outpatient department, I called him into a consultation room, and a slightly older lady followed. I closed the door and introduced myself, informing him of my role. As I sat down, I glanced at the lady and, without thinking, asked, "Is this your mother?"

"No. I'm the ex-wife," she responded with a laugh.

Oh! I felt so embarrassed, I just wanted the ground to open up and swallow me whole! Thankfully they both laughed, and I managed to scramble through an apology and collect whatever shred of professionalism remained.

As I reflected on my day, a verse from James flashed through my mind and reminded me it is important to be "quick to listen, slow to speak" (James 1:19, 20, NIV). The tongue is one of the smallest muscles in the body but can cause the most damage. The wisest man wrote, "The tongue has the power of life and death" (Proverbs 18:21, NIV) and "Kind words are like honey. They are sweet to the spirit" (Proverbs 16:24, NIRV). Let us quit gossiping, criticizing, or sharing hurtful opinions and choose to keep our words kind and sweet. God wants us to "be kind and compassionate to one another" (Ephesians 4:32, NIV) and build up one another for His glory!

Jenny Rivera

June 6

The Parking Space

But love ye your enemies, and do good . . . and ye shall be the children of the Highest: for he is kind unto the unthankful and to the evil. Be ye therefore merciful, as your Father also is merciful.
—Luke 6:35, 36, KJV

I was hot, tired, hurt, and frustrated. Earlier in the day I had been verbally attacked by an angry family member. It had been vicious. Though I had not done what I had been accused of, getting things straightened out would take time and money—both of which I was short on. And now I was on my way to yet another of many doctor's appointments. It was not a good day.

I pulled into the parking lot and noticed the perfect parking spot right in front of the door. At least one thing was going my way. As I eased toward my parking place, another car slipped in ahead of me, claiming my spot. Irritated by the nerve of the rude driver, I stopped and glared at the woman behind the wheel. It was obvious I was headed for that spot. How dare she steal my spot? After making sure she saw my displeasure, I drove to another parking spot much farther from the door of the doctor's office. At least this thoughtless woman knew I was unhappy with her.

As I got out of the car, I saw the same woman walking toward me in the parking lot. I prepared myself for her verbal assault and planned to tell her just what I thought of her. And then she spoke.

"I'm so sorry. I didn't mean to get your parking place. I'll move my car, and you can park there. It's just that my arthritis hurts me so badly, and when I saw that spot, I just went for it before I realized you were headed for the same place."

Standing in that hot parking lot, I realized I had completely misread her intentions. I knew that this stranger was showing me much more of the love of Jesus than I had offered her. And I was ashamed. My angry words remained unspoken. Quietly I asked her to forgive me and told her she did not need to move her car. How humbling to realize that I was the one in need of forgiveness for my harsh, too-quick-to-judge spirit.

In that parking lot I had a change of heart. God had sent me a message of mercy and forgiveness. A message I share with you in the hope that, like me, you will never forget to be kind and merciful—then the world will know that we belong to God.

Faye Acuff

June 7

Like a Child

*Don't worry about anything; instead, pray about everything.
Tell God what you need, and thank him for all he has done.*
—Philippians 4:6, NLT

After a busy men's ministry weekend in Gatlinburg, Tennessee, USA, my husband was headed back home. Our son, with his five-year-old son in tow, was a few miles ahead of him when he called his dad to let him know he was on the side of the road with a flat. My husband caught up to them, picked them up, and headed to the closest supercenter to pick up a lug wrench. They attempted to loosen the lug nuts, and when they could not, they headed home for some nourishment before trying again with a wrench of a different size that my husband had at home.

After eating and gathering some tools, my husband tempted me to join him with the promise I would see both grandchildren. I headed back to the site where my son's car still stood. We met our son, daughter-in-law, baby granddaughter, and grandson, and for the next few hours, the men worked to try to loosen those stubborn lug nuts. As the hours passed, my grandson pretended to drive me from one fast-food restaurant to the next. We ordered all types of treats, and he was completely content sitting on his Bibi's lap while the adults became increasingly frustrated. Before making another trip to an automotive store to purchase a different-sized wrench, my husband prayed for patience and deliverance.

We returned to the stranded car on the side of the interstate, and the new wrench managed to remove the lug nuts, but now they were lodged inside the wrench! While back at the pretend restaurant with my grandson, I heard my son say, "Just forget it, Dad. I'll call a tow truck!" But my husband persisted, and I continued to pray. I watched my grandson—he was completely happy! He knew daddy's tire was broken, but he knew his daddy and his G-Pop would take care of it. And they did. After much time and persistence, lost car keys, more prayer, and found car keys, the saga ended well.

In Matthew 18:3, Jesus encourages the disciples not to be concerned with the things of the world but to be like a child and trust Him completely. Like my grandson, we have a Father who will take care of our problems, so we do not have to fret. Friends, when we ask God for help, we do not need to stress or worry. Our heavenly Father has it under control!

Donna L. Tucker

June 8

The Lost Keys

Jesus said to the servants, "Fill the jars with water"; so they filled them to the brim.
—John 2:7, NIV

Recently I have been creating my own gift baskets, making them as personalized as possible. I had just finished with one basket and started to pack away the extra wrappers, ribbons, and other goodies that I keep on hand. As I filled the storage bag, I heard a clinking sound but thought nothing of it—I have all kinds of paraphernalia in the bag, and it could have been any number of things.

Later that evening someone called to tell me they were delivering something to me and were close by. I headed for my bunch of house keys, which I always keep in a specific place. I went to the stairwell, which is where I keep them during the day. It makes for quick access in any emergency, whether I am upstairs or downstairs, but the keys were not there. Surprised but not alarmed, I calmly went to the lock on the inner doorknob of my bedroom door, which is where my keys are placed at night. Nothing!

Panic began to set in because these two places were home to my keys. Although I was locked in my house, door and grill, and I had a set of duplicate keys, I had no intention of sleeping in the house without knowing where my keys were. In major panic mode I checked several unlikely places, including my refrigerator! Only then, I am ashamed to say, I prayed. Soon I remembered hearing the clinking sound earlier in the day. I found the storage bag and emptied it, and there I found my bunch of keys. Evidently they had been on the table as I packed up everything for my baskets, and I had picked them up with the rest of the things I was putting away.

A few days later I heard one of my favorite preachers, Pastor Debleaire Snell, say that Jesus, when performing His first miracle in Cana, told the servants to fill the jars to the brim with water, and it all turned into wine. If they had filled the jars only halfway, they would have ended up with only half jars of wine. Likewise we should not limit ourselves in what we ask of God because in so doing we may limit the blessings He has for us. I have often prayed for minor things and received answers, but unfortunately panic over my keys made me forget to pray right away. Let us not use God as a last resort but go to Him immediately. He is willing and able to supply all our needs, major or minor.

Cecelia Grant

June 9

God's GPS

Whether you turn to the right or to the left, your ears will hear a voice behind you, saying, "This is the way; walk in it."
—Isaiah 30:21, NIV

My husband and I were driving around Rocky Mountain National Park in Colorado, USA. We turned onto the Old Fall River Road and drove until we came to the one-way stretch that goes to the top of Trail Ridge. Since it was closed, we circled through a nearby picnic area and rejoined the road going east. Suddenly the GPS began to exclaim, "You are going the wrong way!" It must have "thought" we were going the wrong way on the one-way stretch of road. We just laughed and ignored it. After some thought I realized God has a GPS: God's Personal System, the Holy Spirit. We can see it at work in several Bible stories:

When Elijah, exhausted and frightened by a wicked queen's death threat, ran for his life, he found himself in a cave. Finally he heard God's GPS as a gentle whisper, "What are you doing here, Elijah?" (1 Kings 19:12, 13, NIV).

King Balak of Moab offered Balaam a large sum of money if he cursed God's people. Balaam knew he could not curse what God had blessed, but he wanted the money so badly. He ignored God's GPS and ended up having a conversation with a donkey! (Numbers 22).

God had told Jonah to go to Nineveh with a message of repentance—not something he wanted to do, so he ignored God's GPS and ended up in the belly of a fish with seaweed wrapped around his head (Jonah 1; 2).

Peter—on-again, off-again Peter. After denying he even knew Jesus three times, God's GPS rang loud and clear in his conscience when Jesus turned and looked at him. He went out and wept bitterly (Luke 22:54–62).

Judas spent three years fighting God's GPS. At the Last Supper he was given one more chance to repent. "But the last appeal of love was unheeded. . . . And the feet that Jesus had washed went forth to the betrayer's work."* It was Judas's last supper, for he hung himself the next day.

If we are lost at last, we would have to have spent a lifetime fighting against God's GPS. The Holy Spirit's convicting power does not easily let go. How much better to listen and spend eternity with Jesus.

Sharon Oster

---

* Ellen G. White, *The Desire of Ages* (Nampa, ID: Pacific Press®, 2005), 720.

June 10

GPS: God's Positioning System

The mind of a person plans his way, but the LORD directs his steps.
—Proverbs 16:9, NASB

A few years ago I found myself relocating to a foreign land. This relocation was the result of my family's decision. Even though we prayed about it and felt God was leading us in that direction, the question remained of what God wanted us to do in this new land. I obeyed His lead but still felt uncertain about the purpose. A year after the move, as I stared through my kitchen window, I began to reflect on some of the areas I currently served in and how God's hand was guiding me. Though I still had many questions about the future, I began to experience an overwhelming sense that God was directing me.

You might have many questions, as do I, about where God is taking you and what He wants you to do, but rest assured—God has His own system for directing our lives. Being led by God does not mean life will always go smoothly or that we will execute His plans with precision. But if we stay on course, God will take us to the destination He has planned.

Depending on where you live, it might be necessary to rely heavily on a Global Positioning System (GPS) in your vehicle to take you to unknown and distant places. The Global Positioning System is extremely helpful and is usually correct, but there are those few occasions where it leads you into a route that is longer than necessary. The GPS can lose its satellite connection at times, and sometimes it directs you to a completely wrong destination.

While a GPS cannot always be entirely relied upon, there is a better navigation system that is completely trustworthy, reliable, and correct—that is God's Positioning System. In this system our heavenly Father, who created us, carefully maps out the course of our lives and plots each turn, curve, bump, and hill in a way that will ultimately lead us to His kingdom. Though there may be times when we do not follow God's lead and end up lost, our God mercifully reroutes us and reissues His directions so we can get back on course.

So whatever you are experiencing physically or emotionally, whatever you feel anxious or concerned about, remember that you can rely on God to show you the way He has created for you. He can be trusted to lead you in the right direction. God's Positioning System never fails, and it will lead you home.

Taniesha K. Robertson-Brown

June 11

Lost in the Forest

How gracious He will be when you cry for help! As soon as he hears, he will answer you. . . . Your ears will hear a voice behind you, saying, "This is the way; walk in it."
—Isaiah 30:19–21, NIV

We were lost while hiking in the Pygmy Forest in Van Damme State Park, California, USA, for our upper-grade science camp. I was leading the group of kids, and we were happily following the trail, chatting and observing the surroundings. As the path broadened into a wide, sandy area, the remnants of the trail disappeared. As we tried one way, then another, anxiety rose within me, though outwardly I tried to remain calm. Which way would lead us out rather than deeper into the forest? No matter which direction we turned, we could not find the path, and the map was no help.

Finally I admitted, "Kids, we need to pray. We're lost, and only God knows how to get back."

They gathered closer.

In Bible class students often journal Bible stories in their own words, answering such questions as, "What do you think God might be saying to you here?" Now it was time to put those questions to the test in a real-life situation.

I prayed, "God, we're lost. We don't know the way back—but You do. Would You please let us know? We're listening." With heads bowed and eyes still closed, I said, "OK, kids, we're going to take a few moments to just listen and ask God if He would give us a direction to go. If He does, just lift your arm in that direction."

After a few moments, we opened our eyes. Several arms were lifted, pointing in the same direction! We had all heard the same thing. I was amazed!

I should not have been. God's promises are there for the taking: He is "an ever-present help in trouble" (Psalm 46:1, NIV). He invites us, "Call to me, and I will answer you" (Jeremiah 33:3, NIV). "Christ is ever sending messages to those who listen for His voice."* We knew He had answered. He had spoken to all of us. Elated, we praised Him and thanked Him on the spot! Down the path we went in the direction He had indicated. Of course, it led us to our destination.

God made Himself real that day. He grew our faith and gave us a story to tell.

How gracious He is. When we cry for help, He hears and promises, "Your ears will hear a voice behind you, saying, 'This is the way; walk in it' " (Isaiah 30:21, NIV).

Speak, Lord . . . your daughter is listening.†

Marilee Serns Dalton

---

* Ellen G. White, *The Ministry of Healing* (Mountain View, CA: Pacific Press®, 1905), 509.
† This devotional was adapted from the author's chapter, "The God Who Reveals Himself," in *Revealing Jesus in the Learning Environment*, ed. Peter W. Kilgour and Beverly J. Christian (Cooranbong, NSW, Australia: Avondale Academic Press, 2019). Used with permission.

June 12

Count Your Blessings

*I remember the days of old; I meditate on all Your accomplishments;
I reflect on the work of Your hands.*
—Psalm 143:5, NASB

For the past year I have been going through boxes of photos that have been stored away in my closet from years gone by. I have begun to mount them in albums so our children and grandchildren will have a record of their ancestors on both sides of the family. We all make memories every day.

I have been reminded of many blessings and of the protection and care that I have taken for granted throughout my eighty-three years of life. Through all the travels and moves our family has made, God has never stopped protecting, loving, and caring for us.

In our early married years, my husband, my two little children, and I lived in a small trailer, fulfilling tree planting contracts with a team in the high mountain areas of the states of Oregon, Washington, Idaho, and Montana in the United States of America. We would move about every four to six weeks, beginning in Oregon and working our way up toward the Canadian border.

When the snow melted enough for the team to plant seedlings in the forest, the team would move north a little farther. Bundling up our little son and daughter, my husband and I sent them to play outside in the fresh air. We enjoyed the wonderful wildlife and being surrounded by nature. One place we camped was at the base of a waterfall that originated in warm springs above the falls. It created a warm creek where the children spent hours playing. There was an old tub from the early logging days and a pipe that brought warm water to the bathtub. After the men left to plant trees each day, the children and I would enjoy a warm bath.

From 1970 to 1973, this was our "home away from home." We collected and pressed wildflowers and made many happy memories. When we finally returned to our home in California, our children had to learn about flush toilets and showers. What a wonderful life we were able to provide our children. We all have such fond memories of the times we enjoyed in the wilds of the northwest.

We thank God for every precious memory and each wonderful blessing. Let us all remember to count our blessings. As we name them we will be reminded of all God has done in our lives.

Marcella Lynch

June 13

My Little Trailer

The heavens and the earth quake. But the LORD is a refuge for His people.
—Joel 3:16, NASB

After some rained-out camping trips, my husband and I bought a little used trailer. It was to be our home away from home, and we enjoyed camping in it many times. We also used it when an overflow of company came. Our son even lived in it for a couple of summers during his academy years.

One memorable night, the trailer was shaken like a leaf by a blowing gale. We had to get out of bed and tow our trailer farther away from the wild Atlantic shore. A thick tree thicket provided a sheltered, safer spot.

Eventually it became an extra bedroom when we acquired a cottage on Grand Manan Island, New Brunswick, Canada. After several years we were ready to retire it, and a neighbor bought it to use as a playroom for his grandchildren. By then the trailer had reached a ripe old age.

One day we were surprised to see our little trailer being hauled out of the neighbor's yard. The owner shouted, "Say goodbye to your trailer. Its new life will be as a chicken coop." I felt a little sad to see the end of my trailer but grateful for the many happy memories it provided.

As I thought about my little trailer, I was reminded of my Christian walk. I began as a curious seeker. My search took me through many experiences. The more I learned, the more I needed to find answers. The library, various pastors, several versions of the Bible, and fellow young Christians all played a part in my walk with the Lord, so much like my camping experiences.

Whether I was camping in my woods, on an ocean beach, or finally at my little cottage, I learned many things. The more we camp, the better we become at camping. The more time I spend with the Lord, the greater my understanding of God's plan for me.

During my camping years I went to many spots and experienced the fun of raccoons peeking in my trailer windows, deer walking quietly past the trailer, and many quiet hours of listening to birds, blowing whales, and the sounds and scents of the breezes.

As my adventure with God changes my life, I am becoming a seasoned believer. I have a peace in my heart that I never knew was possible. I have learned that my faith is a free walk with Jesus—no campground fees, no planning needed. As I turn my thoughts heavenward, my faith grows. How I long for the day He will welcome His children home to the new earth.

Patricia Cove

June 14

Deception Personified

You will destroy those who tell lies. The LORD detests murderers and deceivers.
—Psalm 5:6, NLT

I think most people who have learned the story of Jacob know his name means "he deceives." But when you read the entire story, the deception did not begin or end with Jacob. Genesis 25 tells the story of Esau selling his birthright for a bowl of lentils, and chapter 27 tells of Jacob's mother, Rebecca, putting a plan of deception into play; Jacob goes along with it, successfully deceiving his father and receiving the blessing. Esau is not happy, and Jacob has to flee.

When Jacob arrives at his uncle's home in Paddan-aram, Laban immediately recognizes possibilities. He stops treating Jacob as a relative but rather as hired help when he sees how eager Jacob is to marry Rachel. After seven years of labor, the deceiver is deceived—Jacob finds he has married Leah rather than Rachel. After seven more years of work, and as son after son and wife after wife follow, he continues to work for Laban until he has had enough. He complains that Laban has cheated (deceived) him ten times. So Jacob comes up with a plan.

Chapter 30 tells of Jacob's scheme of putting fresh-cut poplar, almond, and plane trees cut in stripes before the water troughs. Commentaries suggest that Jacob knew enough of animal husbandry that he did not believe this would make the goats bear striped or spotted—he deceived Laban, making him believe it could work for him too.

Finally the Lord told Jacob to return to the land that had been promised to Abraham and Isaac. When Laban discovers they have fled, he accuses Jacob of deceiving him (see Genesis 31:26). Rachel steals her father's gods, and when Laban searches her tent, she says, "Don't be angry, my lord, that I cannot stand up in your presence; I'm having my period" (Genesis 31:35, NIV). The idols are in the camel saddle on which she is sitting. Deception personified.

The deception continued when Jacob's sons deceived him, showing him Joseph's coat and claiming Joseph had been killed by a wild animal. When did the deception end? Perhaps with Jacob's wrestling with the angel or in the honest life of Joseph. But regardless, it never paid. Nor does it now. Revelation 22:15 tells us that those who practice deception/lies/falsehoods will not be in the New Jerusalem.

Ardis Dick Stenbakken

June 15

Granted a New Lease on Life

And call upon me in the day of trouble: I will deliver thee, and thou shalt glorify me.
—Psalm 50:15, KJV

I live alone, and with that comes the responsibility of taking care of many chores, one of which is mowing my lawn. I do it joyfully and consider it a part of my exercise regimen. It takes approximately two to three hours, including trimming the hedges around the fence.

One hot, sunny afternoon in the middle of June, I embarked on my regular mowing. I finished the front yard and had completed half of the back portion when I felt tired and drained. Wearing socks, a sun hat, and gloves, I was drenched in sweat but felt determined to push myself to finish. Suddenly an unusual uneasiness and dizziness overwhelmed me. All alone, with no one to call for help, I staggered toward the back porch and held on to a wooden bar for support. Gasping for breath, I whispered, "Jesus, please help me. Jesus, please help me," over and over. That is all I remember until I fainted.

When I came around, I found myself face down on the grass beside the lawnmower. I had no idea what had happened and had likely been out in the heat of the sun for at least fifteen to twenty minutes, unconscious and oblivious to my surroundings. I injured my shoulder blade but did not feel it until hours later. In my weakened condition I dragged myself into the house and crashed on the couch. Shortly after, the phone rang. God put it on my son's heart to call me. He was shocked to hear my incoherent speech and scared that I was still out of breath and experiencing such low energy. He prayed for me over the phone.

It was clear my life's chapter on earth could have ended at that moment. But the Lord sent His angel to wake me up. He heard my prayer. He touched me and lifted me up. He alerted my son to call and support me at just the right time.

Thank You, dear God, for restoring my soul and giving me a new lease on life for a reason.

Dear friends, in times like these we all need the touch of Jesus. Life is fragile. Tomorrow is not guaranteed, but the Lord promises to restore our souls and give us a new lease on life for as long as He keeps us here. May we all feel God's touch and experience the new life He longs to grant us in our time of need. Amen.

Ekele P. Ukegbu-Nwankwo

June 16

The Golden Years

The Lord has made everything for its purpose. . . .
Gray hair is a crown of glory; it is gained in a righteous life.
—Proverbs 16:4–31, ESV

The golden years—what a misnomer! Gold is precious and desired by all, but too often, after you turn sixty, no one wants you around. Your advice is disregarded, and your presence is ignored. What is so great about growing old? Well, let me tell you. Believe it or not, *you* are. You are what is great about growing old. Aging is a gift not afforded to everyone. If you are fortunate enough to receive this gift, praise the Lord! Your eyesight may diminish, but your vision is clearer. Youthful inhibitions have long faded, and you can respectfully speak your mind. This shame in aging is a ploy of the enemy. So, too, is the fear of death.

Hindsight is twenty-twenty, and as you age it is easier to look back and be filled with gratitude. Seniors are not deluded by thoughts of finding the fountain of youth. They know it is a myth. They also realize that no one lives forever. Quite the opposite, in fact. As our physical body ages and we realize that we have more years behind us than before us, we have a greater appreciation for the gift of life.

The good news is that no matter our age, we can start now—start to take care of our body but be wise enough to recognize its limits. Before we entered these precious golden years, we pushed and worked and achieved much—but now we are here. Older and wiser. It is good to slow down a bit more, smell the roses, and appreciate all we have. Let us choose to keep learning, stay curious, and foster a positive attitude and a joyful spirit.

The wisdom gained in living this life is far superior to anything we can acquire from books. We are smarter now than we have ever been. Instead of seeing all the negativity associated with aging, why not enjoy our golden years? Stay active and involved. People want us to stick around more than we realize. Enjoy the gift of time with family and loved ones. Find the blessings and remember the promise,

> Even to your old age I am he,
>   and to gray hairs I will carry you.
> I have made, and I will bear;
>   I will carry and will save. . . .
>
> Remember this and stand firm. . . .
> for I am God, and there is no other;
>   I am God, and there is none like me (Isaiah 46:4–9, ESV).

Let us thank God today for the gift of life and celebrate the golden years.

Kathy-ann Best

June 17

When the Unexpected Happens

*The Spirit of God has made me,
And the breath of the Almighty gives me life.*
—Job 33:4, NKJV

If I can just get on my knees, I will be able to stand up, I told myself. With my ninety-sixth birthday around the corner, I had recently had a few falls but had always been able to get up unassisted. But now, try as I might, my right arm would not cooperate, and all I could do was wait for someone to find me.

It was my habit to contact some of my family members each morning, and it was still early enough that I had not done so. I had been preparing breakfast and, with no warning, had awakened to find myself lying on the kitchen floor. I heard the phone ring several times, but I was unable to answer it.

At last I heard men's voices—it was my son and a couple of other men. They soon had me loaded into an ambulance and headed toward the local hospital, only to discover the CT scanner was not working. We then went to the next closest hospital. On the way, the ambulance stopped, and the female attendants frantically pulled me on the stretcher out of the vehicle. I asked if the ambulance was burning, and they replied, "Yes!" We waited on the interstate for another ambulance to complete our trip.

My shoulder had been dislocated, and there was a small well-aligned fracture. After a couple of doctors tried unsuccessfully to get the shoulder back into place, my daughter Marie, an employee at the hospital, contacted the orthopedic surgeon, and the job was soon done.

After two nights in the hospital, I was discharged to my home under the care of my daughter Ann and her husband, who canceled their vacation plans to be with me and help with my practically useless right arm. My sister took over shortly before they left, and I am now back to living alone. With the invaluable help of a physical therapist and lots of exercise, I am making good progress and hope soon to be back to normal.

In retrospect it seems providential this incident occurred when family members were free to help. I am thankful my heavenly Father is surprised by nothing. My desire is to be filled with His Spirit and to make my life count for Him for as long as He gives me breath.

Lila Farrell Morgan

June 18

Rain

Ask, and it shall be given you; seek, and ye shall find; knock, and it shall be opened unto you: For everyone that asketh receiveth; and he that seeketh findeth; and to him that knocketh it shall be opened.
—Matthew 7:7, 8, KJV

The summer was almost over, and I still had not scheduled my daughter's graduation celebration. It had to be soon because everyone would be headed back to college, leaving us with no friends or family with whom to celebrate her achievements.

Invitations were sent out digitally, asking everyone to RSVP—ASAP. The response was rapid. About forty people confirmed they would attend. Due to time constraints, no venue was available for the celebration, so my backyard would have to suffice. Not a problem. We have a big backyard and had successfully hosted several events.

On Monday before the event, while away, I received a frantic call from my daughter to say the weather forecast predicted a 100 percent chance of rain on Sunday. She was genuinely concerned because she knew the event was scheduled to take place in the backyard. I calmly told her I was aware of the forecast and had already taken it to the Lord in prayer.

She laughed and said, "I guess you could host the event inside. Just be prepared." Then more seriously, "Mom, the rain has been falling since you left and is expected to keep falling until Monday."

I repeated that my God had been made aware of the situation and my needs. My daughter added her sister to the call, and they both said, "Only mom and her crazy faith." We laughed as they hung up the phone.

The rain fell all week until the Sunday morning of the celebration. My husband noted that the backyard was saturated, and even if the rain held up, it would not be suitable to host an event. I asked him to put up the tents on the front lawn.

"It will stop raining soon," I said. "I have already spoken to God in prayer."

A little before ten o'clock, the rain stopped completely. The sun came out, and the graduation celebration was an enormous success. It was not until all the guests had left and everything cleaned up that the rain came down again and fell until the next morning.

My sisters, Jesus said, "Do not be afraid; only believe" (Mark 5:36, NKJV). Let us continue to trust God. Know that all things are possible through Christ Jesus.

Christie Simon-Waterman

June 19

From Oddball to Special

But you are chosen people, a royal priesthood, a holy nation, God's special possession.
—1 Peter 2:9, NIV

I stood in line with several other College of Education students preparing to enter Garrison Hall at Henderson State University in Arkadelphia, Arkansas, USA, where I would be officially recognized as a graduate—an educational specialist. Unlike my previous graduation from a master's program, this time I would be hooded. My professor, Judith Jenkins, had sent out an email instructing me to carry my hood over my right arm, but as the line moved along, I noticed that none of the other graduates carried their hood. I saw several wearing their hoods. I felt a little strange, but my daughter and stepdaughter reassured me it was OK. I was not so sure. I felt tempted to put my hood on so that I would be like all the others. But I did not. I chose to follow my professor's instructions, even though I did not understand.

The families of the graduates marched with them up to the front of the Garrison Center before moving to a designated spot. Each graduate presented their card to the announcer, who read the degree and the name of the candidate. When my turn came, I handed my card to the announcer, and then, before I could move forward to receive my diploma, my professor came over to me, handed me a book, took my hood, placed it on me, and hugged me. Suddenly I no longer felt like an oddball. I felt special—it was an experience I will never forget. My daughter recorded the event, and when I sent it to friends and posted it on Facebook, no one had any idea of the story behind the hooding. Perhaps they thought everyone did that. All I can tell them is that I went from feeling like an oddball to special in the blink of an eye.

Then I realized that as God's child and an Adventist believer, there may be times when we feel like oddballs because we do not walk the same path as the rest of the world. We may even feel uncomfortable being different. We may be tempted to follow the world instead of following God's instructions. But in God's eyes we are very special. We are His "chosen people, a royal priesthood, a holy nation, God's special possession" (1 Peter 2:9, NIV).

Help me, Father, to remember that when I feel like an oddball, in Your sight I am special—as are all who follow You and not the world. Help us to always hold fast to Your hand, Father.

Sharon (Clark) Mills

June 20

Just Say Thank You

Encourage one another and build each other up.
—1 Thessalonians 5:11, NIV

Sincere compliments have been essential to my growth as a woman and a Christian and in ministry, but I have had a hard time learning to accept them graciously.

When someone has said, "I love your outfit!" I might feel pleased and reassured, but I have often responded with something like, "Oh, this old thing? I have a blue sweater that goes better with it, but it is in the laundry." Or "Do you think it makes me look fat? I really feel fat in this outfit." Why couldn't I just smile and say, "Thank you"?

When someone has said, "You have a beautiful touch on the piano," I may be encouraged to keep playing. However, I often have said something like, "But I made so many mistakes on that closing hymn!" Why couldn't I just smile and say, "Thank you"?

When someone says, "You sure did a great job on that children's story today—I loved it!" I do feel affirmed, but I am tempted to say, "But I forgot to tell the part about . . ." Why can't I just smile and say, "Thank you"?

We sometimes think we are being humble by putting ourselves down in response to a compliment. How humble is it to disagree with someone, essentially begging them to argue with us and reassure us that we are wonderful?

At face value the compliment is about me, but I have learned that it is really about more. It is also about the other person, who has offered me friendship and connection. When I reject it, I have rejected that connection or friendship and have shown disrespect for their opinion.

Compliments can be awkward to accept when we feel we do not deserve them, when we feel insecure, or if we are afraid to admit we are feeling pretty cute! If we think of them as opportunities to affirm and connect with the person who offers us one, we will be more gracious. Maybe we will say, "Thank you, I got the skirt on a great sale!" Or "What a sweet thing to say! Thank you, I've been practicing!" Or better yet, we will simply smile and say, "Thank you!"

When someone seeks to live biblically and offers kind words to encourage and build us up, we will bless them by graciously accepting their affirmation. In doing so, we may be living more humbly and biblically ourselves.

Cheri Corder

June 21

Called by His Name

If My people who are called by My name will humble themselves, and pray and seek My face, and turn from their wicked ways, then I will hear from heaven, and will forgive their sin and heal their land.
—2 Chronicles 7:14, NKJV

What is in a name?

I find it quite amusing how, on my trips back home after having been away for a while, I use my dad's name as a reference to help establish my identity. The sudden epiphany and exclamation, "Oh! You are his daughter!" never fails to make me smile. Dropping my father's name can also open doors faster than usual in some areas. Amusing as those moments are, it is also sobering to realize I am traced and known through my connection to my father. It is even more sobering to realize the spiritual implications of being known through the connection we have with our heavenly Father.

In 2 Chronicles God clearly states that His people are called by His name (2 Chronicles 7:14, NKJV). In this statement He provides a point of reference to help establish our identity. When we call ourselves Christian, we carry the name of His Son, "Christ," and claim it as being central to our new identity. We align ourselves with Him. We belong to Him.

What incredible opportunities are now available to us. When we call ourselves by His name, the doors of heaven are opened to us as His children. Jesus wants us to realize what this means. Long ago He told the disciples, "If you ask anything in My name, I will do it" (John 14:14, NKJV). Nothing has changed in the intervening years. His promise and His power remain available to you and me—today.

When we are called by His name, when we ask in His name, we are vested with ambassador status backed by all the power of Heaven. Scripture reminds us, "Now then, we are ambassadors for Christ" (2 Corinthians 5:20, NKJV).

Did you notice the thought-provoking manner in which our verse for the day begins? God says, "*If* My people . . ." There is much implied in that small word. The Lord asks us to take a good, hard look at ourselves. He invites us to consider the implications of the name we carry. His name. His identity. His character. Are we carrying His name well?

Jessy Quilindo

June 22

Consider the Birds

How precious is your unfailing love, O God!
All humanity finds shelter
in the shadow of your wings.
You feed them from the abundance of your own house,
letting them drink from your river of delights.
—Psalm 36:7, 8, NLT

In her mid-nineties my mother became less able to undertake active pursuits due to declining mobility. However, she found great pleasure in watching birds, whether from the kitchen window or from the car when we took drives to semirural areas near our home. There is a good deal to be learned from observing birds, and some make excellent role models for Christians. Here are some particular favorites.

Willie wagtails go about their work whole-heartedly, leaping and running energetically while waggling and fanning their tails to disturb the insects on which they feed. They are also known for collecting the softest materials they can find for lining their nest to make a cozy place to raise their young.

Rainbow lorikeets are loyal to each other and tend to mate for life. With their cheerful chattering and gorgeous glowing colors of blue, red, green, and yellow, lorikeets also seem intent on making the world a happier place.

Australian magpies, in their neat black and white plumage, stride purposefully about the yard, gathering food for their families or teaching the young ones how to find food for themselves. They are fearless in defending their families from potential intruders—not just other birds but humans too! Magpies appear responsible and industrious, but they do have a lighter side. They always greet the morning with a joyful caroling call that brightens the day for everyone.

Wood ducks make their nest in a hollow tree, which can be as far as a kilometer (0.62 miles) from water and may also be quite high above the ground. The ducklings leave the nest very soon after they hatch and long before they can fly. The mother duck simply flies to the ground, and at her call the ducklings leap out of the nest and follow her. Now, there is an example of unquestioning trust and obedience!

Scripture assures us that God, who made the birds in all their wonderful variety and cares for their needs, will abundantly care for our needs too—just like a devoted parent bird.

Jennifer M. Baldwin

June 23

A Shining Promise

Keep yourselves in the love of God, looking forward to the mercy of our Lord Jesus Christ to eternal life. And have mercy on some, who are doubting.
—Jude 21, 22, NASB

The love of God shines down through the valleys of the Venice canals in Italy this morning and shines on the occasional person stepping into the early morning brightness. All are illumined: believers, atheists, Christians, Muslims, happy, sad. Whatever the mental state, belief system, ethnicity, or personal identity, God's love beams down, encloses, and physically breathes each breath into that person.

"God said, 'This is the sign of the covenant which I am making between Me and you and every living creature that is with you, for all future generations' " (Genesis 9:12, NASB). Long ago God doubled down on His covenant to us, His promise to never give up on us, to always be there for you and me. God made the promise to a worn-out, exhausted Noah, who probably had PTSD from being tossed about in a huge boat with loudly terrified animals, birds, insects, and humans for forty days and nights and then drifting around for what seemed like forever. *I'm here*, God said. *You and your descendants will never have to go through this again.*

"I have set My rainbow in the cloud, and it shall serve as a sign of a covenant between Me and the earth" (verse 13, NASB). The covenant of love always comes with a concrete gift of remembrance, and God's gift is the shining rainbow that sparkles across a misty sky, glowing above us in the rain and cloud and eliciting joy. I have never heard anyone growl with disdain or grumble with irritation at the sight of a rainbow, but I have heard involuntary aahs of delight and even cries of wonder at the barest hint of those mysteriously beautiful manifestations of God's immovable promise to all of us.

That promise shines down on believers, atheists, Christians, Muslims, happy ,and sad; it shines down on all people, without exception. "For God so loved the world, that He gave His only Son, so that everyone who believes in Him will not perish, but have eternal life. For God did not send the Son into the world to judge the world, but so that the world might be saved through Him" (John 3:16, 17, NASB).*

Gail Wettstein

---

* Adapted from *familytexts*, "August 17, 2024," https://familytexts.wordpress.com/2024/08/17/august-17-2024/. Used with permission.

June 24

Rainbows

I have placed my rainbow in the clouds. It is the sign of my covenant with you and with all the earth.
—Genesis 9:13, NLT

I live in Houston, Texas, USA, where storms, especially hurricanes, are a part of the weather experience. It is not an uncommon occurrence to have a severe downpour in one section of town while only a few blocks away—nothing! A recent weather experience was unique.

Storms were all around, but none in our neighborhood. Our pastor was holding a crusade, and my husband and I planned to go to the church for the evening meeting. We discussed whether we should go early, just in case the weather worsened. We do not live too far from the church, but often it will rain at the church while it is still clear at home.

On this particular evening the sun shone brightly around our house, and we were praising the Lord for His hand in calming the storms in our area. We prayed that the people who planned to attend the evening meeting would have safe passage. As we neared the church, we turned a corner and were startled to see a perfect rainbow arching the sky. It was unique because we often see partial rainbows, but a complete one was something special. I wanted to remember this experience, so I took several pictures. We both rejoiced as we continued down the road, following the rainbow all the way to church.

When we reached the church doors, I asked the greeter if she had seen the rainbow. She was quite surprised and asked me to stand at the door while she took pictures. Everyone who came through the doors that evening had their attention drawn to the rainbow.

At the sermon's close an appeal was made. A young lady came forward, requesting prayer and study. When I looked up, I realized I had not seen her before. She seemed troubled when she came forward but appeared at peace as she returned to her seat.

When I arrived back home, I received a call from one of the elders. She stated the young lady had told her that she had seen the rainbow and had followed it for twenty minutes to the church. The rainbow seemed to be positioned right over the church, and she felt the Lord had provided the rainbow especially for her!

Friends, our God is still a covenant-keeping Savior! When storms arise, look for the rainbow.

Wilma Kirk Lee

June 25

Angels

*For he will order his angels
to protect you wherever you go.
They will hold you up with their hands
so you won't even hurt your foot on a stone.*
—Psalm 91:11, 12, NLT

I am convinced that angels come in many guises.
One summer my daughter and I enjoyed time together camping at a lovely campsite. Toward the end of the week, I needed to pick up a few things from the local supermarket. It was not far from the campsite, so I knew I would not be gone for long. I asked my daughter if she would like to come along with me, but she declined. She wanted to stay and hang out with her friends. I was slightly surprised but brushed it off as just being one of those things. After all, camping is about making and enjoying new friends.

I had not gone far down the road when I noticed a little red sports car in my rearview mirror. As I turned off the traffic circle, he began to flash his headlights at me furiously. I could not imagine why, but I pulled over to the side of the road. Uncertain of what he could want, I got out of my car and walked the few yards back toward him.

Though I do not remember his exact words, he told me that he had seen flames coming out from underneath my car. I remembered I had a gas canister for camping in the trunk of my car! I told the stranger, and he quickly ran to my car and removed it. We stood back and watched the car go up in flames. It was a terrifying experience.

Once the fire had burned out and the situation had settled down, the man drove me back to the campsite. There I notified the necessary authorities and made the necessary arrangements to have the car moved. In all the activity I had forgotten the stranger. I quickly turned around to look for him, but he was nowhere in sight. He had gone, and I had not even thanked him!

You might think anyone would do the same as the man in the red sports car had done if they noticed a car in some sort of trouble, but that is not necessarily true. To this day two things stand out clearly in my mind. The fact that my daughter decided to stay with friends was unusual for her, but how glad I was she was not in the car with me. The second thing was that despite almost no traffic on the country road that day, there was a car behind me at just the right time. So was he an angel, or was it God's provision? I believe that sometimes those are one and the same thing.

Laura A. Canning

June 26

The Goodness of God

For we ourselves were once foolish, disobedient, led astray, slaves to various passions and pleasures. . . . But when the goodness and loving kindness of God our Savior appeared, he saved us, not because of works done by us in righteousness, but according to his own mercy, by the washing of regeneration and renewal of the Holy Spirit.
—Titus 3:3–5, ESV

While driving to work the other day, I was brought to tears by a song that played on the radio. The words told how faithful the Lord has been all my life and how He has been so good to me. It reminded me of a situation I had tried hard to forget over the years.

When I was younger and not so wise, I dated a guy I should never have allowed into my life. I soon discovered he had a drug habit, and like all addicts, he would do almost anything to get his drugs. One evening he stopped by my apartment and demanded money I did not have. The situation became very tense. When he did not get what he wanted, he pulled out a knife and thrust it toward my abdomen. I braced for the impact and inevitable pain, but instead the knife hit something that sounded like rubber and flew out of his hand. The knife bounced on the floor and into the sink around the corner in the kitchen. The guy was so shocked that he abruptly left without making any further demands.

Unbelievable! How in the world did the knife bounce around the wall and into the next room? All I could say was "Thank You, Jesus!" I know He saved my life that night. When it comes to possible and impossible, Matthew tells us, "Jesus looked at them and said, 'With man this is impossible, but with God all things are possible' " (Matthew 19:26, ESV).

Everything happened so quickly, and I do not remember having time to pray; however, Isaiah reminds us, "Before they call I will answer; while they are yet speaking I will hear" (Isaiah 65:24, ESV). I believe God sent an angel to stand in front of me and block the knife. There is simply no other explanation.

"For I know the plans I have for you, declares the Lord, plans for welfare and not for evil, to give you a future and a hope" (Jeremiah 29:11, ESV). The Lord spared my life and has blessed me with many more days, and I will thank Him for the rest of my life. I will praise Him because my life has a purpose, and I will continually sing of the goodness of God!

Sylvia A. Franklin

June 27

Kitty's Angel

"May the Lord watch between you and me when we are absent one from another."
—Genesis 31:49, NKJV

Today was a most interesting day. In the morning I had a doctor's appointment, and as my husband and I stepped out onto the porch to leave, I noticed a young boy in our driveway. We startled one another.

I asked, "What are you doing? What do you want?"

He mumbled a response, and all I could make out was, "Nowhere." Then he took off running.

I followed him through our backyard. He tried to get through the side fence but could not do it, so he ran and tried to climb over the back fence. It was too tall, so he hurried back to the side fence and dashed out onto the street. I told my daughter when she came out. She was concerned.

We drove to my appointment and made a few other stops before going to the bank. There I noticed a group of people gathered around our vehicle. They motioned for me to roll down my window and asked if we knew there was a cat under our car. Surprised, we answered, "No!" My daughter became frantic because she thought she was killing a cat.

A young man asked my daughter to open the hood. I got out to listen and heard a very soft meow. The young man instructed my daughter to turn the wheel, and he caught a glimpse of the kitty. He asked for a jack and jacked up the car on one side. The kitten moved farther back, and all he could see was its paw. He tried but could not reach the poor kitten. My daughter was afraid he would hurt himself, but he was determined to rescue the kitty.

He went to a store across the street and came back with some cat food. Kneeling down, he held out some food between the tire fender and the wheel. She smelled the food and stuck her head out to receive it. She ate but stayed out of reach. That did not stop our angel in disguise. He continued to talk and encourage the kitty, and after almost an hour-long ordeal, the kitten climbed into his hands and meowed. I attempted to hold her, but she would not leave her angel.

God works in mysterious ways, His wonders to perform. The young boy in our driveway was not being mischievous but was looking for his runaway kitten. The kitten remained unharmed after being trapped under our vehicle for miles, and an angel helper refused to leave until he had rescued the kitten. What an awesome God we serve.

Elaine J. Johnson

June 28

The Angel and a Cat's Paw

But my God shall supply all your need according to his riches in glory.
—Philippians 4:19, KJV

My cell phone rang as I left the doctor's office. My husband, Norman, was calling, and he explained, "You need to come home. Mario has been injured." He went on to say that after he had come into the house, he heard my cat crying loudly from the garage. He opened the garage door to find him hanging by his right back leg. Mario did not resist as Norman carefully removed him from the garage door. My very frisky cat had apparently jumped from the roof of my car up onto the garage door and did not get down fast enough as I remotely closed the door and left for my appointment.

When I arrived home, I found Mario painfully dragging his injured leg. At the emergency vet his leg was carefully cleaned and shaved. A deep one-inch cut revealed the tendons and bones, along with a tibial fracture. Upon discharge I was given medications, daily dressing supplies, and instructions to have him rechecked by our vet in three days.

With Norman away on a trip, I enlisted the help of my friend Trish. First, we wrapped Mario in a blanket, leaving his injured leg exposed for me to redress; however, he resisted us every step of the way. Tears ran down my face as I removed the dressing stuck to his wound. Trish soothed me by saying, "Rose, you can do this." This routine went on for fourteen days in an attempt to save the injured leg.

One evening at ten o'clock, I found the dressing had come off his foot. I attempted to contact three friends for help. Lifting Mario and his little basket bed onto the table, I sat there and cried out to the Lord, "I need help badly, Lord. Please help me." I stood up while stroking his little head and suddenly realized he was holding up the injured leg for me to dress. It was as if an angel helped him hold still as I redressed his wound. As I moved his bed to its usual place for the night, my grateful tears of joy flowed freely.

Despite our best efforts, we were unable to save the leg. Due to a severe infection, an amputation became necessary if we were going to save his life. He is currently happy and healthy, whether inside, sleeping on my bed, or outside, chasing birds. I know God cares for His little creatures. He notices when the sparrow falls. But how much more He loves you and me, the ones He calls His own!

Rose Neff Sikora

June 29

Luna

Don't look out only for your own interests, but take an interest in others, too.
—Philippians 2:4, NLT

I love having a garage. Is it raining or snowing? The garage has you covered—literally! Once safely inside I can close the door without even getting out of my vehicle. It is safe and secure, a real convenience, especially at night.

One evening my husband and I returned from town as darkness settled over us. He pulled in but did not immediately close the garage door. I opened my door to get out, and a big furry thing surprised me! Was it a bear? I screamed and slammed my door shut. My husband, thinking I had seen a spider, walked confidently around the vehicle and came face-to-face with a Caucasian shepherd dog. If you are not familiar with this breed, its average weight is between 99 and 170 pounds, and it is usually 23 to 30 inches tall at its shoulder.

Luna lived down the street, and we had seen her impressive presence on our walks. Here in our garage, instead of a dominating demeanor, she seemed utterly vulnerable, unsure of where she was or how to get home. We felt for her collar, but it must have fallen off. Her fur was so soft and fluffy. Had I really been intimidated by this gentle giant? So, with no collar or leash, the three of us walked down the dark road. She would whine and stand questioningly at the front door of every house we passed. Each time, we said, "No, Luna, not that one." About halfway down the street, Luna caught the scent of home and raced off. Arriving at her house, we found no one home. Since Luna seemed happy and did not try to follow us, we left her, praying she would be a good girl until her family returned.

Garages are safe only if you close the door. However, if you always keep yourself closed off, you will miss out on meeting and helping others. Jesus made sure to spend private time with God, and He also prioritized ministering to people. These are not two mutually exclusive things. Jesus spent time with God so He could better help others.

Dear Lord, help me recognize the visible and invisible doors I use to isolate myself. Open my heart and my home to Your Spirit and Your people. "Those who refresh others will themselves be refreshed" (Proverbs 11:25, NLT). Amen.

Deidre A. Jones

June 30

Open Door Faith

However, as it is written:
"What no eye has seen,
what no ear has heard,
and what no human mind has conceived"—
the things God has prepared for those who love him.
—1 Corinthians 2:9, NIV

I have been reflecting on my faith journey lately, trying to articulate what I see God doing in my life. The following object lesson helped me to understand.

Not too long ago my family went on a cruise with friends. One night we were visiting with one of the families we were traveling with. We all sat and chatted as we left port. The father opened the balcony door to feel the breeze and watch the waves. At the same time their daughter decided to go downstairs to find something to drink. When she went to open the suite door, it would not budge. She planted her feet and pulled with all her might, but still the door would not open. We tried to figure it out. She had opened it just a few minutes earlier. What had changed? Then we realized the reason. With the balcony door open, there was something about the pressure and movement of the ship that prevented both doors from being open at the same time.

God whispered to me, "Keisha, that's part of your testimony. Just like that balcony door, you want some things to remain as they are. You want to enjoy the comforts of the experience. But there's another door you are praying to open. On the other side is all you need—and possibly more. You get frustrated because it won't open, but sometimes one door has to close for another to open."

This has been a profound realization for me. Often in life we cling to what is familiar and comfortable, even when we sense that something greater awaits. The closed doors in our lives can be sources of frustration and confusion, but they are also opportunities for growth and new beginnings. By letting go of the familiar, we make room for the new and potentially more fulfilling experiences God has in store for us.

In our faith journey this means trusting God's perfect timing and plans, even when we do not understand. It requires faith to release our grip on the past and embrace the unknown future. As we navigate life, let us remember that sometimes one door must close for another to open, leading us to the blessings and growth God has prepared for us.

LaKeisha Williams

July 1

Abide in Love

"As the Father has loved Me, so have I loved you. Abide in My love."
—John 15:9, ESV

Every spring, my mother-in-law sets out to find Boston ferns to decorate her front porch. She searches for the best price for the lushest ferns. Handpicking each one, she brings them home and begins the process of replanting them. She frees them from the original housing and rehomes them into beautiful, black, wrought iron hangers with coco mat liners for visual appeal and optimal growth. To add the final touch, she places a clear plastic dish that hooks onto the bottom of the hanger. She fills it with water, providing a constant water supply to her beloved ferns. My mother-in-law lovingly performs this ritual each year.

After the effort she puts into giving the ferns a lovely, healthy environment, she makes sure to check the water dishes under the plants regularly, and she turns the plants every few hours to help each side of the plant receive equal amounts of sunlight. Feeding them when needed and stripping away any dead leaves that would deprive the healthy leaves of nourishment are also part of her horticultural duties.

One might think this is way too much work to put into a plant, but she has the biggest, most beautiful ferns I have ever seen. Her love and attention are evident in each of those fern fronds. They abide in her love, attention, and care and respond in kind by producing a luxuriant abundance of beauty as they flourish and blossom under her loving touch.

When we abide in the love of Jesus, we, too, will thrive and flourish. Jesus said that He has loved us with the same love His Father loves Him. We need only to abide in that love. It offers all the nourishment and attention we need to blossom and grow. John reminds us, "We have come to know and to believe the love that God has for us. God is love, and whoever abides in love abides in God, and God abides in him" (1 John 4:16, ESV).

Jesus is the Living Water and the Bread of Life we need to receive each day, and this is His assurance to us: "God will supply every need of yours according to his riches in glory in Christ Jesus" (Philippians 4:19, ESV). When we remain close to Him, He promises to continually supply our daily needs. We simply need to receive the love He offers. There is no greater love than Jesus' love.

Cyndi Woods

July 2

Weeds in My Life

So put to death the sinful, earthly things lurking within you. Have nothing to do with sexual immorality, impurity, lust, and evil desires.
—Colossians 3:5, NLT

These days gardening is my hobby. When I take good care of my plants, I get to enjoy the beauty of the flowers I have planted and also, literally, eat the fruits of my labor from my garden. But I have come to realize that if I want my flowers, vegetables, herbs, and fruits to do well, I need to take good care of them. Some of the basics include giving them manure, watering them, and pulling out the weeds, which often grow faster than the plants.

I have also learned that weeds are deceptive. You may not notice them at first, but soon they are choking out your plants, stealing water and nutrients, and reproducing. The rule in the garden is simple: if you see a weed, pick it! You should not wait for "weeding day" because by then there will be more of them, their roots will be deeper, and it will be harder to get rid of them.

The same is true in my Christian life. I have to weed out sin before it becomes a habit. Daily confession and repentance are musts if we want to keep sin from growing in our lives. Rather, we want to produce the fruit of the Spirit, which is "love, joy, peace, patience, kindness, goodness, faithfulness, gentleness, and self-control" (Galatians 5:22, 23, NLT). These beautiful fruits make us agreeable to one another, as well as make us happy. The fruit of the Spirit show that we are led by the Spirit of Christ.

If we compare the fruit of the Spirit with the works of the flesh, we will know what to cherish and cultivate and what to weed out of our lives. This is the sincere endeavor of all real Christians. "The fruits of the Spirit will be borne by the man who loves God and keeps the way of the Lord, as the rich clusters of grapes grow on the living vine. Christ is his stronghold. Christ lived the law of God in humanity, and so may man do if he will by faith take hold on the strong and mighty One for strength. If he realizes that he cannot do anything without Christ by his side, God will give him wisdom. But he must cherish the love of Christ in his heart, and practice His lessons."*

Dear Lord, please give me the wisdom I need to keep sin out of my life. May the fruit of Your Spirit grow within my life and testify of You. Amen.

Betty Lyngdoh

---

* Ellen G. White, *Testimonies to Ministers and Gospel Workers* (Mountain View, CA: Pacific Press®, 1923), 282.

July 3

The Cost of Praise

"I have been praying here out of my great anguish and grief."
—1 Samuel 1:16, NIV

Growing up in Haiti, I did not have an exercise regime. I exercised most of the day by necessity through the various duties, activities, and responsibilities I carried. I walked miles and miles to school and back. Then I would come home to help cook, clean, and care for my younger siblings. Now that I have grown older and life is different living in the United States of America, I find it necessary for my health to go back to the exercise of my childhood. It is hard for me to start walking, though I enjoy it once I begin.

I often walk at a nearby park where I am comfortable. I bring my music and sing along, using American Sign Language (ASL), the unique language of people who are deaf or hard of hearing. I learned ASL as a young adult.

My walks often take me along various spots in the park where my now-deceased sister, Gina, and I would walk and talk, especially during the last few months before she died. There have been times when the memory of her, mingled with mourning, would take my breath away, and I bent low in agony and anguish. But the songs of hope and victory comfort me as I lift my hands to praise the One who holds me through it all.

As I walk and sign, it may appear that I have lost my mind. But the truth is, I am praying and praising God. His heart and mine are attached by an invisible, indestructible thread, which keeps me steady in solitude, sadness, and sorrow.

First Samuel 1 records the story of Hannah, who prayed so desperately and fervently for God to give her a child. The priest Eli misunderstood her cries and thought she was drunk, but she was just pouring out her heart to the Lord (verses 14, 15).

Mary Magdalene poured out her gratitude by washing Jesus' feet with her tears and wiping them with her hair as she anointed them with the perfume of praise to the One who saved her from sins (Luke 7:37, 38). She must have looked strange to others, but Jesus saw her heart.

My sisters, when life is hard, stay connected to the Savior. Pray consistently and praise God—no matter how it may seem to others. The Lord sees us. He knows the worth and the weight of our worship, and He loves us.

Rose Joseph Thomas

July 4

Hair Journey

Thou shalt have no other gods before me.
—Exodus 20:3, KJV

My weekly visits to the hair salon started in 1992 when my daughter, Evelyn, left home to attend a boarding academy. It was finally my time to be pampered. I loved having my head massaged while my hair was being washed. I loved sitting under the dryer while reading or crocheting. The curling and styling were the icing on the cake. Once every six weeks my hair was relaxed (permed) and cut. My weekly social hour was delightful. I slept on a satin pillowcase and with a satin hair bonnet on my head to preserve my "do." I could not swim nor enjoy water aerobics because my hair would get wet. I could not exercise outside when the humidity was too high. My small fan diverted any steam on the stove while cooking. Looking good on the weekend was worth any inconvenience.

When I moved to Atlanta, Georgia, USA, in 2012, it took longer to find a hair stylist than it did to find physicians. I did not like the place, the price, the parking, the way my hair looked, or how long the appointment took. Finally, after eight months and seven different hair stylists, a salon ten minutes from my home was recommended, and I was very pleased for several years. Then the COVID-19 pandemic came, and the salon closed. I had not washed my own hair in over thirty years and had no idea where to start.

This was the perfect time to transition from straightened hair to natural hair. When I saw a style I liked on an unknown lady, I had no shame in asking what products she used. I found cute natural styles on Google, watched many "how-to" natural hair videos, and purchased many of the products they recommended. My cabinet looked like a mini beauty supply store. Over time I learned that just because the styles, videos, and products looked amazing on others did not mean that they would look amazing on me. After two years of trying to figure it all out, the new me emerged, and now I can finally swim, cook, exercise outside, and walk in the rain with confidence. I feel free. The bonus is that my hair maintenance budget has dropped 75 percent.

This life-changing realization reminded me that the devil knows what resonates with each of us. He knows our gods and our weaknesses. May we not be so consumed with the cares of this world that we forget to keep our hearts, minds, and souls stayed on our Savior.

Shirley Sain Fordham

July 5

Christ's Beautiful Robe

"I will save you from all your uncleanness."
—Ezekiel 36:29, NIV

It was a beautiful, sunny day in Bermuda, and I looked forward to providing a guided island tour in my minibus for a group of eight people. My clients were a little late disembarking from the cruise ship, but finally I stood on the dock with six clients. *Where are the other two?* I wondered. At last, a lady arrived and mentioned her husband would be along soon. She apologized for being late and said he was not feeling his best. Farther down the pier an older gentleman, wearing a frown, walked slowly toward me and the rest of the group. As he approached the van, I reached out to assist him, as I usually do. He stepped up into the van and settled in his seat.

As we were preparing to leave, we noticed a terrible odor permeating the van. The man's wife said, "Excuse me, but my husband needs the restroom right away."

Quickly, I drove to the restroom on the pier, which was quite a distance from the cruise ship. He shuffled out of the van and was gone for at least fifteen minutes. It saddened me to hear his companions complain about the tour being delayed.

Soon his wife returned and said her husband had not made it to the bathroom in time. He emerged from the bathroom, looking dejected. It was true. He had not made it in time. His clothes were badly soiled, and he smelled terrible. My heart went out to him. His wife said, "He's going back to the ship."

I looked at his appearance and thought, *He can't walk back to the ship exposed and looking like that.*

I grabbed a large beach towel from my van and offered it to him. To my amazement, he said, "I don't want it." I offered again, and he refused my offer once more. Then he turned and slowly made his way down the pier, his soiled, smelly clothes visible to all. As I watched him trudge away, my heart hurt for him. I could not believe he had refused to cover up with the towel I had offered.

At that moment God placed a thought in my mind. His heart hurts for His children when He offers to cover us with His beautiful robe of righteousness, and we refuse. Our righteousness is as soiled rags. Friends, let us not refuse His offer! Thank Him today and accept His covering.

Julie Richardson

July 6

A Drive-By Prayer

Confess your trespasses to one another, and pray for one another, that you may be healed. The effective, fervent prayer of a righteous man avails much.
—James 5:16, NKJV

"Excuse me?" The woman said, rolling her car window down as she came to a stop in front of me. She was about my age, thirty or so, and had a bright, warm smile.

I was pulled out of my reverie. "Yes?" I asked, walking a little closer to her car so I could hear her better. I was on my way back to the office building where I worked after checking the mail, and my thoughts were miles away.

I thought she must want directions because multiple other facilities surrounded the building where I worked. Not all of them were marked with signs, and it was not uncommon for a GPS to lead someone to the parking lot and then abandon them with a final "You've arrived" without guiding them to the facility they were trying to reach. So I was taken aback when, instead of asking for directions, the woman said, "I just wanted to ask how I can pray for you?"

I was surprised and touched. I let her know some general things and, in turn, asked how I could pray for her. She told me a few things and then said goodbye with a friendly "Have a blessed rest of your day!"

The interaction made me consider my attitude toward prayer. Although I pray for the people in my life, I am rarely so intentional as to ask how I can pray for them. Sometimes I am short on time or struggle to remember a request, so I pray a quick and general drive-by prayer, knowing God knows the specifics of the situation. Yet here was this lady, taking time out of her day to ask for the specific prayer requests of a total stranger! I felt convicted.

While it is true God knows every situation and considers the spirit with which we pray above the words we use (see Romans 8:26, 27), the interaction left me with a desire to be more intentional about praying for others. Will you pray the below prayer with me now?

Dear Lord, I know the importance of intercessory prayer. I know You are a caring God who wants to hear the prayers of Your children. Thank You for knowing my heart and receiving my prayers, even when I don't have all the words to say. Please help me to be sensitive to Your prompting and lift others up in intercessory prayer. In Jesus' name I pray. Amen.

Kristin Beaven

July 7

God Still Works Miracles

Praise the Lord, *my soul,*
and forget not all his benefits—
who forgives all your sins
and heals all your diseases.
—Psalm 103:2, 3, NIV

When my daughter Daria was only eighteen months old, she suffered a severe head injury that, unfortunately, later affected her brain. A year later our family found her unconscious, and the pupils of her eyes were barely responding. Paramedics arrived immediately after a call to the medical emergency center, but all attempts to revive her were unsuccessful. She remained unconscious for thirty-five minutes. In our desperation we called on God to help and prayed fervently throughout this time. We remembered the instructions in the Bible about the power of prayer: "Therefore confess your sins to each other and pray for each other so that you may be healed. The prayer of a righteous person is powerful and effective" (James 5:16, NIV). We confessed our sins and promised to serve God for the rest of our lives if only He would save Daria.

Daria was diagnosed with epilepsy, and I stubbornly refused to believe it—until the next seizure. We learned that when the brain swells for a length of time, it no longer functions as it should. This often leaves a person severely impaired and unable to function cognitively. But God can still work miracles. Tests on our daughter showed that her brain was completely unaffected by the seizure.

Daria's second seizure was a time of great sorrow and despair. But once again the Lord showed His power and authority over illness and our lives. The first time, He gave us back a healthy child. The second time, we anointed her according to the Word of God, and the Lord healed her completely. The doctors could not believe their eyes after the examination. Her brain was completely healthy! And I could not stop telling everyone how the Lord had healed her.

Thank God, my daughter is now seventeen years old, and we have never had to think about her severe diagnosis again. The Lord healed her completely, and I will be forever grateful to Him. While we do not always understand the way God chooses to answer our prayers, let us not forget that He is still the same loving God today as in times past. Let us remind others that "Surely the arm of the Lord is not too short to save, nor his ear too dull to hear" (Isaiah 59:1, NIV).

Yana Kosian

July 8

The Scar

He heals the brokenhearted and binds up their wounds.
—Psalm 147:3, NKJV

For a Christian, scars can be a reminder of God's providence and grace. Yes, God's grace and providence are inseparable, and we can have scars that give evidence He has worked all things together for our good.

Several years ago I was admitted to the Southern Philippines Medical Center in Davao City with a heart problem. I was diagnosed with severe aortic stenosis, and my cardiologist told me open heart surgery was my only option.

Aortic stenosis is a congenital heart disease that is asymptomatic in younger people. It surfaces when the aortic valve narrows and blood cannot flow normally. A normal heart has three divisions in the valves. Mine had only two.

At first I felt hesitant to undergo such a major procedure. For my family and me, it was a big deal to make such a decision because we knew the outcome was uncertain. We prayed so hard, asking God for intervention, for a miracle to happen. I remembered that God performed miracles in Bible times, and I felt sure He could still do the same in our time because He is the God who sees and hears, and nothing is too difficult for Him. He promised, "For with God nothing shall be impossible" (Luke 1:37, KJV).

I claimed God's promises in the Bible to give me hope, courage, and strength. I submitted to whatever His plans for me might be. He reminded me,

> "Fear not, for I am with you;
> Be not dismayed, for I am your God.
> I will strengthen you,
> Yes, I will help you,
> I will uphold you with My righteous right hand" (Isaiah 41:10, NKJV).

I held on to this promise as I was brought to the operating room, fully entrusting my life to Him, casting everything into His care. Twenty-four hours after my surgery, I had not gained consciousness and was bleeding internally. They reopened my heart to save me, and after the second procedure was done, I regained consciousness after being in a coma for three days.

Today I am back to work, serving the Lord at Southeastern Philippine Union Mission as Women's Ministries and Family Life director. Every time I see the scar on my chest, it reminds me of God's providence and saving grace. My scar is a testimony to His goodness.

Lindy Lou S. Magdadaro

July 9

Channels of Light and Blessings

"I am the light of the world. Whoever follows me will never walk in darkness, but will have the light of life."
—John 8:12, NIV

I knocked and entered her room, where she sat in the hospital recliner, postoperative, day one. I introduced myself, but she barely looked at me. There was such sadness about her. *Was it from the surgery?* I wondered. She was scheduled to be discharged the next day. *Why is she so sad?* I went over her plan of care for the night and inquired about her expectations. She had none except to be left alone.

I returned to her room with her scheduled medications and offered her some apple juice with which to take her pills. She was thankful and took her medication. I could still feel sadness in her as I made her comfortable and inquired if she needed anything else. "No," she said. "I'm fine."

Before I knew it, it was five o'clock, thank the Lord! The night had passed without any incidents. As I entered the sad lady's room for the last time, I saw she was awake. She said had slept well, and her pain level was good. She allowed me to assist with her basic needs, and I made her comfortable in the recliner. She took her morning medications. As I sat across from her, the room felt so peaceful.

She looked at me and very quietly said, "My son." Then everything came tumbling out. Her heart was in such pain. I held her hands and allowed her to purge her soul. When she was done, I shared the love of Jesus with her and told her of His wonderful promises. I prayed and committed both her and her son to our loving Jesus. Smiling, she apologized for the previous night. I smiled in return and told her God had a sense of humor in allowing us to meet.

Sometimes our pain causes us to miss opportunities to point others to Christ. When we commit ourselves to God, He will place us where we can glorify Him.

> Everyone who is connected to God will impart light to others. If there are any who have no light to give, it is because they have no connection with the Source of Light. . . .
>
> God has appointed His children to give light to others. . . . We have been called out of darkness into His marvelous light, in order that we may show forth the praises of Christ."*

May we allow the Holy Spirit to use us as channels of light, pointing others to Christ, who is the Source of Light and peace. All for His glory and praise!

Jannett Maurine Myrie

---

* Ellen G. White, *Christian Service* (Washington, DC: Review and Herald®, 1925), 21.

July 10

An Appointed Time

There is a time for everything, and a season for every activity under the heavens.
—Ecclesiastes 3:1, NIV

Our kitten Tator was sick and getting worse. I called my husband, Ron, and asked if he would take him back to the emergency vet in the city, nearly an hour away. I brought the kitten down and gave it to my husband. He then began the long drive to the vet. Then I had some time on my hands because I had two hours before my first appointment. I drove around a bit and talked with God about how to use this extra time. He impressed me to find my friend Martha at her work. So I pulled into the parking lot and went to her office, but she was not there. As I began to leave, I received a phone call from my friend Melanie. She reminded me that today was the first anniversary of the death of Martha's granddaughter, who had been killed in a terrible accident. I had forgotten. Then I knew why God impressed me to find her.

Martha pulled into the parking lot, and I got out of my car and waved. She opened her window to greet me and then invited me to sit with her. As I joined her I prayed that God would give me the right words to say to my friend. At first we talked about general things, and then I said, "This day must be very difficult for you."

She looked at me with tears in her eyes and said, "Yes, this is one of the most difficult days of my life." She began to review that terrible day a year before. We sat together for over an hour as she talked, and I mostly listened. Then we prayed together. She was much encouraged to have a friend listen to her pain and suffering and to pray with her. What a privilege it was for me.

It is so encouraging to realize how attentive God is to the needs of His daughters. He is always leading and directing our lives, day by day. We must listen to His still, small voice and respond. God needs us to be His hands, feet, and voice. It is a humbling experience to realize His specific timing in our lives. Tator's emergency provided the gift of time with Martha, and the medical intervention saved Tator's life. He is now happy and healing.

This precious time happened in God's appointed time. "I have seen the God-given task with which the [daughters] of men are to be occupied. He has made everything beautiful in its time" (Ecclesiastes 3:10, 11, NKJV).

Sharon Follett

July 11

Together We Stand

Whatever your hand finds to do, do it with all your might.
—Ecclesiastes 9:10, NASB

Over the years I have been blessed by the devotionals shared in these books by women all over the world. When I read the profile of each sister, I find a sweet unity, for no matter which country we call home, we all join in using our talents for service to God. We all have so many stories to tell. God has called us individually and provided us with talent, time, and capability to work for Him. He can use us, blended together, to help finish the work so Jesus can come.

I relate well to Priscilla, who shares she is getting older and slower. How often I have uttered those same words, yet she writes that "her budgies . . . keep singing, no matter what!"* Yes, we can be thankful for what we are blessed with each day, no matter what limitations we may have, like Glenda-Mae in her wheelchair, who delights us with her devotionals. God bless her.

I smile when I read about Elizabeth and her chimney sweep business. This brings the memory of childhood days when the chimney caught alight and roared so fiercely that I thought my family's house would burn down. It was Dad to the rescue, who put a hose down the chimney. What a mess. I have deep admiration for Deborah and her commitment to Sonny. Your stories have given us much inspiration over the years.

Sonia tells us she has driven the school bus for well over thirty years. That brought vivid memories of when I had my four children to get ready to meet the school bus at a set time. That was easier said than done, and the driver often had to sit a moment while the Welk kids did their morning dash. Sonia also tells us she lives in the rugged but beautiful state of Alaska. It must be picturesque. My husband and I love the rugged places and have traveled much of Australia in our four-by-four and our caravan. We live on the side of a hill in the foothills of the Mount Lofty Ranges in southeastern Australia. It was once rich, cultivated land but is now well built on.

My friends, wherever you live, or whatever your passion, God bless you and thank you for blessing us with your stories of God's love and faithfulness! Someday soon, I pray, we will all be living together in the mansions above. I am really looking forward to meeting you all.

"Beloved, if God so loved us, we also ought to love one another" (1 John 4:11, NASB).

Lyn Welk-Sandy

---

* Priscilla E. Adonis biography, in *Covered and Carried*, ed. Carolyn Rathbun Sutton (Nampa, ID: Pacific Press®, 2021), 373.

July 12

Platforms

"Therefore keep watch, because you do not know on what day your Lord will come."
—Matthew 24:42, NIV

The night before the church beach trip, my son and I were filled with anticipation and excitement. My four-year-old son loved the beach, and I knew he would have a wonderful day.

I had prepared everything beforehand, so when we woke up on Sunday morning, all we had to do was go to the train station. I made sure we got there early. Upon arrival at the station, I checked the departure board to see when our train would arrive. It always departed from platform one, so I went there and waited peacefully because I knew we had plenty of time.

Fifteen minutes later I saw a train arrive on platform three. A man began to run from platform one to platform three, but I did not think anything of it. I continued to wait calmly as I watched him run, still confident it was not our train. A moment later I heard a woman frantically inquire of the conductor if it was the train to Bedford that had arrived. I tried to tell her not to worry, as the train to Bedford always departed from platform one. Then she turned to me and exclaimed, "That's the train to Bedford!"

In disbelief I ran to the departure board and realized she was right. I hurried back to my son, grabbed our bags, and told him to run up the stairs. I charged ahead of him to the top of the stairs, and he ran as fast as his little legs could go, screaming for me to wait. We caught up to each other, locked hands, scrambled, and screamed our way to the final flight of stairs to platform three. I saw the conductor and called for him to hold the train. He smiled and motioned us to get on board. We flew down the stairs and burst onto the train with racing hearts. The doors shut behind us.

As I sat on the train hugging my son for his bravery, I reflected on what had just happened. Though I was certain we were on the right platform, I discovered at the last minute we were not. On our spiritual journey we know we need to be ready for Jesus' return, yet how many of us are peacefully waiting on the wrong platform? The conductor kindly held the train for us, but when Jesus returns, it will be too late to change platforms. Let us draw close to our Savior today and every day. He will safely lead us home.

Shantel Stephens

July 13

Believe in God's Promise

"I will come back and take you to be with me."
—John 14:3, NIV

A Chinese couple was married less than a month before the husband was called to serve in the military during wartime. Before leaving he promised his beloved wife he would return and urged her to wait.

As the war intensified he was severely injured and spent a long time recovering in a special care unit. When he was finally discharged, he rushed home, only to find that his wife had moved from their shared home. After searching the area in vain, he decided to remarry and start a new family.

Fifty years later he discovered that his first wife had never stopped waiting for him. Despite being told he had died and being forced to relocate for safety, she held on to his promise, believing he would return.

While human promises can falter, God's promises remain steadfast. After His resurrection Jesus reassured His disciples of His reality and the certainty of His return. In John 14:3 He promises, "And if I go and prepare a place for you, I will come back and take you to be with me" (NIV).

We can fully trust in God's assurances. For those who are faithful, facing death with faith is possible, knowing that God never lies and will fulfill His promises, even in their rest (see Hebrews 11:13). Belief is a manifestation of faith and love. Moreover, believing in God's Word leads us to live with purpose. Faith provides hope that propels us forward.

Finally, the promise of God's return offers profound inner peace. In a world filled with turmoil—marked by conflict, injustice, and natural disasters—it can be challenging to thrive spiritually. The environment often feels unwelcoming, and people may easily stray from their Christian values, conforming to the crowd instead.

We must remember that God has set us apart. He has promised that He will return to take us home with Him. His Word is filled with promises we can hold on to. His Word has the power to transform us. As Paul reminds us, "And being fully persuaded that, what he had promised, he was able also to perform" (Romans 4:21, KJV). Friends, we can believe in God's promise!

Orathai Chureson

July 14

Missing Socks

"He will turn the hearts of the fathers back to their children and the hearts of the children to their fathers."
—Malachi 4:6, NASB

One of my most frustrating and tedious chores is to sit with a pile of socks, still warm from the dryer, hoping to match each pair. It baffles me. We put pairs of socks in the washing machine but something mysterious seems to happen between when we put them in the washing machine and when they are taken out of the dryer. Even with them tied together, they still manage to wriggle free and go missing. What happens to them during the washing and drying cycles?

My challenge is to unite the pairs. The sorting begins by separating them according to color. Blues, browns, blacks, and whites are all placed in their respective piles. Then they are sorted by the matching patterns and details. I keep sorting and matching until I find each pair. It is so satisfying to find the first pair and then the next, until all the pairs are reunited. When they are all matched, I feel a burst of joy that none were missing.

The simple experience of sorting socks and finding their match reminds me of a time when we will be reunited with our loved ones. Parents who were separated from their children, siblings who were separated from each other, and friends who have lost contact with each other will eventually be reunited. What a celebration that will be!

Are you in a situation where you have been separated from a loved one, for whatever reason? It may have dragged on for years. Do you have a loved one, a colleague, or a friend you have not heard from in a long time? I encourage you to reach out to them. Ask the Lord for wisdom, tact, a tender heart, and courage to take that first step. I pray you will experience joy over a relationship restored.

Dear Lord and Father, healer of all broken relationships, thank You today for searching and finding me, for the joy of a relationship with You, and for Your tenderness and love. Give me the strength and tact needed to reach out to the person You have placed on my heart. May we both feel the joy that a mended relationship can bring.

Lord, we all look forward to the time when we will be reunited with You. Dear Savior, may it be soon. We long for You to take us home.

Gloria Barnes-Gregory

July 15

Lost Tooth

Many believed in his name, when they saw the miracles which he did.
—John 2:23, KJV

Remember the parable of the lost coin? Well, this is a true story about a lost tooth. I had been praying about how to show God's love to my coworkers when a friend at work lost a baby tooth from a necklace. It had fallen off her necklace somewhere between the office, a long hall, an elevator, across the parking lot to the sandwich shop, and back. A near-impossible find, and we were unsuccessful at first.

I went back to my desk and silently prayed to find the tooth for her so that her faith would be enlarged. Immediately I began to sneeze. In a room of seventy people, I had to leave. My friend was still in the hall, looking for the lost tooth.

I walked down the hallway toward the restroom while I searched and prayed. The floor was black and white and sprinkled with speckles due to a construction project. As I thought we should ask the custodian to help, my eyes were directed to something white and gold. I picked it up and ran back to my friend, saying, "Tell me this isn't a piece of popcorn!"

She swept me off my feet and while practically crying, told me her grandma was waiting for her to find it before she returned to Italy to have it dipped in gold for her. Her grandma would never understand how she lost the tooth. When she put me down on the ground, I said, "I prayed to Jesus to find that tooth for you. God caused me to sneeze, so I had to come out into the hall just to find the missing tooth."

She agreed.

We went back to our meeting, and at the end of the day, I told her I had never been hugged so hard. The next day she brought a gift to me. When I opened it, I found a leather band with some strange squiggly letters on it.

I asked, "Does this mean something?"

She told me to turn the band over, and I read, "Ask, and it will be given to you; seek, and you will find; knock, and it will be opened to you" (Matthew 7:7, NKJV).

She explained she thought the Scripture was appropriate because of the situation in looking for the lost tooth. I thanked her and told her God loved her very much. He not only had heard my prayer but also would hear her prayers too.

What prayer is on your heart today? God hears, and He hears *everything* that concerns us.

Melinda Smith

July 16

Wisdom of the Ages

"So, in everything, do to others what you would have them do to you, for this sums up the Law and the Prophets."
—Matthew 7:12, NIV

When my husband and I celebrated our sixtieth wedding anniversary, we received many congratulations from friends and family, near and far. Our children and grandchildren organized a wonderful family picnic by the river near our home.

We were asked to share the secret of a long and enduring marriage. My response was that when we would disagree on issues, my husband would not argue or retaliate. He would quietly head for the back door, disappear outside, and busy himself with the various chores that always needed to be taken care of on the farm. Sometimes he would be gone for quite a while.

An old adage says, "It takes two to tango." Over the years, we have found it is often best to put the discussion aside and wait to calm down before seeking to resolve our differences. While waiting did not always resolve the issue at hand, it helped more often than not.

Our son has a degree in psychology, and his wife has a degree in sociology. They both have a lot of "book learning" and used that as their guide for resolving differences when they were dating, seriously considering marriage, and beyond.

One day they asked me to serve as referee while they discussed several major issues they were dealing with between them. They asked me not to say anything but simply to listen. Then, when all the talking had finished, they turned to me and asked for my opinion. Who was right? Which one had the best perspective on things? Of course I was smart enough not to take sides. I carefully affirmed each of them and reminded them of the Scripture which admonishes us, "So, in everything, do to others what you would have them do to you, for this sums up the Law and the Prophets" (Matthew 7:12, NIV).

Putting others before oneself is the biblical admonition. The writer of Hebrews says, "Let us consider one another in order to stir up love and good works" (Hebrews 10:24, NKJV).

God's Word truly is filled with the wisdom of the ages. We can apply it to every situation we face in this world. And it turns out that the golden rule is still the best advice for getting along with others.

Marcella Lynch

July 17

Ask Abba First

Make me know Your ways, LORD; teach me Your paths.
—Psalm 25:4, NASB

Do you have a Scripture for every decision you make?" This is the question I heard quite often from a pastor serving at a Seventh-day Adventist Church in Maryland, USA, where I worshiped. Since then I have tried to let God's Word lead in all my decisions.

One day I received a call from the first elder of my church. He informed me that I had been nominated to serve as an elder. My initial reaction was to decline because I disliked attending board meetings. I said to him, "Let me think and pray about that, and I will get back to you."

As the day wore on, Abba drew my attention to one Scripture in three different photos stored on my cellphone. The images were taken three days apart, almost four years earlier. The Scripture records Jesus saying, "With God all things are possible" (Matthew 19:26, NASB).

In the first picture, I noticed the Scripture on a faceplate covering a light switch. I had taken the photograph while visiting someone's home. Now as I looked at it, I could hear Abba saying, *Go ahead, turn the light on.* I dismissed it, still resistant to the idea. As I continued to scroll, the very next picture was a page from one of my journals. I felt like I was running from something and running toward it at the same time. The journal entry contained excerpts from a book I read by Barry Black, and the section was titled "What do you fear the most?" It was based on a conversation that Pastor Black had with a minister. As I pondered the minister's response, the imprint on the page of my journal caught my attention. I had written, "With God all things are possible."

Later that day I returned to my phone for an encouraging message to send a friend. I noticed a picture of her old business card and decided I would send it to her as a reminder to hold on to the dreams that were deferred. When I opened the image file, her tagline said, "Nothing Is Impossible." At that moment I paused, realizing that Abba had shown me the same Scripture in three different forms on the same day.

He had spoken to my fears and assured me that with God, all things are possible. The answer was clear, and with that, I said yes to the request to serve.

Desrene L. Vernon

July 18

I Am Not the Lead Character

The LORD did not set his affection on you and choose you because you were more numerous than other peoples. . . . But it was because the LORD loved you and kept [his] oath.
—Deuteronomy 7:7, 8, NIV

I was serving as a volunteer when I met a drama queen. I am sure you know what I mean. I remember looking up the signs of histrionic personality disorder I had learned in school, and while I was unable to reach a conclusion, I wished she would take the test.

And then I began to wonder if I was any different. Most books and movies are centered around a main character or a lead character—be it a person or a group fighting for a common cause. The weak fighting the powerful and evil. And even movies with multiple leads center around the lead character.

I concluded that I saw myself as the main lead in the story of my life. Not that I was more selfish or self-centered than others. I have volunteered throughout my life, but as I thought about my deeds, my service, my own good, and my salvation, I realized there was nothing I could bring before the Lord. I had no contribution to make for my salvation. It is His gift alone.

Though I am the lead character in my own life, I am the second lead in the lives of those closest to me and an extra for most other people. Understanding this truth helped me put things into perspective. I realized that not everything is about me. People have bad days. What I think may be the best option is likely just one of many options. We do not always choose the best option, but hopefully we will choose to help one another and move forward together.

But these were not the greatest revelations, even though I am grateful for the changes they brought to my life. The greatest discovery was that my life needed to have a different lead character. Jesus is where my focus needs to be. He is the One who has made all things possible through His sacrifice. I am a lump of clay in His hands that He is molding and making into a vessel fit for the purpose He has chosen. "Does not the potter have the right to make out of the same lump of clay some pottery for special purposes and some for common use?" (Romans 9:21, NIV). The One who has set His affection on you and me does it not because of what we can offer but because of who He is.

Anamaria Maier

July 19

Best Laid Plans

Many are the plans in a person's heart, but it is the Lord's purpose that prevails.
—Proverbs 19:21, NIV

My father was one of the best logisticians known to mankind. Perhaps I exaggerate, but making exquisite plans, schedules, and itineraries was part of his skill set. Although many people exemplify Robert Burns' adage, "The best-laid plans of mice and men often go awry," my family never expected that my father's plans would go awry. That is, not until one day in 1975 when our family began the journey home to the United States of America as permanently returned missionaries.

It should have been simple. Departing from Manila, Philippines, my parents planned to fly to Bangkok, Thailand. They would arrive an hour before my sister, Sharon, and I arrived from Singapore. Sharon and I, still teenagers, were packed and ready to leave our school when Sharon remembered something important she had not done. Her flight was rebooked for the next morning. I flew alone to Thailand. Plans had gone awry.

When I arrived in Bangkok, my parents were not there to meet me. Their flight had been turned back to Manila after an engine caught fire. I waited in the airport alone. Plans had gone awry. My parents arrived the next morning, and we waited for my sister. Her expected flight arrived an hour early without her. She arrived that afternoon. Plans had gone awry. Nothing my father had planned worked according to the schedule. Life is like that.

Carefully laid plans often go awry. The question is, How do we respond? My sister learned to be prepared; I practiced two days of patience sitting in the airport; and my father kept calm and carried on. He had already placed his plans in God's hands, and now he prayed for God to guide each one's journey and safely reunite us as a family according to His plan.

This reminds me of how our heavenly Father, the greatest logistician, made careful plans for creating a perfect world. Yet we ended up separated from Him. His plans went awry.

Thankfully, through Jesus, He made an alternate plan for us to be reunited with Him. Every day He patiently rearranges things—overcoming countless obstacles—so that our journey will bring us closer to Him. Someday soon all the delays and rerouting will end, and we will forever rejoice that God's eternal purpose has prevailed.

Rebecca Turner

July 20

When God Blesses His Children

The LORD declares, "Far be it from Me—for those who honor Me I will honor."
—1 Samuel 2:30, NASB

My daughter, Haadiya, and I had an opportunity to honor the Sabbath after she asked to enroll in gymnastics when she was seven years old. A year later, she was ready to join the team and participate in the competition season. Of the five mandatory competitions, four meets were on Sundays. For the only Saturday meet, she was allowed to participate with another team on Sunday. She only received a participation medal for that meet, but she was still happy. Now watch what God did: At that specific meet they competed to see who could hold the longest handstand. Guess who won? Yes, God loves to honor His children!

After taking a break during the pandemic, she returned once things opened up, and her competition season began in January 2023. She had five mandatory meets, with mandatory registration and payments before the schedules were created. The coach warned me about the probability of forfeiting any Saturday competitions and losing the nonrefundable $200 fee each time. Despite the financial constraints, I just knew God would come through! The first four competitions were scheduled for either Friday afternoons or Sundays. The coach, aware of our Sabbath-keeping, texted me about a Friday meet and said, "I think the sun will set around six o'clock and the meet ends just before seven o'clock, so I guess Haadiya will leave by six o'clock." My daughter finished her four events right before six o'clock! *God, I cannot explain the way You work, but even when we do not see it—You are working.*

But the enemy was also at work. The final meet was scheduled for six o'clock on Saturday, with warm-up starting at five thirty. I told the coach we would arrive after sunset, and she said we might have to forfeit this meet because the decision was out of her hands. We took a leap of faith and arrived after sunset. Haadiya was able to participate in three events and was allowed to make up the missing one. She placed in every event, and we glorified God all the way home!

Pathfinders met the next day, and my exhausted kids begged to skip it. We spoke about how God had honored them, and the next morning they were up and off earlier than usual. Yes, we can do all things through Christ—and He will honor and bless us as we serve Him faithfully.

Caren Henry Broaster

July 21

The Costly Choice That Counts

"If you love Me, keep My commandments."
—John 14:15, NKJV

My family's relocation to Malaysia marked an exciting adventure, particularly for my daughters, who were about to start at a new international school. Nevertheless, as a mother, I wrestled with a deep sense of unease. They had always attended an Adventist school. In the previous Adventist school where they studied and where I taught, I knew their teachers personally and trusted the spiritual foundation they received alongside their academics. In the new environment, I was not as familiar with or involved with the educational system, and I felt concerned about the influences my daughters would face.

It did not take long for us to see how challenging it would be. Most, if not all, extracurricular activities, including sports day and concerts, were scheduled on Saturdays. However, this did not place our daughters in a dilemma because they understood the importance of keeping the Sabbath, even if it meant missing out on fun activities.

On one occasion both our daughters qualified for the national level of an English Olympiad. Their accomplishment meant much to them, but their excitement turned to disappointment when it was revealed that the national finals would be held on a Saturday. As I dropped them off at the school that morning, I jokingly suggested that they decide whether they wanted to participate in this competition. However, deep in my heart, I prayed fervently for their decision to honor God.

That afternoon they came home with the news that they had chosen to withdraw from the competition. Their decision was met with dismay and questioning from their teachers and classmates. "Why forgo such an opportunity? Can you join just this once?" they asked.

Yet my daughters stood firm, understanding that true faith sometimes demands tough sacrifices. Despite worldly pressures their choice reflected their commitment to honoring God above all else.

This experience reminded me of Daniel, who faced intense pressure to conform yet remained steadfast in his faith. It is easy to profess faith without cost, but genuine faith often requires us to forfeit what the world values most. Mark 8:36 admonishes us, "For what will it profit a man, if he gains the whole world, and lose his own soul?" (KJV). Are you confronted with choices that test your faith? Remember, honoring God yields a far greater reward, even if it comes at a high cost.

Vivian C. Bana

July 22

It Only Took Fifteen Minutes

Wait for the Lord and keep His way, and he will exalt you to inherit the land.
—Psalm 37:34, ESV

I moved from New York, with its A+ public transportation system, to the US state of Florida, not realizing how hard life would be without a driver's license. For nine-and-a-half years, I found a ride with friends, which worked well enough, until they decided to move to Brazil.

With my immigration form dated, I went to the Department of Motor Vehicles (DMV) to get a temporary license. The supervisor granted it to me and said the permit would arrive by mail. I immediately started to plan all I would see and do. But two days before I was to take the DMV road test, a letter arrived canceling the permit—which had not even arrived. I went to the DMV main office and was told I could take the test but I had to produce a work permit before they would issue my driver's license.

When I arrived for the test, my instructor looked at her watch and said, "We are too early. Your test is at 2:15 p.m."

I showed her the driving school text message, which stated my test was scheduled for two o'clock.

"That's weird!" she responded. "We'd better go."

We arrived, only to be told by the security officer no driving test had been scheduled for two o'clock. The first one listed was for 2:15 p.m. After reading my text notification, he let me in.

I handed my Brazilian passport to the lady at the desk and she exclaimed, "My best friend is from Maranhão!" She saw the cancellation letter and asked, "Why has this been canceled?" She picked up the phone and smiled.

I asked, "You found someone to cancel the cancellation?"

She nodded and smiled again. "Now go and pass your test! I must leave now, but I will make sure you receive your temporary license after your test."

I passed the test, and while we waited for the papers, I told my instructor, "I still can't believe what just happened."

To my surprise, she said: "God is honoring you because you did what was right by not driving without a driver's license for all these years."

I eventually received my work permit—and my driver's license. God's timing is absolutely perfect, don't you think?

Today I invite you to surrender your all to God and do what is right while you wait for Him to act. He knows what you need. He is not sleeping. He is working on your behalf.

Kênia Kopitar

July 23

Just a Moment

"I will trust in him and not be afraid."
—Isaiah 12:2, NLT

Have you ever taken a detour? On the road, at work, school? How about God's detours or the detours we encounter while living on this earth where the devil "reigns"? How do we face these difficult times?

Sasha* considers herself extremely blessed, despite life's challenges. She thanks God every day for everything and trusts Him in the good and the bad times. Sasha believes our time here is temporary.

One morning she woke up and could not see. The ophthalmologist sent her immediately to a specialist, where she was diagnosed with retinal detachment. She needed emergency surgery. The prognosis was bleak—she faced blindness. Her sight would never be the same, not even with glasses. Life had taken an unexpected turn, a huge detour she had never expected. In just a moment her world had been turned upside down.

And so began a journey that still continues. The next ten months were full of doctor's appointments and multiple surgeries. Recovery has been difficult, but Sasha still praises the Lord. "God is in control of my life. He has my back. The painful, unexpected moments are just that—moments. Though they are challenging, I'm not alone. God is ever-present on this journey, and through it all, I'll continue to trust Him."

Sasha believes in prayer, and before going to the hospital, she reached out to her family and a few friends to pray. Her request: "I want to see, but I want you to pray for God's will, even if it means blindness. Please remember to pray for my family."

Sasha knows that God is not deaf to our prayers. He hears and will answer at the proper time. He promises to walk with us. After five surgeries her vision is slowly returning, though it is not perfect. She has some side effects and more surgeries scheduled, but she continues to depend on her heavenly Father. Sasha's confidence is in God. When she measures her detour, her challenging moment, and her "Goliath" against God—they are of little consequence.

God will always come to our aid because He is faithful. We just need to call on Him, for "God is our refuge and strength, always ready to help in times of trouble" (Psalm 46:1, NLT).

Z. Kathy Cameron

---

* The name Sasha is a pseudonym.

July 24

I Needed a Miracle

"Have I not commanded you? Be strong and courageous. Do not be afraid; do not be discouraged, for the LORD your God will be with you wherever you go."
—Joshua 1:9, NIV

My husband had started to experience severe blurriness in his right eye. This led to an afternoon of numerous medical appointments in quick succession, and by six o'clock he was undergoing emergency surgery. His retina had detached and was badly torn. Throughout the surgery I sat alone, praying for God to guide the surgeon's hand and begin the healing process.

Afterward the ophthalmologist said all the right words, but I sensed a lack of optimism that the eye could be saved. My husband and I began the long drive home on icy roads and falling snow. *Lord, I don't need this!* I silently cried.

"Have I not commanded you? Be strong and courageous [Joshua 1:9, NIV]."

The night seemed endless. I sat with my husband, making sure he kept his head in the exact position needed to prevent any further damage, inserting drops at the prescribed times.

Morning broke. We had to leave for a follow-up appointment, so I quickly got ready and went out to start the car and warm the engine a little. I stepped out to find our driveway had turned into an ice rink, and our car resembled an ice sculpture. The snow had turned into freezing rain overnight. My heart sank, tears welled, and I felt alone and afraid. "Lord, I don't need this!"

"Once again, 'have I not commanded you? . . . Do not be afraid; do not be discouraged, for the Lord your God will be with you wherever you go' [verse 9, NIV]."

I bowed my head and called out to God for help. Miraculously I was able to open the car door and start the car. The ice was another problem. With the scraper I started to scrape and chip it away but quickly realized the enormity of the problem. "Lord, I don't need this!" I cried again!

"My child, 'what is impossible with man is possible with God' [Luke 18:27, NIV]."

With mixed emotions, I ventured inside to help my husband. As he held tightly to my arm, we moved slowly toward the door. My heart was racing. *Lord, I need a miracle!* And He delivered, for all around our vehicle lay piles of shattered ice. The car and driveway were ice-free. God had delivered my miracle at the precise time it was needed. No cry for help goes unnoticed. He is always with us wherever we go!

Dorian Honey

July 25

When Hope Runs Dry

May the God of hope fill you with all joy and peace as you trust in him, so that you may overflow with hope by the power of the Holy Spirit.
—Romans 15:13, NIV

I had so much hope at the start of the year. A surgery for my chronic health condition was on the horizon, promising an end to my pain and struggle. I was looking forward to a future filled with possibilities, eagerly anticipating life post-hospital. However, reality painted a different picture. Post-surgery, I received devastating news—the operation had not been successful. My carefully laid plans fell apart. A heavy weight settled on my heart as hope slipped through my fingers. *Why is this happening?* I asked myself. *How am I supposed to carry on with my life now?* To top it all off, my much-needed summer vacation had to be canceled. I simply did not have the energy to travel.

Then an unexpected opportunity arose. A women's retreat, previously out of reach due to my planned vacation, still had a few available spots. Torn between longing for some encouragement and fearing exhaustion, I decided to attend. And let me tell you, our God is good. He finds opportunities to bless His children in all places, at all times! That weekend provided an unexpected turning point in my life. Through genuine conversations, insightful workshops, and quiet moments of prayer, God began to mend my broken heart and reignite my dreams. He did not heal me or take away the challenges that I was facing, but He gave me renewed hope. It was like a gentle whisper that assured me, *I am with you, and I still have so many plans for you. Yes, even after all you have been going through, I have not given up on you. Your time will come. This isn't over yet.*

We often become so preoccupied with our plans and expectations that we overlook God's limitless creativity. We crave immediate solutions that align with our vision, forgetting His capacity to work wonders beyond our comprehension. Remember, if God could conquer death and restore life in just three days, surely He can transform our circumstances! Sometimes the greatest act of faith is surrendering our agendas and trusting in His perfect timing, even when it feels like our world is falling apart. Remember, "Those who know your name trust in you, for you, LORD, have never forsaken those who seek you" (Psalm 9:10, NIV). Keep trusting!

Karin Tegeman

July 26

When I Cannot—He Can

But I am poor and needy;
Yet the LORD thinks upon me.
You are my help and my deliverer;
Do not delay, O my God.
—Psalm 40:17, NKJV

I felt terrified as I stared at the list in my hand. It outlined symptoms I had been experiencing from chronic liver disease over the past several years. Profound exhaustion, brain fog, aching joints, heart palpitations—it went on and on. I had presented this list to other liver specialists, but the answer was always, "You're sick, but not sick enough for a liver transplant." As I remembered all my failed attempts to find help, a shroud of discouragement settled over me.

In my misery I angrily cried, "God, You have to figure this out for me! I'm tired of trying." I cannot say that I felt peace at that moment, but I did feel something akin to relief that I had let go of the responsibility for my care.

Proverbs 3:5, 6 reads,

> Trust in the LORD with all your heart,
> And lean not on your own understanding;
> In all your ways acknowledge Him,
> And He shall direct your paths (NKJV).

Up to this point, I had not completely trusted God. Sure, I had let Him handle some of the smaller details while I acted as the master of my fate. But when I completely surrendered, profound change took place. It was as if He had been patiently waiting for me to become so desperate that the only place to look was up.

I walked into Dr. Gilroy's office, clutching my list and an outline of my demands. My husband and I had emotionally and mentally prepared to double-team this poor soul if he tried to dismiss my situation. Several minutes later the door swung open, and a sharp-looking gentleman entered the room. Before I could even open my mouth to say hello, he said, in a rich Australian accent, "OK, Mrs. McCluskey, I've looked through your images, and you need a liver transplant. I think my hospital is the best fit for you, and this is why."

I looked at my husband and burst into tears as joy and relief flooded through me. The Lord had done it—without my help. The moment I surrendered, He said, "Let Me supply all your needs" (see Philippians 4:19). When we cannot—He can! Why do we wait so long to surrender?

Katie McCluskey

July 27

Two or Three

*"For where two or three are gathered together in My name,
I am there in the midst of them."*
—Matthew 18:20, NKJV

I want to underscore the importance of intercessory prayer for friends and family, for my story is a living testimony to its power.

Whether the need for help is related to physical, spiritual, financial, or relational needs or a mix of all of the above—people need prayer. I am convinced beyond a shadow of a doubt that my prayer warriors brought me through my liver transplant journey. There are times when we simply do not have the strength to pray for ourselves. When life gets so hard that just making it through the day demands all our focus, knowing you have a team of God-fearing, loving Christians bolstering you up in prayer brings such a sense of peace and calm.

Paul reminds us, "Be anxious for nothing, but in everything by prayer and supplication, with thanksgiving, let your requests be made known to God; and the peace of God, which surpasses all understanding, will guard your hearts and minds through Christ Jesus" (Philippians 4:6, 7, NKJV). Ironically it has been during the worst storms in my life that I have experienced the deepest peace. We can rest assured that, though the storm may rage all around us, it cannot dislodge us from the boat if Jesus is present with us.

If you are struggling and trying to control the course of your life, I would kindly ask if you have surrendered all to Jesus. There is such power and joy in letting go. Jesus can be trusted to guide your life because no one loves you more. He loves you best. In this sinful world we will endure broken bodies and spirits, but the Master Creator and Healer can use our infirmities to further His work in our lives and through our stories.

Jesus is just waiting to answer our prayers. It may not always be in the time we wish or in the way we expect, but it is always exactly the way we need. And while we may not all be physically healed on this side of heaven, we can have perfect healing, perfect peace, in our hearts.

Does someone need your prayers today? Then lift them up, and remember to "pray for each other so that you may be healed. The prayer of a righteous person is powerful and effective" (James 5:16, NIV). Amen!

Katie McCluskey

July 28

Pushing Buttons

*I waited patiently for the L*ORD*;*
And He reached down to me and heard my cry.
—Psalm 40:1, NASB

A few weeks ago I was in Memorial Hospital with my husband, who was recovering from surgery. The new surgery unit was large and impressive. I had to go downstairs to my car to retrieve something, leaving my husband in recovery with our son and grandson. Getting on the elevator, I pushed the button for the ground floor. When the elevator stopped, the door did not open. After waiting for a few moments, I pushed a different button, thinking it might solve my problem. I could hear the elevator trying to open its door, but there was no response. After a total of five attempts to escape, I realized I was stuck in the elevator and began to look for an emergency button on the panel in front of me. I found nothing.

I searched the wall of the elevator for an emergency phone and then noticed an elevator door behind me standing open. Five times it had opened and closed before I discovered I had been looking in the wrong place for the answer to my cry for help! I felt so stupid as I stepped out of the elevator, wondering how many people had walked past and noticed the woman inside, standing with her back to the open door instead of simply turning around and walking out.

How often in life do we begin pushing God's "buttons," expecting a swift and specific answer to prayer? We wait impatiently, pushing the same button repeatedly, wondering why God is so slow to answer our plea for help. Often He has already provided the answer, but we do not recognize it because He did not respond in the manner we expected He should.

In his book on prayer, M. L. Andreasen writes, "Another reason why God does not answer all questions immediately is found in the fact that it is not best for us to have Him settle all questions. He wants us to wrestle with the problem ourselves and attempt to find the solution."*

Sister White writes, "We are to rest in the Lord, and wait patiently for Him. The answer to our prayers may not come as quickly as we desire, and it may not be just what we have asked; but He who knows what is for the highest good of His children will bestow a much greater good than we have asked, if we do not become faithless and discouraged."† Let us wait patiently on the Lord. He hears and will answer.

Dottie Barnett

---

* M. L. Andreasen, *Prayer* (Calhoun, GA: TEACH Services, 2006), 81.
† Ellen G. White, *Sons and Daughters of God* (Washington, DC: Review and Herald®, 1955), 92.

July 29

Hannah's Surrender

"Go in peace, and the God of Israel grant you what you have asked of him."
—1 Samuel 1:17, NIV

Hannah was barren—a woman of affliction. For a woman in Bible times to have self-worth or value, she needed to bear a son, just as it is today in some parts of the world. The Bible is pretty stark: her husband "had two wives; one was called Hannah and the other Peninnah. Peninnah had children, but Hannah had none" (1 Samuel 1:2, NIV). Year after year Hannah went to the tabernacle with the family to pray, seemingly in vain. Her frustration, sadness, and grief were aggravated as "her rival kept provoking her in order to irritate her" (verse 6, NIV).

Hannah's husband, Elkanah, loved her dearly. He was sympathetic, tender, caring, and kind, giving her a double portion of the peace offerings and doing everything he could to encourage her. But nothing could fill the void in her life. She lacked the most precious gift life could offer—a child—more specifically, a male child. Why had God closed her womb?

One year, when she went to the tabernacle, she wept in anguish. She poured out the bitterness of her heart and soul. She believed that the God of heaven alone could lift the burden off her shoulders, so she cast it upon Him through prayer—for God had promised to meet His children at the tabernacle. And she made a vow as to what she would do if God answered her prayer.

Her vow: "LORD Almighty, if you will only look on your servant's misery and remember me, and not forget your servant but give her a son, then I will give him to the LORD for all the days of his life" (verse 11, NIV). Then, "in the course of time Hannah became pregnant and gave birth to a son. She named him Samuel, saying, 'Because I asked the LORD for him' " (verse 20, NIV).

Why did God answer her only after she made the vow? I do not think making the vow was the difference maker. I believe God waited until He knew she was ready to keep the vow—when she was ready to surrender *all* to have what God wanted to give her. Have we ever vowed to surrender ourselves completely to the Lord but failed to fulfill our vow? I am so glad that when God promised to send His Son, He fulfilled His vow to us. May we surrender our all—and fulfill our vows to Him.

Ardis Dick Stenbakken

July 30

Manoah's Wife, Nameless, Childless

Delight thyself also in the LORD: *and he shall give thee the desires of thine heart.*
—Psalm 37:4, KJV

Manoah's wife was a godly woman who remained nameless in the Bible. She was also barren, which, for a Hebrew woman, was the greatest calamity. But she was a privileged woman who experienced a preincarnate appearance of the Messiah. The angel of the Lord visited her with the happy message that her barrenness would pass and she would become the mother of an unusual son.

Some of the greatest men of the Hebrew nation were born of formerly barren women, including Sarah, Rebekah, Hannah, and Elizabeth. In a special sense these children were gifts from God given to parents who were wholly devoted to God. He could trust the children would be reared in a way that would enable them to be used as special instruments of the Lord on behalf of His people.

To the childless wife of Manoah, "the angel of the Lord" appeared with the message she would have a son through whom God would deliver Israel. The angel gave her instructions concerning her health habits and the rearing of her child. "Now therefore beware, I pray thee, drink not wine nor strong drink, and eat not any unclean thing" (Judges 13:4, KJV). The same prohibition was to be imposed upon the child from birth with the addition that his hair should not be cut, for he was to be consecrated to God as a Nazarite from his birth.

The woman shared the message from the angel with her husband. Then, fearful that they may make some mistake in the important responsibility committed to them, the husband prayed, "Let the man of God which thou didst send come again unto us, and teach us what we shall do unto the child that shall be born" (verse 8, KJV).

When the angel reappeared, Manoah's anxious inquiry was, "How shall we order the child, and how shall we do unto him?" (verse 12, KJV). The previous instruction was repeated, and nine months later, the Divine promise to the God-fearing parents was fulfilled with the birth of a son, whom they named Samson. God granted them the desires of their hearts.

Today's scripture invites us to find our delight in the Lord. When He is our greatest desire, we find we have all we need. He alone is the desire and delight of all the ages.

E. May Clarke

July 31

God's Face and the Wind

They will see His face.
—Revelation 22:4, NIV

"Will you please talk with Becks?" Melissa asked.

I had stopped by Melissa's home with a dinner casserole. If I needed to make one, I might as well make two—and share. Glancing at my watch, I knew it was possible to spare a few minutes, so I nodded.

"Hallelujah!" Melissa fairly shouted, jumping up and down. "She'll have an answer for you, Becks," she said excitedly, running into the family room. "She always has an answer!"

Groaning inwardly, I thought to myself, *Yes, I usually have a comment or two. But, no, I do not always have an answer.* And then I was introduced to Becks. Masses of curly red hair made her green eyes pop. Freckles dotted her turned-up nose, giving her an impish look.

"I don't believe in God anymore 'cause I've never seen his face," Becks said. "Not on TV or in magazines and definitely not in person. My aunt and uncle are visiting, and they say it's safer to believe only in things you can see."

Melissa turned her expectant eyes to me.

Taking a deep breath and offering a quick prayer for wisdom, I said, "Well, Becks, I've met other people with the same perspective as your aunt and uncle."

Becks threw an I-told you-so glance at Melissa.

"Do you believe in the wind?" I asked.

Becks tilted her head to the side. It was obvious she was thinking. Finally she nodded vigorously, red curls bouncing around her head.

"Have you ever actually seen the wind?" I asked.

"I've seen what it can do," she replied promptly. "The wind blew the roof right off our chicken coop," Becks said, laughing. "We were collecting chickens from neighboring yards for a couple of days." She paused. "But, no, I've never seen the wind."

"There," Melissa said decisively. "You see, Becks? I told you I believe God exists because I've seen what He can do—even if I've never seen His face in real life."

"You will see His face someday, along with Job and many others," I said (see Job 19:26, 27). "That is going to be one amazing experience!"

"I want to see His face too," Becks said slowly.

And then we talked about examples of what we have seen God do. No matter I was a bit late for my earthly appointment . . .

Arlene R. Taylor

August 1

Mean Ol' Mrs. M

He shall give His angels charge over thee, to keep thee.
—Psalm 91:11, KJV

The whole summer long I shuddered as my two older sisters told me how mean my fifth-grade teacher, Mrs. M, could be and that I should be prepared to have a very bad year in her classroom. Over and over I heard the horror stories they told, and I felt so afraid.

On the first day of school, I timidly walked into my fifth-grade classroom. Surprised at how good everything looked, I was happy to see all my classmates and eager to begin the new school year.

My mother was a school bus driver, and I always rode the one-hour route with her, even though we lived only two blocks from school. Now that I was in fifth grade, I wanted to walk to school. Finally Mom gave in and allowed me to walk to school. I arrived early and was the first student in the classroom. Mrs. M was quite OK with my being there, and we were able to chat a bit. The year progressed, and I continued to arrive early each day. Mrs. M and I would talk; she would give me help when I needed it, or we would just sit quietly in our seats. I liked Mrs. M. She was not mean at all. Though my grades were not good in my earlier years, they soon began to improve, and I slowly grew in confidence. I still felt shy, did not like to read aloud, and was afraid of spelling bees.

The year passed quickly. On the last day of school, Mrs. M told the class she had been taking a college class and that her big assignment was to study one student and write a monthly paper about that student. She asked if anyone could guess which student she had chosen. Several students thought she had selected them, but I knew in my heart she had chosen me. I was just too shy to say so. Finally she admitted I was the one. She said that on the morning she had to choose, she decided the first student who walked through her door would be the one she would select to study. That was the very first day I came to school early. Though I never read any of her papers, my fifth-grade year with mean ol' Mrs. M gave me a love of lifelong learning.

Thank You, dear Savior, for sending Your human angel to watch over me for that most important school year. My mean ol' Mrs. M has left me with fond memories that I love to reminisce over in my old age.

Avonda White-Krause

August 2

A Fish Called Nemo

"Look at the birds of the air: they neither sow nor reap nor gather into barns, and yet your heavenly Father feeds them. Are you not of more value than they?"
—Matthew 6:26, ESV

For the ten years I taught early childhood classes, my classroom always had plants; small, manageable pets; and such natural objects as rocks, sand, seeds, nuts, pinecones, and shells. I often had a beta fish to help teach the children responsibility as they learned how to take care of a living creature. If a parent agreed, a child could take the fish home during the Easter, Christmas, or Thanksgiving holidays. I took it home for the summer.

Several years ago our fish, named "Fishy Nemo" by the class, died suddenly. The children were very disappointed, but I assured them we would get another one. When I went to the pet store, I was surprised to discover they had closed for good. I asked my coworkers to help us find a new fish but without success. It never occurred to me that God's plan was being worked out. The good Lord, who knows the end from the beginning, was teaching me a lesson.

The children kept asking for a fish, so I decided to get one during the Easter break. On March 13, 2020, we all went home for an ordinary weekend—but we never came back. A robocall informed us that all schools in the district were closed until further notice.

Honestly I do not know why our fish died suddenly or why the pet store closed at the same time. But I took it as it came, and all I said was, "It is the Lord. Let him do what seems good to him" (1 Samuel 3:18, ESV). I waited for schools to reopen—but they never did. The coronavirus pandemic prevented them from reopening for a very long time.

What would have happened to "Fishy Nemo" if it had not died before we left for that fateful weekend? A little fish does not cost a lot, but it is still a living creature, and God has His eyes on all His creatures, no matter how small. He knew ahead of time about the shutdown. If we had a fish in our classroom, it would have died. No wonder we never found one, despite our best efforts.

God is an all-knowing Father. He cares for His children. When we trust Him day by day, He will prove His love for us. He knows the end from the beginning, right? So we can confidently say, "Thank You, Father, for being in control. We can leave everything in Your able hands!"

Mabel Kwei

August 3

A Reminder From Crayon Art

Whoever has no rule over his spirit is like a city broken down, without walls.
—Proverbs 25:28, NKJV

Recently my four-year-old child drew a picture of me, as only a preschooler can draw. Scraggly, wiggly lines somewhat resembled a human figure, but it was difficult to make sense of the drawing. I pointed and inquired about various points of the drawing, trying to figure out which lines represented my head, face, legs, arms, and tummy. I asked if the lines at the end of the arm represented my hand, and my child confidently replied they were my phone. My heart skipped a beat.

My conscience had been pricked. Through a four-year-old's crayon drawing, my problem was pushed to the forefront and grabbed my attention. It was a problem I had chosen to ignore. I did not want to acknowledge that my smartphone and social media usage were out of control. But now even my child saw me and my phone as inseparable. I needed a good dose of self-control.

But self-control is easier said than done. For some it may be a second slice of cake they cannot resist. For some it might be yielding to the temptation of an admirer other than their spouse. For others it may be telling a lie in order to look good in the eyes of their colleagues. And what about the familiar flash of anger during rush hour traffic that results in twisted words flowing from your mouth?

Galatians 5:22–24 tells us that self-control is part of the fruit of the Spirit. Without the Holy Spirit to guide us, give us strength, and remind us when we forget the importance of self-control, it is very difficult for us to be able to control our appetites and passions. We need the Holy Spirit if we truly want to change.

I had previously attempted to use self-help techniques to get rid of my addiction. Lists of dos and don'ts did not help me curb my social media addiction. I had to accept that, in my own strength, I am weak. I need the Holy Spirit to give me the power to overcome. So began my journey to reduce the time I spent in that bottomless pit called the internet and, instead, to connect with my family, pursue my ambitions and hobbies, and above all, spend time seeking the kingdom of God by studying His Word and praying.

Shylet Chabata Dzvene

August 4

A Cell Phone Story

Train up a child in the way he should go,
and when he is old he will not depart from it.
—Proverbs 22:6, NKJV

I love going to church with my nephew, Prince. I am happy to see him learn new things about God and bond with his cradle-roll classmates. One fine Sabbath morning, as we went to church, I realized I had left my cell phone at home. As I frantically looked for it in my bag, Prince politely said, "It's OK because we are going to church. I think you said that we should not use a cell phone while we are in the church."

His words shocked me, and I immediately stopped going through my bag. I said, "Oh, I am glad you remembered! Thank you for reminding me."

He was referring to an incident that had happened sometime earlier. I felt humbled to be corrected by a child and happy, at the same time, to know how well he had retained the lesson I had taught him. How amazing he was able to recall those exact words. I did not realize he had been listening so closely to what I said.

This experience reminded me just how crucial our role as grown-ups is to children and young people in training them for life and Christ. Sometimes we think they are oblivious to our words and actions, but they are not. They remember what we do and the words we speak. Our deeds and speech are powerful, and we can use them to create ripples of joy, hope, faith, and love in the hearts of our children instead of sowing sorrow, pain, hate, and discouragement. The lessons they learn from us can last a lifetime.

In our roles as Christian women, as mothers, grandmothers, guardians, caregivers, tutors, and teachers, we have a great responsibility. Through God's grace, may we never waste the blessing and opportunity to participate in Jesus' great commission as we minister to the children He has entrusted to us.

Lord, thank You for the golden opportunity to train and make a positive impact on the lives of the young people entrusted to our care. Thank You for the chance to engage with them in meaningful conversations and to teach and model to them valuable life lessons. Please continue to inspire, guide, and equip us with Your Holy Spirit. Amen.

Ebonie Barde Base

August 5

God Uses Ordinary People

"Speak, Lord, for your servant is listening."
—1 Samuel 3:9, NIV

Have you ever felt you were not living up to what God expects of you? Maybe you think there are so many other people out there who are much better at being instruments God can use. It sure seems like He hears their prayers more than your own. I have felt that way.

One day after the church service, a woman I know rushed in, looking flustered. Her phone had gone missing. Several of us immediately started to help her search for it. We looked everywhere. The senior pastor and various deacons were involved. I took her to the lost and found with the hope that someone had found it and turned it in. No one had.

We went back into the sanctuary and started to search the pews again, with the help of many people. A young boy even offered to lie on the floor and look beneath the pews to see if the phone had managed to slide down. No luck there, either.

As the woman grew more distressed, her brother told her that perhaps she should just accept that her phone had been stolen. I decided to look in the foyer again. As I headed back there, I whispered a prayer, "God, you know where that phone is. Please lead me to it." The words were barely uttered when I noticed a dark shape on a small cabinet at the back of the church. I walked over, and it was indeed a phone. I held it up and yelled, "I have a phone here."

She ran toward me with so much hope on her face. She took it out of my hand and, with the biggest smile, confirmed it was her phone. To prove it, she showed us the family photo that served as her wallpaper—and all the missed calls from her brother who had called, hoping we would hear the phone ring. It had been on silent for the church service.

When she thanked me, I told her it was God's doing because I found the phone just after I had asked Him to lead me to it. It was all God.

I was amazed. I have witnessed answered prayer before, but this time it came as a jolt. God had used ordinary me to make someone's day better. So many had been involved in looking for the phone, but God had shown me where to find it. God wants to use all of us. He delights in choosing and using ordinary people like you and me—people who are willing to hear His voice and do what He says.

Jean Arthur

August 6

Come, You Will Be Fine

"Come," he said.
Then Peter got down out of the boat, walked on the water and came toward Jesus.
—Matthew 14:29, NIV

I'm sure I will never get to that national park; it is so far away," I said to a friend one day. The Dry Tortugas National Park is two and a half hours by boat from Key West, Florida, USA. My mom and I were making our way through the national parks, and I was just a little leery of going so far out into the ocean in the middle of nowhere. Then, one day, we called a friend we did not realize had moved to Florida.

"Come to Florida, and we will take you to the three national parks here," my friend excitedly shared.

As the time grew nearer, I upheld our trip to God, and He began to give me signs and assurances that it would be OK to go out into the middle of the ocean.

One morning I read Matthew 14:29, where Jesus calls Peter out onto the water to walk toward Him. And I felt impressed that it would be OK to leave the familiar solid ground and trust. Another time I walked into the house as my husband, Ron, was listening to a man on a ham radio from the Dry Tortugas Island. Ron had never before heard anyone from there. On yet another occasion, while driving and listening to the radio, I heard a man say, "We shouldn't spend our time in fear but instead crowd it out with praise and songs." Then one day I walked into Costco, and on those big TVs at the entrance, I saw a plane soaring over glaciers in Alaska. As memories came flooding back, God reminded me, "*You've done that—and you were fine!*"

On the night before our departure, God gave me yet another assurance. Our friends wanted to do a dry run from our hotel to the boat check-in place. As we rounded the corner to the dock, I saw the boat arrive. Pretty amazing odds to see it there at that exact moment. It felt as though God were saying, "Picture the boat coming back. It does come back." The next day, we experienced seven- to eight-foot swells on the way back from the island, but I had no doubt the boat would safely return.

Now, consider the many signs and assurances God has given us about His return. Here are just a few reminders: Acts 1:11, Revelation 1:7, and 1 Thessalonians 4:16, 17. Let us sing and praise Him while we wait. Rest assured—it will happen, and we will be fine.

Diane Pestes

August 7

Denomination Versus Jesus

And I, if I be lifted up from the earth, will draw all men unto me.
—John 12:32, KJV

I recently received a phone call from a long-lost cousin. He lives in the state of California, and I live in the state of Georgia, USA. Neither one of us has a social media presence, and over the years, we lost contact with each other. He called because he planned to visit Atlanta, Georgia, and wanted to know if we could get together. When I asked him the purpose of his visit, he informed me that he was coming to check on a friend who had "turned his back on God."

I responded, "Has he truly turned his back on God, or has he just decided he no longer wants to be a member of our denomination? Because those are two totally different things."

Allow me to explain. I was born, bred, and raised in the denominational faith. I am a fourth generation on my maternal side and a third generation on my paternal side, which includes ministers, head elders, and pastors' wives in the ancestral mix. I was that kid who was always in front of the church, singing at tent revivals, telling the children's story, and being active in all the children's ministries. As a young person I served as a youth church clerk and on the editorial staff of the church newspaper. In college I sang with one of the choirs and served in the student government body. But even though I did all those things, I was just going through the motions when it came to adhering to denominational doctrines.

Most of the time I resented all the rules and regulations. Honestly I did not have a personal relationship with God. And because of this lack, it was easy to eventually turn my back on the church and go searching for "freedom," similar to the prodigal son in Luke 15.

However, God is merciful and always seeks to redeem His lost children. I attended a revival, where I was introduced to Jesus as my Friend. For the first time I saw Him as my loving Creator, Savior, and Lord rather than as a harsh dictator who did not want me to have any fun. In time the doctrines became guidelines that have helped me live a richer, fuller life with Him. I still stumble, but it is easier to live within the boundaries set by Him because I love Him—and am loved by Him.

Do you know someone who needs to be introduced to Jesus as a loving Savior? Perhaps that someone is you.

Kristina E. Smith

August 8

The Way

Jesus answered, "I am the way."
—John 14:6, NIV

I woke up one bright spring morning and thought of my friends and family and how much I loved them. I enjoyed being with them, and it was important to me that they always have the very best in life. I did not want to think of them having anything less. Yet had I ever felt comfortable enough to tell them about the Way?

It concerned me that if I loved them as much as I claimed, why did I find it so hard to talk to them naturally about Jesus' love for us and His Word to us? Times together came and went, and still I did not share Jesus. Did they even know there was a way for us to be together forever throughout eternity?

Was it enough just to pray? Has God not called us to action? Even to the point of what might feel uncomfortable? They are my adult children and grandchildren, friends and family—do I just leave it and assume they will find out for themselves or hope someone else tells them? Our lives are so easily filled with fussing over incidentals, but what about helping our friends and loved ones find their way to Jesus? To heaven? Surely nothing matters more than this. Nothing is more important than this.

Surely this is what we must do! Opportunities to speak of our heavenly Father can be found at every turn. Our adult children look to us for guidance on many things, so why not tell them the most important thing? Why not share Jesus?

It does not matter if we find it hard to begin or if we start out feeling uncomfortable. Jesus speaks these words of life to all: "I am the way" (John 14:6, NIV). When we acknowledge Him and His power to forgive us for all the things we have messed up on, and when we can have His courage to be honest with our families about His great love, we allow Him to shine through our lives. Then sharing Jesus will become the focus and joy of our lives. It will become the most natural thing for us to do. And we can look forward to living with those we love through all eternity.

Help us, Lord God, to step forward boldly and let the beauty of Your love shine through us to our loved ones. May we all know You personally as the Way.

Laura A. Canning

August 9

Skippy the Horse

"'Rejoice with me, for I have found the piece which I lost!' Likewise, I say to you, there is joy in the presence of the angels of God over one sinner who repents."
—Luke 15:9, 10, NKJV

Scrolling through social media, I noticed a local posting, an appeal for people to look out for a horse on the loose. Skippy had arrived at a new home in my town and had jumped a fence the same day. A phone number was provided in case anyone spotted the runaway animal. Many responded with well wishes, and I brought Skippy to the Lord in prayer. He who sees the sparrow fall could bring a horse safely home. But days went by and Skippy was nowhere to be found.

It seemed like everyone in our town of thirteen thousand people was talking about Skippy. Families went for car rides on the rural back roads searching for the wayward animal. People with drones volunteered to search for Skippy. But this was not the only story in the local news. A major storm was approaching—a nor'easter was heading straight toward our town.

Our area was pummeled with snow, sleet, and ice. High winds and freezing rain toppled trees and electric poles, leaving many without power and blocking roads. Over a foot of snow covered our previously bare ground, and schools closed for two days. Again, I mentioned Skippy to the heavenly Father. Online postings showed local storm damage and expressed concern for Skippy.

When the storm finally ended, I went to my regular exercise class, where everyone spoke about Skippy. One woman felt he would probably be dead by the time he was found. I disagreed and remarked horses are intelligent animals, capable of finding shelter and pawing down through the snow for grass to eat. However, on my drive home, I contemplated our discussion and felt melancholy as I realized the possibility of bad news about Skippy.

Once home I saw a wonderful announcement on social media! Skippy had been found safe on top of Green Mountain, outside of town, and was now home! Joyfully I read the many messages rejoicing and praising God! Yet how much more joy there is when God's children turn to Him! We bring joy to God whenever we surrender and commit our ways to Him. "He will rejoice over you with gladness, He will quiet you with His love, He will rejoice over you with singing" (Zephaniah 3:17, NKJV).

Marsha Hammond-Brummel

August 10

Do You Have a Favorite?

But if you show partiality, you commit sin, and are convicted by law as transgressors.
—James 2:9, NKJV

With a nine-year-old daughter and two boys aged eight and five, my mother found herself expecting again at age forty. The story goes that when she found out she was having twins eight months into the pregnancy and called to tell my dad, he fell off his chair at work. It was a mighty big surprise. But into the world we came, a month early, my sister and I. We were labeled as fraternal, or unidentical, twins. We were small enough to fit in a shoe box. Our older sister was thrilled that the girls now outnumbered the boys in the family.

We grew up in the same household. Yet we both had our individual and unique personalities. We responded to the events in our lives differently. Our parents loved all five of us the same and showed no favoritism.

The Bible tells of a different scenario concerning a set of twins born to Isaac and Rebekah. Esau was born first and was a skillful hunter. Jacob came second and was a mild man, dwelling in tents (see Genesis 25:27). Unfortunately this difference proved to be a downfall in the family. Isaac loved Esau because he enjoyed eating the game Esau brought home, but Rebekah loved Jacob (see verse 28). Favoritism never fares well in a family, and the children are often the first ones to recognize it is happening. Unfortunately they often take advantage of the situation.

The first mistake came about due to Esau's impulsiveness. He sold his birthright to Jacob because he was hungry and tired. Jacob took advantage of his weariness (see verses 29–34). The second mistake was made by Jacob. By right, as the firstborn, Esau was to receive the blessing from Isaac before he died. Jacob, however, was convinced by his mother to deceive his father into thinking he was Esau. With this conniving plan in place, Jacob brought savory meat to his father under pretense and received the blessing (see Genesis 27:1–29).

Favoritism is defined as the practice of giving unfair preferential treatment at the expense of another. The Bible tells us to "train up a child in the way he should go, and when he is old he will not depart from it" (Proverbs 22:6, NKJV). Let us make sure as Christians that we treat our children and one another equally as our Father in heaven treats us.

Karen M. Phillips

August 11

Evaluating Ourselves

But you, beloved, building yourselves up on your most holy faith, praying in the Holy Spirit, keep yourselves in the love of God, looking forward to the mercy of our Lord Jesus Christ to eternal life.
—Jude 20, 21, NASB

Jude is a book of the Bible that is not well known to many, and I had never read it through, even though it is only twenty-five verses long. When I decided to read it, I was glad to discover some of the following teachings.

In verses 14 and 15, Jude writes that Enoch had already prophesied that God would "execute judgment on all, and . . . convict all the ungodly of all their ungodly deeds which they have done in an ungodly way, and of all the harsh things which ungodly sinners have spoken against Him" (NASB). I like that these verses describe God's justice. He will come to judge everyone, each according to his work.

Did you notice that God judges not only what we do but also what we say? How many times do we give more importance and value to what we do and forget the importance of what we say?

Jude goes on further and helps us understand a little more. In verse 16 he writes, "These are grumblers, finding fault, following after their own lusts; they speak arrogantly, flattering people for the sake of gaining an advantage" (NASB). How many of these characteristics do we have? That is something to think about, particularly as Jude continues with, "These are the ones who cause divisions, worldly-minded, devoid of the Spirit" (verse 19, NASB).

Jude then urges the "chosen ones" to do right and says, "Save others, snatching them out of the fire; and on some have mercy with fear" (verse 23, NASB). "But you, beloved, building yourselves up on your most holy faith, praying in the Holy Spirit, keep yourselves in the love of God, looking forward to the mercy of our Lord Jesus Christ to eternal life" (verses 20, 21, NASB).

Do we build ourselves up in faith, praying as we are moved by the Holy Spirit? Do we stand in the love of God, showing compassion to those who doubt and sharing salvation with others?

It is good to evaluate ourselves, for we want to become like the One who is good, faithful, and filled with love and compassion as we share the good news of salvation with others. May this describe each of us. Amen.

Cecilia Nanni

August 12

El Roi, "The God Who Sees Me"

So she called the name of the Lord *who spoke to her, "You are a God of seeing," for she said, "Truly here I have seen him who looks after me."*
—Genesis 16:13, ESV

Sarai and Abram were married for many years but remained childless. Sarai suggested that her husband sleep with Hagar, her maidservant, so she could have a child through her. Abram complied and slept with Hagar, and she conceived. Now that Hagar was in the coveted position of expecting Abram's child, she despised her mistress. Sarai complained to Abram about Hagar's attitude, and he responded that Hagar was her problem. Sarai dealt harshly with Hagar, who then ran away.

The angel of the Lord found Hagar by a spring of water in the wilderness on the way to Shur. The angel asked her, "Where have you come from, and where are you going?" (Genesis 16:8). Hagar admitted that she was fleeing from her mistress, Sarai. Hagar was told to go back home and submit to Sarai. Then the angel told her, "I will multiply your descendants exceedingly, so that they shall not be counted for multitude" (verse 10, NKJV). He said she would have a son whom she was to name Ishmael because the Lord heard her affliction. That is when Hagar realized that God is a God who sees. She called Him *El Roi* and returned home.

Just as God saw Hagar, He sees you and me today. At times I, too, have felt like running away. I am the third of seven children. My older brother and sister were outgoing, and my four younger brothers were typical boys. I always felt disconnected from my siblings, so I found solace in books.

Growing up, I would always be asked, "Are you so-and-so's sister?" I did not seem to have an identity of my own. I was not an only child, but I was a lonely child. When we feel vulnerable or less than, we can find hope, strength, and power in our *El Roi.*

Hagar was at a well in the desert when she had that encounter and realized God saw her. We may feel invisible at home, church, school, our workplace, or life in general. Do you feel your life is parched due to the circumstances you find yourself in? Do you need confirmation that *El Roi* sees you? Rest assured, my friend, *El Roi* sees you right at this moment. Right where you are. He does not sleep nor slumber, and He has promised never to leave you nor forsake you.

You are the apple of His eye!

Sharon Long

August 13

Trust and Obey

"Blessed is the man who trusts in the Lord, and whose hope is the Lord."
—Jeremiah 17:7, NKJV

God is our Father, and His greatest desire is that we trust Him. God longs for our trust, which fosters closeness and intimacy, just as our human parents do. Trust is about togetherness and mutual agreement. It requires obedience, for trust and obedience go hand in hand, as the hymn reminds us: "There's no other way to be happy in Jesus, but to trust and obey."* This combination produces true happiness because it deepens our relationship with God, bringing us closer to His heart. God's greatest desire is to see us filled with joy—a joy that springs from deep internal happiness.

Obedience means complying with God's requests and submitting to His will, which is always for our benefit. Each of us has a unique calling—a purpose only we can fulfill. While it may be daunting to obey God, especially when His call seems beyond our capabilities, we must remember that when He calls, He also equips us. The foundation for success is trust. We do not need to wait until we have all the answers or see the entire path ahead; we just need to believe and trust Him for the strength we need to be obedient.

We are God's hands and feet on this earth, and He calls us to partner with Him in His work. God desires that everyone live with Him in heaven, and He uses us to reach out to others, to bring them into His kingdom. The Bible teaches that if we are not willing to leave everything behind for Him, we are not worthy of Him (See Matthew 10:37, 38).

God called me to leave New York City and minister in the nearby state of Pennsylvania. At first I was afraid, but I chose to obey. Though I live alone, I am not lonely because I feel His presence with me. Since obeying His call, God has opened doors of opportunity. In my first week in a new town, He gave me my first Bible student. Now I have twelve, and more are coming. Friends are bringing friends.

My friend, you do not need to fear the unknown; simply step forward in faith and trust Him to provide and equip you with all you need to walk in obedience. God is with you, and He will bless your obedience in ways you cannot even begin to imagine.

Julie Williams

---

* J. H. Sammis, "Trust and Obey" (1887).

August 14

Trust the Lord With Your Teens

For he will command his angels concerning you to guard you in all your ways.
—Psalm 91:11, ESV

Transitioning to high school is always a big deal for teenagers and can be quite stressful for families. Raising a teenager is demanding. My husband and I constantly questioned our approach to parenting.

Our son's senior year got off to a great start. He joined the theater club and track and field, and he looked forward to graduation. Then the COVID-19 pandemic struck and shifted everything. Our son had five online classes and soon became overwhelmed by the daily barrage of emails and endless assignments. Organization and self-guided learning became so complicated, and we watched him slowly fall further and further behind. Yet he clung to one thing. "I'm graduating! I don't know how, but I'm graduating." His faith was unmovable.

My husband and I cried out to the Lord. We prayed, "Lord, we have done everything we could! We have family worship, respect the Sabbath, and have sent our boy to VBS, summer camps, Bible Bowl, and Pathfinders. We have given him unconditional love." My anxiety levels soared, and through it all we sensed the Lord asking us, "Do you trust Me?"

Then God sent us an angel. With school ending in eleven days, our son's AP English teacher, Mrs. Cicero, called.

"Mrs. Wellington, your son has been in our school district since K5, and we love him. We know his potential. With all the turmoil surrounding the Black Lives Matter movement, we refuse to allow your son to fall through the cracks within our school district. What can I do to help?"

Amid the pandemic, she came over to our house and drafted an academic plan to assist him in completing the missing assignments. She invited him over to her house and helped him stay focused and on task. With her help and a lot of hard work on his part, he completed every assignment. He graduated in the class of 2020, went on to start his college program in Atlanta, Georgia, USA, and continues to talk about how God used one person who was willing to say, "Lord, use me."

Friends, trust God! Do not give up on your teenager. God will bless your children. He has promised to command His angels concerning our families. Be patient and trust Him.

Domaz Wellington

August 15

For Our Eternal Good

And we know that in all things God works for the good of those who love him.
—Romans 8:28, NIV

I used to claim the promise in Romans 8:28 for my life, knowing that no matter what life brought my way, it would ultimately be for the best. I did not doubt that God had more interest in my life than even I did.

Because I felt so certain of this, I had the confidence needed to skip an exam that had been scheduled on Sabbath. Missing the exam could put a stop to, or at least pause, my education at the age of fourteen. I knew my decision would have consequences, but at that point it simply meant that God had something better for me.

God was, indeed, good to the more than eight hundred students who did not attend the Sabbath exam. The Education Ministry organized a second session for those who missed it, and we were able to continue our studies. Nevertheless, it changed the lives of many of us. We had a decision to make. For many of my classmates, it meant they would choose to attend a different school. For me I simply continued to trust God was working for my good. The experience gave me the confidence to refuse to take the many other exams scheduled on Sabbath over the years. And God did not fail me.

As I have grown in my walk with the Lord, I now see things a little differently, as my understanding of the passage has deepened. I still claim God's promise and ask Him to work for my good, but now the time frame changed. While I know that God is interested in my temporary good, He also has my highest good at heart—my eternal good.

A few years ago I needed to go through an inevitable and irreversible surgery. A second surgery was required due to what seemed to be the surgeon's negligence. During this trying time I could stop to think about how God would work things out in ways that would impact my eternal good. And not just my eternal good, but for the eternal good of those who occupied the beds next to mine—and even the surgeon's eternal good. By then I knew that God had the highest interest, our salvation, in mind for each of us.

He has your best interests in mind too. He sees the big picture, and He wants to bring all His children home.

Anamaria Maier

August 16

Amid Chaos

*The righteous cry out, and the L*ORD *hears them;*
he delivers them from all their troubles.
—Psalm 34:17, NIV

Several years ago the school where I teach experienced challenges that tested the faith of the staff in unexpected ways. One night the Lord gave me a dream, warning of a potential death at school. Disturbed, I woke up and prayed fervently for God's extended mercies. Little did I know how soon this warning would manifest.

The next day a staff member rushed into my office with urgent news. During recess two of our students, a fifth-grade boy and a third-grade girl, were involved in a head-on collision. The accident happened in a blind spot on the school grounds. The boy suffered from severe headaches, but Lindiwe's condition was much worse. She had sustained a serious brain injury, turning pale as she was quickly rushed to Lady Pohamba Hospital in Windhoek, Namibia.

Lindiwe was admitted to the ICU and quickly placed on respiratory support. The doctors were deeply concerned about the bleeding in her brain and the potential danger it could bring. The situation was dire, and the weight of it all pressed heavily on our hearts. Lindiwe's family had recently suffered the loss of her father, and we hated to think of the added sorrow her accident would bring the family.

In response we halted everything at school to intercede for her. We fasted and prayed, crying out to the Lord to spare her life. As we lifted our voices in unison, the miraculous happened—the bleeding stopped. The medical staff were baffled and could not explain how this had occurred. But we knew the great Physician had stepped in to intervene on behalf of His child. We were so grateful.

A few weeks later Lindiwe returned to school, fully healed. What a miracle! We joyfully gathered to celebrate her life and God's incredible faithfulness. This experience reminded us that the Lord hears the cries of His children and still performs miracles today.

To anyone who is unwell or facing a challenge that seems insurmountable, hold on to your faith. The God who healed Lindiwe is the same yesterday, today, and forever. He has done it before, and He will surely do it again for you.

Emma Nangula Kakona

August 17

Business Partners

But my God shall supply all your need according to his riches in glory by Christ Jesus.
—Philippians 4:19, KJV

One morning, as I was browsing the internet on my laptop, I came across an article with the subject line, "Would you allow God to be your business partner?" After reading the article a whirlwind of thoughts and questions swirled through my mind. I began to wonder whether I could make God a partner in both my business and personal life. How might I invite God to be my business partner? As these thoughts and reflections took hold, I remembered my time as a student at university.

While at university, I encountered many significant academic challenges, and I struggled to meet the extensive demands required to excel and be a top-performing student. During that time I met with the dean to discuss the obstacles I faced. Leaving the meeting, I felt overwhelmed, disheartened, and dejected, especially after failing to successfully complete my first year of studies. Though I cannot recall the exact moment I prayed and invited God to become my senior study partner, I remember the positive changes that followed.

Entrusting my dreams, goals, and aspirations to Him was one of the best decisions I have ever made. Investing my academic pursuits with God, particularly my grades, had a profound effect on my university experience. The dividends derived as a result of God's faithfulness in our partnership propelled me toward the successful pursuit and completion of my degree.

I do not consider myself the most financially adept person, but one thing I do understand is the idea of a return on investment. When you invest your time and money in God, you will always receive a return on your investment. This is how the economy of the kingdom of God works. When we invest in a partnership with God, it will never fail.

No matter what challenges we are facing right now, remember that when we invest our time, energy, and finances into God, He promises to return our investment abundantly—often multiplying it tenfold. We serve an awesome, amazing God. How good He is to each of us.

I want to invite you today to make God your senior business partner in all aspects of your life. It will be the best decision you ever make.

Tamia A. Griffith

August 18

Unexpected Blessings

The Lord will command the blessing on you in your storehouses and in all to which you set your hand.
—Deuteronomy 28:8, NKJV

I had many engagements booked, including a wedding, the wedding shower, birthday celebrations, and speaking appointments. So many of these were close together, and I felt a little stressed. I looked at my wardrobe and realized I needed a few new outfits for the events.

Each day I prayed for God to meet my needs. My budget was somewhat challenged, but I determined that after I had completed all the engagements, I would not be in the red. I disliked red at the end of my budget line. So frugal I would be!

My accountant had good news regarding my income tax return. The Canada Revenue Agency would be refunding me some money I had over-contributed. I praised the Lord for His many blessings. The amount would increase my ability to meet my needs, and the bottom of the budget line would definitely be black.

Unexpectedly it was brought to our church's attention that there were "empty baskets" at the church, mainly from job losses and other unmet needs. The funds budgeted by the church for these emergencies were inadequate, so members assisted privately. I knew I had to contribute. The extra money in my budget was just enough to help. I broke even.

A few days after meeting these needs, I went online to do my banking. My shock was palpable as I noticed a few thousand extra dollars had been deposited into my account. Because of the notation beside the deposit, I suspected it had come from the Canada Revenue Agency. Twelve years prior, my tax return was questioned, and after all my appeals were refused, I decided to pay the amount being challenged, including the interest. The Lord knew my desire to be honest, and I hoped He would one day vindicate me. As the years passed my hope waned. A few days after the deposit, a letter came from the Canada Revenue Agency stating that my twelve-year-old tax claim had finally been approved and refunded. My heartfelt praise and thanks ascended to God. The bottom line of my budget was again black.

God vindicates His children. We should not lose hope. He tells us in Psalm 37:5, "Commit your way to the Lord, trust also in Him, and He shall bring it to pass" (NKJV). And at exactly the right time too. Amazing!

Sonia Kennedy-Brown

August 19

Ever a Father

"And you saw how the Lord *your God cared for you all along the way as you traveled through the wilderness, just as a father cares for his child."*
—Deuteronomy 1:31, NLT

Several years ago, my husband and I were with a friend and his family at Mount Saint Helens, a volcano in southwestern Washington State, USA. It is an active volcano, having last erupted spectacularly in 1980. It is a popular tourist attraction, and most visitors to the area want to see it.

The family included our friend Robert, his new wife, and their infant daughter. Also present were her two daughters from a prior relationship and Robert's fifteen-year-old daughter, Megan, who, through circumstance, had only recently become a part of his life.*

There was a high, steep hill a few miles from the mountain, and it looked like there would be a fantastic view from the top. Everyone but the new mother, the baby, and I chose to make the climb. And everyone started strong. We could easily see their progress from below. Fairly early on, though, Megan began to flag. She slowed down, frequently stopping to look fearfully about. Her body language fairly shouted, *Danger! Terror! Big Mistake! Someone get me off this mountain!*

Robert was bringing up the rear, and it did not take him long to realize what was happening. Remember that he was a brand-new dad to a teenager and an infant. His experience at "dadding" was extremely limited. But while the others went on ahead, he caught up to Megan from behind and held her around the waist, steadying her. Gently he guided her to the top, stopping whenever she needed to stop. From below we could see him talking reassuringly to her.

And they made it. They remained at the summit for a long time with the others, enjoying the view, spending time with each other, taking photos, and just relaxing. The trip down went much better and far more quickly.

Watching them, I thought of our heavenly Father, who is always watchful; always available; and ever eager to help, steady, and support us. That is what loving fathers do. As Robert did not leave a frightened, overwhelmed Megan to navigate the pathway by herself, our Father will not stand by and watch us struggle. He will always step up and do what needs to be done to get us through. We can count on it. He, like Robert, is ever a father.

Carolyn K. Karlstrom

---

* All names are pseudonyms.

August 20

Be a Giver

*And do not forget to do good and to share with others,
for with such sacrifices God is pleased.*
—Hebrews 13:16, NIV

Pakistan is blessed with great beauty. The northern part of our country is particularly mesmerizing and full of the wonders of God's nature. My husband and I were traveling back from north to south Pakistan, and while we descended from the mountains, we noticed someone roasting corn on the roadside.

"Let's stop and get some corn to eat," I said to my husband, and he quickly stopped the car and went to the roadside vendor to buy corn.

I remained in the car, and a little girl with a pack of chewing gum came to my window and asked if I would help her by buying a pack of chewing gum. I looked at the child and noticed she was very young, no more than seven or eight years old. I looked for some loose change in the car and found a few coins. My husband was quite far from the car, and I was not able to call him and ask for some money. I gave the change to the little girl and told her it was not enough to pay for the gum, so she could keep the gum and sell it to someone else. I could tell by the look on her face how happy she was.

She came back to the car again and again to thank me, and even as we drove away, she continued to wave.

God wants us to help others. He loves it when His children are generous. It is good for us to keep Jesus' words in mind, "For I was hungry and you gave me nothing to eat, I was thirsty and you gave me nothing drink" (Matthew 25:42, NIV).

Sometimes we do not realize that what we consider to be very little is very valuable in the sight of the needy. Their needs are great, and our help brings them joy. Whenever we have the opportunity to do good and share with others, we should make the most of the opportunity. We can also look in our neighborhoods, church, and the world around us for those we can help. When we see someone in need, we should not delay in helping. I believe that if we help others and share our blessings, God will bless us. We can never outgive God. The more we share, the more He gives us so that we can share again. As He reminds us in His Word, "Whoever is kind to the poor lends to the LORD, and he will reward them for what they have done" (Proverbs 19:17, NIV).

Farzana Yaqub

August 21

My Surprise

"For I know the plans I have for you," declares the Lord, *"plans to prosper you and not to harm you, plans to give you hope and a future."*
—Jeremiah 29:11, NIV

My husband and I were blessed with a son and a daughter, but when they left home to attend an Adventist boarding school, we became empty nesters.

One day my husband received a call from the Children's Aid Society, asking if we would be willing to take care of two boys, ages eight and ten, for three days. My immediate response was, "I'm not ready to start taking care of children all over again." But my husband convinced me, saying it would be for only three days. Long story short, we ended up having the boys for almost ten years.

The children came with a lot of emotional and behavioral baggage. It turned our home into something quite different from what we were used to. As a pastor my husband was busy with church work, so the responsibility of raising the boys rested on my shoulders. I cried many times and asked the Lord to give me strength to get through the day.

Our daughter, who had married and was living in a different city, moved back home with her husband. This time they brought a dog along with them. One day the dog nipped one of the boys, and when the Children's Aid Society learned of the incident, they felt that the children were not safe living in a house with a dog. We were given the weekend to decide between keeping the children or the dog.

We were in a really great battle. Prayerfully my husband and I approached our daughter and explained the situation. We said, "If the children remain with us, they can receive salvation." Our daughter started to sob and said we should keep the boys but to please make sure the dog would be given to a loving, caring home. Praise the Lord, we did find a really good home for the dog.

Over the years the boys learned about Jesus and began to develop a relationship with Him. Soon they were baptized. Now both have grown and are settled in life, married with two children each. Please remember them in your prayers.

While it may be scary to take the road less traveled, as we follow God's leading, it will always lead to the best rewards.

Alice Emerson

August 22

What If I Had Asked?

Bear ye one another's burdens, and so fulfil the law of Christ.
—Galatians 6:2, KJV

Death affects us all. Sometimes it comes through illness; sometimes it is due to an accident. Death can be expected, but sometimes it arrives suddenly. However we experience it, the questions arise: What will I do with the time that I have left? How will I impact the lives of those around me? How can I be a blessing or a safe place for those I meet or know intimately? I have been thinking about this a lot.

Several years ago the school where I teach had our biannual sports day, which kept us busy all day. At one point I interacted with one of my colleagues as she moved around the sports field. I could tell that her mind was preoccupied. She looked sad, which was a far cry from her normal demeanor. I felt impressed to ask her if she was OK, but it was neither the time nor the place. I told myself I would talk to her the next day.

The next day she was not at work, and we assumed it was because she was exhausted. The following morning I awoke at four thirty to several missed calls. I called back and received news that forever changed my view of the world. Our colleague had been found murdered, along with her eldest daughter and two others. Disbelief, shock, and sorrow washed over me. Anger came next. Later I would experience fear as a woman living in a world where women are often seen as expendable. Our staff room struggled to process the loss, tormented by the death of our fellow teacher. Later that same week two more women were killed in domestic violence disputes. But I was haunted by the loss of my colleague because I will forever wonder, *What if I had spoken to her? Would it have made a difference?*

As women many of us live in unsafe situations. Some of us hide it so well that we fool those around us into thinking everything is all right. God has given us eyes to see and a heart to discern—if we would just look. We are our sisters' keepers. If we see any warning signs, let us not assume everything is well just because we see a smile. It takes so little to genuinely ask, "Are you OK?" If you know someone or if you are someone who needs a safe place—please reach out. There are resources available. May none of us experience the pain of having to question, "What if I had asked?"

Greta Michelle Joachim-Fox-Dyett

August 23

The Lost Keys

Because You have been my help, therefore in the shadow of Your wings I will rejoice.
—Psalm 63:7, NKJV

One day I had a three-thirty appointment at a therapy office, and I left early to do a little shopping. Because I was in a hurry, after closing the door, I put the keys in the sleeve of my cart, which, although the zipper was broken, was halfway fastened. I went into a shop and bought a bowl. I thanked the shop assistant and gave her a spiritual book, *God With Us*, which she happily accepted.

I left in a hurry so that I could get to my appointment on time. After the treatment, at 4:45 p.m., I looked for the keys. But surprise! The keys were not in the cart handle. I took out my purse and everything, but nothing! I did not know what had happened, but one thing was certain: without the keys, I could not get into the apartment. God inspired me, and I called my children, who were getting ready to go on vacation. My darling daughter-in-law answered, and I told her briefly what had happened and then asked her to leave the spare set of my keys with her mother.

The burden was lifted from my heart, and I went for another little shopping trip. When I came out of the shop, something amazing happened. A lady stopped me and asked, "Have you lost your keys?" It was the sales assistant from the shop next to the one where I had bought the bowl. She was already on her way home, but when she met me, she accompanied me to the first shop. When we arrived, the shopkeeper had put a notice in the window about the lost keys in the hope that I would stop by again and she could return them to me. It was a providential meeting! I hugged them both and said to the lady who gave me the keys, "Do you see that God is with us?"

I believe that this experience marked them both, and I pray that the Holy Spirit will work further and convince them of the truthfulness of His Word. For me it was a new confirmation of the wonderful way God's angels synchronize the encounters of those who know the Lord with those who do not know Him yet desire Him.

Thanks be to Him for the opportunities He gives us to confess Him before our neighbors! I pray that the Holy Spirit may water the sown seed so that it may bear rich fruit to His glory and the salvation of as many souls as possible!

Magdalena Toma

August 24

Will Your Anchor Hold?

This hope we have as an anchor of the soul, both sure and steadfast, and which enters the Presence behind the veil.
—Hebrews 6:19, NKJV

I live in Alabama, USA, where we say, "If you don't like the weather, just wait a day; it will change." Today the forecast warned that severe weather was coming. Severe weather is expected when warm air meets cold air. This particular system, we were told, would bring strong winds, hail, thunder and lightning, and lots of rain. The newscaster said to take precautions. So I moved some of my outdoor furniture inside and secured anything that might fly away. Just before I went to bed, I watched the news for the latest update.

Sometime later I was awakened by my cat's loud meowing. Outside, the winds rapped against my house. I felt like Dorothy in *The Wizard of Oz*, afraid my house might start to swirl and fly up into the night sky! I felt anxious, but then the song "Will Your Anchor Hold?" came into my mind, and I started to sing. I pulled out my tablet, looked up my Advent Hymnal app for the words, and read through them.

I was amazed to see I did not know the words as well as I should. I knew the refrain well:

> We have an anchor that keeps the soul,
> Steadfast and sure while the billows roll;
> Fastened to the Rock which cannot move,
> Grounded firm and deep in the Savior's love.*

I kept repeating the refrain as I read through the verses. The fourth verse talks about death and how when we take our last breath, He never fails. Verse five reminds us that when He comes back, we will anchor fast to the heavenly shore.

During the storm I realized that if I could not trust God to protect me in this small storm, how would I be able to trust Him when things get really bad? In Matthew 24, Jesus tells us what to expect in the last days. Tornadoes, pestilence, wars, and rumors of war are nothing compared to the troubles that are coming upon the earth. How will our anchor hold to the Rock of our salvation at that time? As we trust Him today through life's storms, we will find His strength to face tomorrow's storms.

Eva M. Starner

---

* Priscilla J. Owens, "Will Your Anchor Hold?" (1882).

August 25

Fuel for Our Journey Home

And while they went to buy, the bridegroom came; and they that were ready went in with him to the marriage: and the door was shut.
—Matthew 25:10, KJV

How suddenly the mood in the airplane changed after the captain announced we were running out of fuel. Sleeping passengers suddenly awoke. Mothers clutched their babies, eyes wide with terror. The normally subdued hum of the engines gave way to the concerned chatter of fearful passengers. "Are we going to die?" was the question on everyone's lips. Thankfully we survived and landed at an alternate airport to refuel. But we had already missed our connections. Would we also be stranded for the night?

Yes! We found ourselves stuck at an unfamiliar airport, at our own expense, since the airline determined the delay had been caused by a storm—"an act of God." We could get on a flight leaving twelve hours later, but the airline would not put us up at a hotel. They would not even give us a meal ticket or coupon for a taxi. They thanked us for traveling with them and wished us a good night. We were left alone to take care of our out-of-pocket expenses for an overnight hotel room and tips for the shuttle to and from the airport.

Here is an interesting comparison. In the parable of the ten virgins (Matthew 25:1–13), all was well until five ran out of fuel. Suddenly the quiet wait for the bridegroom became a plea of concern as they begged the other five, "Give us some of your oil. We are running out of fuel." But sharing the oil would not be a wise decision. It would result in all the virgins running out of oil. The bridegroom would arrive to find everything in darkness.

What about us today? Are our lamps filled with oil for the journey home? We know the oil in our lamps represents the Holy Spirit. How do we know when we are running out? We can check the light from our lamps, and here is the test: "The fruit [light] of the Spirit is love, joy, peace, longsuffering, gentleness, goodness, faith, meekness, temperance" (Galatians 5:22, 23, KJV). Are we running low on patience, joy, or any of these?

Let us refuel and trim our lamps before the imminent return of the Bridegroom. Better still, let us determine to stay filled with the Holy Spirit, seeking an infilling each day. Only then can we be sure not to run out of fuel.

Annette Walwyn Michael

August 26

Finish the Race

Do you not know that in a race all the runners run, but only one gets the prize? Run in such a way as to get the prize.
—1 Corinthians 9:24, NIV

Earlier this year I had the privilege to attend the last sermon presented by a previous pastor of mine, who is also my very good friend, at his current church before he left for an assignment to Kenya. His sermon, as always, really touched me. He is a powerful speaker whom God is using in great ways. His sermon title was "Finish the Race," and it inspired and blessed me greatly. As I reflected on his message, I was reminded how important it is for us to learn how to persevere.

We are all running a race. At times it feels like a marathon, filled with many hills and valleys, twists and turns. Sometimes it is hard to see what lies around the next bend. We are not always sure we want to continue because of the uncertainty of what may be ahead. Distractions pull at us, often leading us to change direction. We become hungry and feel the need for sustenance. We feel thirsty and just want a bottle of cold water. We grow tired and want to quit the race and switch it out for a comfy chair.

If your race feels overwhelming right now, I want to encourage you. Do not stop. Determine to finish the race. It may be long, but the reward at the end is great. Have faith when you cannot see around the next bend. Have trust in His guidance and protection. Have faith in Him. Stay focused on Him. He will never lead you astray but will keep you on the narrow path, the right path. Feed on His Word; it will provide you with the best sustenance you need to endure. Drink His living water, and you will never be thirsty again. Let Him be your strength, and He will comfort you.

"The Saviour's words to them [His disciples] were full of hope. He knew that they were to be assailed by the enemy, and that Satan's craft is most successful against those who are depressed by difficulties. Therefore He pointed them away from 'the things which are seen,' to 'the things which are not seen.' 2 Corinthians 4:18. From earthly exile He turned their thoughts to the heavenly home."*

At the end of the race, He will be there, coming from the sky to bring us home. Finish the race, my friend. His love is without end; the prize is eternal. Finish the race!

Shannon J. Pigsley

---

* Ellen G. White, *The Desire of Ages* (Mountain View, CA: Pacific Press®, 1898), 662.

August 27

God's Repair Business

Heal me, O LORD, and I shall be healed;
save me and I shall be saved, for You are my praise.
—Jeremiah 17:14, NKJV

My career is in Christian education, and sometimes, as an administrator, the decisions you make are not always popular. One particular case had left a parent very angry and bitter.

As I transitioned from that job locale to another, out of state, I had to travel back to take care of some business before the new person came to fill the empty position. I stayed at a nearby hotel, which happened to be where this angry parent worked. I prayed that I would run into her because I did not want to move away and leave her holding on to her anger. I asked God for an opportunity to use me to help provide healing and relieve her of the bitterness that I knew she harbored against me.

On the morning of my departure, I checked out and was leaving the hotel when I glanced down at my receipt. I realized that they had charged me incorrectly and had not applied the room discount that came with our corporate account. I quickly went back to the front desk to have it corrected. As I waited for the manager to verify the rates, this parent walked by. Remembering my prayer, I called out her name. She turned around and was obviously surprised to see me.

Without hesitation I immediately leaned forward and hugged her. She was a bit apprehensive but remained reserved and polite.

"I heard that you were moving away. I hope it's a good move for you," she said.

I told her I was happy because it meant I would be closer to my grandchildren and family. And then I said, "I've been praying that I'd see you before I left."

Instantly she melted and responded, "Well then, I will give you a huge hug."

And she did. It was a warm, whole-hearted embrace that said everything I knew she could not say out loud. She was choosing to let go and move on.

It was healing for both of us as we felt God lift not one but two burdens before I left—her burden of bitterness and my burden of desire to see her set free.

God is always in the business of repair. When we give Him our heart's permission, He will find the way. Is there anything you want God to free you from?

Nicole Mattson

August 28

A Testimony of Faith and Perseverance

Do not be anxious about anything, but in every situation, by prayer and petition, with thanksgiving, present your requests to God.
—Philippians 4:6, NIV

As I reflect on my academic journey, I realize that I was finding my way home, in terms not only of completing my studies but also of finding my spiritual destination. My story is a testament to God's faithfulness and guidance, even when the path ahead seems uncertain.

In my second year I discovered my passion for internal auditing and envisioned a future in this field. I had pinned all my hopes on attending the University of Pretoria's honors program in Pretoria, South Africa. It is one of two institutions in South Africa that offers a program aligned with the Institute of Internal Auditors in the United States of America. For this reason it is known as a center of excellence. However, during my final year the competitive nature of the honors program left me feeling discouraged. With only sixty spots available and over five hundred applications, I wondered if my dream was unattainable.

To make matters worse I had put all my eggs in one basket. I had applied only to this program. If I was not accepted, I had no backup plan, no direction, and no clear future. The uncertainty felt overwhelming. I left my final exam in tears, lost and uncertain about my future.

At that moment I had given up hope but somehow mustered the faith to ask God for a miracle. Despite my doubts I asked Him to intervene, to open doors and make a way where none seemed possible. Little did I know that God was working behind the scenes.

Through the Ten Days of Prayer and Fasting initiative, I surrendered all my worries to Him, even though I had resigned myself to the idea that the door might be closed. Final decisions were being made, and I had not received any communication from the department. Then the unthinkable happened. God surprised me with an invitation to interview shortly after the Ten Days of Prayer ended. His faithfulness became evident soon after as I received my acceptance letter.

This experience taught me that even when we feel lost or uncertain, God's faithfulness and provision are unwavering. He proved Himself to be a God who opens doors and makes a way for His children where none seems to be possible. So ask yourself today, What am I struggling to surrender to God? What can I present to the Lord in prayer—with thanksgiving?

Minenhle Lindelwe Mlilo

August 29

Even at My Worst

But God put his life on the line for us by offering his Son in sacrificial death while we were of no use whatever to Him.
—Romans 5:8, *The Message*

God made me a doer, and I am going to stop apologizing for it. I have a million ideas, and there was a time when I had the energy to carry most of the good ones to fruition.

It is fun to tell people I went back to college with nine credits at age sixty-four and started a new career at seventy. My goal is to try hard consistently. There are no illusions though. I am so aware that none of this comes from me. I am also slightly socially awkward, and though unintentional I have been known to hurt feelings in a minute and only realize it after the damage is done. My self-criticism sometimes just spills over onto others. And anyone who knows me well will tell you I talk too much. How God chose me is something I will never understand. But He has, and every day He is growing me in new ways for new tasks; I love that about God. He takes the time to show me a better way.

This morning He taught me a new prayer. Right in the middle of praises and requests, I felt an overwhelming sense of the way God loves me in the terrible—those awfully messy seasons we all experience. However, I am not in the terrible now. Life is going well; a new ministry path is opening. But in my life there are moments when loneliness, self-loathing, and a sense of spiritual failure come over me like the wagging finger of doom.

This morning I felt God was saying to me, *"When you feel sorry for yourself, when you barely cling to hope, when you feel a failure, I want you then too. In those weak moments, you are still Mine. I still want to hear from you."* How amazing is that! I love the wording in *The Message* of Romans 5:8: "while we were of no use whatever to him."

It is my earnest desire to be of some use to Jesus, but I have no illusions of who I am. Quite often I pray, "Lord, please don't let me get in Your way!" But He continues to find use for me. Every Christian, at some point, has had the question of why God, in His limitless wisdom, knowledge, and power, would possibly crave companionship with any human. We all know one particular human best, which makes the question more specific and more intense. Despite all the reasons we can give Him for loving us less, He chooses to love more.

Carolyn Huffstickler

August 30

Choose Kindness

If you are kind only to your friends, how are you different from anyone else?
—Matthew 5:47, NLT

No one liked Margaret.* She stood taller and was stronger than anyone else in the fifth grade. She arrived like a whirlwind soon after the school year began, and while her fierce red hair and freckles were enough to get her noticed, it was her meanness that truly set her apart.

Pencils vanished, erasers and crayons snapped in two, and spit wads flew through the air with marksman-like precision. She seemed to enjoy being obnoxious. Recess became a nightmare, for Margaret ruled the playground like a tyrant. Even the boys seemed intimidated.

In those days needlepoint was still taught in school, and it was my favorite class. Every Wednesday Miss Vera taught my class the intricacies of embroidery as we worked on tray cloths and pillow slips. While we stitched she spoke to us about the roses in her garden and the books she loved to read.

"Remember girls," she would say, "the only thing you can take to heaven with you is your character."

I glanced pointedly at Margaret, but she seemed not to notice.

One week Margaret fell ill and missed needlepoint class. Someone mentioned her name, and soon we all shared our Margaret horror stories. After we had finished we waited to hear what Miss Vera would say. Threading a needle, she said thoughtfully, "Margaret has such beautiful handwriting."

With those gentle words Miss Vera showed us how to be kind. Instead of reprimanding us, she quietly demonstrated how to love and gave us a glimpse of Christ's loveliness. No one had ever shown me so clearly what it meant to be like Jesus.

We finished the school year, and I completed my tray cloth. Miss Vera said my lumpy daffodil showed potential. Margaret never returned to school, and memories of our troubled classmate eventually faded. As I grew older, however, I discovered a world full of Margarets—wounded hearts in a wounded world—searching desperately for evidence of love.

Kind words are a balm for broken hearts. Kindness quietly reveals Christ's heart of love toward the hurting women around us—and to the hurting woman within us. It changes us. The kindness we show to others and to ourselves gives a glimpse of Jesus that heals and restores. Let us always choose to be kind.†

Karen Pearson

---
* Margaret is a pseudonym.
† Adapted from Karen Pearson, "The Ministry of Kindness," *Lake Union Herald* 100, no.8 (August 2008): 16. Used with permission.

August 31

Be Perfume

For we are to God the fragrance of Christ among those who are being saved and among those who are perishing.
—2 Corinthians 2:15, NKJV

I was just visiting my spiritual birthplace last week. It is really hallowed ground for me! The line from the great hymn "Amazing Grace" comes to mind: "I once was lost, but now I'm found, was blind but now I see."* Do you remember when that moment happened for you? Some of us have dramatic conversion stories, and others have walked with Jesus from their earliest memories. Both experiences are amazing in their own way, and both get better over time as they deepen and grow.

My family is a product of evangelism. We still praise God for the little church in Ankeny, Iowa, USA, that took the gospel commission seriously. We were the classic yuppie family—you know, the stereotypical young adults who were obsessed with material objects and financial success. We had two babies, two cars, one dog, and a new house. On the outside you could not tell we were interested in biblical things, but God had been preparing our hearts in many unseen ways. Life was hard without Jesus and the Holy Spirit, and when we learned about God's love and His abundant power, it changed our lives!

This church had the nicest people; they provided care for our little, full-of-energy kids over and above anything we had experienced before. We had actually had to leave more than one church elsewhere because our kiddos were so disruptive! But now our emotional and spiritual hunger was being satisfied meeting by meeting. The enemy was losing ground as the prayer warriors lifted us up nightly.

The warm welcome was hard to resist, even though I tried. One night a persistent member wanted to get to know me better, so she followed me into the bathroom. I don't suppose she knew I had gone in there to sneak a cigarette. Sensing her presence, I did not light up. A little frustrated, I came out to wash my hands, and with her bubbly personality, she greeted me with, "Hi, I'm Chris!"

Everyone needs a friend when making difficult lifestyle changes. She knew exactly what to say and made sure I always had the support I needed. She was the fragrance of God to me. No judgment—just a friend to hold me up! I want to do that for others too!

Cheri Gatton

---

* John Newton, "Amazing Grace" (1779).

September 1

Six Feet of Grief

And the peace of God, which surpasses all understanding, will guard your hearts and minds through Christ Jesus.
—Philippians 4:7, NKJV

When I learned my mother had stage 4 cancer, my heart clung to hope. I believed with every fiber of my being that she would get better. After all, I had been raised by a mother whose life was bathed in prayer. She had taught me to trust in God's providence, and we had witnessed His hand at work countless times. Surely, even in the face of this dire diagnosis, we would see a miracle. Surely we would witness God's goodness, and my mother would emerge a cancer survivor.

When the call came for me to return home because she was unlikely to make it through the night, even then my faith did not waver. With all the fasting and praying we had done, surely we had accumulated enough grace and favor from the Lord. But hours before my departure, I learned she had passed away. It tears at my soul that I never got to say goodbye. The pain of losing the anchor of love in my life is unbearable. She was the light that warmed our home and my partner in faith because she and I were the only Adventists in our family. I miss her laughter and her love that flowed into every corner of my life. When she died, I fell into a deep depression. The depth of my sorrow is more than I can bear.

But, beloved, my grief is carried by God. His promise is true. He can give us a peace that transcends all understanding. His peace is not the absence of sorrow; it is a promise He will gently walk beside us through the pain, whispering solace into our aching hearts and weaving His grace into the very fabric of our suffering until His light transforms our darkest hours into a testament of enduring hope.

Without God this grief would have consumed me. In the midst of my sorrow, I found no place for the question of "Why?" Instead the Holy Spirit wrapped me in a peace that transcends all understanding and reminded me that even in her passing, God is still God.

Beloved, trust in His Word, for it is truly a lamp unto our feet and a light unto a dark, lonely, anger-filled path. As Psalm 34:18 says, "The Lord is close to the brokenhearted and saves those who are crushed in spirit" (NIV). To you who are crushed in spirit, I say, rest in the Lord, for "He heals the brokenhearted and binds up their wounds" (Psalm 147:3 NKJV).

Sibongile Tshabalala

September 2

Soon and Very Soon

We look forward with hope to that wonderful day when the glory of our great God and Savior, Jesus Christ, will be revealed.
—Titus 2:13, NLT

I shudder at the thought of losing someone close. It is difficult not to let sadness, perhaps fear and anxiety, rule our hearts. But during life's hardest moments, we often feel God's presence most powerfully. When hope grows thin, God is strong. He is present, and He is good.

After my husband and I had been together for more than thirty-six years, he died unexpectedly. I had the privilege of washing and dressing him before the funeral home undertaker came to take his body. He and I had talked about death and had made a pact to meet in heaven. Now that he is gone, I could say that losing Walter has been brutal, and grieving hurts. Grief is horrific and comes in like a tsunami. I feel we are never prepared to bid farewell. It was not God's plan for us to experience the utter despair of separation. But then I remember that God also felt the pain of losing His Son. I am sure He cried, and His heart ached like mine. I am comforted, however, because He reassures us that loss is temporary.

Grief is real and needs to be embraced in order for us to move forward on the journey of loss, for loss is unavoidable. If we are alive, we will all experience loss. One of our nephews introduced me to the study by Elisabeth Kübler-Ross, in which she proposed the five stages of grief.* It has helped me navigate the steps within the grief process.

Writer Thomas Moore reminds us that "earth has no sorrow that heaven cannot heal."† God's presence is palpable; it surrounds me and those who call upon Him. He is faithful to grant solace, comfort, and peace. He breathes His love and hope into our grieving hearts. We can be bent, yet not broken. Overcome with grief, but not conquered (see 2 Corinthians 4:8, 9).

We were not created to die, but sin brought death. God does not enclose us in puffy packing material to protect us from experiencing loss. But when we hold on tightly to Him, we can trust His life-giving promises. We know how the story ends. God already won the battle over death!

I am sorry that death exists, that grief is experienced, and that emptiness ensues. One day death will be no more (see Revelation 21:4). I grasp that promise as I continue to grieve my own loss, and I remember that soon and very soon, "joy comes with the morning" (Psalm 30:5, NLT).

Z. Kathy Cameron

---

* Elisabeth Kübler-Ross, *On Death and Dying* (New York: Macmillan, 1969).
† Thomas Moore, "Come, Ye Disconsolate" (1816).

September 3

Goodbye for Now

We want you to know what will happen to the believers who have died so you will not grieve like people who have no hope.
—1 Thessalonians 4:13, NLT

I watched someone pass away last night. While I thought it would be the most awful thing, it really was not because we know death does not win. "We are of good courage and prefer rather to be absent from the body and to be at home with the Lord" (2 Corinthians 5:8, NASB).

We cannot earn our salvation, and we do not go to heaven because we are good people. We are saved because Jesus paid the price we could never pay. Bad things happen to good people, and in that way, and plenty of others, the gospel does not make much sense on a human level. An elementary belief about walking with Christ assumes that life will be a lot easier and happier with Him. But that is not always true. A life lived for Christ does not guarantee happiness or freedom from things that cause pain. It often seems more like the opposite.

But I can tell you confidently that while walking with Jesus might not make life easy, it does make it bearable. The peace He gives when storms come does not make sense from a human perspective. Neither does the understanding that He walks right beside us, lifts us up, and carries us in His arms through the most painful times.

There is an assurance, an unshakable hope that cannot be taken away because we know that death does not win. Jesus defeated it when He left the grave, and because He did, it no longer has the final say for us either. And it did not have the final say for my gentle friend, Cindy.

When by all accounts it looks like the end and the final breath is taken, it is truly the beginning. An incomprehensibly beautiful beginning. I do not know how it all works. I still struggle when His plans do not look like mine. I do not know why people get sick or die too soon or get in accidents or suffer. I have no answers. But I know that Jesus made a way for this life to give way to an eternity spent with Him, and watching someone take their last breath on earth, knowing their next breath will be taken when He returns to take them home, is really beautiful.

Of course it was sad, and as I looked at the faces of the people she loved most in the world, I cried for and with them. But the overwhelming feeling was not sadness. It was awe that this life is not all there is and gratitude that there is life beyond that final, ragged breath.

Carol McLeod

September 4

Claim the Promise

Train up a child in the way he should go:
and when he is old, he will not depart from it.
—Proverbs 22:6, KJV

When I was the young mother of two small boys, my husband and I had friends who could not have children. Although the wife did not say anything, I knew she did not always approve of the way I dealt with my children. However, her attitude changed after they adopted children of their own. One day, I felt discouraged and said, "Sometimes, I think I should never have been a mother."

Startled, she said, "I thought I felt that way because my children are adopted!"

Parenting can be tough and is not made easier by self-appointed experts. Maybe you have heard advice from someone like Larry. He had very young children, and one day he gave a talk at church about how to raise the perfect child. After church one father of a teenage son dryly commented that he would like to hear Larry make that same talk in fifteen years. Larry's words are forgotten, but I remember the older minister who pointed out that Proverbs says when the child *is old* he will not depart from the way he should go—not when he is seventeen.

Prayer is a mighty resource for parents. After graduating from high school, the young man who later became my husband, Ted, found a good job with a bright future, although it meant working on Sabbath. He had forsaken Sabbath keeping in his high school years. However, he had a praying mother. At the youth congress a quartet from Southern Missionary College (now Southern Adventist University) sang of the wonderful love God has for each of us, and it won his heart. The following week he talked with his superior, who reminded him that the job required working every Saturday. Ted gave two weeks' notice, and the sympathetic boss assured him that he could have Saturdays off while working his notice. Not long after he made that decision, Ted enrolled at Southern Missionary College and began the long, hard journey of working his way through college. After he graduated Ted served the Lord he loved for many years.

Mothers, when the way seems hard and the parenting journey has us feeling worn out, keep praying. Claim the promise, "I will contend with him that contendeth with thee, and I will save thy children" (Isaiah 49:25, KJV).

Mary Jane Graves

September 5

Sacred Love

"Before I formed you in the womb I knew you, before you were born I set you apart; I appointed you as a prophet to the nations."
—Jeremiah 1:5, NIV

Before we were formed we were loved. Even before we were a thought in our parents' minds, God had a plan for us. No matter how difficult our lives may be or how challenging our childhood, God's plan for us does not change. David reminds us, "The LORD gives victory to his anointed. He answers him from his heavenly sanctuary with the victorious power of his right hand" (Psalm 20:6, NIV). We have been chosen and anointed. The Lord will save us.

The story is told of a woman who went through a difficult labor. For almost a week she went back and forth between the hospital and her home. The doctors were afraid of losing both her and the baby, so they decided to induce labor. After a successful delivery, they were immediately faced with another challenge. The baby was silent. By God's grace one of the doctors had the wisdom to sharply tap the baby's feet, and after a while the baby started to cry.

Centuries ago, in one of thousands of stories in the Bible, a young boy died after his parents had waited many years to have a child. The boy cried of a headache, and his father sent him to his mother, confident that she would know what to do to help their son. Unfortunately the little boy died anyway. The desperate mother gently placed him on the bed and hurried to the prophet Elisha. She begged him to come and help her child. Elisha returned with her and prayed over the boy, and by the grace of God, the child sneezed seven times and opened his eyes, fully restored to health and life (see 2 Kings 4:11–37).

God loves us so much, and He longs for us to trust Him to take care of us. We are children of the heavenly King. We are a chosen generation, a peculiar people. Not even death nor any challenge we face in life will have the final say. We were seen and loved before our existence. God, in His greatness, holds the power of life and death in His hands. He will come through for us and will fill our hearts with joy.

The Lord has a sacred love for mankind that no language can ever explain or express. "God loves His children with infinite love. To Him, the dearest object on earth is His church."*

Nokukhanya Ncube

---

* Ellen G. White, *Christ's Object Lessons* (Washington, DC: Review and Herald®, 1900), 165.

September 6

Olivia, Jessie, and Me

The eternal God is your refuge, and underneath are the everlasting arms.
—Deuteronomy 33:27, NIV

The strawberry blonde exploded into the children's Bible class the morning that a no-show teacher had turned me instantly into a reluctant substitute teacher—of one three-year-old. "Where's my teacher? Can I play with Tiny Bear?"

I handed Olivia a small teddy bear, hoping its fluffy softness would calm her. There had been no time to unearth flannelgraph figures. A craft-drawer survey yielded only random sheets of paper, a stapler, and nearly dry markers. I hadn't taught for years, so I felt awkward in this role. I began the day's Bible story: "One time some mothers brought their children to Jesus—"

"I know Jesus!" Olivia's honest gaze emphasized her confident words. "He's always with me." Tiny Bear slipped from her lap to the floor. "And I talk to Him—it's called pray."

Nice!

After our Bible lesson Olivia and I began working on a craft. Reaching for a wayward marker, I noticed something at the other end of the worktable: a weathered, white-framed picture.

I smiled at that old picture from my childhood days: Jesus, a little girl on His lap, surrounded by people all wearing 1950s-era clothing. As a child I naively envisioned myself as the little one in those arms—at peace, protected. I shook off old memories and set the white-framed picture before Olivia.

"So, who's that nice Man with all those people around Him?"

"That's Jesus," Olivia said.

Then I asked who was in His lap, expecting her to say "A little child" so I could visually reinforce the lesson. But Olivia responded, matter-of-factly "That's Jessie."

Huh?

"Well, let me look again. Yep, that's Jessie. Don't you think it looks like Jessie?"

She never could tell me who Jessie was. Now, I must choose my words carefully. Jesus once said, "Let the little children come." But in faith, Olivia already seemed to be "there"! And with Jessie securely seated in His lap . . . where I had once sat, though I had never considered how spacious that lap really was, how wide the encircling expanse of those arms or how eternal that Refuge.

Quietly I responded, "Let me look again. Yes, that could be Jessie."

Olivia's nod affirmed my response.

Eternal God, You've just reminded me, through a child's faith, that this now-weathered and widowed "little girl" is still secure in those everlasting arms.

Carolyn Rathbun Sutton

September 7

Our Greatest Victories

Rejoice always, pray without ceasing, in everything give thanks;
for this is the will of God in Christ Jesus for you.
—1 Thessalonians 5:16–18, NKJV

Out of all the Christian disciplines, prayer seems to be the one we struggle with the most. Not because we do not believe in prayer or understand its necessity but because we have not learned to prioritize intentional time for it. Our calendars are filled with things we consider important and a priority. But what if we put prayer time in our calendars or set alarms reminding us that it is time to pray? What if we did this until prayer became as natural as eating and sleeping?

Most surveys on how often Christians pray reveal that, on average, most spend little time in prayer. The enemy of our soul knows well that if we truly understood the power of prayer, his influence in our lives would be broken, and we would see more victory in our Christian walk.

"The greatest victories to the church of Christ or to the individual Christian are not those that are gained by talent or education, by wealth or the favor of men. They are those victories that are gained in the audience chamber with God, when earnest, agonizing faith lays hold upon the mighty arm of power."*

Did you get that? Our greatest victories are gained in the audience chamber with God! How is it possible that we are not running to meet with God more often to commune with Him? Jesus, the Son of God, felt His need to pray. No wonder the angels marvel at how little we weak humans pray. Jesus left us an example to follow—He prayed often, always, and in every situation.

When we are consumed with the cares of this world, let us not neglect to pray. We can cast our burdens at the feet of our heavenly Father, who cares for us and longs to comfort and deliver His children. Why should we wait until we have exhausted our human efforts before we finally turn to God in earnest prayer? Satan dreads to have us pray. Remember, "at the sound of fervent prayer, Satan's whole host trembles."†

Satan constantly seeks to keep us away from the audience chamber with God because he knows it is where we are connected to the Source of strength, grace, and wisdom. Let us spend time in prayer and be filled with awe of the majesty, glory, and splendor of God.

Lillian Torres

---

* Ellen G. White, *Patriarchs and Prophets* (Washington, DC: Review and Herald®, 1890), 203.
† Ellen G. White, "The Power of Satan, *Advent Review and Sabbath Herald*, May 13, 1862, 187.

September 8

God's Providence

"This is what the LORD Almighty says: 'If you will walk in obedience to me and keep my requirements, then you will govern my house and have charge of my courts, and I will give you a place among these standing here.'"
—Zechariah 3:7, NIV

God gifted me with a life partner who shares my desire to serve Him. He blessed us beyond measure as we navigated life and its challenges, working on our careers and raising a family. In the thirty-seven years my husband and I have been married, God has shown us that anything is possible when we put our trust in Him and walk in His ways. One of the things my husband and I enjoy doing together is going on mission trips to the Philippines, where we help provide medical, dental, and optical services.

After our children graduated from high school, they decided to attend Columbia Union College (now Washington Adventist University) in Takoma Park, Maryland, USA. They were both excellent students and earned partial scholarships, but we did not want to burden them with college loans. God provided for our needs even before we asked. Isaiah says, "Before they call, I will answer; and while they are still speaking, I will hear" (Isaiah 65:24, NKJV).

My husband, Jun, who served in the United States Navy, was offered a job where he was able to apply the experience he had gained while in the service. God blessed his decision to retire from an outstanding military career after twenty-five years and pursue a career in the civilian world. This has enabled us to travel together and serve God and our fellow men.

We have proven God's faithfulness throughout the years. His grace has brought us this far, and He has blessed our lives in so many ways. Both our kids finished their education without college loans. They are blessed with life partners they met in college and graduate school, who share their beliefs and are now raising their own families.

God is good all the time. He hears and answers prayers when we earnestly seek Him. We just need to surrender our lives to Him and trust that He can make all things possible for us if we let Him.

> Trust in the LORD with all your heart
> and lean not on your own understanding;
> in all your ways submit to him,
> and he will make your paths straight (Proverbs 3:5, 6, NIV).

Rhona Grace Magpayo

September 9

Recipe for Happiness

Seek the Lord, *all you humble of the land, who do his just commands.*
—Zephaniah 2:3, ESV

I love to travel. One of my greatest joys is to experience other cultures. But even if you think you know everything about yourself, there are some things you can learn only when you find yourself face-to-face with other people. One day, when I was in Switzerland on a trip, I was part of a group waiting to tour the city cathedral. Most of our group sat at a table on the terrace of a restaurant and exclaimed, "What are we going into churches and museums for? We came here to relax." So, in the end, it was just me, the guide, and his wife who went on the tour. Everyone else went on strike—coffee strike.

I realized then that I am different from many others. My highest priority is not like theirs. My dearest focus is found in seeking God. And because I want to know more about Him, when I am away from home, my eyes are immediately drawn to places of worship. I have learned so much from these magnificent buildings about how Christianity and culture are lived out around the world. Once home, I write a column to share what I have learned on the radio.

Something else I love to do is to pray, and I have invited my girlfriends to join me in prayer. In response I heard the classic, "I don't have time," and the famous, "I'm not mystical." I have gone through a few rejections, including, "I don't have the patience," or "I don't know how to pray," and even, "No matter how much I pray, I never get an answer." Someone once told me, "You pray enough for both of us!" Yet prayer is the only way we can communicate with our heavenly Father.

He is interested to hear what we think and what we long to do. He answers when we ask for wisdom. Through prayer we can learn to listen and understand what He tells us. In prayer we can hear His voice clearly. Yes, He walks beside us on the street. He watches over us as we sleep, but it is when we come to Him in prayer that we can hear His clear voice.

"In secret prayer the soul is free from surrounding influences, free from excitement. Calmly, yet fervently, will it reach out after God. . . . By calm, simple faith the soul holds communion with God and gathers to itself divine rays of light to strengthen and sustain it to endure the conflicts of Satan. God is our tower of strength."*

Bianca Timșa Stoicescu

---

* Ellen G. White, *Steps to Christ* (Mountain View, CA: Pacific Press®, 1892), 98.

September 10

The Most Expensive Plane Ticket

For God so loved the world that he gave his one and only Son,
that whoever believes in him shall not perish but have eternal life.
—John 3:16, NIV

The week after I buried my mum was so tumultuous, on every level. In fact the whole trip was turbulent. My mum passed away one hour after I arrived in the country, and instead of being able to say a last goodbye, I found myself, together with my sister, preparing for her funeral—and cleaning her cluttered apartment. On top of that, just eleven days after I arrived, countries around the world began to close their borders. Flights were canceled as millions of people fell sick with something called COVID-19. An earthquake shook the city and woke me up. But it was the phone call I received in the middle of the night that proved more shattering.

I had been asleep for only two hours when my husband called to tell me to pack immediately and get to the airport for my flight back home. It was time to evacuate. He would purchase my ticket as I made the three- to four-hour drive to the airport—regardless of the price. Adding to the complications was the weather. It was the middle of winter, and snow and gale-force winds had been predicted along my route to the airport. Councils had closed local borders, and I needed an official pass to get through, which I did not have. We all prayed. What else could we do?

Angels were very busy, keeping me awake and focused while making sure to keep other vehicles at a safe distance from me as I drove. All the while I did not know if I had a ticket or how much it would cost. Only when I reached the check-in counter did I discover I had a ticket, and it routed me through to my destination—another forty-eight hours away. It was the last flight in. And the price? Almost three times as much for this one-way ticket than what I would usually pay for a return ticket.

I wondered, *Why on earth would my husband pay so much for a ticket?* It was exorbitant! It was not difficult to realize the answer to my question. He did it because he loved me and wanted me to be safely home with him. He also knew that once international borders had closed and flights were canceled, there would be little chance of my getting home any time soon.

His love reminded me of Another's love. One who paid the most expensive price of all to show me His love. He made a way for me to return home to be with Him forever!

Danijela Schubert

September 11

Let Me Be My Own Person

Whether you turn to the right or to the left, your ears will hear a voice behind you, saying, "This is the way; walk in it."
—Isaiah 30:21, NIV

Our children teach us some of life's most important lessons. My eldest daughter, at six years old, came to me with one of those "Oh Mom, let me be my own person" moments. I sat down with her and said, "I'll let you, but first I just want to ask you a question. Do you know what it means to be your own person?"

She answered, "No, I don't."

"Well, let me explain it to you," I replied. "The first thing you need to do is get a good job so you can pay for your school, piano lessons, food, clothes, shoes, and toys—everything you need and like." I continued explaining it to her and then calmly asked, "Do you still want to be your own person?"

She shook her head and responded with an emphatic, "No, I don't!"

I had a hard time trying to control myself not to laugh. Children!

Though it happened many years ago, I still remember our exchange. It leads me to reflect on how often we have a rebellious attitude toward our heavenly Father. He kindly tells us, *"Daughter, do it My way; I know what is best for you."*

And we, full of our own will, answer "Oh Father, let me be my own person! I want it that way!" And without listening to God's voice, we go ahead—but not without consequences. Many times, we do not stop to reflect and recognize what we did wrong, and we wonder, *Oh! My Lord, why did You allow this to happen to me? What went wrong?*

The best thing to do during these times is to sit at the feet of Jesus, like Mary, and cry out for help to choose to follow His plan. His plans are always best. Rebellion hardens the heart and distances us from God. Whenever we have decisions to make or obstacles or challenges to overcome, we must first go to the Father in prayer; study and meditate on His Word; and then, with faith and trust, wait for His instruction. God is patient and kind to all His children. He cares about each one of us. Just as my daughter came to understand and accept her need for dependence on her mother, we must recognize our dependence on our heavenly Father.

Dear Father in Heaven, do not let us stray from Your path. May our ears hear Your voice that leads us in Your straight paths. We want to see Your face. Amen.

Aparecida Bonfim Dornelles

September 12

Head, Shoulders, Knees, and Toes!

For you created my inmost being;
you knit me together in my mother's womb.
I praise you because I am fearfully and wonderfully made;
your works are wonderful,
I know that full well.
—Psalm 139:13, 14, NIV

I usually wear socks around the house, but on this night I was already in bed and felt too lazy to put them on to go get some water. As I sleepily headed downstairs, my bare feet gliding across the carpet triggered a thought.

"Mom!" I called out.

"Yes, child," my mom replied from her office downstairs.

"Does each person have unique toe prints just like fingerprints?"

"Mmm, I don't know," she answered, without apparent interest in my random question.

I was content with not knowing the answer, at least for the time being, but before I had finished filling up my water bottle, Mom answered again.

"Whoa! Yes, each person has unique toe prints. In fact there are nine body parts and characteristics that are as distinctive as your fingerprint."

Mom had stumbled upon an article online that listed them all. As we delved into the list, I could not help but feel awestruck. Our toe prints, irises, ears, lips, tongue, voice, teeth, and retinas are all one of a kind!

When we reached the ninth item on the list, I could not contain my disbelief.

"No way!"

Did you know that even an individual's gait is unique? The article explained that "even if you've never noticed anything unusual about how you stroll, sophisticated systems can. When an international team of bioengineers analyzed the foot pressure patterns of more than 100 participants, they identified individuals with a 99.6 percent accuracy rate. Though more research is needed, gait identification could eventually be a way of identifying individuals from a distance—such as camera footage that identifies a robber walking out of a bank."*

Our infinite God has unlimited ways of creating, working, and saving each one of His precious jewels. My existence, your existence, neither is an accident. Just as God carefully molded the soil to create Adam (Genesis 2:7), He intricately formed each one of us in our mother's womb. We are fearfully and wonderfully made. All His works truly are miraculous.

Kendi Callender

* Kelsey Kloss, "9 Body Parts as Unique as Your Fingerprint," The Healthy, last updated Feb. 6, 2018, https://www.thehealthy.com/bodies/unique-body-parts/.

September 13

Are You Holding Her?

"And when he has found it, he lays it on his shoulders, rejoicing."
—Luke 15:5, NKJV

My daughter and her family were visiting. Without disturbing his mommy and me as we chatted in the living room, my grandson Jahnus climbed onto my back and put his arms around my neck. It was the signal for a piggyback ride, and I willingly got up and started to amble around the room while still listening to Ndala. Very soon baby Jahrra crawled toward us, clearly wanting to join the fun. I scooped her up, and with one child on my back and another in my arms, I continued the piggyback ride.

Engaged in the adult conversation, I focused on the urgent question only when he repeated it. "Grandma, are you holding her?" At my affirmative Jahnus jumped off my back. Dear little man! He had been gripping his beloved baby sister firmly. Over my shoulders he could not see that she was secure in my arms. Nor did it occur to him that, with his barely five-year-old strength, he would not have been able to keep her from falling.

The moment was an epiphany. I glanced involuntarily at my daughter as she continued to share her ideas with little concern about the familiar scene in front of her. But from my perspective it had not been that long since she and I had negotiated her challenging years of adolescence. I had been as uncertain as Jahnus. My frequent, tearful prayer had been, "Dear Father, please hold her for me!"

I wondered now whether His response might have been, "*My child, I've got her. Relax and enjoy your ride on My shoulders.*"

With our children we sometimes forget the all-encompassing injunction to "be anxious for nothing, but in everything by prayer and supplication, with thanksgiving, let your requests be made known to God" (Philippians 4:6, NKJV). His promise is sure: "For I will contend with him who contends with you, and I will save your children" (Isaiah 49:25 NKJV).

As for Jahnus he has never lost his caring and loving disposition. Six months ago, now twenty years after that stressful piggyback ride, he chose to work remotely and move to Alabama, USA, in response to my need for live-in help. Praise God from whom all blessings flow (see Psalm 147). "I will sing of the mercies of the LORD forever" (Psalm 89:1, NKJV).

Lela Moore Gooding

September 14

Taste and See

*Taste and see that the L*ORD *is good; blessed is the one who takes refuge in him.*
—Psalm 34:8, NIV

Monsoon season in India is awesome—and beautiful—though often destructive. India, being a tropical country, is hot and humid, and the rains are welcomed with gladness. The agriculture depends on rain, so the farmers are happy when the rains begin. They anticipate a good crop and harvest. It is also a busy time for those in the medical field because many sicknesses occur during this time, and they have many patients to help.

It was during this season that I became ill. I praise God for His wonderful healing touch and the recovery He brought me. I developed chikungunya, a viral disease, after a mosquito bit me. It is a very painful illness, and I experienced fever, joint and muscle pain, and loss of taste. Though the pain was terrible, I felt more able to endure it than the loss of taste. I found that to be unbearable—at least, it was for me.

Indian foods are spicy, savory, and sweet. But it did not matter because everything tasted bland. I tried everything I could to make my food tasty, but to no avail. I remembered the words from our text for today and wondered, *How does the Lord taste?* As I lay sick in bed with nothing to do, I remembered my past experiences with God over the many years He has led and guided my footsteps. I reflected on every aspect of my life, from my single years when I experienced His merciful protection to my married life and the joy and sorrow I shared with my husband as we trained our children through life and experienced the joy of seeing them serving the Lord. We were so thankful when they found their life partners, and now here I was, waiting to become a grandmother. What a life. What a blessing.

Among life's sweetest joys is the privilege of having been chosen by God to work for Him. I have experienced renewed joy and peace in my life. My heart exploded in thanksgiving as I sang from my sick bed, "O taste and see that the Lord is good" (Psalm 34:8, NIV).

No matter that my tongue could not taste anything—I had tasted the goodness of the Lord! How great are His mercies and His grace; His love endures forever. I have found my refuge in Him. May we continue to taste and see how good He is!

Priscila Kandane

September 15

Might in the Night

Trust in the Lord forever, for the Lord God is an everlasting rock.
—Isaiah 26:4, ESV

I often travel for work, and sometimes, by choice or chance, I arrive at my destination during the darkness of night.

On one trip I traveled from Alabama to Florida in the USA. Delayed connections pushed my arrival through the night and into the early morning hours. Every interaction and transaction seemed fraught with difficulties. I claimed my luggage and walked what felt like miles to the trolley that would take me to the bus, which would drive me to the rental car place. When I arrived at the trolley stop, a lady in uniform signaled for me to wait. After several minutes I was directed to take an elevator, padded with heavy brown cloth on all sides, to the bus stop.

The ride felt dangerous as the bus drove through heavy rain and over the hilly curves. I was relieved to finally get my car, but it took a long while to locate the exit and make my way to the hotel nearby.

After my trip, as I prepared to return home, I was surprised at how well I negotiated my way in the daylight. There were no curves or hills on my way to the car rental place. The trolley was there and worked perfectly. The way to the airport felt shorter. I walked with confidence as I bathed in the beauty of the sights and the sunshine. I could not remember the location of the damp and dim elevator, but it did not matter. The day was clear, the path was safe, and my heart was glad.

This experience reminded me of my life's journey. I thought about the times when I stumbled in the dark, filled with sadness, sorrow, and self-doubt. Times when life was unjust and unkind to me and my loved ones. Times when disasters overwhelmed my soul. Then there were bright periods when I experienced miracles, moments of pure elation, and God's favor beyond my imagination. I sensed the Lord reminding me that He is always with me. The One who led me in the night was now leading me in the light.

My sisters, whether you are on top of the world or struggling in the valley, God is with you. He is the Way in the day, and most comforting of all, He is our Might in the night!

Rose Joseph Thomas

September 16

Alarming

"Therefore you also must be ready, for the Son of Man is coming at an hour you do not expect."
—Matthew 24:44, ESV

A few years ago a family celebration required a drive to the other side of the state. My husband, Steve, and I took a few days off, visited a couple of attractions, and stayed over in hotels.

One night, just before midnight, a blaring alarm sounded along with a flashing strobe light. After having a full day, we had been sleeping solidly. It took a few seconds to realize it was a fire alarm. Steve called the front desk, thinking the issue was in our room. I fumbled for my cell phone and purse as Steve repeated the word: "Evacuate?"

Apparently when the alarm goes off in one room, the entire hotel is alerted. In addition, the elevators lock, preventing people from using them. Thankfully we were only on the second floor, so there was no problem using the stairs. When we reached the lobby, the hotel staff were trying to figure out the cause of the alarm. They were simultaneously on the phone and fielding questions from barefoot guests.

Each time they reset the alarm, it would just start all over again. The fire department had been called but had not arrived. The staff assured us that if they could not pinpoint the problem, there was likely a malfunction in the system. Steve and I went back to bed. In the morning we learned that a microwave from the second floor was now lying on the hotel lawn. I don't know whether the microwave malfunctioned or someone simply burned a bag of popcorn.

One takeaway from this experience was that I need to keep the essentials together in case there is an actual emergency. This could work at home as well. We took too long to leave our room and were among the last to reach the lobby. If there had been a fire, I would have been barefoot in my nightgown until I could buy an outfit. At least I had my purse, my phone, and my life.

The Bible tells us we need to be ready always. "Behold, I am coming like a thief! Blessed is the one who stays awake, keeping his garments on, that he may not go about naked" (Revelation 16:15, ESV). We know Jesus is coming soon. Let us get ready, stay awake, and watch for the signs. Can you hear the alarm sounding?

Ann Trout

September 17

Fire Across the Pond

And we know that God causes all things to work together for good to those who love God, to those who are called according to His purpose.
—Romans 8:28, NASB

My son Adam was awakened at two o'clock by the howling wind. He suddenly remembered the portable basketball goal in the driveway and went outside to put it down. Once back inside he looked out the window to check the backyard. Across the pond he saw something that looked like a fire. This startled him, and he woke his wife up. "Wake up! Look! What is that?"

A minute later the two realized something was burning. Adam got into his car and quickly drove toward the houses on the other side of the pond. He parked and ran to the house on fire, which had started from the back porch of the house. He pounded on the front door, and when it opened, a woman, two children, and an older son were scrambling to get out of the house.

What are the odds that of all the houses by the pond, the house on fire belonged to their friends? In the meantime Adam's wife, Danielle, had called 911 to report the fire. The smoke alarms did not go off until they were outside the house. In that short period of time, they were able to drive two of their cars away from the house.

Adam ran to the next-door neighbor's house and pounded on their front door. It seemed like the longest five minutes before someone came to the door. He ran to the other neighbor's house to wake them up too.

After the family was safely outside, as the flames were engulfing the whole house, Adam held hands with the family and prayed, "Lord, let Your will be done. Please minimize whatever damage is done to this house, but in the name of Jesus, don't let the houses on the left or right catch fire."

The house was engulfed in flames so fast. A propane light at the back porch had exploded, causing the fire. But thank God the fire did not spread to the other houses, and everyone was safe.

God has a way of placing us in the right place at the right time to be a help to others. Let our daily prayer be, "Lord, please give me the opportunity to help others and direct my every step. And please give me Your protection always. To You, Lord, be the glory!"*

Reva Lachica Moore

---

* Adapted from "The Fire Across the Pond," Adopt a Minister International on Facebook, Oct. 20, 2022, https://www.facebook.com/story.php?story_fbid=1059743427987549&id=121366765158558&_rdr. Used with permission.

September 18

The Profound Principle of Unfolding

(If we look forward to something we don't yet have, we must wait patiently and confidently.) . . . For example, we don't know what God wants us to pray for. But the Holy Spirit prays for us with groanings that cannot be expressed in words.
—Romans 8:25, 26, NLT

We often hear that God answers prayer with *yes*, *no*, or *wait*. I can understand *yes* and *no*, but for me the answer *wait* is problematic. How do I know if an answer is *no* or *wait*? If I cannot "hear" His answer, how do I eventually know when I have received one?

I finally came to understand that God answers my prayers by using His profound principle of unfolding. Unfolding is about stories. God unfolds stories with His sense of timing, not ours. For example, at the beginning of the Bible, God unfolded an answer to Adam's unvoiced prayer for a mate of his own. First, God introduced Adam to all the animals and told him to name them. Sometimes God sets up our desires to pray for certain things.

That was called discovery learning, and Adam discovered that he was only a half. Then Jesus let Adam help create his other half with a part of himself. This was an unfolding story as well as an answer to prayer.

Job and God were part of another unfolding story. As far as we can tell, Job never got an answer to his prayer asking why he was going through all his troubles. He was depressed; he wanted to die, but he trusted that God was not out to punish him. For some people God's lack of answer to prayer for Job is troublesome. But I have come to believe that it is not necessarily those with the strongest faith who receive the biggest miracles. I think dramatic answers to prayer are often for the benefit of the weak in faith. God wants us to trust Him with the slowly unfolding answers to prayer that we may or may not ever see with our own eyes.

In prayer we do not try to manipulate a whimsical God. We join His story, trusting He knows the storyline better than we ever could. My smaller story always falls inside that bigger one. He wants to weave them together, and for that He needs my trust in His omniscience.

So the best way for me to hear the answer *wait* is to stay tuned in to the story God is unfolding all around me. When I trust patiently for His profound principle of unfolding, his apparent *no* answer often transforms into a resounding *yes*!

Kathy Beagles Coneff

September 19

Spiritual Jumper Cables

One of those days Jesus went out to a mountainside to pray, and spent the night praying to God.
—Luke 6:12, NIV

I especially like the places in the Bible that describe Jesus slipping away from the chaos and crowds that followed Him to find a solitary place to pray and connect with His Father. We all need those times, but sadly, in the hustle and bustle of work, family, and life, we often put quiet, focused prayer time at the bottom of our daily list.

My husband and I own a tractor-trailer. It is a machine, and machines wear out and break, and I dread the days when he tells me the truck will not start. This happened recently, and while I wondered how the bills would get paid, he jumped in to troubleshoot the problem. He connected jumper cables between the big truck battery and our pickup truck battery, and the big truck fired right up! But when he disconnected the cables, the truck stopped running. When he hooked them back up, it started right up again. He soon figured out that the big truck battery was so dead it needed a longer time hooked to the other battery to build up enough charge to keep it running. After enough time had passed, he unhooked the cables, and the big truck continued to run, now fully charged with help from the pickup truck battery.

"But Jesus often withdrew to lonely places and prayed" (Luke 5:16, NIV). Jesus spent His days eating, sleeping, and living with twelve men of various personalities who, let us be honest, were exhausting at times. Crowds of needy people pressed in close as they followed Him. People wanted to be healed. They wanted to be fed. They wanted to ask questions and hear Him preach.

The Pharisees who followed were always challenging and criticizing Him. He was pushed, pulled, and stretched every day in every way, and while He never complained, He often withdrew for long moments to plug back in to His Father.

Prayer is our spiritual jumper cable. We cannot run on an empty battery, no matter how hard we try—and we do try! Instead we need to remember the example Jesus gave us. We need to make it a priority to step away, find a quiet place, and recharge every day. Jesus did, and He was both God and Man. If God recognized a need to recharge, we, my human friends, are no different.

Pam Carbaugh

September 20

My New Car

And my God will supply all your needs according to His riches in glory in Christ Jesus.
—Philippians 4:19, NASB

When I graduated with my bachelor of social work, I desperately needed a job. I was a single parent with student loans. I lived in Montréal, Québec, Canada, and just before my graduation, human resources representatives from the Government of Alberta conducted interviews on campus. I figured I had nothing to lose, so I applied. Shortly after being interviewed I was offered a frontline social work position in Edmonton, Alberta. One of the conditions of employment was that I had a vehicle. I did not own a car, nor did I know how to drive, but I thought that would be an easy fix.

The driving school at the end of my block made it convenient to sign up for lessons. I wanted to learn to drive a stick shift, but time was against me. I completed the required lessons and prepared for the road test. When my appointment was changed from the morning to the afternoon, it gave me time to practice. One of my younger brothers, Wesley, took me out in the morning and had me do all sorts of maneuvers until it was time to go for the test. To my surprise I passed after the first try. Wesley was not so confident in my newfound driving abilities, so he declined my offer to drive home.

Now that I had my permit, I just needed a car. Wesley took me to a Ford dealership to look around. When the salesman asked what we were looking for, my brother did not give me a chance to speak. He explained that I needed something small, inexpensive, with great miles per gallon. We were shown a new Ford Escort, a two-door hatchback. I wanted four doors, so I protested a bit. Wesley quickly reminded me that as the driver, I had a door, and I did not need to worry about passengers.

He sold me on the idea, and we proceeded to purchase the car. We went into the office to do the paperwork, and the salesman inquired how much money I intended to put down.

"Nothing," I answered and quickly explained that I was relocating to Alberta as I had a job with the government there.

The salesman contacted my employer and confirmed my position and my salary. He handed me the keys, and off we drove.

Isaiah 55:1 says, "You who have no money come, buy. . . . Without money and without cost" (NASB). We can trust God to supply all our needs!

Sharon Long

September 21

The Gift

"Again I say to you, if two of you agree on earth about anything they ask, it will be done for them by my Father in heaven."
—Matthew 18:19, ESV

Around the end of July 1994, a mysterious thing happened. I was unemployed and resided at the home of Janice and John in Tallahassee, Florida, USA. I started a garden, and John became interested. Together we worked in it, and the Lord blessed us.

One night John's mother summoned him to her home. She had a beautiful baby boy whose mother had abandoned him, and she needed help to care for the child. I was in the right place at the right time to babysit little Edward. In this wonderful way God provided a job opening for me. I was able to care for the child and receive a salary from the government.

One Monday afternoon Janice returned home from work very distressed. When John asked what the matter was, she shared the many problems she had with her car on the way home. She said it was only through the grace of the good Lord that she had been able to return home safely. I was working in the garden and overheard their conversation. I walked up to the back door and said to my friend, "Janice, you are working with millionaire bosses. They are the very people who work to resurface and build roads in Tallahassee, and you should have no reason to be struggling without a car."

She came through the door, stood on the steps, and said, "That is very true Sister Johnson."

I continued, "The company can give you a new car."

"Yes, they could!" she replied.

I stepped closer to her and we touched each other's hands as a sign of agreeing in presenting this request to the Lord.

The next morning, around ten o'clock, Janice called and said, "Sister Johnson, guess what?"

I said, "I can't guess; you tell me."

She responded that she had just been given a brand-new Ford, and the title had been made out in her name.

"Praise God! Hallelujah!" I exclaimed.

She told me that when she arrived at work, her boss said he and his wife were taking her to the Ford car company, and she could choose whichever car she liked. She chose a beautiful Ford Escort. God really blessed Janice—and He wants to bless you today. Let us be faithful, my friends, for He is so faithful to us!

Sheila Johnson (deceased)

September 22

Frogs, Fear, and Faith

Fear thou not; for I am with thee: be not dismayed; for I am thy God: I will strengthen thee; yea, I will help thee; yea I will uphold thee with the right hand of my righteousness.
—Isaiah 41:10, KJV

I do not fear frogs. At least not like my mom did. At least that is what I thought, until . . .

I had just kissed my husband goodbye and returned to work on my to-do list when I saw it. An enormous frog! For a moment I froze with fear and then dashed for the phone.

"Honey," I half screamed, "you have to come back and get this frog. It's on the wall beside the kitchen. It's huge!"

"Calm down, honey. You'll be fine," he tried to assure me. "If I turn around, I will be very late and probably won't find it."

As it turned out, he was right.

Freaked out, or more accurately, "frogged out," I felt thankful it was time for my hourly prayer. But "because fear hath torment" (1 John 4:18, KJV), I changed my usual prayer place. I was not going to walk past the frog. I grabbed my *Clear Word*, my favorite devotional Bible, ran to my bedroom, and locked the door.

"God," I prayed aloud, "I need Your help now. I know You see my fear, and You are concerned about it. I trust You to do this. It concerns my peace."

And yes, the fear diminished when I got off my knees, and honestly an hour later it had completely gone. I could even face walking past the wall. When I did—that frog was nowhere in sight. In fact, when my husband came home, he searched for it. With his cell phone flashlight, he went through every room, closet, cabinet, and dark spot. The frog was gone. I went to bed and slept like a baby.

While having my devotion the following morning, I heard something.

"What was that?" I called.

My husband was going to his devotional spot and had stepped on it! Yes! The *frog*! It had come out of its hiding place before dawn, as it had done the day before. Suffice it to say I had a real praise service. Ellen White writes, "Nothing that in any way concerns our peace is too small for Him to notice."*

Do you have something that is causing you to fear? I encourage you to "give your frog" to God. He reminds us, "Fear thou not . . . I am thy God" (Isaiah 41:10, KJV). He is with you today, tomorrow, and forever. Go forward and face your frogs in Jesus' name.

Claudette Garbutt-Harding

---

* Ellen G. White, *Steps to Christ* (Mountain View, CA: Pacific Press®, 1892), 100.

September 23

Saved!

*The LORD is my rock, my fortress and my deliverer; . . .
I called to the LORD, who is worthy of praise,
and I have been saved from my enemies.*
—Psalm 18:2, 3, NIV

I lived with my family in Kyiv, the capital of Ukraine. In February 2022, on the first day of the war, we decided to leave immediately because our city was the main target of the enemy. We thought we would be safe in our country house in Bucha. Unfortunately the town was soon occupied, and what followed were two of the most terrible weeks we have ever experienced, fully aware our lives could end at any moment. We stayed in the basement without electricity, water, or heat. We melted snow into water and had hardly anything to eat. I constantly feared my children would starve to death.

Living under constant bombing, we knew our every breath was in the hands of the Lord, and it brought us very close to God. Though our house was not hit, we knew it was impossible to continue living with the terrible fear, so we decided to escape. The alternative would be to starve to death.

It was terrifying. We were warned the occupying forces would not let any cars through and would shoot ruthlessly. But the desire to leave was stronger than our fear, so we drove off. Others saw us leave and joined us. We ended up in a convoy, knowing we could be shot at any moment and very aware of the high probability of death. We prayed fervently.

At the first roadblock our convoy was stopped. And then the Lord performed a miracle! The driver of the first car was led away at gunpoint while we prayed incessantly. I have no idea what words the Lord put in that driver's mouth, but when he returned, the Russian soldier got behind the wheel of the car and drove ahead of our convoy, signaling everyone not to shoot at us. In this way he led us through every checkpoint. Outside the car windows we saw many who had tried unsuccessfully to escape. Both sides of the road were littered with the remains of shot-up and burned-out cars.

We had faced death and escaped. God gave us a new life! We remember with deep gratitude the day God saved us in His great mercy. We will never forget as long as we live.

Thank You, Lord, for Your great mercy toward us.

Yana Kosian

September 24

Sweet Sleep, Quiet Rest

"Come to Me, all you who labor and are heavy laden, and I will give you rest."
—Matthew 11:28, NKJV

I wonder how well I slept as a baby. My mother is no longer alive for me to ask this question, but I am curious. Did I sleep soundly, oblivious to surrounding noises? Was I a light sleeper so that everyone had to tiptoe once I was in bed for fear I would awaken? Did I enjoy taking naps as a child? (Ask me that now, and I will tell you at this stage of my life, I yearn for more sleep.)

I recall stopping at a friend's house. As I met the mother at the door, she put her finger to her lips and stepped outside, fearing our conversation at the door would awaken her newborn baby. It seemed he reacted to the slightest noise and had a hard time sleeping soundly.

One day my husband and I took our motorhome and stopped overnight before reaching our son's place in Illinois, USA. We both slept in. Have you ever heard that phrase before? We slept for almost ten hours. I could hardly believe it. It felt luxurious to have been given the gift of extra sleep. I felt so rested.

And my—did that feel wonderful. I am typically lucky to get seven hours of sleep at night. Rest. I just love that word! R-E-S-T. What does it look like to you? A quick word search defines *rest* as "cease work or movement in order to relax, refresh oneself, or recover strength."* Some synonyms include *slow down, recharge one's batteries*, and *take a load off*.

So what does *rest* mean for our spiritual life? Do we fully let go of our burdens? We pray—but do we pick up our burdens at the end of prayer? Some people are born worriers, but being a worrier is like rocking in a rocking chair and expecting to go somewhere. Instead, why don't we picture God gladly taking on our burdens, allowing us to rest assured that He knows and cares about each one? What a glorious mind picture of His willingness to take all that weighs us down and give us complete and perfect rest.

Rest—it is what we all need. Most of us need physical rest, and more likely than not, all of us need spiritual rest. Jesus says He wants our cares and worries. And guess what? He knows what to do with them anyway. So go grab some z's. Rest well!

Valerie Hamel Morikone

---

* Encyclopedia.com, s.v. "rest (v)," last updated May 21, 2018, https://www.encyclopedia.com/literature-and-arts/performing-arts/music-theory-forms-and-instruments/rest.

September 25

TGIF (Thank God It's Friday)

Don't worry about anything.
—Philippians 4:6, NLT

One Friday evening I sat down with my mom for family worship to welcome the Sabbath. In the middle of singing the first song, an overwhelming wave of tiredness hit, and I started to yawn. By the time we started the reading, I could barely keep my eyes open. I was exhausted. After we had prayed it dawned on me that this occurred frequently. I hustled all week, sleep-deprived but strong, trying to stay on top of things. It was as if my body were holding itself together because it knew the Sabbath finish line was coming. Can you relate? Have you experienced the "thank-God-for-the-Sabbath" moment on Friday evenings when you can drop all cares? Then you can rest and sleep peacefully, knowing you do not have to hustle the next day.

While reflecting, I remembered a pastor saying, "If you're exhausted on the Sabbath, you're breaking the fourth commandment." I felt insulted by his comment and wondered what he meant.

Let us take a look. What does the commandment say? "Remember the sabbath day, to keep it holy. Six days shalt thou labour, and do all thy work: But the seventh day is the sabbath of the Lord thy God. . . . For in six days the Lord made heaven and earth, . . . and rested the seventh day: wherefore the Lord blessed the sabbath day" (Exodus 20:8–11, KJV). The pastor emphasized that the Lord rested not because He was tired or exhausted but because His work was complete. God set aside a day to spend quality time with us.

The commandment instructs us that we have six days to "do all thy work." When we arrive at this sacred time and feel frazzled, we have likely done more than our own labor, whether working for God or man. It is incredibly easy to micromanage life and worry about things we cannot control. What will happen next? Where will this come from? Why did that happen? How can I realize my dreams on my timeline? That. Is. Exhausting! No wonder our bodies are impacted.

Once I let go of the worries that belonged to God and set realistic goals for myself and boundaries for the ways I help others, my health improved and I was able to attentively spend time with God during the Sabbath (see Philippians 4:7). My friends, may the Holy Spirit help us live intentionally and align with God's will; then we shall prosper as He envisions.

Kendi Callender

September 26

Do Not Let Good Things Get Away From You

Now all glory to God, who is able, through his mighty power at work within us, to accomplish infinitely more than we might ask or think.
—Ephesians 3:20, NLT

Self-care.

People, particularly Christians, seem to have trouble deciding whether the self-care movement is a good thing or not. Any mention of "self" within a church setting raises red flags and sets off sin detectors like smoke bombs. Is there a difference between selfishness and practicing self-care? According to the Merriam-Webster dictionary, being selfish means you care for yourself "without regard for others,"* and self-care is to "care for oneself."† What the definition of self-care does not say is to disregard the needs of others.

Jesus teaches us to "love your neighbor as yourself" (Matthew 19:19, NLT). Do you want your neighbor to collapse from overwork or not get enough rest? No! So do not imagine God wants that to happen to you. Jesus cautioned Martha to focus on what truly matters and reprioritize, even though she thought her service to others was more important (Luke 10:38–52). Jesus went off alone to pray (Matthew 14:23). He slept (Mark 4:38). He wept (John 11:35). He ate (Luke 5:29). Jesus is fully God and fully human. He practiced self-care for His human needs just like everyone else, and He continued to minister to others. The Bible speaks against selfishness. What the Bible does not say is to neglect yourself.

God calls us to treat ourselves with as much love as we treat our neighbors because He loves us (John 16:26, 27). God is working through us to accomplish His goals (Ephesians 3:20, 21). One of His goals is to make sure we are fit to serve. He knows our needs. In 1 Kings 17, God provides food and water for Elijah. Self-care is not a sin; being selfish is. Falling off either side of the selfish/self-care path is easy. If you question whether something you do for your well-being is right or wrong, I encourage you to pray and look to the Bible. Friends, family, pastors, church members, authors, and strangers all have their own opinions on the self-care movement. Only you get to determine what God wants for you, the child He loves.

Remember, not all ideas are evil, nor are they good, so be sure to "test everything and do not let good things get away from you" (1 Thessalonians 5:21, NLV).

Deidre A. Jones

---

* *Merriam-Webster's Collegiate Dictionary*, s.v. "selfish," accessed Mar. 5, 2025, https://unabridged.merriam-webster.com/collegiate/selfish.

† *Merriam-Webster's Collegiate Dictionary*, s.v. "self-care," accessed Mar. 5, 2025, https://unabridged.merriam-webster.com/collegiate/self-care.

September 27

Your Word I Have Hidden in My Heart

"You shall teach them diligently to your children."
—Deuteronomy 6:7, NKJV

I was on the streetcar in Bucharest, Romania, returning from a missionary visit. The journey was long, but I enjoyed a special surprise along the way. A poorly dressed young man boarded the tram and began to recite *Luceafărul,* a very long Romanian poem of ninety-eight verses written by renowned Romanian poet Eminescu. Everyone listened with amazement as we watched his flawless rendition, which left many in tears. I thought, *How nice it would be to know whole pages of Scripture by heart! There would be little room for the enemy to sow his tares!*

I used to memorize biblical texts, but now I've set my sights higher and have begun to learn whole psalms and paragraphs from the Bible and the Spirit of Prophecy. As a mother I made it a point to help my children at a young age memorize Bible verses after I read about the way Barry Black's mother taught him.

When he was thirteen, Barry had to memorize, "My son, if sinners entice you, do not consent" (Proverbs 1:10, NKJV). That very day two young men in the neighborhood asked him to help them "give a spanking" to another boy. Barry recounted that he remembered the memorized text and refused to accompany them. The next day he learned the two boys had not only beaten the other young man but had killed him. Though one of the two young men confessed to Barry that it was his friend who was the murderer, they were both arrested and sentenced to prison. Barry's memorizing and practicing Proverbs 1:10 saved him from prison. Today Barry Black is the sixty-third chaplain of the United States Senate and, to date, the only Seventh-day Adventist to hold this position.

By storing up in our minds the marvelous promises of God, we prepare effective weapons to defeat Satan's schemes. When we no longer have our Bibles, we will be able to recall all we have memorized. "None but those who have fortified the mind with the truths of the Bible will stand through the last great conflict."*

Let us make it our daily goal to gather pearls of dew from the meadow of Scripture and store them in the cup of a pure mind, from which heavenly glory will spring forth to enlighten those around us.

Magdalena Toma

---

* Ellen G. White, *The Great Controversy* (Mountain View, CA: Pacific Press®, 1911), 593.

September 28

The Bible

All Scripture is given by inspiration of God, and is profitable for doctrine, for reproof, for correction, for instruction in righteousness, that the man of God may be complete, thoroughly equipped for every good work.
—2 Timothy 3:16, 17, NKJV

In all honesty, sincerity, and humility, does anyone know of a book that transcends the wisdom, relevancy, and sacredness of the Bible? There are thousands of books on bestseller lists that are captivating, informative, and even inspiring. One such book, for me, was about a grandmother who, in her late sixties and into her seventies, hiked the entire length of the Appalachian Trail, which passes through fourteen states and at that time was 2,168 miles long. Since walking can be enjoyable, it stirred a desire in me to walk at least a portion of that trail because it starts in my birth state. That has not become a reality though.

Even though the Bible is the best-selling book of all ages, are we so inspired and captivated by it that we can hardly put it down? It is full of narratives that are relevant to every situation we face in life, and it offers solutions for anything we may encounter.

The narrative about Eli's sons, Phinehas and Hophni, tells us how very wicked they were. They took the ark of God with them into battle against the Philistines, thinking that it would protect them and give them victory over their enemy. It mentions nothing about them repenting and turning away from their sins. That act had disastrous results. You can read about the account in 1 Samuel 4.

Then there is dear Abigail in 1 Samuel 25. God used her to keep David from committing a heinous act against her household that he most surely would have regretted later. She recognized and acknowledged that David was a man of God, and God was able to use her mightily. How did she acquire that wisdom and courage, considering her circumstances? Such wisdom does not come overnight but from a lifetime of walking with God.

There are lessons for us to learn in each of these narratives. We are all human and make mistakes. While we can see God's displeasure in many biblical narratives, many accounts in His Word illustrate how He delights in us and loves it when we choose to obey. So let us walk with God each day because following Him will lead us to eternal life.

Sharon M. Thomas

September 29

Ladies Advice Panel Discussion

*Trust in the L*ORD *with all your heart,*
and do not lean on your own understanding.
In all your ways acknowledge him,
and he will make straight your paths.
—Proverbs 3:5, 6, ESV

One January I was included on a panel with three other senior ladies as part of our women's ministry program. What follows are a few of the topics we were asked to address.

My first piece of advice? Do not marry before finishing college. Being naïve about protection, I fell pregnant six months later! My professors advised me to finish my senior year, but having a baby was too exciting! Now mind you, I had no experience with little kids, but I had taken those child development classes and read all the baby books, right?

Wherever possible, be a stay-at-home mom. Our second son came less than twenty months later. Those boys were my life. I wanted to be the mother to them that I never had. Sabbath School class and the church building became their other home. On many Sabbath afternoons we would play Sabbath School by putting felts on a flannel blanket against the back of the sofa while singing their songs. Both boys always knew their memory verses for the whole quarter. When my oldest son was eight, he learned to play the ukulele at junior camp. He then played for Sabbath School and for our worship each evening. Pathfinders came later, and how they enjoyed participating!

One real fear I had as a young mother was that my boys would not make wise choices. I knew about Eve's boys, Cain and Abel. That story would haunt me on days I felt I had not made the right decision dealing with them. Then there was Eve's major bad decision at the tree. What if I made a decision that would be harmful to my boys' future? I prayed lots of prayers for my boys to be good citizens in this world and the next. Praise the Lord; they are successful men today, loving the Lord.

My advice at forty years old: Get a job to pay for your children's church school tuition. Pray more with and for them, their friends, and their life partners. Stay involved in church life. Make time to read God's Word and pray daily. Talk less to friends and family about being discouraged, frustrated, or worried, but tell God about it. Keep a gratitude journal more faithfully. Spend more time listening to and singing uplifting songs.

What advice would you give? I pray we will meet many in heaven whom we have influenced.

Louise Howlett Driver

September 30

Dancing Among the Ivories

A joyful heart is good medicine, but a crushed spirit dries up the bones.
—Proverbs 17:22, ESV

Music class at Calvert Junior High progressed as usual. That is, until our instructor sat down at the piano with her back to most of the class. Moments later I noticed the girl seated directly to my left roll up a spitball. She placed it in her left hand and sent it to the front of the room, where it danced merrily along the keyboard between the nimble fingers of our instructor. I held my breath as the spitball appeared to be propelled along by the interactive energy of those keys and fingers. Suppressed giggles erupted among the students until our teacher turned to face the class and asked sternly, "Who shot the spitball?"

A blanket of silence covered the students. The girl beside me gave the appearance of perfect innocence, but I could not restrain my giggles. As a result I was asked to leave the class! With my rather spontaneous personality, it took me many years to learn to rein in my humor.

What causes laughter? Why are we created to laugh? Medical science tells us laughter triggers healthy physical and mental changes in the body: it strengthens the immune system, boosts energy while diminishing pain and stress by relaxing muscles and producing endorphins, and improves heart function and blood flow.

Our Creator has set up this complex mechanism within our brain that triggers spontaneous humor from the unexpected. Now I know why a spitball dancing among the ivories on the piano long ago was so funny to the group of early teens.

A prescription given by our Creator to enhance better health is found in His manual for living, the holy Bible. My paraphrase of Proverbs 17:22 reads something like this, "A happy heart is the best medicine!" Commenting on the same verse, Ellen White writes, "There is a physiological truth—truth that we need to consider—in the scripture, 'A merry [rejoicing] heart doeth good like a medicine.' Proverbs 17:22."* He fills our prescription each morning as we take His Word into our hearts through reading, meditation, and prayer. His abiding presence brings us joy and wellness. We become more conscious of His blessings, the voice of the meadowlark, the playfulness of His creatures, and the innocent humor around us. Life's sorrows and burdens seem a little lighter. Remember, laughter begins with the birth of a smile. Let us become infectious!

Dottie Barnett

---

* Ellen G. White, *Education* (Mountain View, CA: Pacific Press®, 1903), 197.

October 1

Healed From Breast Cancer

And whatsoever ye shall ask in my name, that will I do,
that the Father may be glorified in the Son.
—John 14:13, KJV

Almost ten years ago my mother received a devastating diagnosis—cancer of the right breast. Faced with this frightening reality, she turned to us, her family, and asked for prayer. She sought God's guidance and direction, as she was uncertain of her path. My sister, who was an administrative nurse at the time, quickly arranged for a surgical consultation. However, my mother hesitated, expressing a fear that "most people die within one year after a breast cancer operation." Instead of rushing into surgery, she asked us to commit to a month of prayer on her behalf.

With unwavering faith we prayed consistently—night and day—for an entire month. Family members, friends, and even people across the United States of America, Canada, and the Caribbean joined this prayer chain, lifting my mother to the Lord in earnest petitions for healing.

At the end of that month, my mother felt a profound change. She told us, "I feel good. I want to see what is happening in my body. I want to be x-rayed."

Trusting in the power of prayer, she returned to the same doctor who had diagnosed her illness, and she requested a new X-ray examination.

After the assessment the doctor was astonished. He said, "Ms. S, there is scarring on your right lung as if it has been healed."

The cancer was gone, and my mother's body showed signs of recovery that could be explained only as divine intervention.

We rejoiced and shared the incredible news with everyone who had been praying for her. From that day forward my mother never experienced any symptoms of breast cancer again. Her healing was a powerful testament to the truth of God's Word and the strength of fervent prayer.

In James 5:16, we are reminded, "Confess your faults one to another, and pray one for another, that ye may be healed. The effectual fervent prayer of a righteous man availeth much" (KJV).

Indeed God's words are true and consistent. This experience taught us the importance of praying without ceasing, confessing our faults, and partnering with others in prayer. Through intense and earnest prayer, we witnessed God's healing power firsthand, transforming my mother's health and our entire family's faith.

Jazmin Wildman

October 2

Jesus' Spoiled Child

"The LORD himself goes before you and will be with you; he will never leave you nor forsake you. Do not be afraid; do not be discouraged."
—Deuteronomy 31:8, NIV

If anyone had asked for my favorite Bible verse before 2020, it would have been Psalm 46:1, "God is our refuge and strength, an ever-present help in trouble" (NIV), for I loved the assurance that God was my refuge and strength and that He was very present with me in trouble. However, after a period of illness and doctors' inability to diagnose my problems, I turned to the Scriptures to search for some hope. That is where I found today's scripture reading and fell in love with its beautiful promise.

In October 2020, during my annual screening and mammogram, the doctors noticed something that caused them some concern. They ordered a biopsy for me, and although I'd had procedures done before, I felt extremely scared about this biopsy. My family and close friends could see how anxious I felt and did their best to reassure me of God's goodness, but the thing that helped most was this promise: "The LORD himself goes before you and will be with you; he will never leave you nor forsake you. Do not be afraid; do not be discouraged" (Deuteronomy 31:8, NIV).

I held on to that text and immediately felt a sense of calm. I repeated the promise throughout the procedure, and an inexplicable peace replaced the anxiety I had struggled with. I knew I was not alone. My fear disappeared.

At the beginning of this year, while preparing to have another annual mammogram done, the anxiety returned, and I felt uneasy once more. On the morning of my screening, as I opened my morning devotional app, there it was again! Would you believe it? His special message for me that day was the promise in Deuteronomy 31:8. What a sweet reminder. I felt like His spoiled child. I am JSC—Jesus' spoiled child. I thank God daily for His love for me.

Friends, whenever you feel alone, scared, or worried, always remember God goes before you. He is with you, and He will *never* leave you nor forsake you. No matter what you may be facing, remember that each one of us is Jesus' special child. We do not need to fear. Allow His peace and strength to replace the fear and anxiety. We are His, and we are loved.

Jill Springer-Cato

October 3

Your Guardian

The Lord shall preserve you from all evil;
He shall preserve your soul.
The Lord shall preserve your going out and your coming in
From this time forth, and even forevermore.
—Psalm 121:7, 8, NKJV

During the divine service one Sabbath morning, I received Psalm 121:7, 8 as a promise from the Lord. I thanked Him and felt happy, not knowing how much this promise would come to mean over the following months.

I remembered the Jewish custom of writing Deuteronomy 6:4–9 and 11:13–21 from the Torah on the doorposts of their homes so that every time they left or entered, they would remember that they were people who lived in a covenant relationship with God. To this day they still keep the custom of touching the mezuzah, which contains the scripture passages placed on the doorpost, and reciting Psalm 121:8.

So I began to memorize the verses the Lord had given me. However, my interest in deeply understanding the message was heightened eight months later when I was diagnosed with breast cancer. My first reaction to hearing the news was to remember the promise from the Lord. I came home, retreated to the library, grabbed my Bible, and read Psalm 121 a few times.

I prayed, wept, and tried to figure out what God was trying to convey to me in the context of the illness ravaging my body. I stayed there until a few thoughts came to my mind. First, God is my Keeper who will not allow my feet to slip. He never slumbers or sleeps. He is awake 24/7 and watches over me. And finally, God is trustworthy because He is the Creator. He knows me and knows exactly the path of my life—so why should I fear?

Armed with these assurances, I felt encouraged and energized to walk through the valley of the shadow of death with peace, not fear. I began to investigate what I needed for the fight ahead: surgery, chemotherapy, and radiation. With the moral support of my family and the promises of God, I got through the ordeal. Now, six years later, I feel well. But the most important thing I learned was that God cared for not only my body but also my soul. He taught me to trust in His promises and to overcome my fear, anxiety, and discouragement.

My dear ones, love the Word of the Lord. Hold fast to His promises and rejoice in each day, for it is a gift from Him.

Elena Petrescu

October 4

Like A Weaned Child

I have certainly soothed and quieted my soul; like a weaned child resting against his mother, my soul within me is like a weaned child.
—Psalm 131:2, NASB

The news of our daughter's stage four non-small-cell lung cancer hit my husband and me like a devastating storm, leaving us grappling for understanding. Chipo had never smoked in her life. She had lived a healthy life the best she knew how. Intelligent, she graduated summa cum laude with a bachelor of science in nursing. She was only thirty-three, a hard-working nurse who had recently become engaged and was busy planning a wedding. Immediately we cried out to God for a miraculous healing. Through prayer we moved from despair to hope as we called upon Jehovah Rapha, God our healer (Exodus 15:26). Family, friends, and colleagues sought God's healing favor upon Chipo. For weeks the situation remained dire, but we did not give up hope.

A breakthrough came when the doctors confirmed her type of cancer could respond to genetically targeted therapy that cost between US$10,000 and US$15,000 per month. Our joy turned to panic when we learned that insurance would not cover the cost.

"Lord, have mercy on Chipo," we pleaded earnestly. Miraculously Chipo found a sponsor for the costly medication. How we celebrated! For eighteen months Chipo was back on her feet. She worshiped, got married, and visited friends and family. We were sure God had answered our prayer and that she would remain cancer-free. But that was not to be the case.

When her body stopped responding to treatment, she passed away. How my heart wrestled with this loss. However, God gently reminded me of the many miracles He had performed during Chipo's remission, and I started to find peace and slowly began to trust His wisdom and timing.

While Chipo did not receive the complete healing we longed for, those eighteen months were a profound gift I will forever cherish. Like a weaned child, I came to a place of full surrender, recognizing that God is the Creator and I am His child. Like a weaned child resting on my mother's breast, God's provisions—though different from my desires, brought healing, peace, and acceptance. I reaffirmed my trust in God's sovereignty even when His answers do not align with my deepest desires. Like a weaned child, may we all find peace in surrender, trusting the God who knows our deepest needs, even in the most challenging circumstances.

Earlymay Chibende

October 5

Three Rolls and a Divine Thud

Hitherto shalt thou come, but no further: and here shall thy proud waves be stayed.
—Job 38:11, KJV

After an eventful time preparing for a much-anticipated union-wide youth congress in Namibia, I settled into my seat as we departed from the Botswana-Namibia border. The group of seventeen, mostly young people, fell back into our two-vehicle convoy, excited to have begun the final leg of what had already been a twenty-four-hour trip from our home country of Eswatini. We had already traveled through two countries, and now we had entered the third one—Namibia.

We still had about a nine-hour drive remaining before we would reach our destination. All hope of making it to the opening ceremony had been dashed by many delays along the way. We had made peace with the fact that we would arrive at six o'clock on Sabbath morning and had already planned to skip the post-road-trip rest in order to jump into a shower, get dressed in our Adventist Youth uniform, and go to worship the Lord with throngs of other young people from Lesotho, Namibia, and South Africa. At least, that was our plan.

Hours later, after a stop in Windhoek, the capital city of Namibia, those of us who were traveling in the seven-seater vehicle fell into a deep sleep, induced mainly by the fatigue and sleep deprivation of two days of traveling. I was not sure how long I had been asleep when I woke up to the scraping sound of the tires trying to grip the edge of the narrow, tarred road and the descending dirt area that ran alongside it.

The van had rolled, and I was upside down. As it rolled the second time, I screamed for Jesus, and when it rolled the third time, my only thought was, *So this is how it ends*. In response to my resigned conclusion, I heard a loud thud. The van had stopped turning. Miraculously we all survived with only minor to moderate injuries. We missed the Sabbath service that we had long anticipated. But we experienced a divine service of a special kind that day—a service of deliverance on the Lord's day.

What delays, frustrations, and unexpected overturns have you experienced along this Christian journey? Give them to God, my friends. He is able to minister to you even as the billows roll.

Nolwazi Gumbi

October 6

Be Vigilant—Watch and Pray

Take ye heed, watch and pray: for ye know not when the time is.
—Mark 13:33, KJV

A few years ago, after a Women's Ministries Advisory meeting, eight of us directors of the different sections within our union headed for the railway station. Excited to return home after a week of meetings, we enthusiastically chatted and shared the experiences of the past week. We had arrived early to catch our train, and after a while we heard an announcement informing us that the train had been delayed by an hour. No problem! We continued our chatting.

After an hour had passed, another announcement informed us there would be an additional hour delay. But after the second hour had ticked by, there were no further announcements—and still no train. We all began to grow tired. Along with everyone else who waited on the platform, we were sleepy. Some began to stretch and settle down as they dozed off.

It was past midnight when suddenly an announcement split the air. The train was arriving—on another platform!

We scrambled, hurriedly gathering our luggage, and ran to the new platform. The train had finally arrived. People rushed here and there, desperate to reach the train and find a seat. Confusion reigned everywhere as I prayed, thanking God that everyone in our group had managed to board the train—just in time!

This experience reminded me of Jesus' story of the ten sleeping bridesmaids who were waiting for the bridegroom to arrive. I reflected on the condition of those waiting for the second coming of the Lord. We await our Lord's return. Is the love and enthusiasm we had at the start of our spiritual journey still vibrant, or is it slowly fading away? Has the delay in Jesus' return left us feeling lethargic? We are tired, I know. Are we falling asleep?

When the trumpet of the archangel sounds, splitting the air, will we be found ready to meet the Bridegroom? Did we remember to put extra oil in our vessels? Are our lamps trimmed and burning? My friends, any moment now, the announcement may sound, "Behold, the bridegroom cometh; go ye out to meet him" (Matthew 25:6, KJV). If we are vigilant, we will be ready when He calls. Let us not slack in keeping ourselves ready. Let us watch and pray, that we may be filled and strengthened by the Holy Spirit! Jesus is coming soon!

Jeyarani Sundarsingh

October 7

The Day the Bell Did Not Ring

Being confident of this very thing, that he which hath begun a good work in you will perform it until the day of Jesus Christ.
—Philippians 1:6, KJV

It happened a long time ago, but it is something that has never been forgotten. My husband, Ted, was a ministerial intern and served as assistant pastor of the large Southern Missionary College church in Collegedale, Tennessee, USA. Back in the 1950s, a ten-day camp meeting was held each year on campus. Much preparation was required, including pitching tents for the campers. A ministerial intern was kept very busy from morning until night—before, during, and after the meetings—until the last chair was folded and the campus was put back to normal.

One of Ted's duties was to ring the rising bell in time for the campers to be ready for the early morning meeting. After ringing the bell he would go to the far end of the campus to assist in the youth meeting.

One morning the unthinkable happened. We both overslept, waking just in time for him to ring the bell. Frantic, knowing that our conference president, Elder N., was well known for his opinion that unless you were at least five minutes early, you were late, Ted wanted me to put on a robe and go ring the bell while he got dressed. I protested that I did not even know where the bell was! He made it to the youth meeting but overheard two of the campers talking. One said, "The bell never did ring!"

Fortunately for Ted, Elder N. happened to be away from the campus that morning. Years later Ted confessed to that very fine gentleman what had happened. With a straight face and a twinkle in his eye, Elder N. said, "Ted, if I had known, you wouldn't be in the ministry today!"

Fortunately for us, the bell incident did not end Ted's years of ministry, youth work, teaching, and counseling. For many of those years, the two of us enjoyed working side by side.

Now both he and Elder N. are peacefully sleeping, awaiting the next rising bell, which will be when "the Lord himself shall descend from heaven with a shout, with the voice of the archangel, and with the trump of God: and the dead in Christ shall rise first" (1 Thessalonians 4:16, KJV). Now that is a real rising bell, and there will be no oversleeping when it rings!

Mary Jane Graves

October 8

Guided by the Light

The entrance of thy words giveth light; it giveth understanding unto the simple.
—Psalm 119:130, KJV

In the quiet solitude of my dimly lit room, I found myself grappling with a simple task—charging my laptop. The process should have been routine. It is a task I have done countless times before. But on that evening it proved to be a source of annoyance and frustration.

I reached for the charger plug and cord, plugged them into the outlet with ease, then turned to the laptop. I knew where the charging port was. Yet I found myself fumbling for the elusive port as if it were hidden treasure on a dark, unknown path. Each attempt to connect the cord to the port left me more perplexed. How could such a straightforward task be so challenging? Only after surrendering to the stubborn darkness and reaching for the nearby light switch did I finally see the port. The light revealed the way, and my fingers, no longer searching blindly, found their mark.

As I sat there, pondering this brief but perplexing moment, a whisper of realization brushed against my heart. God often speaks to us in simple everyday occurrences, and in these moments His voice resonates, teaching us profound lessons.

In the dimly lit corridors of our lives, we, too, often fumble and falter, searching for direction, purpose, and the power to carry on. The burdens of life can wear us down, leaving us battered and bruised, just like my laptop's neglected battery. At times like this we need the light of God's Word, for it is a guiding beacon in the darkness. It provides direction and strength. When we are spiritually drained, it is His Word that offers us the power to persevere. Just as my laptop needed a source of power to recharge, we need spiritual renewal to face the challenges life presents.

Here is the clincher. I had allowed my laptop's battery to go completely dead before plugging it in, so the process of revitalization took longer. In the same way, when we allow our spiritual batteries to go completely dead, it can be a lengthy and arduous journey to restore our faith, our purpose, and our spiritual vitality. But God's Word is always there, ready to be our guiding light, offering us the power we need.

Father, keep my connection to You constant and consistent, lighting my path daily.

Florence E. Callender

October 9

Training Wheels

And He said to her, "Daughter, your faith has made you well. Go in peace, and be healed of your affliction."
—Mark 5:34, NKJV

When I was a little girl, I had a bike with tall, curved handlebars hung with tassels, a long banana seat—and training wheels. As I grew older I no longer wanted those training wheels on my bike. After begging my dad to take them off and let me try to balance on my own, he finally gave in. I was so excited!

My family lived on the top of a hill at the end of a dead-end road. With Dad holding on to the back of my bike, I started to ride on two wheels ever so slowly. Dad kept holding on, but eventually I was going so fast that he could not keep up, and he let go. When I realized I had left Dad at the top of the hill and that I was now on my own, panic set in, and I crashed. Despite the fall, I gained confidence in my ability to balance on my own, and off I went.

Faith drives us to try. I had faith in my father's willingness and ability to help, and that motivated me to do something bold.

Similarly a woman in the Bible had faith that Jesus could heal her. She knew that if she could only touch His garment, He had the power to heal her disease. If she did it quietly, perhaps no one in the pressing crowd would notice, and she would avoid being punished for making them unclean.

The woman had faith she could be healed even without Jesus being aware that she had touched Him. But He was aware—He felt her faith. He felt her faith so strongly that He experienced the energy leave Him and transfer to her. If she had not had faith in Jesus' willingness and ability, she would not have been made whole. Her life would have remained unbalanced. In the same way, I would have stayed on training wheels if I had not had faith in my dad to teach me how to balance my bike.

We all have doubts and fears, but if we do not grow in our faith in Jesus, how are we ever going to find balance? The woman in the story did not touch His garment because she knew He would heal her—she touched His garment because she knew that He could heal her. Faith motivated her effort; she believed in the only One who could bring balance to her life. Do we believe?

Pam Carbaugh

October 10

Sitting in a Corner

Their strength is to sit still.
—Isaiah 30:7, KJV

I came across a TV show about a group of British nannies who were each assigned to work with American families. Observing their professional disciplinary techniques proved interesting. In our home my parents did not practice "time out," nor did they yell at my siblings and me. My parents often quoted a Bible verse and connected it to our salvation. Their intent was to "train up a child" (Proverbs 22:6, KJV). If emphasis was needed, a brief tap on the legs two or three times with their hands might be in order. Being the eldest child, I hated to disappoint my parents, and I hated to be rebuked in front of my siblings.

At my public school, though, I remember one frightful day in kindergarten when my best bud and I were making clay or paper snakes. To show Kenneth how much I appreciated the realistic appearance of his creation, I screamed. The young and overzealous teacher mistook my scream, snatched me up, and took me into the coat closet, where I had to remain for the rest of the hour. I remember sitting alone among the coats, crying and feeling abandoned and misunderstood.

This year I found a reference to "sitting" as a form of discipline in the Bible and relived that kindergarten moment all over again. In Isaiah, as an attempt to dissuade Israel's warriors from receiving military aid from Egypt, God says, "Their strength is to sit still" (Isaiah 30:7, KJV). To sit still is an acknowledgment of God's voice as the final authority on right and wrong.

Couched with parental disciplinary language, the counsel recorded in Isaiah 30 was aimed at a rebellious and lying nation that refused to hear God's law. At that time Jerusalem despised God's Word and practiced oppressive and perverse actions in its dealings with others. They were counseled that "in quietness and in confidence shall be your strength: and ye would not" (verse 15, KJV). Instead they looked to Egypt for help.

Ellen White gives some insight into what works in discipline: "We must individually hear Him speaking to the heart. When . . . we wait before Him, the silence of the soul makes more distinct the voice of God. He bids us, 'Be still, and know that I am God.' Psalm 46:10, KJV."* Despite the style of discipline, when I sit down with Him, I know I am loved. The Holy Spirit gives the victory.

Elinor Harvin Burks

---

* Ellen G. White, *The Ministry of Healing* (Mountain View, CA: Pacific Press®, 1905), 58.

October 11

Lessons and Blessings

"But watch out! Be careful never to forget what you yourself have seen. Do not let these memories escape from your mind as long as you live! And be sure to pass them on to your children and grandchildren."
—Deuteronomy 4:9, NLT

Today I realized just how blessed I am for being an instant mommy, a *Titang Ina*.* One of my greatest desires is to share and teach my nephews, especially Prince, who stays with me, about important life lessons and values. I want to teach them about the love of God. I want to show them the way to Jesus' feet. Nevertheless, I realize that I am often the one who has something to learn, including some hard but golden lessons from an eight-year-old nephew.

One time he said, "Mommy, I have a question."

"What is it?" I said.

He continued, "Why is it that when I take a bath first, I leave more water in the pail for you, but when you take a bath first, you leave only a small amount for me?"

Dumbfounded, I said, "Oh, I am so sorry. I didn't mean to do it. Don't worry; tomorrow I will leave enough water for you."

One afternoon I arrived to pick him up after school and saw him playing basketball with his friends. As we left, Manong Guard, the security guard, said, "Are you not going to get your ball?"

At first my nephew was hesitant to get it because his friends were playing. I urged him to keep the ball lest it get lost or damaged by the other kids. He did so that afternoon but not the next day. I learned he wanted to leave the ball at school so the other kids could play even without him. It seemed he did not mind others using his ball.

This morning we rode a van to Tamban, our hometown, for the long weekend. I learned that our reserved seats were not together. I felt apprehensive about being separated for an hour-and-a-half ride on public transport. I also thought the space assigned to him was too tight to sit in. As I commented anxiously he calmly said, "It's OK, Mommy. I can fit and sit comfortably."

These are just a few examples of when I have been humbled and honored to learn from a child. They remind me of the golden rule. May we learn lessons in giving and sharing and being patient. Like the Israel of old, may we guard our hearts, words, and ways lest we become detrimental to the spiritual journey of the young people we care for.

Ebonie Barde Base

---

* *Titang Ina* is a colloquial Filipino term for aunts who serve as mothers or guardians to their nephews or nieces.

October 12

Weeds and Thorns

"The seed falling among the thorns refers to someone who hears the word, but the worries of this life and the deceitfulness of wealth choke the word, making it unfruitful."
—Matthew 13:22, NIV

I have always enjoyed a good story, and Jesus' parables are among my favorites. Do you remember the one about the farmer who sowed his seed on four different types of soil? Some fell on the pathway, others on shallow ground, some fell among the weeds and thorns, and "still other seed fell on good soil, where it produced a crop—a hundred, sixty or thirty times what was sown" (Matthew 13:8, NIV).

Confused as to the meaning of the story, the disciples asked Jesus to explain it. He told them the seed represented the message of God's kingdom, and the soils, the various conditions of the hearts of His hearers.

I have experienced each of the soils listed at different seasons of my life. Perhaps you have as well. We love the farmer, we want the seed to be fruitful in our lives, but somehow life surprises us as it unfolds in unexpected ways. Once tender hearts can harden under the burden of disappointment and prevent the seed from taking root.

Or, after a promising start, we grow disillusioned when stubborn character traits remain unchanged. Surely, a transformed life and victorious living should not be so hard.

But at this stage of my life, the condition of heart that trips me up most often is the one overwhelmed by the worries and cares of life. Anxiety seeps into every area of my internal world, stealing my joy, depleting my energy, and leaving me tired and discouraged. I begin to ruminate on the thought that if I could just find a way to earn a little more money, life would be so much easier. And it's true—it would! However, circumstances have limited my options. Life is harder than I had hoped.

Farmers are patient. They understand soil and seasons. They know that not every seed sown will bear fruit. They don't reprimand the seed lost among the weeds and thorns. They look to the seed sown into good soil and anticipate a rich harvest. Even so, the Lord knows we will not always be fruitful. We will miss opportunities, grow weary, feel betrayed by the condition of our hearts. But in due season, His Word will fall into the welcoming soil of our lives and bear much fruit for His glory. Don't lose hope! God sees our hearts. We are safe in the farmer's care.

Karen Pearson

October 13

Caring About Others

Let each of you look not only to his own interests, but also to the interests of others.
—Philippians 2:4, ESV

Mumtaz began working as an outpatient volunteer in the Acute Treatment Unit Department at the hospital. After some months she became a permanent staff member when she was hired as the public relations officer. Her work involves the registration of patients' confirmed schedules at the registration kiosk. She gives them a number tag to take when they have chemotherapy treatment. After treatment the patients return the tag and place it into a slotted box.

Mumtaz is friendly and has a good rapport with all her patients. She has a gift for remembering their names and treats each one with dignity and respect. Sometimes she pushes patients in wheelchairs and helps them check their weight and height using their registration numbers. She also wheels them to a taxi stand or bus shuttle service. When I look at her diligence and her manner of dealing with people, I am reminded of God's tender love for me.

The apostle John reminds us, "But if anyone has the world's goods and sees his brother in need, yet closes his heart against him, how does God's love abide in him? Little children, let us not love in word or talk but in deed and in truth" (1 John 3:17, 18, ESV).

Paul exhorts us to "encourage one another and build each other up, just as in fact you are doing" (1 Thessalonians 5:11, NIV). Paul also urges us to "bear one another's burdens, and so fulfill the law of Christ" (Galatians 6:2, NKJV).

Ellen G. White writes, "Men may speak fluently upon doctrines, and may express strong faith in theories, but do they possess Christianlike meekness and love? If they reveal a harsh, critical spirit, they are denying Christ. If they are not kind, tenderhearted, long-suffering, they are not like Jesus; they are deceiving their own souls. A spirit contrary to the love, humility, meekness, and gentleness of Christ, denies Him, whatever may be the profession."*

I appreciate Mumtaz's example of Christlike love. I want to be more like her as she serves each day as the hands and feet of Jesus. I pray many will come to know and love Jesus as they see His love shine through us in our kindness toward them.

Yan Siew Ghiang

---

* Ellen G. White, *Evangelism* (Washington, DC: Review and Herald®, 1946), 632.

October 14

The Ultimate Antidote for Stress

I will give you rest.
—Matthew 11:28, KJV

The world is full of stressors today. The devil is angry and on the offensive because he knows that he has but a short time (see Revelation 12:12). People are angry and irritable and need only half an excuse to explode. Even in churches this irritability is demonstrated in the way we tend to deal impatiently and unkindly with each other. The world is on edge. We have lost the graces that once defined us as Christians. The world prizes blunt speech, passion, and rage. It is baptized as confidence and assertiveness. People do not care how many lives they have to trample over to get what they want. Profit and personal gain are the bottom lines. "The end justifies the means" is the ruling philosophy.

Jesus knows this experience very well. He was reviled by those he had come to save. "When he was reviled, reviled not again; when he suffered, he threatened not; but committed himself to him that judgeth righteously" (1 Peter 2:23, KJV). The apostle Paul counsels us that when we are reviled and verbally abused, instead of being reactive, we should bless others. When we are persecuted, we should endure it with patience (see 1 Corinthians 4:12).

Jesus is our example and the only effective antidote for a stressed world. "A Christian reveals true humility by showing the gentleness of Christ, by being always ready to help others, by speaking kind words and performing unselfish acts, which elevate and ennoble the most sacred message that has come to our world."*

The psalmist reminds us, "Great peace have they which love thy law; and nothing shall offend them" (Psalm 119:165, KJV). May this peace fill our lives as we determine not to allow things to so easily offend us. Let us have the incorruptible beauty of a gentle and quiet spirit that is precious in the eyes of God.

Dear sisters, Jesus in us is the cure for all sinful conditions: selfishness, a quick temper, a competitive spirit, and a superiority complex. He is the ultimate antidote for the stress of this world. He invites us to open our hearts to Him so that He may come in and dwell with us. His invitation is given to all: "Come unto me, all ye that labour and are heavy laden, and I will give you rest" (Matthew 11:28, KJV). How will we respond today?

Minsozi Sibeso-Mweemba

---

* Ellen G. White, *Christian Experience and Teachings of Ellen G. White* (Mountain View, CA: Pacific Press®, 1922), 74.

October 15

The Power of Healing Words

A word fitly spoken is like apples of gold in settings of silver.
—Proverbs 25:11, NKJV

When I studied communication in school, I learned that words are only 7 percent of effective communication. The other 93 percent of our communication is credited to voice tone, facial expression, and other nonverbal means.

How do we use the 7 percent of our verbal communication? Several texts in the Bible remind us of the need to be vigilant with our words. The tongue needs to be controlled. Here is a good reminder: "Let your conversation be gracious and attractive so that you will have the right response for everyone" (Colossians 4:6, NLT). Another verse reminds us that "gentle words are a tree of life; a deceitful tongue crushes the spirit" (Proverbs 15:4, NLT).

Recently I longed to see a friend who no longer communicated with most of the church members, including myself. I wanted to enjoy sweet fellowship with her once again. Over the years she had designated me as her sister, friend, and counselor, but personal challenges and circumstances in her life had made her bitter.

Many of my attempts to reestablish communication failed. So, once again, I prayed as I texted her.

"My Sister, it has been too long. Can we meet somewhere?"

She responded, "I am in this world alone and just want to leave it there. I will survive alone."

I was shocked. I could hear her anger, pain, and disappointment speaking. After much thought I decided not to respond in kind. I told myself, *Take time to pray for her.*

Forty-eight hours later I saw this text from her, "Thanks for the concern, very much appreciated!" A few days later she sent another positive text that ended with, "Lots of love, stay blessed."

I replied, "Your response brings joy!"

Though I originally had been tempted to respond in kind to her initial text, I gave praise to God for restraining my tongue.

My restraint was confirmed when I read the following quote: "If impatient words are spoken to you, never reply in the same spirit. . . . There is wonderful power in silence. Words spoken in reply to one who is angry sometimes serve only to exasperate. But anger met with silence, in a tender, forbearing spirit, quickly dies away."*

Let us always choose to speak healing words.

Sonia Kennedy-Brown

---

* Ellen G. White, *The Ministry of Healing* (Mountain View, CA: Pacific Press®, 1905), 486.

October 16

The Battle Is Real

For we do not wrestle against flesh and blood, but against principalities, against powers, against the rulers of the darkness of this age, against spiritual hosts of wickedness in the heavenly places.
—Ephesians 6:12, NKJV

Having grown up in the Seventh-day Adventist Church, I knew very well the devious methods employed by Satan and his goal to destroy God's children. Having memorized Bible texts as a child, I felt confident I would never be deceived by the supernatural and would easily recognize an evil spirit should it ever present itself.

However, Satan seems to know when we are the most vulnerable and watches for these openings to deceive us. After my husband died, while getting a massage, my masseuse began to tell me that she had spirit guides on her shoulders that could help me get through this tough time. I did not think too much of it at the time, but it continued to bother me as I was reminded of a familiar Bible text: "For Satan himself transforms himself into an angel of light" (2 Corinthians 11:14, NKJV). Could I be experiencing this angel of light for myself? The thought was frightening, but I wanted to know more.

A few weeks later I returned for another massage, and my masseuse began to tell me that my deceased husband had spoken to her about me. She excitedly shared his extensive message with me. His words were comforting. He assured me that he was fine and that I should move on with my life. In the moment it felt good to hear from him. But wait a minute! Was this coming from one of those evil spirits I had read about in the Bible? As I thought about it, I felt mortified that I had almost been sucked into believing my husband was talking to me from the grave. I knew in my heart this was Satan seeking to deceive me. I recalled the Bible text, "For the living know that they will die; but the dead know nothing" (Ecclesiastes 9:5, NKJV). I was fully convinced Satan was trying to trick me into doubting the Bible, which made me really angry.

I quickly prayed for forgiveness for doubting God's Word and seeking comfort and guidance from an evil source. Satan knew I was vulnerable, hurting, and wanting answers, and he attempted to take advantage of my condition. I praise God that I knew what His Word teaches. The battle is real. Let us determine to constantly keep our eyes focused on Jesus.

Judy Casper

October 17

God's Good News

Do not grieve like the rest of mankind, who have no hope.
—1 Thessalonians 4:13, NIV

Several years ago, my husband of almost thirty-nine years died after battling with Parkinson's disease. In a journey of ten to twelve years, we tried to figure out what illness he had. Appointments with a neurologist and other specialists throughout this disease process helped with the diagnosis. My three sons, parents-in-law, and friends helped me navigate this difficult time. Near the end we decided to place him in a hospice care facility. It was then we realized who our close friends were. They supported our family in so many ways.

One Friday evening a lady who was a fellow Seventh-day Adventist brought us some homemade potato soup and a puzzle. It was a wonderful surprise since I had not planned what we would have for supper. I thanked her and asked why she had brought the puzzle. She said it would give us something to do when my husband was resting. She would occasionally come and visit my husband and bring us another puzzle after we finished the last puzzle. At the hospice center I noticed that other staff and visitors would put in some pieces when they came into the room to care for him or visit. Seeing the progress of the puzzle made me smile.

Recently I went to a memorial service for my friend's mother. The pastor talked about the state of the dead and gave an in-depth Bible study on what happens when a person dies. I was impressed by how clearly he presented what the Bible teaches. He made an altar call and asked people to renew their relationship with God and invited them to ask him any questions they had after the service. I sat beside a Catholic friend and wondered what she thought. I saw her go up to the pastor after the service to thank him and let him know how much she enjoyed his talk.

Yesterday my cousin asked if she should get anointed because of the extreme pain she has after surgery on a broken leg. She is in a nursing home for physical therapy and has leukemia. I told her I thought it was a good idea. She said that it gives her peace to know that her family, church, and friends are praying for her. My husband, cousin, and friend's mom know death is a "sleep," and the next thing they will know is when Jesus comes to wake them before going home to heaven with Him! God loves each of us with an everlasting love. We do not need to grieve as those who have no hope.

Gyl Bateman Walker

October 18

Landmines

*When my spirit grows faint within me,
it is you who watch over my way.
In the path where I walk
people have hidden a snare for me.*
—Psalm 142:3, NIV

I lived in the small Ukrainian town of Gorodnya, not far from the Belarussian border and thirty kilometers, or almost nineteen miles, from Russia. Right from the first days of the war that started in 2022, Gorodnya was under occupation for more than a month. At that time there were no border controls, and many people tried to leave the country through Belarus.

My friend's daughter Sasha was visiting her father in our region while her mother remained in the western part of the country. Due to the danger in our area, Sasha decided to go to her relatives in Gomel, Belarus, when her father left to join the army. Because she was a minor at seventeen, officials from the city guardianship service went to her grandmother's home and said, "We have received a report from Belarusian customs that a girl crossed the border as a minor. Do you have any guardianship documents?" Without proof of guardianship, Sasha would be taken to an orphanage if her parents did not come for her. It was an impossible situation.

When the Russian troops were leaving the Chernihiv region, it meant Sasha could return to our area once the town was liberated. My friend called and asked if Sasha could live with me. Of course I said yes. I arranged for a car to take me to meet her at the border. I called all my friends to pray for Sasha's safety. With no border controls and a no-man's land of two kilometers, she was in great danger. Her grandmother and aunt had loaded her with food and clothing, and she had many bags to carry. She had to go back and forth, moving the bags. As she did, she saw a sign with the words, "Be careful, the road is mined." In the middle of a war, anything could happen.

Our prayers for her safety were answered. She made it across the border without stepping on a landmine. We were all so relieved. This was an incredibly stressful experience for Sasha. She had heard a lot about God but did not have a personal relationship with Him. But in this troublesome time, she experienced firsthand how God protects us and walks beside us on the way. But we need not wait for difficult times to start praying to God. He is always ready to answer our prayers. Even when it seems to us that God is silent, He knows the best way to answer our prayers, and He watches over us.

Natalia Nikolenko

October 19

Walking With Jesus

And they said . . . , Did not our heart burn within us, while he talked with us by the way, and while he opened to us the scriptures?
—Luke 24:32, KJV

Jesus' friends exclaimed the words of Luke 24:32 after they recognized who had walked with them to Emmaus. Does your heart burn within you after spending time in God's Word?

The friends rushed back to Jerusalem to tell the disciples. There Jesus appeared to the group. They were shocked and could not believe He was alive. He reminded them, "All things must be fulfilled, which were written in the law of Moses, and in the prophets, and in the psalms, concerning me" (Luke 24:44, KJV). Likewise, we must study God's Word for ourselves to know what the future holds.

Jesus stayed for forty days after His resurrection to encourage and strengthen His followers. By the time Jesus ascended to heaven, they were fully on fire for Him. Daily they got together to pray and humbly plead with God. They worshiped daily in the temple, met in homes, and generously shared their meals with joy (see Acts 1:14; 2:46). My friends, now is the time to order our lives so we can study together in homes, sharing meals and uniting in prayer with others seeking a closer walk with God.

Through the power of the Holy Spirit, the early believers grew in their faith and gained the gifts of preaching and healing with boldness. We can expect to receive the same and more as we seek to know Him deeply.

Using their gifts resulted in Peter and John being thrown in jail. At their trial the next morning, the leaders were amazed at their boldness, for they knew the men were uneducated, ordinary people. But they recognized them as friends of Jesus (see Acts 4:13).

The council was afraid to sentence Peter and John for fear of a riot, so they ordered them to stop preaching and healing in the name of Jesus. The apostles replied, "We cannot but speak the things which we have seen and heard" (Acts 4:20, KJV).

Sisters, can others see that we are friends of Jesus? As I write these words, my heart burns within me with longing to be bold like Peter and John. Like them I want to exclaim, "I can't stop sharing my experiences." What about you? Do you long for the same experience? Let us determine to follow on to know Him; then, as we walk beside Him, our hearts will burn like fire.

Elizabeth Versteegh Odiyar

October 20

Making Tea

When you walk through the fire of oppression, you will not be burned up; the flames will not consume you.
—Isaiah 43:2, NLT

Finally I felt like writing. I put water on to heat for blueberry tea and sat down at the computer. Since my husband's death a few months before, I had not really wanted to be alone with my thoughts, so writing was not on the menu. But today felt different. I sat in front of my desktop computer, and surprisingly the words began to flow. It was good to get them out. Without my realizing it the water heating on the stove left my mind completely as I poured my heart into writing.

By the time I remembered, it was far too late. With one look at the pan beginning to turn red, I knew it was just minutes away from bursting into flames. I frantically turned off the heat and should have stopped there—but no! I thought it would be a good idea to cool the pan in the sink, and I began to move it. Now, this was a special pan specifically designed to heat more efficiently, and although made almost entirely of stainless steel, the bottom outside of the pan had a sunburst of aluminum inserts. By the time I had the pan hovering toward the sink, I realized with horror that liquid metal was falling from the pan onto the floor, creating small spurts of flames on the vinyl flooring. Panicked, I thrust the pan back toward the stove.

It was only later, after I had extinguished the small flames on my floor and stood surveying the damage, that horror and gratitude both surfaced at once. What if that liquid aluminum had landed on my as-usual bare feet? And at the same moment, why had it not? The only explanation I can find came from the pattern I discovered on the damaged floor. When I examined it, I noticed the two semi-circle burn marks right where my feet had been— a heart-shaped safety margin of almost two inches around my feet.

Maybe a woman lacking the sense to leave a fiery red pan on the stove had the composure to hold that pan at a safe distance from her feet, but, to me, an easier-to-imagine scenario is that God's protection covered me at that moment. And though there were many more trials to face after my husband's death, which I might have had to deal with from a permanent seat in a wheelchair, the memory of God's intervention in my kitchen on that morning stuck with me. It burns brightly still—an assurance of His love for me.

Carolyn Huffstickler

October 21

Meager Fare

Who satisfieth thy mouth with good things;
so that thy youth is renewed like the eagle's.
—Psalm 103:5, KJV

Following a frenetic move to a neighboring state, the 24/7 needs of my beloved but failing husband had me on an erratic schedule. A sinister fatigue became my constant companion. My health suffered. My devotional time also suffered. I would fall asleep at midnight after reading just half of a Bible chapter. I would re-memorize a text only to "lose" it after a night awakening caused by another "did-I-just-hear-him-fall?" thud. Often my little New Testament dropping from hands to chest jolted me into wakefulness. Just as often the best I could do with my leftover moments was snatch a quick Bible promise and run with it for the next twenty hours. Normally, of course, the standard fare verses: "I can do all things," "My grace is sufficient," "Great is His faithfulness," and the ubiquitous "Lord, help me!" But standard fare became meager fare. How I longed for my former lengthy, uninterrupted spiritual feasts in the Word!

Then I remembered John the Baptist's meager fare (Matthew 3:4) in his wilderness season: wild honey and locusts. That was it. Recently, while browsing a couple of websites, I read that the nutritional value of John's locusts—if anything like today's edible African locust pods—probably contained lipids, protein, fat, calcium, fiber, carbohydrates, carotene, retinol, iron, magnesium, and a variety of vitamins. Honey would have provided John with antioxidants and polyphenols, managing his blood pressure, regulating his heartbeat, and improving cholesterol and triglyceride levels. Wow, that does not sound like meager fare, does it? To me it sounds more like a platterful of well-balanced, life-sustaining nutrition!

As my Jim declined and my Bible "snacks" decreased, I noticed something amazing: even snippets of truth and Bible promises were somehow sustaining me, one dark hour at a time. Though that draining season has now passed, I will never forget the quiet miracle of sustenance through my "meager fare."

Whatever your current life season, do not give up if you have time only for "meager fare" from God's Word. Remember the locusts and honey . . . remember the loaves and fishes . . . remember the power in God's Word that fills our souls with good things and renews our strength.

Carolyn Rathbun Sutton

October 22

A Time for Healing

Fear not, for I am with you;
be not dismayed, for I am your God;
I will strengthen you, I will help you,
I will uphold you with my righteous right hand.
—Isaiah 41:10, ESV

The year 2002 changed my life forever. One night I went to bed married and woke up a widow because my husband had died suddenly in his sleep. My son was only eleven years old. I was so angry with God! I had no desire to live, and all I could do was cry. I wanted to die. I could not care for my son, who was also in total shock and disbelief. I could not pray and did not want to pray, but for whatever reason I still went to church, where I spent most of my time in the ladies room crying. I found myself becoming increasingly suicidal.

One Saturday night, while preparing for bed and weak from crying, I began to formulate a plan to end the pain. I thought of jumping out the window of our two-story house, but the registered nurse in me reasoned I would hit the pavement but not necessarily die. I decided against jumping. At that point I realized my thoughts were terribly unhealthy; I needed professional help.

I cried myself to sleep and woke up crying. I cried as I drove to work. When I arrived at the nursing staffing office for my work-location assignment, I was told I had been assigned to the Medical Psychiatry Department. I was dumbfounded. "God, You can't be serious!" I said out loud.

My first patient was a middle-aged woman who had been admitted for attempted suicide. She was living with chronic pain. I spent the first part of my assessment listening to her describe her desire to die. My second patient, a young woman, refused to eat or care for her personal needs because her boyfriend had left her for another woman. My other patients were also suicidal.

I found myself sharing the love of Jesus and promises from the Bible that He can and will heal our pain and strengthen us each day. I forgot my own pain as I ministered to each of my patients. I could not believe what a great day I had! I felt the Lord's presence and sensed Him say, *"Jannett, trust Me. I know you're hurting, but I will take care of you. I will never leave you."*

I have never again thought of hurting myself. God has been the source of my strength and comfort. He continues to care for me and my son.

Whatever your crucible, my friend, remember God always keeps His promises. He will take care of you, and we can trust Him with our children.

Jannett Maurine Myrie

October 23

We Will Never Part Again

Give all your worries and cares to God, for he cares about you.
—1 Peter 5:7, NLT

With the pandemic behind us, for the most part, it is easier to see the impact it had on millions of families around the world. My family is no different, specifically when it comes to my twin sister Valeria, my only sibling. We lived seven hours apart, she in Baton Rouge, Louisiana, and I in Huntsville, Alabama. Separated and masked as we were, staying in touch became all important as the sense of isolation felt overwhelming.

I kept in touch with family as much as I could through free conference calls, Zoom, and texting. This worked with everyone except Valeria because she had no cell phone or internet access. I purchased a phone for her birthday, and she was able to connect by way of a nearby cell tower. She was ecstatic.

Every Sabbath morning we were able to meet together through technology and study the Word of God. My sister had many health challenges and had been on dialysis for seven years. I remember one Sabbath in particular when she really enjoyed our Sabbath School study time with family and friends. She seemed to be doing well, so what happened next came as a big shock.

That same Sabbath evening I received a call from my brother-in-law, James, and my nephew, Patrick. They told me they had found Valeria on the floor. James had come into the house and could not find her. After looking through the house, he found her lying beside the bed on the floor. She was alive. The ambulance came, and the emergency medical staff said she may have had a stroke. They rushed her to the hospital in critical condition.

I felt petrified. Because of the pandemic the hospital personnel would not allow me to see her, and because I lived so far from her, I could only communicate through Google Duo or Zoom with the assistance of the health providers.

Valeria could hear me, and once when I asked her to raise her hand if she could hear my son, Nelson, she did. We were so excited. Three weeks later the doctor called to say I should come to Baton Rouge to say goodbye. I was able to see her once before she passed away.

How I cherish the blessed hope we have in Jesus. Friends, we will see our loved ones again and will live together forever—and we will never part again. Hallelujah!

Vivian Brown

October 24

Knowing God

"Now this is eternal life: that they know you, the only true God, and Jesus Christ, whom you have sent."
—John 17:3, NIV

Cheri Keaggy performed a song many years ago titled "What a Privilege." The lyrics show the listener how it truly is a privilege to personally know the Creator of the universe. He is the same God who spoke this planet into existence yet made humankind with His hands and breathed the breath of life into our bodies.

We are talking about the God who parted the Red Sea so His people could cross over on dry land, and then, once they were safely on the other side, He closed the waters over the pursuing Pharaoh and his army, drowning them. Our God will always make a way out—even when it seems there is no way.

So why am I too busy, too often, to spend time with God? This great God is more than the Eternal King of all creation. He is our heavenly Father who longs for a close and true relationship with me and you. And just like any relationship, it can grow solid and strong only when we spend adequate time with each other.

I have always loved to spend time getting to know God. I read the Bible, enjoy going to church, and love to pray privately. I fellowship with other Christians, and we share our faith and journey in this world. However, I have recently realized I need to work on spending more quiet time with Jesus and ask Him to fill me with the Holy Spirit. The worries of this world and the necessity of work have gotten in the way of really lingering in God's presence and waiting for Him to speak to me instead of rushing off to the next thing on my list to do each day.

When God helped me realize this, I started on a new journey of drawing near to Him and staying in His presence. No relationship survives a quick hello followed by prompt goodbyes, yet we often do so with God. Think about this: We have the King of the entire universe waiting to speak to us and give us instruction every day He wakes us up. Why do we rush our special times with Him? If this were an earthly king or queen, we would do our best to soak up every moment we are in their presence. We have the privilege of spending time with the King of kings! Let us be intentional in getting to know our God.

Alexis A. Goring

October 25

His Extended Hand

"When you pass through the waters, I will be with you;
and through the rivers, they shall not overwhelm you;
when you walk through fire you shall not be burned,
and the flame shall not consume you.
—Isaiah 43:2, ESV

My husband, Ken, and I decided to celebrate his birthday by spending the weekend in Thermopolis, Wyoming, USA. *Thermopolis* is Greek for "hot city"—the town is home to many natural mineral hot springs. Ken's birthday is in February, which often means extremely cold, snowy, and possibly icy conditions. We looked forward to spending some quality time at the hot springs.

We arrived at the Hot Springs State Park before the water park opened for the day. Rather than wait in the car, we decided to walk around the boardwalk. It is always fun to cross the suspension footbridge, also known as the swinging bridge, and view the Bighorn River and the waterfowl. We walked along briskly in the bracing cool winter air, yet we had not thought about the possibility of coming across ice patches. Suddenly we both slipped on one. Thankfully neither of us fell because we caught ourselves in time. After we had steadied ourselves, Ken reached out his hand to me and said, "Let me help you as we walk." Immediately I grabbed his outstretched hand.

We walked hand in hand for quite a while, and I felt more confident once more and eventually let go of Ken's hand. I felt safe and thought I no longer needed his steadying hand. As you have probably guessed, we came across another patch of ice, which was just as slippery as the first one! Again Ken offered his hand for support, and I gratefully took it. Holding his hand made me feel safe and secure once again. Why had I let go?

In that moment I thought of God and His extended hand. "Behold," writes Isaiah, "the LORD's hand is not shortened, that it cannot save; neither his ear heavy, that it cannot hear" (Isaiah 59:1, KJV). There have been countless times He has picked me up when I have stumbled. I am so grateful for His never-ending love.

My prayer for each of us today is that we will never let go of His hand and that we will stay in constant communion with Him. May we trust Him in every situation—and keep holding His hand.

Gayle Cochran Wright

October 26

At Home With Jesus

Now Jesus loved Martha and her sister and Lazarus.
—John 11:5, NKJV

Jesus appreciated the atmosphere of the home in Bethany where He was often invited. It was not uncommon for Jesus to seek rest at the home of the sisters Mary and Martha and their brother Lazarus. There He was treated as an honored guest, and the family rejoiced in His presence.

The Savior left his home in heaven to join the human family. He was never drawn to a home because of its architectural or decorative beauty. Everywhere He went He searched for those who longed for a Savior. It was His joy to bless such, whether they lived in a hovel or a mansion. Human magnificence was never a condition for the visit of the greatest Teacher the world has ever known. He always enjoyed being in the company of His friends in Bethany. Not that it was a perfect home, but Jesus loved those who loved to be found at His feet.

The sisters were women of different temperaments but united by blood ties. Mary is identified in the Gospels as the person from whom Jesus cast out seven devils. She was considered by many to be a great sinner. Martha was a helpful woman, hardworking, honest, and decent. But in seeking to be the perfect hostess, she showed an anxious, restless spirit. Lazarus was responsible for the home and guardian of his sisters. He was a personal friend of Christ.

Each, in their own way, needed Jesus. Mary needed forgiveness and a fresh start. She also needed to be freed from the dark forces that plagued her, making her life miserable. Martha also needed to be set free—free from the cares and anxieties of life. Jesus wanted her to learn to leave her worries at His feet. Lazarus needed healing and, literally, a new birth. This he received from his Friend.

The home, although calm and peaceful, was not a perfect place, but it was there that Jesus found comfort. Despite the sisters' challenges, their home remained a place where Jesus felt special and was welcomed to find rest whenever He needed it.

All homes are, in some way, fiercely attacked by the enemy of God. But when Jesus is the guest of honor, there is no chance for Satan to gain victory. In every home where the Savior can be found and where people seek Him, there will always be light, harmony, and love.

Sueli da Silva Pereira

October 27

House Number 1504

But God chose the foolish things of the world to shame the wise; God chose the weak things of the world to shame the strong. God chose the lowly things of this world and the despised things—and the things that are not— to nullify the things that are, so that no one may boast before Him.
—1 Corinthians 1:27–29, NIV

In 2012 I moved from New York to Florida in the USA. About a year later some family friends came to visit. Gabriel, their younger son, loved to watch lizards and all the other wildlife Florida residents live with on a daily basis. After a few days they decided to move to Florida as well, and we started the process of finding houses for sale.

Gabriel insisted they should not live anywhere else but on my street. I explained this was impossible. I live on a small circular street, and no houses were available for sale. But then I remembered something. When the developers had started to build on my street, I had looked at the only two houses that existed: the beautiful model homes built to impress. One of them, number 1504, was a beautiful two-floor home I had never seen anybody move into. I called the Realtor and asked about it. He told me the house had been sold.

"Are you sure?" I asked. "Because I can see it from my window, and all this year I haven't seen anybody there."

He double-checked and called me back. He said I would not believe what he had discovered: Someone made a down payment of US$30,000, and the house went off the market. Then the buyer disappeared. If this was not crazy enough, it seemed everyone just forgot about it! God had miraculously held the house for Gabriel's family for all that time! This was not presumption. It was pure childlike faith we would do well to learn from.

The Bible is filled with amazing stories of how God works on behalf of His children. For example, the one about a powerful country that chose a foreign slave to be next in line to the throne was the same place that ordered all the baby boys to be slaughtered. Yet Moses was adopted by a princess and raised to be the future pharaoh, though God ultimately had other plans for him.

Our loving Father heard the wish of my young friend Gabriel and made provision for it even before it was asked. What is your heart's desire? God can do some crazy things to further His will!

Kênia Kopitar

October 28

Homeowners in Heaven

"Let not your heart be troubled; you believe in God, believe also in Me. In My Father's house are many mansions; if it were not so, I would have told you. I go to prepare a place for you. And if I go and prepare a place for you, I will come again and receive you to Myself; that where I am, there you may be also."
—John 14:1–3, NKJV

Part of the great American dream is owning your own home. I had the privilege of owning my own house before, and it was a great feeling knowing I had a place to call my own. I could decorate it how I wanted and know it was my safe place. In this season of my life, I do not own a home. I have a place to live, but I do not own it and cannot really make it the way I would like. While I am grateful to have a place to live, I am longing for my own place someday soon. It is a desire shared by many people.

I have been thinking about homes a lot over the past year. I recently listened to a sermon in which the speaker referenced John 14:1–3. It is a familiar passage. I started to think about what Jesus is really saying in these verses. He reassures His disciples that things will be OK and that He is going away but He will come back for them. Embedded within these verses is something that reminds me that I am already a homeowner, and so are you. In verse 2, Jesus says, "In My Father's house are many mansions," letting us know He is preparing them for us. Let that sink in.

You, friend, are a homeowner now, even if you do not own one here on this earth. Too often we get so caught up in this world and what we want here, we forget what is most important—we have a home with Jesus. We have a home without all the headaches of a mortgage, upkeep, property taxes, and maintenance. Though definitely an enormous price was paid for it, our heavenly home does not cost us a thing. Christ wanted us with Him so much that He paid the price to ensure we could all have a home with Him forever.

So when you feel down, longing for the good things in this world more than anything else, remember—you own a home in heaven. Jesus is preparing the perfect home for you, where you will love all your neighbors, and it will be located in the best neighborhood. Your home in heaven was bought and paid for by the One who could not live without you. All we need to do is take ownership of it. I am ready, how about you?

Debra Snyder

October 29

Let God and Let Go

He leads me beside peaceful streams.
He renews my strength.
He guides me along right paths,
bringing honor to his name.
—Psalm 23:2, 3, NLT

At the age of fifty-four, I was retired on disability after working for twenty-one years at the Internal Revenue Service. Suddenly cast out of management ranks with no immediate plans for the rest of my life, I was filled with misgivings and anxiety over the unwanted drama in my life. I moved to Florida in the USA, but after six months found myself uprooted again to Lansing, Michigan, USA, where my mother resided. Neither of these moves were planned.

Jimmy and Rosalyn Carter's book *Everything to Gain—Making the Most of the Rest of Your Life* helped change my thinking. It forced me to consider that if the president of the United States could find purpose after the American people had thrown him out of office, I should be able to make sense of my forced early retirement and do likewise.

For a year and a half, I worked as a secretary-bookkeeper for one of the Adventist church schools. Then I found a job as a tax preparer for a tax franchise, and during the off-season I became an accountant for the franchise's year-round clients. I worked at a certified public accountant office and spent several years working for temp agencies. At church I was a co-organizer for singles, taking camping trips and canoe trips and enjoying fall colors in northern lower Michigan. It was fun to provide Thanksgiving dinner for Michigan State University students who could not go home for the holidays. I also trained for a chaplain assistant position at a local hospital.

My physical health improved, and I no longer needed medication. Though at first I did not understand why retirement had been thrust on me, I now saw how the Lord had worked in my life all along. I became the women's ministry leader and headed up the communications committee at my church. The grief I felt at being turned out to pasture turned to gratitude.

Fast-forward thirty years—I have my own business preparing taxes for about eighty to ninety clients. Every day I walk five miles. My youngest son lives with me in California, helps with my computer and internet problems, and drives me around on California highways. We love to work together in the kitchen, preparing our favorite vegan dishes. When we let God, He renews our strength and guides us along the right paths. With God life is good!

Patricia Hook Rhyndress Bodi

October 30

Facing the Storms With Jesus

But I trust in your unfailing love. I will rejoice because you have rescued me.
—Psalm 13:5, NLT

Why does it feel like getting closer to God is so hard? I once heard the expression, "A good crisis is something to take advantage of." And while no one likes to face a crisis, there is Someone who can use it to help us advance in our journey of faith. If we are willing, God can take advantage of a storm to transform us. He will allow a storm if it means He can use it to help us grow in character and be strengthened in Him.

When the disciples found themselves in a wild storm on the Sea of Galilee, they forgot Jesus was with them in the boat. Jesus used the storm to teach them He controlled the wind and waves. And when they reached the shore and encountered a crazed demoniac (another kind of storm), Jesus calmed the storm within the man. Did you ever stop to think it was Jesus who led the way? He did not bypass the storm. He did not prevent the storm. He weathered the storm with His disciples.

Storms are not only external experiences. Sometimes they rage within us. Emotional turmoil and stress can make our minds feel as though whatever is holding us together is no longer working. Our storms are deeply personal, impacting those parts of us that others may know nothing about. Still, God can use the internal storms to help us grow. It is probably not a pretty situation, but if we hang on to Jesus, He will use it for our good.

Are you in the middle of a storm? Are you confused by things that were going in one direction changing to a direction you cannot begin to understand? Do you feel tired? Drained of energy and emotion? Do you need to find rest? Jesus knows. He sees, even if we feel like no one else has noticed or cares.

Remember Hagar, bone tired and alone with her son in the middle of an emotional storm? She felt unseen and abandoned in an empty, scorching desert. But her Savior noticed. Just like Hagar, our Savior watches us and makes provision for every step of the way. Be assured of His presence and guidance; He cares for us above all. Storms? Jesus is there. No storms? Jesus is still there. We need him every day, every hour, every minute.

Dear Lord, help us to see Your mighty hand so we never forget You are leading.

Yvita Antonette Villalona Bacchus

October 31

Trusting in God's Plan

For I know the thoughts I think toward you, says the L%%ORD%%, *thoughts of peace and not of evil, to give you a future and a hope."*
—Jeremiah 29:11, NKJV

When my husband of almost sixty-six years was nearing his one-hundredth birthday, he knew he did not have much longer to live. He also knew that he did not want me to be alone. So often he would mention different places I might want to live after he was gone. I did not even want to think about it after spending so much of my life with him.

The day did eventually arrive, and while I was taking care of all the final business, my youngest daughter invited me to come and live with her and her husband. All their children were now grown and had homes of their own. The only problem I could see was that I had been born and raised and lived most of my life in California, in the Southwest USA, and she lived in Maine, about three thousand miles away in the Northeast USA. One of my granddaughters came to help me get ready, and I soon found myself flying to my new home in Maine.

For many years I had enjoyed being busy with church activities, but the church my family attended in Maine was very small. There was one other member about my age, but we could not find much to volunteer for in the church. One Sabbath morning I noticed an older lady slip into church quietly and slip out just as quietly before anyone could speak to her. After a while she stayed for the potluck one week, and we were able to meet her. We felt so happy when she gave her testimony in church one Sabbath and soon joined our group.

As a child I had always wanted a little sister but only had an older brother. Now I had met Sue and discovered she lived not far away from me. We had both been widowed about the same time, and she had also moved to Maine from California, another thing we had in common. Although she was the big sister in her family, she was young enough to be the little sister I had always wanted. For several years now we have enjoyed many good times together in and out of church.

Though I had been hesitant to move to a new place, I found I needed to give God room to send me on life's detours. When I did, I discovered so many unexpected blessings came while journeying on roads I did not expect to take. God has a great plan for your life too. Trust Him!

Betty J. Adams

November 1

I Want Jesus to Walk With Me

And Enoch walked with God: and he was not; for God took him.
—Genesis 5:24, KJV

I sat in the pew, preparing to sing the hymn "I Want Jesus to Walk With Me." It was a song my husband, the church band, and I had practiced for weeks. As I prayed, Genesis 5:21–24 caught my attention. I thought about Enoch's relationship with God and how profoundly close it had been.

First, Enoch was sixty-five when he started to walk with God. He was Methuselah's father, and as a parent he understood the need for parents to turn to God at every juncture. *Have I been calling on God on behalf of my child?* I wondered. *Am I leaving her up to chance?*

The Bible says Enoch walked with God three hundred years—three hundred years? I compared this with my walk, highlighting the times I had allowed the rush of life and following my own ways to keep me from consulting Him on important as well as mundane matters.

I reread the verse, and something else pierced my heart. "Enoch walked with God: and he was not . . ." (verse 24, KJV). Enoch's walk was such a daily part of him that he decreased while God increased. Enoch did not lose his personality; it was not taken away. He gladly gave up his will to God, knowing that to lose was gain. To decrease was to experience immeasurable peace and security. Comparing this with myself, I realized Greta was not decreasing as much as she should. There were times when she increased and pushed God into a supporting role—or out altogether.

I looked at the text once more and found infinite love and reward. "Enoch walked with God: and he was not; for God took him" (verse 24, KJV). God had enjoyed His conversations with Enoch so much that He took him in order to continue talking—face-to-face. What about my conversations with God? Does God enjoy them? Are they meaningful, or do I dominate with my demands and commands? Do I allow God to speak into my life, or do I try to speak into His? Would God want to see me face-to-face? I had weighed myself in the balance and had come up lacking.

As I sang, the song took on a whole different meaning. It became a prayer of desperation, a recognition that my life needed to belong fully to God. We all need to make this our earnest cry: "I want Jesus to walk with me / All along my pilgrim journey / I want Jesus to walk with me."*

Greta Michelle Joachim-Fox-Dyett

---

* African-American Spiritual, "I Want Jesus to Walk With Me."

November 2

Unlikely Heroes of Faith

Fixing our eyes on Jesus, the pioneer and perfecter of our faith.
—Hebrews 12:2, NIV

Many unlikely heroes are mentioned in the Bible. Several of them are listed as heroes of faith in Hebrews, the eleventh chapter. Believe it or not, Rahab, a prostitute, is called a hero of faith. And who could ever imagine God would call Gideon a hero of faith? He was hiding and threshing grain, unsure of God's leading or power, and asked for several signs. God had to let him overhear an enemy's dream before he had the confidence to move forward in obedience (see Judges 6; 7). Barak is on the list. He lacked the courage to go to war, even after the prophetess Deborah told him God was commanding him to form an army against their enemy and would bring them victory (see Judges 4). What did Barak do? He said he would not go unless Deborah went with him. Can you imagine, at that time in history, a man going to battle only if a woman went with him? Yet, in Hebrews, he is named as an example of faith.

Hebrews also mentions Samson, a profane, immoral man who finally did turn to the Lord at the end of his life. And then there is Jephthah, who made a very rash and unwise vow that caused him much pain regarding his daughter (see Judges 11). David is also listed, and while we know he was a man after God's own heart, we also know he was an adulterer and murderer who deeply repented.

While we do not know all the backstories and exactly why each of these people is in God's "Hall of Faith," they remind us that God is not looking for flawlessness but faithfulness and trust in Him, which leads to obedience. We cannot make ourselves perfect. He is the only one who can perfect our characters. How does He do this? Hebrews reminds us to keep "fixing our eyes on Jesus, the pioneer and perfecter of our faith" (Hebrews 12:2, NIV).

So, today, do not be discouraged if you feel you are not good enough. Remember these flawed human beings who are called heroes of the faith. If God can make them into faithful heroes, He can do the same thing for His children today. Let us keep our eyes on Jesus rather than our mistakes. He pardons sin and forgives transgression. He will "tread our sins underfoot and hurl all our iniquities into the depths of the sea" (Micah 7:19, NIV). If He does not remember our sins anymore, why should we? Instead rejoice! We have a loving, forgiving Savior.

Myrna L. Hanna

November 3

No Cooling-Off Time Needed

Neither do I condemn thee: go, and sin no more.
—John 8:11, KJV

Have you ever felt, after you have sinned, that you and God need to take a break from each other? That is often how it works with our human relationships, so it seems logical to feel the same way with God. After we argue with a friend or family member, we often take some time away from them to give each other space to reflect and heal. Then, after both parties have had ample time to process and recover, we resume our relationship. It is interesting that when we are children this process often takes only minutes, while as adults it may take several years, and sometimes our relationships never recover.

The devil tries to convince us that our relationship with God is the same as our human relationships. He tells us that after we sin we need some time away from God to get our act together and heal. So we stay away from church for a while, disconnect from our godly friends, or stop coming to God in prayer. However, this is not biblical at all. We can never heal and recover without God. There is no place in the Bible where God says that we should stay away from Him after we mess up.

Take the story of the woman caught in adultery in the eighth chapter of John. First of all, she was caught right in the act of sin. She did not have time to go off by herself and get her act together before coming to Jesus. Look at the way He responds. He is patient and treats her kindly. He forgives her sins and tells her, "Go, and sin no more" (John 8:11, KJV). He does not tell her how disgusted He is with her. He does not send her away until He has had time to think about the situation. He does not call her a failure or say He does not believe she can ever stop sinning. He does not tell her to clean herself up first, and then He will forgive her. He simply forgives her. Right after she had sinned. No cooling-off time needed!

I am so glad we have a High Priest who constantly intercedes for us. "Therefore let's approach the throne of grace with confidence, so that we may receive mercy and find grace for help at the time of our need" (Hebrews 4:16, NASB). If you have strayed from your heavenly Father, come back to Him now. Do not delay. His arms are open wide. We are His daughters, and He loves us beyond compare.

Mary C. D. Johnson

November 4

Search Me, O Lord

*Search me, God, and know my heart;
test me and know my anxious thoughts.
See if there is any offensive way in me,
and lead me in the way everlasting.*
—Psalm 139:23, 24, NIV

My routine for successfully navigating airport security is to ensure I do not have any prohibited items in my carry-on luggage. One day, while preparing for a flight, I made sure to empty my water bottle and remove my smartwatch from my wrist because the security alarm had sounded the last time I went through security while wearing it. This time I was confident that I would pass the security check without any hiccups.

As I went through, I placed my shoulder bag and backpack into the scanning machine, and the security personnel asked me to open my shoulder bag because the scanner indicated a pair of scissors in it. Alarmed, I wondered how I had been so careless. Then I recalled I had put the scissors in my bag while preparing for a recent children's program. I quickly dug into my shoulder bag and removed them. They told me another pair of scissors was in my backpack. How embarrassing! I consider myself a law-abiding person and would never do anything that is against the rules. I searched the bag and even emptied the contents, but I could not find the second pair of scissors. I asked for a rescan of my bag so I could see where the scissors were. The staff obligingly put my backpack through the scanner and told me they were in the side pocket. I dug deeply to find the offending item and removed it.

It is amazing how these machines can identify the items in one's bag without opening it. They can even indicate whether the object is organic, such as food, or nonorganic. Before these machines were invented, bags had to be opened and their contents physically examined.

Just as we cannot see into our closed bag without one of these machines, our sinful nature and desires often may not be transparent to us. Many times we are in denial and feign ignorance, but like the scanner, God sees all. He knows all and does not let these offenses go without bringing them to our attention. Our text for today reminds us to give God the full authority to search our hearts. When we do, He will pinpoint our wrongs that may be hidden from us. With His help we can address them and remove them from our hearts.

Lord, You know my innermost thoughts and hidden sins. Show me what I need to remove from my life, and empower me to live a life that is pleasing to You. In Jesus' name, amen.*

Debbie Saul-Chan

---

* Used with permission. Adapted from a personal Facebook post, January 21, 2024.

November 5

When Comfort Starts to Make You Uncomfortable

In their hearts humans plan their course, but the LORD establishes their steps.
—Proverbs 16:9, NIV

My husband and I were born and raised in Argentina, a country full of beautiful landscapes and rich in culture. For over ten years we dedicated our lives to Adventist education in our beloved province of Entre Ríos. These years were filled with challenges and blessings. Each day God showed us His faithfulness in challenges both big and small. We saw His hand in the dedication of our colleagues, in the smiles of the students, and in the moments of learning and growth that we shared. Working for the university and the school gave us a very comfortable life. We built our house, made a good income, and had friends and family nearby. Everything was going very well—more than well. We felt satisfied and content with life.

However, amid this comfort, we began to feel an unease in our hearts. It seemed God was calling us to step beyond our comfort zone. We sensed He was preparing us for a new mission. We remembered Proverbs 16:9, "We can make our plans, but the LORD determines our steps" (NLT). Though we had charted our course in Argentina, we understood that the Lord directed our steps. In prayer we surrendered our doubts and fears to God, trusting that He would guide and provide for us in every new chapter of our lives.

We contacted Andrews University in the United States of America to enroll in the English as a Second Language (ESL) program. We prepared to leave, resigned from our jobs, rented out our house, and bought plane tickets with the certainty that God was guiding our steps. However, just before we left, the COVID-19 pandemic disrupted our plans. Opportunities closed, and the university informed us that English classes would be held online rather than in person. This news was a hard blow for us. We had given up everything for an immersive learning experience.

In the midst of uncertainty, we clung to our faith and God's promises. Although our plans had crumbled, we trusted God had a greater purpose for us. The pandemic taught us to depend entirely on God and to be flexible with our plans. He used this situation to strengthen us and prepare us for the future. We learned to trust Him more. Friends, we can be confident in times of uncertainty, for while our plans may change, His love and guidance remain constant. Always.

Nadia Trossero

November 6

Tattoos of the Heart

*"I will put my law in their minds
and write it on their hearts.
I will be their God,
and they will be my people."*
—Jeremiah 31:33, NIV

Nearly half of young adults in the United States of America are inked with tattoos. A powerful motivation for getting a tattoo is to express one's individuality and freedom. Another driving force is to identify with a certain cause or group, culture, or religious tradition. Other reasons can be darker: addiction, seeking attention, or drunken impulsiveness.

The practice of inking the body with tattoos goes back in time across cultures. Some Egyptian mummies have tattoos. Some tattoos were religious symbols, such as the all-seeing Eye of Horus. Egyptian women used tattooing for cosmetic and decorative purposes. When tattooed with the name of a god, Egyptian slaves were marked as property of the god through his priests or pharaoh. In other cultures, past and present, tattoos invoke magical protection from evil or indicate group membership. In 1769 Captain James Cook documented the practice of *tatau* in the South Pacific islands. It was exotic to him because tattooing had been banned in Europe a millennium earlier by Pope Hadrian. It was considered to be sacrilegious because it disfigured God's likeness (the human body).

One might wonder whether Isaiah had tattooing in mind when he wrote, "Some will say, 'I belong to the Lord'; . . . still others will write on their hand, 'The Lord's' " (Isaiah 44:5, NIV). Should I show my submission to God with a religious symbol tattooed on my hand?

The Mosaic law, of course, commands us not to put tattoo marks on ourselves (Leviticus 19:28). We do not live in Egypt of antiquity, we are not God's slaves, and we do not need a talisman to gain His protection. But His people are commanded to observe the Sabbath as "a sign between us" (Ezekiel 20:20, NIV). Sabbath observance is our mark of identity and group membership. It shows our allegiance to Him and acknowledges that it is the Lord who delivers us from the slavery of sin and who sanctifies and redeems us. Keeping the Sabbath shows loyalty to our Creator. This is the right motivation to keep the seventh-day Sabbath.

In turn God provides more than a skin-deep tattoo. He writes His law of love into our hearts and minds, and this is visible through obedient worship, our witness, and our loving acts for others.

Lisa Beardsley-Hardy

November 7

God's Faithful Preparation

What, then, shall we say in response to these things? If God is for us, who can be against us? He who did not spare his own Son, but gave him up for us all—how will he not also, along with him, graciously give us all things?
—Romans 8:31, 32, NIV

At noon on a seemingly ordinary day in November, my life was shaken to the core. My husband was one of two victims of a highway robbery two towns away from where we lived. He received three gunshots from two gunmen, resulting in a close encounter with death. The terror I felt at receiving the news was overwhelming. I rushed to the hospital, praying fervently even as memories of our past trials came flooding back. I remembered the fear, the helplessness, and the desperation that marked the time in our lives when our son had nearly died years before.

As I sat by my husband's side, watching him fight for his life, I could not help but think of how God had brought us through our son's ordeal. I realized God had used that situation to build my faith and deepen my trust in Him. Paul reminds us in Romans 8:28 that "in all things God works for the good of those who love him, who have been called according to his purpose" (NIV). This promise became a lifeline for me, for it reminded me that even in life's darkest moments, God is at work, shaping, strengthening, and preparing us for what lies ahead. Through prayer and trust in God's plan, I witnessed another miracle from God.

Our faith in God teaches us about the power of His providence—that He is always at work in our lives, often in ways we cannot see. Looking back, I can now see how God used the trial with my son to prepare me for the challenge of caring for my husband. The fear was still there, but so was the faith. I knew that God could preserve my husband's life just as he did my son's. By God's grace my husband survived. His recovery is a testament to God's power and mercy. This experience reinforced my belief that nothing in our lives happens by chance.

Every trial is part of God's greater plan to prepare us, grow our faith, and bring us closer to Him. As we cling to His promises, we will find peace even in the storm. We can trust His providence and His purpose for us.

Ardie Diaz

November 8

Fear Not

Fear thou not; for I am with thee: be not dismayed; for I am thy God: I will strengthen thee; yea, I will help thee; I will uphold thee with the right hand of my righteousness.
—Isaiah 41:10, KJV

As the end of World War II drew close, my mother lived with her mother, three sisters, and an aunt in the small town of Rudenhausen, Germany. Their father, like many who had been forced to become soldiers, had been killed on the border of Germany and Russia. At the tender age of eight, my mother learned her father would not return home.

Each day became a fight for survival. During the summer the children went to nearby farms and hoped to find an apple that may have fallen to the ground. However, during the winter months the ground was covered by ice and snow, and many died of malnutrition.

Prayer became essential. One day the family woke up and did not have a morsel of food in the house. The farmers had allowed the girls to search their land, but no apples remained on the ground. Their stomachs grumbled with hunger pains, and their mother wondered whether they could last until the next ration and how long that wait would be. As dinner time approached, my Oma (German for grandmother) gathered her daughters together for evening prayer to thank the Lord for bringing them through another day. As they ended their prayer, there was a knock on the door. One of the girls ran to the door to find a basket filled with salad, fruit, and nuts. They never found out who left the food at their door.

Another answered prayer allowed the family to remain in their home during the war. Many homes were leveled by bombs, and those homes that remained would likely be taken by soldiers who needed a place to stay. Horror stories abound of the atrocities committed by soldiers, so when the American soldiers walked into my mother's home, the girls ran and hid. As the soldiers looked at the girls attempting to hide, they took candy out of their pockets and offered it to them. Though the soldiers only spoke English and my mother and her family spoke German, they overcame the language barrier using sign language. One of the soldiers motioned to my grandmother, pointing to the attached barn. She immediately understood the family would not be harmed by the soldiers and would be allowed to stay in their barn.

We face instability every day, but we can find peace in the promise that "my God shall supply all your need according to his riches" (Philippians 4:19, KJV).

Beatrice Tauber Prior

November 9

Help on a Dark Night

"Be strong and courageous. Do not be afraid or terrifed because of them for the LORD your God goes with you; he will never leave you nor forsake you."
—Deuteronomy 31:6, NIV

When the invasion of Ukraine began, it was terrifying to hear airplanes roar overhead, flying low, just above the rooftops. My husband and I would go to bed fully clothed so we would be ready to jump up and run to the basement whenever the air raid siren sounded. But we lived on the eighth floor, and the elevator often did not work, so we would have to climb eight floors on our way back. In the news we heard stories of soldiers brutalizing and abusing civilians.

At the entrance to all our towns were roadblocks of sandbags and concrete blocks that were manned by armed territorial defense forces. Despite the great risk, we knew we had to leave the country. We climbed into the car in a hurry. We could not take much with us, but we had the most important thing—our documents.

We drove along rural dirt roads as we made our way to our son in Poland. The road signs and village names had all been painted over, and the GPS was not working. Additionally, it began to snow, which soon covered the roads with six inches of snow and ice. We could hardly see where to go, but we pressed on until we came to a steep hill. In the wind and snow, our car stopped halfway up the hill. We were stuck. Surrounded by darkness, with trees on both sides, we could see nothing. How we prayed!

Suddenly eight men appeared out of the darkness, some in camouflage uniforms. They turned our car around in the snow and drove it down the hill. We turned around and drove up again, building up speed, while the men waited for us on the dangerous part of the road. As soon as the wheels started to slip, they were ready to push us up. With their friendly help we made it to the top of the hill and thanked them profusely as they wished us well.

We knew God had sent them to help us in answer to our prayers. It was after midnight on a small country road in total darkness with no one around. On our journey God sent kind people who offered us a place to rest, and when we were hungry, they offered us milk—the only thing they had. All along the way we saw God's hand and His loving care for us. Ultimately we moved to Germany, where we found a welcoming church family. When God is with us, we need not fear, even on dark nights.

Tatyana Zvereva

November 10

Angry People

For the wrath of man worketh not the righteousness of God.
—James 1:20, KJV

Everywhere I turn it seems I find angry people. I go to work, angry people. I head to the supermarket, angry people. I make my way to the bank, angry people. I listen to the news, angry people. I go to church, where we meet with God and should have the spirit of peace more than anywhere else, and what do I find? Angry people. This anger is so pervasive that it presses in on us from every corner, leaving me to wonder whether I am also exhibiting this undesirable attribute.

By God's grace I cannot allow the spirit of anger that is floating around to invade and destroy me. So what am I to do, and where should I turn for help to combat the spirit of anger? How do I stand firm with my feet planted on solid ground? I do not know about you, my friend, but I go to the Rock. Jesus is the Rock of my salvation. He is the solid Rock on which I can safely stand. He is my shelter, and when I need a friend, He is the Rock to which I cling.

To find Him I reach for my Bible, which is the true and living Word of God. Within those pages I find precious promises that give peace in the midst of anger. I discover a calm that sustains me through the storms of life and gives me hope in times of despair. God's Word has the power to lift our hearts and fill our lives with joy. It gives light to our darkness and shows us where to walk in safe paths. Through His Word God envelops us in His loving care.

When I spend time with Jesus, I find myself renewed, strengthened, and filled with the power of His Spirit that enables me to stand in the arena of anger without being harmed, without being consumed. This is because I know that it is "not by might, nor by power, but by my spirit, saith the LORD of hosts" (Zechariah 4:6, KJV). I claim the promise that "no weapon that is formed against [me] shall prosper; and every tongue that shall rise against [me] in judgment [I] shalt condemn" (Isaiah 54:17, KJV).

Therefore each day I go out, having my waist "girt about with truth, and having on the breastplate of righteousness; and [my] feet shod with the preparation of the gospel of peace" (Ephesians 6:14, 15, KJV). Where there is anger I now find peace, gladness, and laughter. I continue to rest and hope in Christ Jesus, our Savior and Redeemer. He is the only remedy for angry people in an angry world.

Elizabeth Ida Cain

November 11

A Decision to Serve

"No one can serve two masters; for either he will hate the one and love the other, or he will be devoted to one and despise the other. You cannot serve God and wealth."
—Matthew 6:24, NASB

My husband and I were surprised when our oldest son informed us he planned to join the army. He had just started his senior year at a Christian academy. I hoped it was just a passing phase; after all, when he was a young boy, he wanted to be a garbage truck driver!

He signed up in December after September 11, 2001, and joined the Army National Guard so he could continue college and still serve his country. I encouraged him to talk to God about this big decision, but he was so influenced by the events on September 11 that there was no changing his mind. Forty-eight hours after graduating from specialized training in the military police, he deployed to Iraq, where he served for fifteen months. The Lord protected him and his company.

My son's decision to serve has been a "journey" for our entire family. He missed many family events, holidays, a wedding, a funeral, and his brother's academy graduation. I know my son believed in his mission while serving in Iraq.

I joined Blue Star Mothers of America, supporting other parents with children serving our country. We sent packages to the troops who were overseas. This support group became very important to me as I learned how to deal with things my son and his unit were experiencing. I served as a chaplain for many years and still serve in this capacity.

In life we make many decisions. Some we make without much thought, such as setting our alarms before going to bed, what to eat for breakfast, or what to wear. However, there are more important decisions we are called to make that will be life-changing for us: which career path to choose, whom we will marry, whether or not to have children, and what church we are going to join.

God calls us to decide whether we will follow Him, and He does not want us to delay. He wants us to study and make an informed decision as to whom we are going to follow. Satan also is calling us to pledge our allegiance to him. To delay making a decision or to "not" decide is still a decision. We cannot sit on the fence when it comes to choosing whom we will serve, as Matthew 6:24 states. So let us choose to follow Jesus each day, and soon we will spend eternity with our Creator and Savior!

Gyl Bateman Walker

November 12

Patience

I waited patiently for the LORD; he turned to me and heard my cry.
—Psalm 40:1, NIV

A hot-tempered person stirs up conflict, but the one who is patient calms a quarrel.
—Proverbs 15:18, NIV

After a meeting at a swanky hotel resort in Scottsdale, Arizona, USA, it was time to find our car in the sprawling parking lot that surrounded the huge building. My husband and I had walked many, many steps when we saw a golf cart driver transporting other weary searchers.

"Can you help us?" we asked the driver, and as the conversation progressed, we realized we knew the owner of the company for which she was driving. We chatted for an extended length of time, with her and the other passengers in the hot, muggy weather (yes, Arizona gets humidity!), when I noticed a huge SUV waiting behind the golf cart. There was no place for the driver to go around us—we occupied the width of the driving area.

As the golf cart drove away, I felt responsible and offered an apology to the patient driver. There had been no coarse language, no beeping horns, no rolling of the tires toward the cart, no hand manipulations—just patient waiting.

I approached the driver and poured out my sincere apologies and gratitude for her patience. I noticed the name badge she wore and knew she was attending the Alcoholics Anonymous meeting that also was being held at the hotel.

She replied, "Well, I've had a rough day. I just sat here and took the time to pray for patience and understanding. I figured that was the smartest thing to do at this moment." She accepted my apology, smiled graciously, and slowly drove away.

A rough day. My imagination filled with all sorts of challenges, temptations, and hopefully victories she may have experienced. Despite it all she had not let the exuberant, time-consuming, inconsiderate lady (me!) rob her of her peace and calm. She maintained her poise through prayer.

When we have a rough day that ends with even more challenges, may our first response be to pause and pray. Praying for this unknown lady has become part of my prayer life. That is the least I can do after her powerful example. *God, thanks for continuing to provide for her.*

Lynn Ortel

November 13

Broken Fences and Answered Prayers

Wait for the Lord; be strong and take heart and wait for the Lord.
—Psalm 27:14, NIV

The backyard fence was badly damaged, and it was time to replace it. To get an idea of the cost and the best price for the replacement fence, I went online to check out some of the fence companies. I earnestly prayed for God to help me find a reputable company with a good price for the fence we needed.

After checking several companies, I contacted and made appointments with two of them to get free quotes. The first man came and gave a quote that seemed reasonable, but I was not happy with his terms and warranty.

I continued to pray for God's guidance when Chris, the man from the second company, came to take fence measurements. He said he would email his quote at the end of the week. In the meantime I kept checking out fence companies online and even made an appointment with another popular company to come and give us a quote the following week.

I felt quite anxious and worried throughout the week as I wondered what Chris would quote us for the fence. I kept checking other fence companies online while pleading with God to help me find the right company. The mixed reviews left me feeling quite confused and a little overwhelmed. While searching on Google, I came across the Better Business Bureau website and was surprised to read all the negative comments regarding the third company with whom I had made an appointment. Suddenly Chris's company's website popped up. I clicked on the popup and read the reviews on their website and saw they were overwhelmingly positive. Reading those comments left me with a sense of calm and peace. I thanked God for giving me this peace and prayed Chris would email me a good quote.

The next day, after praying, I checked the email and was thrilled to see the price quoted was almost the same as the one I had received from the first company. I praised God for answering my prayer for a good price from a reputable company. I knew God was leading and immediately canceled the appointment with the third company.

How amazing that God hears our prayers. We can trust in His leading. No matter what we may face in life, large or small, we can always count on help from our heavenly Father.

Stella Thomas

November 14

A Purpose and a Plan

For I know the thoughts that I think toward you, says the L<small>ORD</small>,
thoughts of peace and not of evil, to give you a future and a hope.
—Jeremiah 29:11, NKJV

Our church visits two nursing homes monthly and sings with the residents there. On one of our visits, some of the children in our Adventurers Club joined us. They sang a song titled "The Commission" by the singing group Cain. The song talks about Jesus getting ready to leave and go back to heaven. Before He leaves He tells His friends that they have a purpose and He has a plan—for them to tell others about Him.

One Sabbath afternoon an elderly resident joined the singing, along with her daughter and granddaughter who were visiting her. The elderly lady brought her well-loved baby doll along with her so the doll could enjoy the singing too. I watched how she tenderly fulfilled her purpose by lovingly holding her "baby," and my heart was touched. As we shared our music, I began to wonder about my purpose.

Shortly after this I received my July copy of the *Adventist Frontiers* magazine. As I read through it, two words leaped off the pages several times. I am sure by now you can guess what those two words were. If you guessed *purpose* and *plan*, you are exactly right. The word *purpose* was used eight times, and the word *plan* was used nine times.

I have been diagnosed with two copies of a variant gene associated with an increased risk for Alzheimer's disease. As my forgetfulness increases, this diagnosis concerns me. However, there are two thoughts that I hold on to. The first is, I love Jesus and He loves me. The second thought is, I love my family, and they love me. As long as I can remember those two things, nothing else really matters.

I have come to the conclusion my purpose in life is to show Jesus' love to others. Is this not God's purpose for each and every one of us? Sometimes it is hard to do this in a world where so much hurt, pain, and sadness exists. *But* (my favorite word) God is in control, and one day soon we are going to see Him return in all His glory. He has a plan, and we have a purpose. Let us show others His love. If you are not familiar with the song "The Commission," I encourage you to listen to it on YouTube.

Kathy Hull

November 15

Are You Lucky?

*"Blessed is the one who trusts in the LORD,
whose confidence is in him.
They will be like a tree planted by the water
that sends out its roots by the stream.
It does not fear when heat comes;
its leaves are always green.
It has no worries in a year of drought
and never fails to bear fruit."*
—Jeremiah 17:7, 8, NIV

I am currently searching for my next career opportunity and have participated in many phone interviews. At an in-person job interview, I was asked, "Are you lucky?" *Why did she ask me that question?* I wondered. *What does this have to do with the position I am interviewing for?* My immediate response was, "No, I am not lucky. I am blessed!"

As I reflect on this exchange, I believe this question was asked to learn a little more about me and was not necessarily about the job. The blessed person trusts in the Lord, while the lucky person trusts in chance to bring about a favorable result. I also realized that I had been allowed to witness for the God I serve, the One who blesses me. As stated in 2 Corinthians 9:8, "God is able to bless you abundantly, so that in all things at all times, having all that you need, you will abound in every good work" (NIV).

While I was not blessed with that position, I know and believe "every good and perfect gift is from above, coming down from the Father of the heavenly lights, who does not change like shifting shadows" (James 1:17, NIV). My career search has been long, yet I know the Lord will bless me with the job that is best for me.

The unexpected blessings I have received in the past led me to exclaim, "Now to him who is able to do immeasurably more than all we ask or imagine, according to his power that is at work within us, to him be glory in the church and in Christ Jesus throughout all generations, for ever and ever! Amen" (Ephesians 3:20, 21, NIV). As I continue my career search, I am encouraged by these words:

"The LORD bless you
  and keep you;
the LORD make his face shine on you
  and be gracious to you;
the LORD turn his face toward you
  and give you peace" (Numbers 6:24–26, NIV).

I am blessed indeed!

Sylvia A. Franklin

November 16

An Address Label Changed Her Life

Cast all your anxiety on him because he cares for you.
—1 Peter 5:7, NIV

In 1968 a teenage girl, traveling alone in a foreign country, sat scared and shivering at the Los Angeles airport in the United States of America. She kept rubbing her arms to keep warm. It was not this cold back home in the Philippines. A man wearing a long coat sat close by and kept watching her. Then he approached her, took off his coat, and gave it to her. How kind! *What a wonderful place the United States must be*, she thought.

Her travel to the United States started with an address label she had peeled off a church magazine. It was because of the person named on the label that her life was changed. At fourteen, with nine brothers and sisters and an endless money problem, her dream of going to college seemed impossible. She had already quit school for two years to help her mother earn a living.

In desperation and after months of prayer, she followed the advice of her older sister to write to someone in the United States. Her sister knew of classmates who were sponsored by generous Americans. But how and where would she find such a person? She spent months checking church magazines and found American names but no addresses.

Then one afternoon an uncle came to visit. In his arms was a package of old *Review and Herald®* magazines wrapped in brown paper. As he laid it down, the sight of an almost peeled-off address label caught her eye. She tore off the label and kept it in her room. That night she wrote to Mrs. Beryl McLarty in Memphis, Tennessee. To her surprise the lady answered. She found out she was a seventy-five-year-old lady who was willing to sponsor her. Soon the girl was on her way to the United States, where Beryl soon became a grandma to her.

Overwhelmed by the kindness shown to her, the girl returned to the Philippines, where she studied hard and graduated from Philippine Union College with a degree in medical technology. After graduation she went back to Memphis to live with her Grandma Beryl. She was able to send two of her younger sisters to nursing school.

How do I know this story is true? Because I was that teenager! And because of my love for Jesus, I started Adopt a Minister International and Help the Needy, Inc., ministries. To God be the glory!*

Reva Lachica Moore

---

* Adapted from Adopt a Minister Facebook page. Used with permission.

November 17

Curiosity Saved the Cat

Let us stop passing judgment on one another.
—Romans 14:13, NIV

You know the old adage "Curiosity killed the cat"? It is another way of saying, "Stop being so curious; it may get you into trouble."

But getting curious has revolutionized my mental health. I spent decades passing judgment on myself and others. However, like many of us, I was often a grueling judge toward myself and much softer on other people.

Part of my journey to better mental health taught me that I needed to remove that harsh judge from having a seat at the table and, instead, invite curiosity to join the conversation. You see, every time I passed judgment on myself, my identity in Jesus was dismissed. I allowed judgment to slap a label on me or my behavior, and then I would sulk in guilt and shame for days. I judged myself as if God were judging me in the same way.

But God is a righteous judge, which means He does not judge me the way I do. He factors in my genetics, my pain, my trauma, my circumstances, and my knowledge, all while keeping my identity as His child intact before making a righteous judgment. His heart is always in my favor. While I might tell myself, *Ugh! You're a failure!* God says, *"My child is hurting; I want to heal the reason behind her pain, acting out, or sin."*

As I learned to invite curiosity into the conversation, the tables turned. Curiosity has shown me the way to discover *why* I do what I do. Asking questions instead of placing labels puts me in the position of a learner, and those discoveries show me what tools I can use to help myself grow. It also allows me to invite God to heal those spaces.

God wants me to get off His seat of judgment and allow myself to be loved by a kind and fair Judge who also happens to be an incredible Healer, capable of turning areas of brokenness into testimonies of His goodness. How freeing is that?

So the next time you are tempted to let self-judgment have the final say, get curious with Holy Spirit discernment instead. Watch God do something special for you as you keep your identity in Him and surrender the root causes to His healing hands.

Sarah Casper

November 18

A Hiding Place

You are my hiding place; you will protect me from trouble.
—Psalm 32:7, NIV

I was living in a big nine-story apartment complex. One afternoon on my way home from work, as I approached the apartment building, I saw a small kitten running toward me. It looked terrified. With its ears pressed flat against its head, its eyes filled with fright, the kitten was trying to escape a big, fierce stray dog that was chasing it. Before I knew it the kitten flew up my pants and snuck under my jacket. I could feel his little body tremble as he clung to my body in the safety of the hiding place he had found inside my jacket.

The dog ran up to me and skidded to a sudden stop. It looked around and sniffed the air. It looked up at me with a perplexed expression and seemed to ask, "Where has that little cat disappeared? I was just chasing it!"

I talked to the dog in a soft, soothing voice, "You're a good dog. You're such a good boy. You can go for a walk now. Come on. Run along. Go for a walk. Go!"

And off it went on its way.

I stood and wondered, *What in the world am I going to do with this kitten?* I was sure he must belong to someone, and they were probably looking for him.

Just then a woman in slippers came out of the doorway. She wore a coat on top of her robe, and as she walked she looked around, obviously searching for something. She saw me and asked, almost in tears, "My son is crying because his little kitten ran away! The door was left open, and he must have scampered out! We have already looked for him in the house and on the street." The poor lady was distraught. She continued, "My husband and I can't find him. He's nowhere to be found, so we prayed and asked God to find him. My son is crying for his pet!"

I unbuttoned my jacket and asked, "Is this your lost kitten?"

Her eyes widened in astonishment. How had the kitten found its way under a stranger's jacket? The whole family was so happy to find their kitten, delighted he had found a hiding place from a stray dog. They thanked God for His help, and the little boy was thrilled to get his beloved kitten back.

A tiny kitten is such an insignificant thing, but God heard and answered their prayer. He hears our prayers, too, when life overwhelms us and we find ourselves in trouble. When we cry out for help, He is always by our side. He is our place of safety. He is our hiding place.

Tatyana Zvereva

November 19

The Lost Dog

*He who did not spare his own Son but gave him up for us all,
how will he not also with him graciously give us all things?*
—Romans 8:32, ESV

My husband, daughter, and I had wrapped up a shopping trip in a nearby town when we decided to take the scenic road home. I drove while my husband, who is diabetic, ate his lunch. We were a few miles from home when I saw a small dog run toward us in our lane. When it did not run over to the side of the road, I slowed down and came to a stop. I waited a while and then climbed out of the car to see what it was doing. The dog promptly ran over to the open door, jumped in, and sat down in the driver's seat.

My husband thought it was likely a neighborhood dog and that we should give it a piece of his sandwich and put it back outside. I thought the dog might be lost. To help solve the dilemma, my daughter texted a picture of the dog to two friends who lived in the neighborhood.

One friend texted her back and said a friend had just posted pictures of the little dog on Instagram, asking for prayers for its safe return. We contacted the young woman and made arrangements for her to pick up the dog at our house. It turned out her husband was a youth pastor at a nearby church, and they had both graduated from the university where my husband taught.

We learned the little dog's name was Luna, and she had dug a hole under the fence meant to protect her. Outside of stopping our car and getting in when I opened the door, Luna did nothing to get home. We texted, messaged on Instagram, found her family, and gave her a ride. Luna could not do any of those things for herself.

I cringe to think of the times in my own life when I, too, dug a hole under the fence meant to protect me and wandered off. Since I am not capable of getting home on my own, I am thankful for my Father "who did not spare his own Son but gave him up for us all" (Romans 8:32, ESV). When we ask God for help, He does everything else. It is His grace, His faith, and the salvation He gives us, not because we are good but because He loves us. And He reminds us in His Word, "By grace you have been saved through faith; and this is not of yourselves, it is the gift of God; not a result of works, so that no one may boast" (Ephesians 2:8, 9, NASB).

Miranda Hadley

November 20

God Cares

May the kindness of the Lord our God be upon us.
—Psalm 90:17, NASB

My precious fifteen-year-old dog, Ms. Molly, died while lying on my lap. A few days later I packed up most of Molly's belongings and took them to the veterinarian's office to give to people in need of doggy things.

While I was there, a lady was walking her dog, Luna, into one of the exam rooms. This huge black dog dragged her owner over to me as I sat with an assistant. Luna laid her doggy head on my lap as her owner tried to pull her off. Dr. Hughes walked out and told the owner to let her dog show me much love because my baby had died two days ago. Then that precious dog jumped up and gave me the biggest hug, wrapping her front legs around me. After the hug she laid her head back in my lap as I rubbed and hugged this beautiful dog. She then took her left paw and placed it on my lap as if to say, *Everything will be OK.* She sat in front of me for a moment, as if to say goodbye, and then walked away. I could not help but cry. I stood up to leave and everyone, even Molly's doctor, came over and gave me a big hug.

As I walked out of the office with one of the assistants, a man came walking in with his cocker spaniel. The dog jumped on me, and the owner quickly said that he had never done that before and told his dog to get down. I asked if I could pet his dog, and he said I could. I bent down and gave his dog some rubs, and then this little doggie took both his front paws, placed them on my shoulders, and lay his head under my neck.

These incidents showed me how deeply God cares for me. He knows what concerns me and how I feel. Neither of these precious animals had no clue what a horrible time I was experiencing on the inside. God can even use animals to help us through our pain.

If you are going through a difficult time, remember that the God who sees the sparrow fall cares about your broken heart. God's Word encourages, "Give all your worries and cares to God, for he cares about you" (1 Peter 5:7, NLT). Nothing that concerns His children is too small or too unimportant for Him to notice.

Thank You, dear Lord, for showing me Your love when I was deeply grieving. Help us to always remember that You care for us, no matter what we are going through. Amen.

Debra Gough

November 21

Call Upon Me, and I Will Answer

And it shall come to pass, that before they call, I will answer; and while they are yet speaking, I will hear.
—Isaiah 65:24, KJV

Recently I had a nagging thought that I should visit my sister, who lives about five hours away from me. Though I tried to ignore the impression, it was relentless. Finally I decided to make the trip. The date was set, and my mind was made up. However, my car became a problem, and I decided not to take a chance driving on the highway before getting the problem fixed.

I took the car in for repairs and was told it would take a couple of days, but they would provide me with a loaner car. When given the paperwork to sign, I noticed they were loaning the car to me for more than a week.

Immediately I asked, "Why are you signing this vehicle out to me for over a week?"

The response was, "Just in case we run into a problem and need more time to repair your car. It is an older model, and the technician may need more time."

The car I was given was a 2024 model, completely computerized, and I did not want to deal with it. But after coming to terms with my resistance, I decided to use the car to go wherever I desired to go. On a Tuesday morning I set out to visit my sister. Before I left I prayed and asked the Lord to keep me safe and hold back the rain. I arrived safely, and we had a wonderful time visiting together. When it was time for me to return home, we prayed, and I made the same request to God, "Lord, please keep me safe and please hold the rain until I arrive home."

About an hour before I arrived home, a light rain began to fall, and as the clouds grew darker, the rain fell heavily. In the oncoming traffic I noticed the drivers had their wipers going full force, and the lanes were covered with water. As I turned onto the last route east, the lanes were dry on my side of the highway, but the oncoming traffic had their wipers going, and their lanes were wet. This pattern held the entire distance until I turned off on the road leading to my home.

Sisters, this was truly a miracle that I witnessed, and it has increased my faith. God is still in the miracle-working business. Trust Him, be encouraged, and enjoy the blessings He has in store for all His children if we come before Him and ask in prayer. There is no request too small, for He cares for us, and He promises, "I will hear" (Isaiah 65:24, KJV).

Mary Head Brooks

November 22

The Ukrainian Family

"Truly I tell you, whatever you did for one of the least of these brothers and sisters of mine, you did for me."
—Matthew 25:40, NIV

One morning during my prayer time, I said, "Lord, please show me if there is anyone who needs help, and show me what to do." The answer was not long in coming.

My car's engine was having trouble, yet I hoped I would be able to run some errands without it breaking down at the most inconvenient time—which it did. When I was ready to return home, the car stubbornly refused to start. The Lord worked in such a way that I met someone who was going to the same place, and they offered me a ride.

When my husband came home from work, we both went in his car to pick up the broken one. He managed to get it started, and on the way home, he drove ahead of me. When we reached the last village before our house, I had forgotten about the car problem and stopped at a pet shop to get some pills for our dog.

A couple entered the store behind me with their thirteen-year-old daughter. The wife, in broken English, tried to explain to the shopkeeper that they needed accommodation for the night because their car had broken down and they had left it with a mechanic. They were from the Ukraine and were going to Bulgaria for a vacation. In response the salesman shrugged his shoulders and said he was sorry, but he could not help them. As I listened I offered to let them stay at my house for the night. The wife started to cry. She hugged me, and we went to get their luggage.

When I tried to start my car, it would not move. I called my husband and asked him to pick me up. While we waited for him, I told the family, "I think God wanted me to meet you."

They were thankful and could not believe they had found a place to sleep.

As we got ready for supper later that night, the wife began to search through her purse. "Oh, you don't need to pay. We just want to help you," I said. I wondered if they were Christians and asked, "Are you Adventists?"

She replied yes, and I told them we were also Adventists. We hugged again.

My husband ended up driving them to Bulgaria while their car was repaired and brought it to them once it was done. We thanked the good Lord for this beautiful experience.

My friends, now is the time to be attentive to how God wants to use us. A sincere prayer and an open heart will bring much joy and blessing to us and others.

Cecilia Voinea

November 23

A Gentle Whisper

*After the earthquake came a fire, but the L*ORD *was not in the fire. And after the fire came a gentle whisper.*
—1 Kings 19:12, NIV

Since the age of seven, I knew I wanted to be a nurse. I also knew that meant I would need to do well in my science classes to fulfill this dream—but I struggled! In years eight and nine, I was barely passing. In fact my year nine science teacher told me never to study anything that involved science because I did so poorly in the subject. I remember praying, *God, I know You want me to be a nurse, but I need to understand science. How will I ever succeed without it?*

Shortly after, I asked my parents if I could change schools. After much discussion they agreed. In year eleven I enrolled in biology, and I will never forget my first day of class. My teacher, a middle-aged woman, stylishly dressed, walked purposefully into the classroom. She opened her textbooks, looked down very briefly, and then proceeded to teach. She never once looked down at her notes. I was inspired and did well in her class. Ultimately, I went on to finish my senior year with a solid B.

To attend university for a bachelor of nursing degree, I knew I had to achieve an overall position (OP) of 10 or less. This was the goal of every prospective nursing student in Queensland, Australia. I prayed desperately that my OP would be sufficient to be accepted into the program. How anxiously I waited for my results. Two days before the grades were due to be released, I knelt beside my bed and prayed once more. In the silence of my bedroom, I sensed a gentle whisper saying, *Eight*. Suddenly I felt hope my dream would become a reality. When the official letter arrived, I had achieved an OP of eight! How amazing!

The Bible says God cares for every detail of our lives. We are more important to Him than the sparrows He cares for (Matthew 10:29). I completed my degree and have spent the last eighteen years as a registered nurse. Though this career journey has had its challenges and can be emotionally draining, when I reflect on all the opportunities God has given me, I am in awe. All I have accomplished is because of God. I am thankful every day for His leading.

I want to remind you, my dear sisters, to "commit to the LORD whatever you do, and he will establish your plans" (Proverbs 16:3, NIV). What a marvelous God we serve!

Jenny Rivera

November 24

Isn't God Awesome?

"For you are to be his witness, telling everyone what you have seen and heard."
—Acts 22:15, NLT

One Sunday morning George found himself in a predicament. He had missed the early service at his local church, so while waiting for the second service, he walked over to his favorite diner for a cup of coffee. In an empty booth he spotted an abandoned book. Picking it up, he curiously flipped through the pages and was immediately captivated. In his more than eighty years, he had never seen anything like it. He wondered where could he find more from the inspiring author.

A few weeks later I stood on George's front doorstep with a bag full of books by the very same author. After George had purchased a thick stack of new reading material, I remember his somber eyes shining.

"Alyssa," he said, "I don't know if I'll live long enough to read all these books, but I know I was meant to have them. I'm living proof that you're never too old for God to seek after you."

Though I only met with George briefly, I thought of him often, and a smile would always linger when I did so. That Christmas a card arrived from George letting me know he was already in need of more books to read. I could not help but cry and laugh as I thought of God's goodness. But the story does not end there.

Almost two years later I found myself unexpectedly stuck in Bakersfield, California, while driving to Prescott, Arizona, USA. My friends and I had decided to make Bakersfield our lunch stop, but when it was time to hop back on the road, my car would not start. What should have been a quick stop turned into an entire weekend stay. But all my frustration went out the window when I walked into church that Sabbath and made eye contact with none other than my sweet ol' George! I could not believe it! Walking over to say hello, I was quickly intercepted by a middle-aged woman who was crying.

"Is this her?" she whispered to George.

He nodded, and soon I was gathered into a warm embrace.

After several long seconds she said, "I'm George's daughter. I've been so curious to meet the girl who has made such an impact on my dad. I thought it was impossible, yet here you are. What are the odds?"

The crazy part is that she was also visiting town. Just think, Someone had perfectly timed things to ensure our paths would intersect at that very moment—thanks to a broken-down car. Isn't God awesome?

Alyssa Morauske

November 25

Looking Back

*Many, L*ORD *my God, are the wonders which you have done,*
And your thoughts toward us;
There is no one to compare with You.
If I would declare them and speak of them,
They would be too numerous to count.
—Psalm 40:5, NASB

Looking back over the years, I am in awe of the miracles of God. First, I was not expected to survive my premature birth, but I did! My family's migration to the United Kingdom brought many challenges. We survived! Quite frankly we not only survived but also thrived. Both mom and dad worked very hard to ensure we had a much better life than they did growing up on the island of Jamaica. We certainly did.

When I decided to immigrate to Canada at age twenty, my parents were distraught. We had no relatives in Canada, and up to that time, I had not ventured out on my own any distance from our hometown of Chorley in Northern England. How would I survive life in a "strange" country, far across the Atlantic? We reached a compromise. Dad suggested I wait until after my twenty-first birthday—the "age of majority" at that time. So I did.

I landed at the airport in Toronto, Ontario, Canada, on an extraordinarily warm spring day, outfitted in a smart wool suit with a matching purse and gloves. The heat that greeted me felt very tropical. I could not have been more inappropriately dressed. Thus began my love affair with my beautiful new home—Canada.

I could not have anticipated the things God had in store for me. I met some extraordinary people, made some exceptional forever friends, including Leon, who asked me to marry him. I also adopted many "parents" along the way, including two special nuns. They attended our wedding ceremony and shared in our wedding day celebrations. I was also blessed by Pastor Rudy and Sister Rhoda James, who invited me to live with them during one of the low patches in my life.

I still cannot explain what drew me to Canada. But I am convinced it was all part of God's plan. How else could I have met my beloved husband of over fifty years? How else would I have been so honored to be appointed the first black female justice of the peace in Canada?

Dear friends, I promise you that this same God, of whom I testify, has an awesome plan for your life. Simply trust Him. You will be amazed at the magnificent future He has in store for you.

Avis Mae Rodney

November 26

God's Priceless Masterwork

For we are his workmanship, created in Christ Jesus unto good works, which God hath before ordained that we should walk in them.
—Ephesians 2:10, KJV

It was Thanksgiving time, and as the family gathered to remember all of God's manifold blessings, one of my twin daughters surprised us with wonderful news. She was pregnant, and we could expect to have a baby joining the family sometime in July. Her news overwhelmed all of us with joy and happiness. This would be the very first grandchild in the family, and we could hardly wait.

When I was pregnant with my twin daughters, I saw them both in an ultrasound, and many years later I had the privilege of seeing my grandchild in an ultrasound. It certainly was an amazing experience to see the mother and then the child. It amazed me to see a tiny poppy-seed-like fetus grow into a fully developed baby of eight pounds. Our God is awesome, and we are each His masterpiece.

Have you ever felt worthless in the eyes of the world? Have you ever felt that you were not really what you could be or what you should be? I know that, at times, I have struggled with this. Often the world looks at us as failures. Whether at school or work, we know how it feels to see the big red F grade on our paper or to receive a poor evaluation at work. But this is not how God views us. I have failed God more times than I would like to admit, but He still loves me and helps me grow. Never once have I received the big red F from God, and I never will if I follow Him. Though we may sometimes feel of little worth—in reality we are priceless in the eyes of the Lord.

None of us are cheap imitation copies of anyone else. We are the masterpieces of God. We are made in the image of God, created by our wonderful Creator. No artist could ever have created us like God has. All of our worth is found in God, for we have been touched by the hand of God, and we are priceless. We have been designed by the Master Artist and paid for with the Master's life. We are priceless creations. Though we have been scarred by sin, we are covered by His love and are priceless in His eyes. When the enemy tries to discourage you with feelings of worthlessness, remember this: You are God's priceless masterpiece!

Premila Pedapudi

November 27

Give Thanks

"Who am I and who are my people that we should be able to offer as generously as this? For all things come from You, and from Your hand we have given to You."
—1 Chronicles 29:14, NASB

One Sunday morning I left the house to go to the market. Changing my usual route, I went down the opposite side. On the second block I noticed an overflowing dumpster. An older man sat among the trash that had fallen to the ground. As I passed I saw he was holding a tub of ice cream in his hands. It still had some chocolate syrup on it. I watched as he ran his fingers through the chocolate syrup and licked it off. The scene made me feel ill. How sad to see a human being, in his old age, eating leftover food from a dumpster.

The convenience store was on the next block, and I bought an ice cream cone and went back to where the old man still sat, licking up the last drop of chocolate syrup. Smiling, I handed it to him and said, "I'm sure this ice cream will taste better!"

He flashed a wide smile at me, and then, with both hands raised to the sky, he exclaimed, "Thank You, Jesus! Thank You, Jesus!" He gratefully took the ice cream and smiled in anticipation. A simple treat while sitting among the garbage gave him reason for joy and gratitude.

I tried to remember the last time I thanked God for something He had given me with the same spirit of praise.

Paul reminds us, "Rejoice in the Lord always: and again I say, Rejoice" (Philippians 4:4, KJV). That is great advice. Rejoice always, no matter the situation. Gratitude leads to happiness, and a grateful heart helps us to see our blessings. "Nothing tends more to promote health of body and soul than does a spirit of gratitude and praise. It is a positive duty to resist melancholy, discontented thoughts and feelings—as much a duty as it is to pray."[*]

Regarding gratitude, Robert A. Emmons, PhD, a professor in the Department of Psychology at the University of California, Davis, notes, "Those who kept gratitude journals on a weekly basis exercised more regularly, reported fewer physical symptoms, felt better about their lives as a whole, and were more optimistic about the upcoming week compare to those who recorded hassles or neutral life events."[†]

Why not try it? Start a gratitude journal and discover the countless ways God shows His love. Nothing is better for us than a spirit of gratitude and praise!

Isabel Cristina de Almeida

---

[*] Ellen G. White, *The Ministry of Healing* (Mountain View, CA: Pacific Press®, 1905), 251.
[†] Robert Emmons, "Gratitude and Well-Being," Gratitude Works, accessed December 18, 2024, https://emmons.faculty.ucdavis.edu/gratitude-and-well-being/.

November 28

Sit at the Welcome Table

*Taste and see that the L*ORD *is good.*
—Psalm 34:8, NIV

I have a confession to make," I remarked as I greeted our visitors at church one Sabbath. "This confession will come as no surprise to my friends and family, but are you ready? Here goes: I am a foodie!"

After the laughter died down and the knowing nods of confirmation stopped, I continued. "I love food. I love to cook it, eat it, and share it with my friends and family. I love shopping for it at farmers markets. I love the colors, the smells, and the tastes. I love going out to restaurants and trying new cuisines. I am often called upon for restaurant suggestions when people come to visit my city or are just looking for a new place to go to celebrate special occasions. My social calendar is full of Sunday brunch dates and weekday dinner dates where I can catch up with what's going on in the lives of the people who are important to me. I love food."

By this time I had the congregation's full attention as they listened to me go on and on about the joys found in good food. Then I said, "And guess what? I believe God is a foodie too!"

Deep down in my heart, I believe this statement. Who else but a foodie God would create delectable treats like mangoes, strawberries, and pineapples? Only a God interested in nourishing and delighting all our senses would create artichokes and spinach and spaghetti squash. Staples like potatoes, onions, grains, nuts, and berries that can be used in different ways to bring joy to our palates, taste buds, and noses all at the same time could only come from the heart of a foodie God.

As a child, while attending youth services held after church, we would often sing the song "I'm Gonna Sit at the Welcome Table," which suggests the image of a God who wants His children to gather together and share good times and good food—a classic trademark for any true foodie.

I look forward to the day when we will sit together at God's welcome table. I do not know what delectable delights He will serve us. Milk and honey? Fruit from the tree of life? Whatever it is, I want to be there. Don't you?

Kristina E. Smith

November 29

I Can Hardly Wait

"Eye has not seen, nor ear heard, nor have entered into the heart of man the things which God has prepared for those who love Him."
—1 Corinthians 2:9, NKJV

I love chocolate, and that is why my friend Jayne hastened to tell me, some thirteen years ago, of a wonderful new chocolate shop she had discovered. She informed me it was called Alexander's and that their sipping chocolate was a must. My husband and I went as soon as we could and were in full agreement about the chocolate. We loved it. However, when we went back, the place had closed. We had no idea where it had gone, and we have spent the intervening years missing it.

Then we moved. Foodies that we are, it did not take long to find a new favorite restaurant in a town about forty-five minutes away. We have been going there a couple of times a month for the past three years. And apparently we are not particularly observant. A couple of weeks ago, we headed over for lunch but were forced to park on the opposite side of the street from the restaurant and down a ways. I got out of the passenger seat, straightened up, and saw a sign on the door of a shop directly in front of me that read, "Artisan Chocolates."

"Rick," I exclaimed. "Chocolate here."

"Let's go in," he said. "Maybe get something for dessert."

We entered the shop, and a man approached, greeting us with a smile and tiny paper cups. "Our sipping chocolate, folks," he said. "Try it."

Mercy! At the first taste we knew we were back in business. When I said, "There was a place called Alexander's where we got this many years ago," he turned and gestured toward a very prominent sign on the wall that read "Alexander's Chocolate Classics." We all had a good laugh. On our way out we counted four different, large Alexander's signs, three of which we could easily see from across the street—if we had looked.

I got to thinking of how easily we humans are taken with a joy that is enticing to our particular tastes. But imagine what we have to look forward to. Or try to. Our text says we really cannot. The delights God has prepared for us in heaven will dim to insignificance the pleasures we know here. We have not seen, tasted, smelled, felt, nor heard anything like heaven's thrills.

I love chocolate. I adore Alexander's sipping chocolate. But. I really am eager for Jesus and heaven. He has something unimaginable planned for our enjoyment. I can hardly wait.

Carolyn K. Karlstrom

November 30

In His Image

Put on the new self, created after the likeness of God in true righteousness and holiness.
—Ephesians 4:24, ESV

I am fortunate that both my daughters live nearby. So when my daughter gave birth to my second grandson, I was able to hold him the day he arrived home from the hospital. At three days old he was completely perfect—smooth baby skin, silky blonde hair, and tiny feet with toes that curled around your finger.

As I stared into his sleepy face, those little eyes squinting now and again at the bright lights around him, I wondered who he looked like. His appearance is quite different from his older brother. When he was born, it was as if I gazed into the face of his mother years earlier. But this little guy did not stir my memory. Maybe his other grandmother would see what I did not—the sleepy face she rocked thirty-plus years ago.

Genesis 1:26 says, "Then God said, 'Let Us make man in Our image, according to Our likeness' " (NKJV). Adam and Eve were made in the image of God—not only to look like their Creator but to share His attributes as well.

My older grandson is a wonderful mix of both his father and his mother. While he may look like his mother, he has the interests and passions of his father. His joy in finding a worm or toad and his interest in all things nature come from spending time with his dad. He loves to walk in the woods. And just as his father taught him, he rolls over logs and looks under rocks because the best worms, spiders, and critters are found in the dark, muddy recesses. Because he spent time with his father, he has become like his father.

We are also made in the image of God. While sin may obscure what Adam and Eve initially experienced, through Christ's light and glory, we may reflect our Creator. Years ago I listened to an Amy Grant song called "My Father's Eyes." The lyrics express hope that when people saw her, they would see she looked like her Father—her heavenly Father.

Just as my grandson becomes more like his dad because of the time he spends with him, may we, too, spend so much time with Jesus that people can't help but see the resemblance. And when we reflect and share the love of Jesus, others will be changed too.

Merle Poirer

December 1

Darkness and Development

"You, LORD, are my lamp; the LORD turns my darkness into light."
—2 Samuel 22:29, NIV

When I was a child, my dad was an amateur photographer. He occasionally took wedding pictures on Sundays. During the week in the evenings, he took photographs in a studio he had fitted out in our basement. Next to the studio was his dark room, where he developed the pictures.

I loved to spend time with my dad and watch the picture developing process. The room was lit with a very dim, reddish-orange light, so we could barely see. My dad would dip the photographic paper into three different solutions. The first solution appeared to have no effect, nor did the second. But to my young mind, the third solution was magical. Very slowly, the picture began to emerge. Finally, after a few minutes, the photograph was fully developed. It was a process that involved darkness, and then some heat, before the picture was placed in a "drying machine."

As I reflect on this process, it seems similar to developing character, which is seen in several Bible characters. For example, in reading about the "darkness" Job went through, we learn he lost his material possessions, his children, and his health. Through it all he remained faithful and could say, "I know that my redeemer lives" (Job 19:25, NIV). By faith, he looked to the future and said, "When he has tested me, I will come forth as gold" (Job 23:10, NIV).

Periods of darkness also surface in the story of Joseph. Sold as a slave by his brothers and imprisoned for something he did not do, Joseph was finally made prime minister of Egypt. He was able to say to his brothers, "It was not you who sent me here, but God" (Genesis 45:8, NIV). In other words, after the darkness, a bright picture emerged.

Paul, too, endured much darkness in his life. He lists all the hardships he went through in 2 Corinthians 11:23–30. Yet he could say everything that had happened to him had "actually served to advance the gospel" (Philippians 1:12, NIV). Through all the darkness, Paul could see a beautiful picture emerging. He knew there would be dark times, but he could confidently say, "The Lord will rescue me . . . and will bring me safely to his heavenly kingdom" (2 Timothy 4:18, NIV).

We live in a sinful world and experience times of darkness, but if we watch long enough, we will see a beautiful picture emerge—eternal life with Jesus.

Sharon Oster

December 2

Severe Storm Advisory

Beloved, think it not strange concerning the fiery trial which is to try you, as though some strange thing happened unto you: but rejoice, inasmuch as ye are partakers of Christ's sufferings; that, when his glory shall be revealed, ye may be glad also with exceeding joy.
—1 Peter 4:12, 13, KJV

The headlines screamed, "East Coast Digs Out from Record-Breaking Snow!"* It was the winter of 2009–2010, and the entire East Coast of the United States of America was blanketed in snow. In some areas the storm brought almost twenty inches, and residents everywhere struggled to shovel in the winter wonderland.

Just over seven hundred miles away, the Bermuda government issued a severe weather advisory. The storm would bring gale-to-hurricane-force winds, and residents should exercise extreme caution when traveling on the slick, slippery roads. As it was the weekend, I decided to take an afternoon nap. When I awoke, the howling wind and huge pelting raindrops sounded like a hundred women in high heels trampling across my roof.

I jumped up and opened my curtains, wanting to see the storm's impact in my backyard. The trees were bending and bowing to the strength of the wind. The tops of my fruit trees had been ripped away, and leaves and limbs lay strewn everywhere. I was amazed at how quickly my yard—which had been beautiful and full of color just days before—was now bare and desolate, hardly a leaf in sight.

Weather patterns resemble our lives in many ways. You are enjoying life—it is beautiful even—and then suddenly a storm appears, and you can barely hold on.

Today's text is one of my favorites. Every time I read it, it reminds me that often the storms that life brings are so unlikely and unbelievable that it truly feels as if a bizarre, crazy thing has happened. But the last part of the text is where I get excited. The Bible says "when" God reveals Himself—notice, it does not say *if, might,* nor *maybe,* but *when.* So I know that if I continue to trust in Him, my "when" will come. It may not happen right away; it might not even happen in my lifetime, but it will come. My prayer for you today is that when life brings severe storms your way, the "when" of God will bring you peace.

Leah J. M. Dean

---

* Associated Press, "East Coast Digs Out From Record-Breaking Snow," NBC News, February 7, 2010, https://www.nbcnews.com/id/wbna35281444.

December 3

How We Learn and Grow

"But seek first his kingdom and his righteousness, and all these things will be given to you as well."
—Matthew 6:33, NIV

When I first heard the song "Praise Him in Advance,"* I did not understand the lyrics. At the time I heard it, I was in the middle of a divorce, and I felt angry. I recall thinking, *Praise Him in advance? How can I do that when I don't know how He's going to work things out?* I was perplexed about how I was going to sell my business, provide for my daughters, and create a future for myself. I was going through so many emotions at the time. I remember asking God, "Why would You allow me to experience this?"

Most of us would describe this experience as going through a storm. In hindsight I allowed my storm to overwhelm me. I became completely consumed with trying to solve my problems. But why did I think I had to find an answer to every problem? It is because the world brainwashes us into believing we must know the answer to everything all the time. God does not operate that way. There are times when we will not see our way forward and the situation seems impossible. But God majors in impossible things.

Now I can see I had become overwhelmed by trying to solve my problems instead of allowing God to solve them. Many of us struggle with the same thing—looking to find the solution. I believe God wants us to learn from the experience we are going through rather than skip ahead to find the solution.

At the darkest time in my life, Jesus Christ found me. He picked me up out of the gutter and loved me even before I had accepted Him into my heart. Now, as I go through life, I am learning to grow in my relationship with God. He loves us more than we realize, and He longs to take our relationship to ever deeper levels.

When was the last time you wore out your pants praying on your knees? Have you ever prayed through the night? If we are honest, few of us have, but before we can receive extraordinary power, we must go deeper in our walk with Christ. Let us commit to deepening our relationship with Christ. Instead of only seeking solutions, let us seek Him first. This is how we learn and grow daily.

Paula Sanders Blackwell

---

* Deon Kipping, "Praise Him in Advance," © 2009, Meaux Hits/Gospo Music Thang/216 Music, admin. at EMICMGPublishing.com.

December 4

Courage in the Storm

God is our refuge and strength,
an ever-present help in trouble.
Therefore we will not fear, though the earth give way
and the mountains fall into the heart of the sea,
though its waters roar and foam
and the mountains quake with their surging.
—Psalm 46:1–3, NIV

Storms can come in many forms. Sometimes they are invisible and rage within, testing the very foundations of our being. Other times they are the kind you can see, like the one that threatened me on a ferry crossing a year ago. I will never forget that day.

Early one morning my husband and I set out to cross the Baltic Sea with our car on a smaller ferry, a catamaran. The previous night we had received an email from the ferry company asking us if we would like to reschedule the journey for free because high seas were in the forecast for the next day. Because we had other scheduling conflicts, we had no option but to cross as planned. We prayed for calm seas, trusting God to protect us, come what may.

It began slowly, but just as we left the harbor in the morning, the wind started to howl. We watched the waves crash against the ferry with a fury that made our hearts pound. The workers in the coffee shop onboard, oblivious to the weather, had forgotten to secure their drinks, and soon soda bottles rolled across the deck. As chaos erupted around me, I started to ask, "Why don't You calm this storm, God?" Desperately clinging to the promises in God's Word, I prayed continuously throughout the journey.

After two hours that seemed like an eternity, the ferry docked safely on the other side. I felt profound gratitude and relief and, at that moment, realized that though God had not promised me a calm journey, He had promised to be with me through the storm—and He kept His promise. The experience taught me that faith is not about avoiding storms; rather it is about finding strength and courage within them. It is about trusting that even when we are surrounded by chaos, God's presence is always with us.

The next time life throws a storm at you, remember: you are not alone. God is with you, offering you shelter from the storm. And when the storm finally passes, you will emerge stronger, wiser, and with a faith deeper than ever before, and you will testify that "He stilled the storm to a whisper; the waves of the sea were hushed" (Psalm 107:29, NIV).

Karin Tegeman

December 5

Herding Cats

When he saw the crowds, he had compassion on them, because they were harassed and helpless, like sheep without a shepherd.
—Matthew 9:36, NIV

I'm currently housesitting for a friend. I am not used to having my midnight trips to the filtered water spigot interrupted by three murky silhouettes emerging from the shadows to silently pad after me. Yes, this housesitting gig came with three cats: Manny, Missie, and Mae (I have changed their names to protect their true identities). They are rescues, having been mistreated, neglected, abandoned, or just in need of a loving home—which they definitely have here! When I discovered, almost immediately, that Missie had lost her supper (which appeared to have consisted largely of a fat orange rubber band), I texted the pet owner, still on her way to the airport.

"Yeah," my friend replied, "Missie eats the most unusual things: rubber bands, cellophane, plastic bags . . . stuff like that . . . you know."

No, I did not know. But I do now!

Mae, due to intestinal challenges, can't always eat just dry cat food. I have to slip her wet food slyly because it disagrees with Missie. And Missie, who loves to cuddle, is jealous of Mae, the newcomer. I remind her that spitting and face-offs aren't polite or inclusive behaviors. And Mannie? I sometimes ride herd on him because he will quickly eat up his five evening treats and then attempt to snatch more from his "siblings."

My friend, Gail, says that cats are like "bad little kids." I sort of agree and would also add that most of them have the attention span of a butterfly—unless the focus is on something they want. After my first week with these felines, I now have gentle strategies to get their attention, though rarely their cooperation. And almost never, their obedience.

So would I do this again? Yes, in a heartbeat! Why? Because I truly hurt for their lonely hearts as they wander about looking for their missing mama. I hope they shadow me because they sense I care and love them just as they are—litterboxes and all.

The "harassed and helpless" referenced in Matthew 9:36 also sensed a vacancy as they wandered about, confused and lonely. They needed a home that only a Shepherd could provide. Despite their bad habits and character flaws, Jesus had compassion. Understanding that changed their lives forever. The Good Shepherd took them in, providing comfort, conviction, direction, and purpose. And on our loneliest wandering days, He takes us in too.

Carolyn Rathbun Sutton

December 6

An Unexpected Gift

Bring all the tithes into the storehouse,
That there may be food in My house,
And try Me now in this,"
Says the LORD *of hosts,*
"If I will not open for you the windows of heaven
And pour out for you such blessing
That there will not be room enough to receive it."
—Malachi 3:10, NKJV

On vacation one summer, I joyfully discovered another dimension to Malachi 3:10, one I had not thought of before.

My family loves hiking in the mountains, and that summer we decided to go to France. My husband and I traveled by car to Chamonix while my daughter, eldest nephew, and a few friends planned to fly. My husband and I made two stops along the way. The second was at a hostel in Austria on the Swiss border. The weather outside was gloomy, and soon it started to rain lightly. We checked in and looked forward to resting in the cozy warmth of our room. Instead our room was quite cold. My husband, tired after the long drive, climbed into the bed and covered himself with the warm feather duvet. It was comforting and restful.

I decided to sit at the table in the room to study my Bible and Sabbath School lesson. But I was cold. I tried to turn on the heater and discovered it was broken. My husband called the front desk, and they brought us a heater. I plugged it in and was soon warm. But then the heater started to leak oil. I unplugged it to prevent further trouble, pulled on a thick wool sweatshirt, and continued my study. When I was done, I got into the already-warmed bed and fell asleep.

In the morning, before breakfast, I notified the landlord about the broken heater. We enjoyed our breakfast and then got ready to check out. As we looked at our bill, we were puzzled to see a single charge for €20, or about US$22.00. It must be a mistake. The owner smiled and assured us that it was the correct charge—for breakfast. He had written off the cost of the room due to the faulty heater. "This is our way of apologizing," he said and wished us a happy vacation.

We were amazed by this kind gesture and reminded how good God is. I realized that the time I had spent studying was pleasing to Him. He is always ready to shower abundant blessings on all who honor Him. My dear sister, be faithful to Him. Draw close to Him, and you will see how much He appreciates your devotion.

Elena Petrescu

December 7

God's Precious Gift

This is my comfort in my affliction, for Your word has given me life.
—Psalm 119:50, NKJV

I am longing for heaven! I would venture to say everyone reading this devotional has that same feeling. As we have seen and heard about sad happenings in our country and the hard times being experienced by other nations as well, we long even more to see Jesus coming in the clouds to take us home.

Several years ago, we had a family reunion. My immediate family, once made up of Mom, Dad, and five children, has now multiplied to fifty-nine and spans five generations. Sadly, five family members are deceased. One of my sisters, Margie, died of a very rare neurological disease at age fifty. The last few years of her life were spent in a nursing home; she needed help with all of her physical and mental needs. Visiting her was more like talking to a two- or three-year-old. She had to be hand-fed, and my parents faithfully went every day to feed her the evening meal.

While Mom would feed her, she would sing some of her favorite hymns, and many times Margie would sing along. Amazingly she remembered all the words and melodies. That always surprised me. Though my sister could not converse with others very well, she still remembered all the words to hymns. Our mother's spiritual training and her Christian example stayed forever in my sister's mind. This always reminded me of the verse in Proverbs, "Train up a child in the way he should go, and when he is old he will not depart from it" (Proverbs 22:6, NKJV).

But I feel God gave Margie a gift—the ability to remember His words. "Therefore hear me now, my children, and do not depart from the words of my mouth" (Proverbs 5:7, NKJV).

What a wonderful God we serve! He gives gifts and encouragement in ways we cannot imagine. Margie singing along with Mom was also a gift to Mom. It made the chore of caring for Margie each evening a delight as her sweet voice filled the air. My sister's faith in God stayed with her all her fifty years. Praise God for His goodness.

Oh, how I long for a grand reunion in heaven, where there will be no more sickness, death, nor sorrow—for heaven will be a happy place. Sweetest of all will be the blessing of worshiping our Lord and Savior together with those we have loved here on earth. How I long to go home and be with Jesus!

Ginger Bell

December 8

God's Desire for Our Lives

He hath shewed thee, O man, what is good; and what doth the LORD *require of thee, but to do justly, and to love mercy, and to walk humbly with thy God?*
—Micah 6:8, KJV

If we want good things to happen in our lives, God gives us a plan and some requirements to open the doors of heaven. He requires obedience. God is gracious in giving us specific instructions through prayer and His Word. The exact application of God's instructions is of utmost value, and it brings us abundant blessings.

First, He wants us to be just and honest in our connections in life. Proverbs 21:3 says, "To do justice and judgment is more acceptable to the LORD than sacrifice" (KJV). Second, He wants us not only to be merciful but also to love mercy. Luke 6:36 tells us, "Be ye therefore merciful, as your father also is merciful" (KJV). Third, He wants us to walk humbly with the Lord. We walk humbly when we give God all the honor and glory. The invitation of 1 Peter 5:6, 7 is to "humble yourselves therefore under the mighty hand of God, that he may exalt you in due time: casting all your care upon him; for He careth for you" (KJV). Remember to be humble, or you will stumble.

To spend a lifetime in pursuit of our Savior, trying to be more like Christ and less like our former selves, is not something we must force ourselves to do—as we walk with Him, it will become a natural response. This is in stark contrast with those who pursue success by chasing after wealth and fame. While these may not necessarily be bad, they can tend to appeal to a sense of selfishness, greed, and pride. They cause us to look for satisfaction apart from God.

Yet God does not ask His children to settle for earthly success, wealth, or fame. He wants what is best for us, even if we quietly think we know better. And throughout the Bible, from Genesis to Revelation, God points His people to true success: their Savior, Jesus. He wants us to discover that in pursuing Christ our desires will fall in line with God's. "Delight yourself in the LORD, and he will give you the desires of your heart" (Psalm 37:4, ESV).

When we do what the Lord requires, we will be blessed. Doing justice, loving kindness, and walking humbly with God are what the Lord desires for our lives. These three things offer us a path to a meaningful and blessed life. The only life that is truly worth living is the life that brings glory and honor to God.

Premila Pedapudi

December 9

Just Do It

And Samuel said, Hath the Lord *as great delight in burnt offerings and sacrifices, as in obeying the voice of the* Lord*? Behold, to obey is better than sacrifice, and to hearken than the fat of rams.*
—1 Samuel 15:22, KJV

A famous company's slogan is "Just Do It." No need to question it. No need to think about it. Just do it.

Does this slogan have anything in common with what God requires from His people? He wants His people to be obedient—to trust that He knows what is best and not question His every word, His works, or His will. Just to be obedient. Surely the God of all creation, of things seen and unseen, who knows the heart and mind of man, who created the heavens and earth, who gives life and breath, and who can alter the path of destruction so no harm befalls man—surely this God can be trusted. "*Just do it,*" He says. "*Just trust Me!*"

Obedience is defined as compliance with an order, request, or law or as submission to another's authority. Disregarding that simple nine-letter word caused the initial destruction of mankind, and its impact is still playing out today. So why do we sometimes find it so difficult to obey the God of all creation? We have all witnessed the result of disobedience in one form or another. Yet it is a natural response to go against the flow, to throw caution to the wind. Just imagine, for a moment, that for one day we were all obedient. Just for one day. Can you imagine how different this world would be? Can you imagine what love would accomplish in just one day? Can you envision a world filled with people who are kind toward one another, living out the fruit of the Spirit?

When I completely severed my rotator cuff, I experienced unbearable pain. En route to the hospital, I requested pain meds. How I prayed, recited Scripture, and asked God to take away the pain. Relief finally came six hours later. It was faith that kept me going—I knew God had heard my prayer. Yet I had to endure the pain until relief came. In this world we experience the darkness before dawn. We know how it feels when weeping endures for a night—or much longer. But it is during the wait that we must remain faithful and obedient. The waiting may feel endless, but oh! The joy that comes in the morning!

Sylvia Giles Bennett

December 10

The Greatest Love

Greater love hath no man than this, that a man lay down his life for his friends.
—John 15:13, KJV

Many of us, myself included, face rejection in all forms, even by those dearest to us. As a result we feel inferior, insignificant, incapable of loving, and unworthy of being loved.

Growing up, I was depressed. I went through high school feeling like an outcast. My friends could not understand me, home was the last place I wanted to be, and I sat there feeling all alone. I would journal to empty myself, pouring myself into a book that paid me attention.

One time I wrote a prayer telling God to reveal the truth to me because I did not understand my life. Years later I stumbled on that prayer and nearly wept. God had answered my prayer: I had finally met the truth, and it was beautiful. It filled my dry soul with joy, and I want to share this precious gift with you so you also may be joyous. I met Someone. He goes by many names, but today I will focus on one: Love (see 1 John 4:8).

When Love speaks, the waves hush and listen, the roaring sea stills with wonder as we ponder, *What manner of man is this?* Surely He is no ordinary man. He bids us to come and be His friend and partake of His love. However, He asks us to count the cost of this friendship before accepting it. "Ye are my friends," He says, "if ye do whatsoever I command you. . . . These things I command you, that ye love one another" (John 15:14–17, KJV).

Ever wondered why we are commanded to love? John tells us that "every one that loveth is born of God, and knoweth God" (1 John 4:7, KJV). When we love, we show that we know God. Those who love know God, and they will inherit eternal life. Jesus wraps up everything in love. The law is washed in love, nature is dressed in it, and all creation shouts God is love. When I understood that He sacrificed Himself so I may have life and enjoy the bliss of love (John 10:15, 18, KJV), I wondered, *Me? The one no one else seemed to love?* Yes! Me! For He says that He loved me too much to watch me die. He would rather die in my stead. Oh! The joy that found my soul. Knowing that I am loved has been the salvation of my life, and it can be yours too.

He bids us, "Come, taste, and see that I am good" (see Psalm 34:8). He is so good, and we can experience no greater love than the love Christ offers us. We can go our way, rejoicing, for we are loved.

Evis Kachana Matali

December 11

The God Who Made Us

For You formed my inward parts;
You covered me in my mother's womb.
I will praise You, for I am fearfully and wonderfully made;
Marvelous are Your works,
And that my soul knows very well.
—Psalm 139:13, 14, NKJV

David, the psalmist, is very moved that our bodies are assembled and formed in our mother's body. In Psalm 139:14 he says he is so grateful to see his own body, which was "fearfully and wonderfully made." Are we, like David, thankful for the amazing creation that is our body, made and kept alive by God's power? Perhaps we have not given this much thought or have taken it for granted, but David reminds us how blessed we are as human beings to be given this gift and to be kept alive by God's gracious care. Consider these facts about our bodies:

Many studies show that the skeletal system of the average adult human is supported by approximately 206 bones, with a quarter of them found in each foot. The bones of the feet are so finely made that they allow the feet to bend flexibly and enable us to walk with good balance. God is a God of details, and our bodies are evidence of His attention to detail.

Another marvel is the circulatory system. An adult body has about 6 quarts (5.6 liters) of blood, which circulates through the body around three times per minute, traveling approximately twelve thousand miles (more that nineteen thousand kilometers) per day. Our hearts pump about 1.5 gallons (5.6 liters) of blood every minute while beating over a hundred thousand times per day. That is amazing!

How thankful we should be to God for creating something so wonderful. What is even more amazing is that our bodies are made according to the image of Jesus, our Creator. It is an immeasurable thing that the Creator formed and shaped us in love. We were created to discover His plans for us, to experience the plan of redemption in our own lives.

"The central theme of the Bible, the theme about which every other in the whole book clusters, is the redemption plan, the restoration in the human soul of the image of God."* He created us to be like Him—and He makes provision to accomplish this, with our cooperation, in each of our lives.

Let us take great joy in the life we have been given and walk boldly with Him.

Mie Hashimoto

---

* Ellen G. White, *Education* (Mountain View, CA: Pacific Press, 1903), 125.

December 12

Running Over

Be careful for nothing; but in every thing by prayer and supplication with thanksgiving let your requests be made known unto God.
—Philippians 4:6, KJV

For years I wanted a brand-new vehicle. I had experienced alternators malfunctioning while overtaking container trucks on the highway, transmission belts that stopped working, and wheels that came loose while driving. I had lived through very interesting and scary experiences over the years in my "old" vehicles. As grateful as I was for them, I had often contemplated having something new, as problem-free and reliable as possible. Unfortunately, given my financial situation, this remained a dream.

In 2020 essential workers were given duty-free concessions to purchase vehicles. A close friend encouraged me to get one. I wondered if it made financial sense. Could I possibly afford it, considering I wanted to pursue another degree? I decided to ask God. His answer to my prayer amazes me still.

Unexpectedly my tax code changed, and my disposable income increased by the same amount I would need to pay toward a monthly car loan. Added to this, around the same time, my husband was relieved of paying a significant amount of money he had paid monthly for years. While we went forward with the vehicle, I continued to struggle with God. I had felt impressed to pursue another postgraduate degree and needed money for that too. Was I asking for too much?

When the deadline for the tuition payment came, I was $5,000 short. I prayed all night. The next morning I was led to call someone. She assured me that I could refinance a small loan I had and pay my tuition fee on that same day. Long story short—I did! This was unbelievable. The car and the tuition were paid for, and my tithe and offering were unaffected. Even my monthly savings remained minimally affected.

The Bible says that God is able to do above and exceedingly beyond what we ask so that our cups run over. I wonder sometimes if we limit God by not asking. Why do we think that He does not care about the things we need? God can solve financial problems, mend broken relationships, and answer us while we are yet praying. God is good all the time. Trust Him with every problem. He will come through for you with unexpected blessings through unexpected means.

Shana Cyr-Philbert

December 13

A Strong Tower

The name of the LORD is a strong tower; the righteous run to it and are safe.
—Proverbs 18:10, NKJV

I have always been fascinated with lighthouses. I like the structure of the buildings. They stand firm, tall, and visible. The light they emit from the top of the tower and reflect on the water has always been something I wanted to see up close. Lighthouses have provided guiding lights for ships for centuries. The light could be seen during the worst weather because of the powerful lamps in them. Very few lighthouses exist today, which is probably one of the reasons I find them so fascinating.

One summer I had a chance to see Mississippi's most famous lighthouse when my son and I went to Biloxi, Mississippi, USA, for a brief vacation. The massive structure was so tall it could be seen all over the city. At night I stood in my hotel room or on the beach and watched the light from the lighthouse rotate on the water. Even though I was not on a ship while I was in Biloxi, the light somehow comforted me.

Our Scripture refers to the Lord as the strongest tower ever. How many times have you turned to Him as your strong tower? It is good to know we can run to Him and be safe. He stands tall and provides us with the light we need to make it safely to our destinations. As our strong tower He provides direction, comfort, peace, joy, and so much more.

Some of the things that make lighthouses so durable are metal plates and brick linings. Life's storms will constantly pound against us, but if we have God's Word (metal plates) and faith (brick linings), combined with prayer, we can continue to stand. If our spiritual foundation is strong, no matter the storms we face, no matter how much we are torn, battered, and bruised, God lovingly restores us after each storm because of His great love for us.

"Jesus will be the helper of all who put their trust in Him. Those who are connected with Christ have happiness at their command. They follow in the path where their Saviour leads. . . . These persons have built their hopes on Christ, and the storms of earth are powerless to sweep them from the sure foundation."*

Dear Lord, thank You for being our strong tower.

Barbara J. Walker

---

* Ellen G. White, *Counsels for the Church* (Nampa, ID: Pacific Press®, 1991), 162.

December 14

Blessings From Pink Lady's Slippers

Oh, taste and see that the Lord is good; blessed is the man who trusts in Him!
—Psalm 34:8, NKJV

One Sabbath morning before church, I was walking a trail that goes around my property. During my walk God powerfully spoke to my heart. There is a small area of about two thousand square feet in the middle of our twenty-five acres where pink lady's slippers grow sporadically. Sometimes the area is hard to locate, so last year my son lovingly flagged the area where they appear so I could locate them better. I was blessed to see my first lady's slipper around mid-April when, instead of just one flower at the flag, there were two. They had been in bloom since mid-April, so I knew this morning's walk in mid-May was at the end of their season.

On the first one-mile lap of my walk, I thoroughly searched the small area to see if there might be just one last late bloom still hanging on. As I expected I found only dried-up flowers hanging from their stems. I continued my next lap and asked God to please give me a special Sabbath blessing. As I neared the same area, I casually looked, and there, much to my surprise, I saw a perfect pink lady's slipper bloom hanging from its stem in the same area I had just searched thoroughly. Of course I began praising God as soon as I saw it.

While crying tears of joy, I stooped down and gently picked my special Sabbath blessing from the Lord. While doing so, I felt impressed to pick a dead one also so I could photograph the contrast between the beautiful bloom and the ugly dead bloom. Gently placing both blooms in my cupped hand, I continued my walk.

As I was about to complete my second lap, the thought crossed my mind to lay the two blooms on the ground while I finished my final lap. However, God softly spoke to my heart and asked me to continue carrying the two blooms to prevent them from getting damaged. In obedience to His prompting, I continued to carry the two blooms on my third lap. As I neared the end of my Sabbath walk, God spoke once more to my heart. He reminded me how He tenderly carries me in His hand just as I had gently carried my pink lady's slipper blooms. Sister, whether life is going beautifully or it is especially tough and somewhat ugly, let us always remember that our heavenly Father tenderly holds us in His hands.

Kathy Hull

December 15

The Perfect Timing

Wait for the Lord; be strong and take heart and wait for the Lord.
—Psalm 27:14, NIV

Waiting on the Lord can sometimes be the most challenging aspect when it comes to exhibiting our faith in God. As I sit nestled in the cozy writing nook in my living room, surrounded by my beloved books, I am reminded of my journey toward homeownership.

During the height of the pandemic, I received notification that I qualified for a mortgage and, more importantly, a home in what is considered to be one of the more affluent communities on the island where I reside. It would prove to be the most arduous journey of my life—a roller coaster of events that would test my faith in God and require me to trust His perfect timing and also to trust He was working all things together for my good during the process.

Many times I found myself frustrated with the process, including the speed at which the contractor was moving throughout the construction process. I wanted to give up more than once. As time went on I found myself arguing with God while trying to rely on His promises. Eventually I chose to surrender to the process and trust God.

Three days before I was notified that the construction was finished and the mortgage process could finally be completed, I found myself in an interesting situation. I received notice that a gratuity payment owed to me five years earlier was available for collection. Talk about perfect timing! I needed these funds to help cover the closing costs of my new home, and there were sufficient funds to help with a down payment I did not think I would be able to make.

Sometimes we fuss and complain about things and processes, forgetting that God orchestrates our lives and has our best interests at heart. He is working everything out for our good, even though we may not see it.

I received the keys to my home earlier this year, and I can now announce I am a grateful homeowner.

Heavenly Father, help us trust in Your perfect timing in all aspects of our lives. Grant us patience and peace as we embrace Your plan with faith, knowing that You are working everything out for our good. In Jesus' name, amen.

Tamia A. Griffith

December 16

When God Uses a Two-by-Four

"Then you will call upon Me and come and pray to Me, and I will listen to you."
—Jeremiah 29:12, NASB

Several years ago I worked as the registered nurse manager of a thirteen-bed medical surgical floor. I had been doing this for six years but did not feel I was doing the best job that I could. One Sabbath I wrote out a private prayer petition and placed it in our prayer box at church. "Lord, I'm feeling ineffective as a manager. What should I do?" In my mind, I thought, *Show me how to do this job better, Lord. Are there any classes I should take?*

The following Thursday my manager asked to talk with me. When the human resources person came in, I knew something was up, so I prayed, "Lord, help me, and don't let me cry!"

The human resources person bluntly stated, "We no longer have confidence in your leadership abilities, and you are relieved from your management position."

I sat quietly, stunned. I no longer had a job.

But then she continued, "We would like to offer you a different position. You can manage the infusion center, or you can transfer to home health."

Home health? I began to pray. *Lord, you know how I hated home health in school and said I would never work there. What are you doing to me? But I can't go to the infusion center—I would be pushing out another employee. Home health is my only option. At least I still have a job.*

"You have tomorrow off and the weekend, and then let us know what you decide."

While the Lord answered my prayer so that I did not cry during the meeting, the tears flowed once I was back in the office. I had not remembered the prayer I had prayed a few days before. But later that evening I finally remembered and thought, *Wow, Lord, you hit me with a two-by-four.* I begrudgingly accepted the home health position.

I now enjoy home health and have a wonderful opportunity to witness in a way I never could as a manager. In hindsight I can see how the Lord was protecting me. I did not recognize at the time how much the stress of being a manager was starting to affect me. The Lord had shown His love and care for me by removing me from that stressful position.

Be careful what you pray for, and trust Him when He answers in ways you are not expecting.

Dawn Goad

December 17

Gifts That Keep on Giving

Give, and it shall be given unto you; good measure, pressed down, and shaken together, and running over. . . . For with the same measure that ye meet withal it shall be measured to you again.
—Luke 6:38, KJV

When I was about seven, Mama taught me how to embroider and sew by hand. We did not have a sewing machine. She gave me a box of sewing supplies, including a small pair of scissors, and she taught me well. I mended, patched, and started to alter clothes and made some for myself. I also embroidered scarves for the Dorcas Society to sell. What I did not know until much later was that my maternal grandmother bought most of my finished work and saved it to give to me later for my hope chest!

After graduating from business college and getting a secretarial job, I bought a sewing machine and sewing table. When I married my husband, Carl, my mother-in-law gave me a box of thread from a sewing factory. She had never used them.

"I was given them because my husband's aunt knew I didn't like to sew!" she explained.

I thanked her for the gift, and over the years I have put the thread to good use! After fifty-seven years of marriage, only a few spools are left. God saw to it that I did not lack for things I could sew with. Only occasionally do I have to buy things I need!

When my sewing machine broke, a friend of my husband gave me his late mother's sewing machine and sewing chair. The seat top could open, and that is where I stored my thread.

Some years later, when that machine died, Carl bought me a new sewing machine for Christmas. Talk about the perfect gift! And when the mother-in-law of Carl's friend died from cancer, I was given cloth, thread, and other fine sewing items from her collection.

More recently a friend brought me a large bag of fabric. I was able to use some of it, and what I could not use, I dropped off at the secondhand store. They were delighted to receive the sewing grab bags I donated. The manager told me, "Ladies love these items! We keep the prices reasonable. Please keep bringing them!" I promised I would.

I feel blessed to help others in this way. God has been so good to me! He has also been good to you, I know it. So what can you pass along to someone else? Let's form a circle of joy, and may our gifts keep on giving as we share God's blessings with others.

Bonnie Moyers

December 18

Thank You—But No Thank You

Every good gift and every perfect gift is from above, and comes down from the Father of lights, with whom there is no variation or shadow of turning.
—James 1:17, NKJV

My son's birthday was coming up, and I was not sure what to get him. He had been planning to buy a house for some time, so I thought it would be a good idea to give him something for his home office. But what exactly? He already had all he needed for his office, so what could I possibly get for him? Then I remembered his chair. It had a low back and was not well suited for an office. My search for the perfect chair began. It took me a few days, but I finally found it—the perfect chair!

Made specifically for use with a computer desk and also for gaming, the chair had an ergonomic high back, cushioned lumbar support, a comfortable black leather racing seat, and an adjustable swivel—a rolling home executive chair! Surely I had found the best birthday gift for him! I felt certain he would love it as much as I did.

I ordered the chair and scheduled it to arrive a day or so before his birthday. A few days later I received notification the chair had been delivered. I could hardly wait to hear from my son. He called, and I expected to hear how much he loved the chair. Instead he said, "Ma, thank you for the chair, but do you think we can return it?"

Shocked and a little hurt, I asked him, "Why?"

He said he already had a chair. I told him I knew he did, but it was not an office chair. It had no support for his back, no headrest; it had to be uncomfortable. He said, "Thanks, but no thanks, Mom."

I felt so upset. This was not the reaction I had expected from him. I arranged for the chair to be returned and tried to forget the incident.

A few days later, while having my devotional time, the incident came to mind. Slowly I realized how many times God finds Himself in the same position with me. How many gifts has He bestowed that I have either rejected or simply not used? What about the best Gift of all, His Son, Jesus Christ? Have we ever rejected Heaven's sweetest Gift?

Let us determine to say yes to the incredible gift of salvation and the promise of eternal life. May we never say, "Thank you, but no thank you!"

Mayra Rivera Mann

December 19

Our Heavenly Travel Agent

*Trust in the L*ORD *with all your heart,*
And lean not on your own understanding;
In all your ways acknowledge Him,
And He shall direct your paths.
—Proverbs 3:5, 6, NKJV

Christmas break was here. All my friend and I could think about was getting on the train and traveling as far south as we could! We were in school near London, UK, so we booked a train ticket to southern Spain. We anticipated a grand adventure. Two days and 1,500 miles (2,400 kilometers) later, we arrived at our destination, tired but excited.

We checked into a hotel and walked around the city, taking in the sights and really enjoying all the history and architecture of the region. Each day we explored and practiced a little Spanish. We were having a great time for several days until we discovered that our cash and food supplies were almost gone. That is when we began to notice several people hanging around our hotel. Something about them made us question their intentions. Suddenly all we wanted was to get back to school. But how? Hitchhike?

Only then did we pray to God for help. It had not occurred to us to pray before the trip—but now we really needed Him. We prayed earnestly for God to intervene, but His answer was not exactly what we wanted to hear. "*Call your parents and ask them to send you money.*" What? How could we admit our stupidity and ask our parents for help? They were not wealthy people and would not easily be able to scrape the money together to bail us out of our predicament.

However, with no other alternatives, we each reluctantly placed a collect call to our parents, and they agreed to wire the money to a local bank. Nervous, frightened, and with help from an interpreter, we found the bank and breathed a sigh of relief as we left with cash in hand. Within a few hours we were back in London, only a few miles from school, a little bedraggled, embarrassed, and tired, but safely "home."

So why does God ask us to "lean not on our own understanding"? And why did my friend and I set off on our adventure without first asking Him for safety and guidance? Could it be that we tend to learn life's lessons only after we have made a mistake and failed? My friend and I were clearly reminded that God cares about everything concerning us, and that He is ready and willing to step in and guide us on the right path. All we have to do is ask. After all, He is the master travel agent!

Judy Casper

December 20

When Wise Men (and Women) Came to Visit

They presented unto him gifts; gold, and frankincense and myrrh.
—Matthew 2:11, KJV

My cardiologist walked in, took one look at me, and said, "You don't look right."

"Doctor, I don't feel right," I responded.

He immediately began to order tests and then came over to listen to my heart. He assured me we would find out the cause of the downturn in my health.

Over the next few weeks, I followed his orders and went for each test he had prescribed. Once the results came back, they revealed that my mitral valve was not functioning at all. Thus began my journey, once again, with heart valve surgery. The surgeon told me without surgery I had five to twelve months left to live. He felt hopeful, however, because there was a chance that new procedures might be available. Through a process called transcatheter mitral valve replacement, my valve could be replaced through the bilateral femoral vein. My surgeon had carried out only three of these surgeries. Ten years before, he had successfully performed my original open-heart surgery. This time would be different. The risks involved were much higher. I had a big decision to make, but I had faith in him.

In the end it was not difficult to choose to have this surgery. There were no other alternatives. My family and friends encouraged me to go ahead and have this frightening procedure. I prayerfully chose to undergo the operation.

As they wheeled me into the big surgical theater, people came at me like a swarm of bees, each with a job to perform. Each one knew exactly what they needed to do. Gently they put me to sleep and worked together to get the new valve in place and functioning properly. As I started to come around, I heard someone say, "All done!" My first thought was, "I lived! Thank You, Jesus!"

I thank the Lord for the "wise men and women" who were willing to study, learn, and invent new and better ways to help people who suffer. My wise men came from far away, not riding on camels but using today's common means of travel: airplanes and cars. These wise men did not bring gold, frankincense, and myrrh to my bedside as they did to baby Jesus. Instead they brought their skill, love for people, and surgical tools to heal my old heart. How grateful I am for their gifts!

Avonda White-Krause

December 21

Wait for It

Wait on the LORD: be of good courage, and he shall strengthen thine heart: wait, I say, on the LORD.
—Psalm 27:14, KJV

My family had just heard the news. One of my beloved aunts had asked the family to meet on Zoom because she had something she wanted us to hear together. In the Zoom meeting, she told us was gravely ill: the cancer in her breast had spread to her brain.

We were all shocked at her news and kept silent the entire time she spoke. Hearing her sad news felt difficult. The accompanying prognosis was even more worrisome.

Grief is not new to any of us. It is the ever-present unwanted companion that lurks in the shadows and creeps up on us unexpectedly, always without fair warning. It comes in only one form—horrific.

Grief, however, is not the only constant in life. Christians have a steady flow of love, laughter, and peace that not even the intermittent disruptions caused by grief can destroy. Paul is right. The enduring reminders of hope travel with us (see 1 Thessalonians 4:13), and it comes in the form of our Savior, Jesus.

In Exodus we read of the children of Israel's exit from Egypt, from slavery and oppression. For generations they had prayed and begged God for deliverance. At times it felt as if God had forgotten them and the covenant He had made with their forefathers. But God saw them. He sees us, His children, through eyes of pity and compassion. God sees all the hardships and injuries we endure. He acknowledges that we are His. God knows everything, remembers all, hears every word and sigh, gathers every tear we shed, and notes everything concerning His people. At this present moment God seems silent, and grief seems to be more present than He is. Nevertheless God knows what He has prepared: For the enemies who torment and oppress His people—a terrible recompense. But for His children—a marvelous, victorious deliverance!

The hard part is waiting for it. In the second chapter of Galatians, Paul states that Christ lives in him and that he now lives by the faith of Christ. It is no longer his faith or life; it is Christ's (see verse 20). This is our assurance as we wait—Christ living in us. Wait on the Lord, my friends. Be of good courage, and He shall strengthen your heart!

Joan Dougherty-Mornan

December 22

Joyous Gifts

"Let's go to Bethlehem." . . . So they hurried off.
—Luke 2:15, 16, NIV

Not long after our mother died, my sister decided being together during Christmas week was the best gift for us. Gifts come wrapped, and wrapped gifts are a surprise. So, of course, I was not told she and her husband were flying from the West Coast of the United States of America to my house on the East Coast, where I lived with my husband and our little son. The incessant knocking in the middle of the night forced me out of bed. I was astonished to see my sister through the peephole, wearing a red bow on her head. What a joyous gift I unwrapped that night!

I am reminded of another joyous Christmas when angels sang praises to God, and shepherds were the thrilled audience. An angel told the shepherds that their newborn Savior was wrapped in swaddling clothes and lying in a manger in the city of David. I have often wondered how they knew which city of David to search—his birthplace in Bethlehem or his capital, Jerusalem. The shepherds got it right when they cried, "Let's go to Bethlehem!" (Luke 2:15, NLT).

Did the shepherds truly comprehend that salvation's joyous gift was the wrapped baby? Were they so excited by the heavenly visitors that they rushed into town, stumbling into the discovery of the rest of the story? Did they wake up the town knocking on doors in the middle of the night? Did they call out questions about a newborn's birth or shout stories about angels singing? Did they ask for directions to the stable? Or were they guided by a divine compass, arriving at the stable to worship the Christ child with reverence and awe?

The shepherds "spread the word concerning what had been told them about this child, and all who heard it were amazed" (Luke 2:17, 18, NIV). Whether this occurred in the middle of the night or after daybreak, whether they spread the word loudly or reverently, they did not keep quiet about the wondrous angelic message nor about their experience in finding the Christ child!

Is finding my Savior so crucial that it keeps me up at night? Do I think knowing Jesus is so vital that I do not hesitate to shake others from the lethargic unawareness of God's plan for redemption? Am I so amazed by the good news that I share it with everyone I meet?

Come, let us go to Bethlehem, worship our Savior, and then tell others about His joyous gift of salvation! Or are you also slumbering?

Rebecca Turner

December 23

Saved by the Bell

"It shall come to pass that before they call, I will answer; and while they are still speaking, I will hear."
—Isaiah 65:24, NKJV

It was the first school day after Christmas break. I was thirteen years old. I sat in my usual seat on the left-hand side near the front of the classroom. Toward the end of the class period, my teacher said, "I would like for each one of you to stand beside your desk and tell the class what you received for Christmas."

Oh no! I thought, suddenly filled with anxiety. My family was very poor. The Good Fellows Organization gave gift boxes only to children until the age of twelve. I was thirteen. I no longer qualified for a gift box, so all I received that year was a much-needed white slip! It was decision time: *Do I tell the truth and have the kids tease me without mercy? Or could I tell a lie and keep the kids off my back?* My mother had taught me that I should always tell the truth, but at that moment it was a very hard decision for me to make.

As the teacher got closer and closer to my desk, my stress and anxiety levels increased. *What shall I do?* He started on my row, and one by one my classmates shared what they had found under their Christmas tree. I was stressed to the limit. Just as he was about to reach my desk, the loud *ring* signaling the end of class filled the air. How do you spell relief? Thirteen-year-old me spelled it B-E-L-L that day. I was so relieved I could have cried. I was literally saved by the bell.

So many times, as adults, we do not understand the circumstances children may be dealing with. It is so easy for us to put them in a catch-22 situation where they feel condemned if they do and condemned if they don't. My teacher was not trying to shame me. He thought he was doing something nice for the class.

How important it is for us to teach children to pray and to share with them that they can turn to Jesus in every situation. Nothing is too unimportant to bring to Him. Let us help them understand that Jesus will be with them in every situation. I am so glad that He understood the anxiety of a thirteen-year-old so many years ago. He answered before I called—and He will do the same for our little ones.

Ruth Cantrell

December 24

Love Like Jesus

"A new commandment I give to you, that you love one another; as I have loved you, that you also love one another. By this all will know that you are my disciples, if you have love for one another."
—John 13:34, 35, NKJV

Ladies, have you ever wondered what true love is? Not sure of the way to find happiness? Do you want to start to feel better or really learn how to love unconditionally?

Maybe you think love is when you are given a new car by your significant other, or when you get to go shopping for a completely new wardrobe, or for sure when a new house with beautiful furniture along with acreage is purchased. Then you would be content and happy, knowing that you are loved.

But soon enough you find out such things are not what makes you feel loved or happy, and they do not take you away from feeling sad or lonely. These things do not give you direction. You begin to realize that instead of wanting earthly materials, you need to have only one thing: a closer walk with God. He says we need to learn to love like He does.

It was Christmas at our home in Chattanooga, Tennessee, USA. My husband and I had not been back from the mission field to celebrate Christmas in more than ten years, and I was excited because every one of our children and grandchildren would be with us. Additionally, some of my siblings planned to join us.

We celebrated Christmas in an amazing way. The whole weekend was focused on the birth of Jesus. Friday evening my daughter led out in worship by reading the story of Jesus' birth, after which there were small gifts to choose from. When we opened the package we had chosen, we had to equate it to something about Jesus's birth. We sang Christmas carols, and each of us said one-sentence prayers to close our worship, starting from the youngest to the oldest.

And yes, we also got to open gifts on Christmas Day. However, the two things that stood out from the weekend were our focus on Christ and family. Material things will come and go, but Christ remains. So, sisters in Christ, hold on to your Savior and Friend. Learn to love like Him. He is our example. Do not let anything remove you from the path He has set for you. Give the gifts of love, kindness, and peace to everyone you come face-to-face with.

Nancy Mattison Mack

December 25

A Christmas Blessing

Those who trust in the LORD will find new strength.
They will soar high on wings like eagles [and fly!].
—Isaiah 40:31, NLT

It was Christmas time again, my favorite time of the year. I love celebrating the gift of God's Son to us to bring us salvation. I also love giving gifts to show God's love to others. Some say my love language is giving. I enjoy spending time selecting the right gift for each person. Something I know they would love to receive. I like to receive thoughtful gifts too.

This particular Christmas I started to feel sorry for myself. I remembered past Christmases when I had been given gifts that were not very thoughtful. They were last-minute runs to the drug store to get a gift card—or socks. You can always use socks and gift cards, but it does not take much thought. It felt like those were the only gifts I received.

I shared with a friend that I did not always feel I was being blessed with thoughtful or useful gifts at Christmas. My friend said, "Your blessing is coming!" He told me that God saw all I was doing and that He had a special gift just for me. He repeated that my blessing was coming and told me to look for it because it was on its way. It was just the encouragement I needed to stop feeling sorry for myself and continue to help others.

The conversation was soon forgotten, and I moved on with the holiday season and all the activities it brought. On Christmas day I received a phone call from my youngest daughter. She is a traveler and loves to go to new places. She was in Africa at the time, and she told me that she was giving me American Express points for Christmas. I thanked her. She went on and said I could use them for travel. I thanked her again. Then she told me I could use them for an around-the-world ticket and fly with her for the trip of a lifetime. And I said, "Thank you!"

Suddenly I remembered what my friend had told me. "Your blessing is coming!" Hallelujah! What a blessing! My daughter used her travel points to pay for my ticket and lodging, and for six weeks we enjoyed a wonderful excursion around the globe.

If you feel discouraged for whatever reason this Christmas season, I want to remind you that God sees you. He has not forgotten you. He is not ignoring your needs nor your desires. Wait on Him. Your blessing is coming!

Eva M. Starner

December 26

Christmas Interrupted

The LORD gave, and the LORD hath taken away; blessed be the name of the LORD.
—Job 1:21, KJV

Among the days that have greatly impacted my life, there is one Christmas day that still stands out like no other. While all around us were festive sounds of people celebrating Christmas with their families, my husband and I held the lifeless body of our son. All the plans and dreams we had for him flashed before us. How could this have happened to us? How could God have allowed it? And, more importantly, why? It all felt so surreal.

My experience of loss and heartache is not unique to me. The world is full of many heartaches. The earth seems to open its mouth to spew out seemingly unending trouble. Evil stretches forth its arm to touch each one of us at one time or another. In my loss the days ahead stretched out before me with emptiness and dread. By God's providence, as I leafed through the pages of my Bible, trying to make sense of the fate that had befallen me, many passages from Scripture seemed to jump out at me and hold me in a loving embrace.

One of my favorites was, "These things I have spoken unto you, that in me ye might have peace. In this world ye shall have tribulation: but be of good cheer; I have overcome the world" (John 16:33, KJV). The verse reminded me to have hope, not to get discouraged, and not to lose faith. It reminded me that Jesus had conquered death, and because of that I could face life with confidence despite my circumstances.

As I surrendered my emotions to God daily, I experienced the peace spoken of in John 14:27: "Peace I leave with you, my peace I give unto you: not as the world giveth, give I unto you. Let not your heart be troubled, neither let it be afraid" (KJV). Despite our prayers and fasting, God had chosen not to heal our son. He did not change our circumstances but, instead, chose to change us in the circumstances. The peace I felt in the days after the loss was supernatural. I found that I could face the dreaded days that stretched out before me. And you, too, can face uncertain days because Jesus lives.

Whatever the circumstances you are facing in life, you can cast your cares upon the Lord, and He will sustain you. He will never let the righteous be shaken. "Weeping may endure for a night," but we are assured that "joy cometh in the morning" (Psalm 30:5, KJV).

Minsozi Sibeso-Mweemba

December 27

Christmas—Canceled

"Therefore, stay awake, for you do not know on what day your Lord is coming. . . . You also must be ready, for the Son of Man is coming at an hour you do not expect."
—Matthew 24:42–44, ESV

The year 2023 will always be etched in my mind. In March my husband and I, along with two of our grandsons, were able to surprise our older son on the occasion of his retirement from the Miami-Dade County Public Schools in Florida, USA. I contacted the school district, and we were able, with God's help and my granddaughter's assistance, to make this happen. My son was amazed to see the four of us walk into the room, and it was such a joyous occasion to see friends and family. I look forward to the joyous occasion when we meet Jesus at His coming.

Just three months later my husband of more than sixty-two years passed away on June 4. He had experienced many health challenges, and now I was left wondering how I could possibly continue this journey without him. Our happy times together turned into sad times, as so often happens in life. But look at God—He gave me the peace I needed. When October came, the month we would have celebrated sixty-three years of marital bliss, I knew God was with me.

Thanksgiving without my husband was another sad time. The grief ministry at church, my family, and my Zoom Sabbath School class helped me cope with my loneliness and sadness. I was determined to keep myself engaged and had friends over for Thanksgiving dinner. It eased the pain.

Then came December. As I continued on the grief journey, I determined, with God's help and the prayers of family and friends, to make it the most enjoyable Christmas possible. My husband would have wanted me to. Then it happened. Family members became ill, and it looked as though Christmas would have to be canceled. "Lord, what can I do?" I cried. I wanted it to be as joyous an occasion as possible.

Then my son said, "Mom, I'll call a restaurant that's open on Christmas, and we can go there for Christmas dinner." So we did and had a great time.

Jesus clearly states that no one knows the exact time of His return (Matthew 24:36). World conditions indicate its nearness. Friends, His return will not be canceled. He is coming on time. Hold fast. We are almost home.

Vivian Brown

December 28

He Is With Us Too

"Behold, I am with you and I will keep you wherever you go, and will bring you back to this land. For I will not leave you until I have done what I have promised you."
—Genesis 28:15, ESV

Have you ever wondered why God has placed you exactly where you are right now? I was born to parents who lived in Tokyo, Japan, and now I live with my husband and three children in a pastor's family. With each move our workplace, home, church, and school changes. While these changes in environment can be exciting, they can also be stressful. And while I want to go wherever God leads me, I do not always feel equipped to handle all the changes. Perhaps today you are feeling overwhelmed, fearful, or exhausted. Remember that the God who says, "Behold, I am with you" (Genesis 28:15), did not say this only to Jacob. Even when we make mistakes and feel alone, the God who created us desires a personal relationship with each of us. He is alive and active, ready to provide strength for each day.

Not long ago I was feeling overwhelmed by work, family, and personal matters. I was so focused on the little things that I lost sight of the goals I had prayed about. I was about to give up when I ran into an elderly woman from a church I used to attend. She was in her eighties and still remembered the names of my three children. Her daughter later told me that her mother prayed for my children every day. It was such a comforting reminder that I do not have to carry everything alone.

No matter where I go, God watches over me and sends me reminders of His presence. Jacob saw a ladder reaching up to heaven and poured oil on the stone he had used as a pillow, calling the place Bethel (House of God). In Genesis 35, we read how God brought Jacob back to the Promised Land. Jacob was instructed to live in Bethel and build an altar there. He said, "Then let us arise and go up to Bethel, so that I may make there an altar to the God who answers me in the day of my distress and has been with me wherever I have gone" (verse 3, ESV).

My friends, God will be with us wherever we go. He will lead us to His house and will never leave us until His promises are fulfilled. The day we will dwell in Bethel, His house, forever is coming soon. May today bring us new goals, new joy, and a new understanding that the God of Jacob is with us too.

Mie Morita

December 29

A Panoramic View

And he showed me a pure river of water of life, clear as crystal, proceeding from the throne of God and of the Lamb.
—Revelation 22:1, NKJV

As I listened to the beautiful, peaceful music coming from my television and caught glimpses of the background scenes, I stopped my work in the kitchen and spent a few mindful moments soaking it in. The aerial panoramic views were breathtaking: Scenes of snow-capped mountains and majestic rock formations that seemed to stretch high up to the heavens. The sight of crystal-clear water flowing over rocks and waterfalls invited even a nonswimmer like me to draw closer. Lush pastures, the ripening buds of barley dancing in the gentle breeze, and the sight of a quaint little church in the forefront of a village on a hillside filled the screen. I remembered the wonder of my childhood memories as I listened to my mother read about the Garden of Eden.

My thoughts then went back to March 2020, when Canada and the rest of the industrialized world entered the "lockdown" after the World Health Organization declared the COVID-19 outbreak a global pandemic. We were ordered to shelter in place. No work, no school, no shopping—except for essential services such as grocery shopping and medical and pharmaceutical needs. No sporting events, no social events, no religious gatherings, no weddings, and no funerals. The world came to a standstill.

The evening news showed panoramic views of many of the major cities. In the United States, New York's Times Square—empty. In England, London's Piccadilly Circus—empty. In France, Paris's Avenue des Champs-Élysées—empty. In Italy, Rome's Trevi Fountain, its Pantheon, and its Colosseum—all empty. It felt eerily disconcerting. I wondered aloud, "Is this a precursor to the Lord's return?"

Scripture assures us that Christ's second coming will be a magnificent event. "For the Lord Himself shall descend from heaven with a shout, with the voice of an archangel, and with the trumpet of God. And the dead in Christ will rise first. Then we who are alive and remain shall be caught up together with them in the clouds to meet the Lord in the air. And thus we shall always be with the Lord" (1 Thessalonians 4:16, 17, NKJV).

Dear friends, I pray we all will be ready to greet Jesus as our "King of kings" and "Lord of lords" on that grand and glorious day!

Avis Mae Rodney

December 30

New Year's Opportunity

It is lawful to do well on the sabbath days.
—Matthew 12:12, KJV

It was the second Sabbath of January 2022. The church congregation had just heard a faith-lifting message in which we were encouraged to ask God to change us from the inside out, to help us be kinder toward our fellowmen, and not to pass by those in need as the priest and Levite did in Jesus' story of the good Samaritan. We had all stood in commitment and pledged to do so by God's grace. The preacher was my husband, the church pastor.

Five minutes after leaving church, my husband, Keith, and I came face-to-face with a good Samaritan situation. We had reached a major intersection at State Road 441 and were stopped at the traffic light. A senior citizen in a wheelchair had been propelling himself along the sidewalk when his wheelchair became stuck in the sand. He seemed to have realized his predicament and was shaking vigorously. He was clearly panicking. Keith carefully eased our car onto the narrow sidewalk and put on his hazard lights. He moved the wheelchair out of the sand and maneuvered it along the narrow edge of the road. The grateful man said he had been trying to get to the other side of the busy street.

As Keith stood at the busy intersection, a policeman in a cruiser arrived on the scene. He turned on his flashing lights and facilitated a safe crossing. The older man was very thankful and went on his way rejoicing. The policeman and all the other drivers gave a thumbs-up for everything they had witnessed.

How amazing that less than an hour earlier, my husband had committed not to pass by anyone in need. He had been given the opportunity to live what he had preached. For the onlookers it may have seemed to be just another good deed, but for me the saying "I'd rather see a sermon than hear one any day"* came to life.

May God help us to open our eyes and ears to see and hear the needs of others this New Year. As Jesus practiced doing good on the Sabbath—and every day—so we have the opportunity to be His hands and feet here on earth. May the Lord help us to follow the Savior's example on the Sabbath—and every day. For us it was truly a great way to start the New Year!

Claudette Garbutt-Harding

---

* The opening line of a poem largely attributed to Edgar A. Guest, "Sermons We See," public domain.

December 31

Future Blessings

Then the angel showed me the river of the water of life, as clear as crystal, flowing from the throne of God and of the Lamb. . . . And they will reign for ever and ever.
—Revelation 22:1–5, NIV

The final chapter of the final book of the Bible summarizes the eternal rewards of God's faithful children. A major focus of the chapter is the "river of the water of life, as clear as crystal, flowing from the throne of God and of the Lamb" (Revelation 22:1, NIV). From the onset, eternal life is guaranteed for those who will drink from the crystal-clear river, but that is only the beginning. There are added blessings on each side of the river.

"On each side of the river stood the tree of life" (verse 2, NIV). Does that suggest that there are two trees, one on each side of the river? Or does the tree of life expand its roots and branches, growing on both sides of the river? Those questions should generate interest in seeing the tree of life. It will bear twelve different fruits, one each month, and will provide food for the redeemed. Its leaves are "for the healing of the nations" (verse 2, NIV). The healing mentioned here encompasses more than physical maladies. Nations will be healed of their animosities, conflicts, and rivalries so that they will dwell in peace, free of resentments and all other opposing forces.

There will be no curse. The evil that generated the curse will have been eliminated because "the throne of God and of the Lamb will be in the city" (verse 3, NIV). Sin and its consequences will have been forever destroyed. There will be no temptation because the tempter will have been annihilated. Therefore God's children will freely love and serve Him.

We "will see his face" (verse 4, NIV). God's constant presence will revive us and remind us of our intimate relationship with Him. We will be loyal to Him. Additionally, because "his name will be on [our] foreheads" (verse 4, NIV), it will be a constant reminder that we are His children.

With God's presence there will be no night, and there will be no need for the sun (verse 5) because God is light. Finally, the redeemed "will reign for ever and ever" (verse 5, NIV).

What wonderful prospects lie ahead for us! Those future blessings will be ours if we surrender to God's pleading and let Him have full control of our lives. There is so much more to gain than to lose. Sisters, let us be faithful. We will soon be home.

Valerie Knowles Combie

2026 Author Biographies

Faye Acuff lives with her husband, Howard Bumgarner, in a quiet valley near Morganton, North Carolina, USA. They have two grown sons and a daughter-in-love. She serves as the lay pastor for a rural Seventh-day Adventist church. She enjoys lighthouses, reading, and chasing waterfalls with her husband. **June 6**

Betty J. Adams was born and raised in California, USA, where she lived mostly until her husband of sixty-six years passed away in 2020. She now lives in Maine, USA, with her youngest daughter, whom she helps with her scrapbooking business. Betty has six children, nine grandchildren, nine great-grandchildren, and four great-great-grandchildren. She is a retired teacher and graduated from Pacific Union College in 1953. **Oct 31**

Taiwo Adenekan is a teacher by profession and a local women's ministries leader. She is married to an elder of the church and has four children. She currently resides in Nigeria. **Mar 21**

Isabel Cristina de Almeida is the retired mother of three young people. She lives in Brazil, where she loves to read, make friends, and be out in nature. **Nov 27**

Sue Anderson is retired from the US Forest Service. She has two married daughters, three grandchildren, and three great-grandchildren. She enjoys writing, gardening, spending time with family and friends, and being outdoors. **Apr 7**

Mirlene André currently lives in Maryland, USA, where she is a full-time caregiver for her mother, who has dementia. She knows God is using this phase of her life as a training field for the work He has for her, which will include praying with and for people. **Mar 12**

Raquel Queiroz da Costa Arrais is a minister's wife who developed her ministry as an educator for twenty years. She serves in South Korea at the Northern Asia-Pacific Division as director of Women's Ministries, Children's Ministries, and Family Ministries. She has two adult sons, two daughters-in-law, and four adored grandchildren. Her greatest pleasures are being with people, singing, playing the piano, and traveling. **Mar 25, Apr 13**

Jean Arthur is a retired attorney. When she received an opportunity she could not refuse, she gladly worked to help students improve their writing skills by joining the staff at a local high school. Her hobbies include traveling, bicycling, running, baking, gardening, and photography. **Jan 6, Aug 5**

Yvita Antonette Villalona Bacchus is a graphic designer living in the Dominican Republic. She works in the music department of her local church and loves to share her faith in God and life in general on social media. Yvita is grateful for the opportunity to bless and be blessed through this devotional book. **Feb 21, Oct 30**

Jennifer M. Baldwin writes from Australia, where she works in risk management at Sydney Adventist Hospital. She enjoys family time, church involvement, and relaxing with crossword or Sudoku puzzles. She has contributed to the women's devotional book series for about thirty years. **June 22**

Vivian C. Bana, originally from the Philippines, now resides in Malaysia. She is a pastor's wife, a mother of two girls, and a former educator who has had the opportunity to teach in the Philippines, South Korea, Malaysia, and Singapore. She currently serves as an administrative assistant at the Malaysia Union Mission and leads various ministries at her local church, including family, women's, and children's ministries. She enjoys reading, writing, gardening, nature walks, and singing. **July 21**

Corletta Aretha Barbar is a native of Jamaica. Currently, she resides in Sacramento, California, USA, with her husband, Michael Barbar. Corletta has a passion for writing. Her involvement within the church varies from serving as the head of the music ministry to being a hospitality team player. Her hobbies are writing, traveling with Michael, crocheting, walking, sightseeing, and singing. **Apr 3**

Gloria Barnes-Gregory is inspired by everyday experiences, especially interactions with her granddaughters. She and her husband, Milton, continue to serve in health, family life, and leadership ministries, enabling others to make positive lifelong changes for themselves and to honor God. **Jan 18, July 14**

Dottie Barnett is retired and lives in a beautiful country setting in southeast Tennessee, USA. For more than fifty years, she has been involved in children's and adults' Sabbath School leadership. For the past several years, Dottie has written a devotional blog called *Whispers of His Wisdom*. She loves working with plants and flowers, mowing her large lawn, photography, and camping with her family. **July 28, Sept 30**

Ebonie Barde Base writes from the Philippines. She has worked in a state college for sixteen years, where she mentors future teachers. In her spare time, she loves to write in her journal, read, paint with watercolors, bake, listen to good music, play the keyboard and ukulele, and sing with her nephews. **Aug 4, Oct 11**

Lisa M. Beardsley-Hardy is currently director of Education for the General Conference of Seventh-day Adventists. She works with the Adventist Accrediting Association and is editor-in-chief of the journal *Dialogue*, which is published in English, French, Spanish, and Portuguese for Adventist university students around the world. **Nov 6**

Kristin Beaven earned a BA in English from Arizona State University, USA. She loves to read and write stories that inspire, uplift, and connect people to Christ. She is currently a member of the Crossville Seventh-day Adventist Church in Tennessee, USA. **May 25, July 6**

Ginger Bell resides in Colorado, USA, with her retired pastor husband. She is also retired, having served in women's ministries in her local church as well as in the Rocky Mountain Conference of Seventh-day Adventists. Ginger and her husband have two children and five delightful grandchildren. She enjoys family get-togethers, flower gardening, and antiquing. **Dec. 7**

Sylvia Giles Bennett, wife of Richard for about forty-five years, is retired from federal and state government. She is from Portsmouth, Virginia, USA, and has now lived in Suffolk, Virginia, for more than twenty-six years. She enjoys reading, writing, gardening, sharing, caring, traveling, and, most of all, spending quality time with her family, especially her five adorable grandchildren. She served various positions in the Seventh-day Adventist Church over the years and is a current member of the Calvary Seventh-day Adventist Church in

Newport News, Virginia. There is no greater honor, she says, than to seek and serve as God directs. **Dec 9**

Kathy-ann Best is a personal trainer and health enthusiast. She has been the health leader at her home church in Grazettes, Barbados, for many years. She enjoyed writing and publishing her first health book in 2024. She is the mother of two and tries to lead by example, teaching her children that God is in control no matter what happens in our lives. **Mar 9, June 16**

Sandra Blackmer is retired after serving more than eighteen years as an assistant editor for *Adventist Review* and *Adventist World* magazines. She and her husband, Larry, live in Idaho, USA. **May 2**

Paula Sanders Blackwell is an educator and writer who resides in Georgia, USA. She is the author of a devotional book titled *Lessons From My Hard Head* and a ninety-day prayer journal. **Dec 3**

Patricia Hook Rhyndress Bodi moved in October 2023 to Mason, Michigan, USA, after living eight years in Southern California. The University Seventh-day Adventist Church in East Lansing, Michigan, welcomed her back. She is very happy to be back home. **Feb 15, Oct 29**

Rhonda Bowen is a Jamaican-Canadian teacher and writer. She enjoys traveling, meeting new people, and watching God work to draw others closer to Him. **Jan 26**

DeeAnn Bragaw is the Women's Ministries director for the North American Division of Seventh-day Adventists. She holds a master's degree in pastoral ministry and a bachelor's degree in education. DeeAnn previously served the Rocky Mountain Conference as its Women's Ministries director and Prayer Ministries coordinator. **Jan 1**

Caren Henry Broaster is a high school English teacher at Houston Math, Science, and Technology High School in Texas, USA. She also teaches Dual Credit English Composition I and II at Houston Community College. Caren loves to interact with her sisters in Christ in women's ministries, compassion ministries, and the church book club. **July 20**

Mary Head Brooks is a retired psychiatric nurse who lives in Georgia, USA, with her husband, Marshall. She has a passion for providing food for those who may suffer from food insecurity. She enjoys gardening, traveling, and spending time with her grandsons, Mason and Maverick. **Apr 26, Nov 21**

Vivian Brown has lived in Huntsville, Alabama, USA, since 2006. Recently widowed, she keeps herself busy studying the Word of God. She is a member of a photography class, coordinates a cousin and family prayer and devotion group, facilitates a Zoom Sabbath School class, and serves as one of the church clerks for Oakwood University Seventh-day Adventist Church. Her three children and six grandchildren are the joy of her life. Nothing is more important to her than to be ready when Jesus comes. She encourages others to join her. **Oct 23, Dec 27**

Brenda Browne-Ashe is from the island of Antigua in the Caribbean, where she serves as the Women's Ministries island coordinator. A wife and mother of three, two girls and one boy, she loves to work with women. **Feb 24**

Elinor Harvin Burks resides with her soulmate, Winfield, a lay pastor in Leeds, Alabama, USA. They enjoy pointing out God's creative genius in nature by demonstrating science experiments for kids in libraries, churches, schools, and community fairs. Mrs. Burks, a church treasurer, loves researching history and making soap. She is a journalism graduate of Wayne State University in Detroit, Michigan, USA. Mrs. Burks retired from the City of Birmingham, Alabama, in 2010 after twenty-four years of service. **Jan 8, Oct 10**

Sarah Burt lives in Maryland, USA, with her best friend and husband, Merlin, who is the director of the Ellen G. White Estate. Together, they have three adult children, all married to wonderful spouses, and seven grandchildren, whom they try to visit several times a year. She is a retired registered nurse and enjoys keeping up the home, cooking, reading, and gardening. **Feb 10**

Helen O. Byoune, EdD, resides in Georgia, USA. She is ninety-two years young. A retired educator, she taught grades two and three and junior high English. Dr. Byoune is a learning-disabled specialist. She lived and worked for six years in the United States/British Virgin Islands as a diagnostician and adjunct professor. Dr. Byoune served for three years in South Korea as a Bible and ESL instructor and teaching supervisor. She is a mother of three, grandmother of one, and has three great-grandchildren. Her leisure time is spent reading, writing, crocheting, and spending time with her granddog, Chi. **Mar 26**

Elizabeth Ida Cain is an administrative manager who oversees the care of employees in the workplace and strives to serve as Jesus would. A professional florist, she enjoys cheering others with beautiful floral arrangements. One of her spiritual blessings is writing devotionals for the women's devotional books. She lives in Jamaica. **June 3, Nov 10**

Florence E. Callender is the "Difference In Learning" speaker, an author, an educational consultant, and a learning specialist. She is the founder of Innovative Lifestyle Solutions and the creator of Learning Made Easy: Success Secrets for Parenting Dyslexia. Florence helps parents work with their struggling children so that they learn faster and easier, have better school experiences, and succeed in life. She currently resides with her daughter in Tennessee, USA. **Mar 28, Oct 8**

Kendi Callender has a passion for finding creative ways to spread the gospel. She works in video production and is a world traveler with an entrepreneurial spirit. Kendi is always looking for new ways to make an impact for God on an international level. Most recently, she has developed Bible affirmation cards and a blog called *The Prudent Mind* to help women build faith and confidence in who God called them to be. When not traveling, Kendi lives in Tennessee, USA, with her mother. **Sept 12, Sept 25**

Z. Kathy Cameron identifies, above anything, as a child of the King, but she is grateful for being a daughter, mother, church administrator's wife (recently widowed), educator, grandmother, aunt, and friend. She served as the Women's Ministries director and Health Ministries coordinator of the Lake Union Conference, in Michigan, USA. Kathy's motto in life is "Hide me behind the cross; I am just a vessel." **July 23, Sept 2**

Laura A. Canning lives in the United Kingdom. She has three children and three grandchildren. Laura enjoys being with her family and her pets, and she loves country life. **June 25, Aug 8**

Ruth Cantrell is a retired Detroit, Michigan, USA, schoolteacher and counselor. She and her husband, Ronald, relocated to Harvest, Alabama, USA. She has two sons, a daughter-in-law, and three grandchildren. She enjoys women's ministry, prayer ministry, reading, flowers, music, and organizing programs. **Mar 22, Dec 23**

Pam Carbaugh believes God can bring balance to her life. She lives in Pennsylvania, USA. **Sept 19, Oct 9**

Judy Casper lives in Idaho, USA, with her husband, Martin. She loves hiking in the summer and skiing in the winter. She is passionate about health and exercise and loves any opportunity to be in nature, especially the mountains. With a degree from Loma Linda University, Mrs. Casper works remotely in the health information management field. **Oct 16, Dec 19**

Sarah Casper is a mental health and spirituality coach at Hey You're Brave, LLC. She lives in Pennsylvania, USA. **May 16, Nov 17**

Eleasia Charles, EdD, MSc, JP, is a reading specialist and literacy coach. She has taught at early childhood and tertiary educational levels and focused her time on writing children's books to provide educational resources for struggling readers. Dr. Charles enjoys family time with her husband, four children, and two dogs, Bella and Spunky, and being active within her church and community. **Feb 11**

Earlymay Chibende, PhD, currently serves as the director for Women's Ministries, Children's Ministries, and Communication at the Southern Zambia Union Conference. She and her husband, Mwewa Chibende, have served in various portfolios in the Seventh-day Adventist Church. Together, they had two children, but now have one beloved son, an amazing daughter-in-law, and two affectionate and energetic grandsons. She is passionate about empowering women to be their very best in God's vineyard. **Oct 4**

Suhana Chikatla is originally from India. She has two master's degrees and a doctorate. She wears many hats as a volunteer with children's and youth ministries at her church. Currently, Dr. Chikatla is the Adventurer area coordinator for the North Alabama region, Pathfinder club director, Master Guide club director for her church, Sabbath School teacher, multimedia personnel, and social media personnel. She and her husband, Royce Sutton, have a beautiful daughter, Rehana. **May 23**

Orathai Chureson was born and raised in Thailand. Prior to her appointment to the General Conference Children's Ministries Department, she served for eight years as the director of Children's and Family Ministries and one year as Ministerial Spouses Association coordinator in the Southern Asia-Pacific Division, based in the Philippines. She obtained her doctorate in curriculum and instruction (cognate in TESOL) from the Adventist International Institute of Advanced Studies in the Philippines. She is married to Saw Samuel, who currently serves as an associate secretary at the General Conference in Maryland, USA. **Mar 7, July 13**

Rosemarie Clardy enjoys nature and is truly blessed to live in the country with her husband and two dogs. Together, they keep their community clean by picking up trash along a mile and a half of road. She is a volunteer and helper at Mount Pisgah Academy Seventh-day Adventist Church in North Carolina, USA. **May 28, May 29**

E. May Clarke was raised in Jamaica and now resides in Rochester, New York, USA. She's a retired registered nurse, mother of two sons and a daughter, and grandmother of five grandchildren. She served as Sabbath School teacher, secretary, and women's ministry leader for the Jefferson Avenue Seventh-day Adventist Church. Her hobbies include reading, cooking, and traveling. **Mar 10, July 30**

Ella Clark-Tolliver, PhD, is a retired college dean. She has authored several articles in various publications, including *Message* magazine; a book, *Transformations*; and contributions to this women's devotional book series. She lives in California, USA. **Mar 1**

Florentina Coman lives in Romania, where she works as a professor of psychology and has a private psychotherapy practice. She has been married for thirty-five years and has a daughter and granddaughter. She has been a member of the Seventh-day Adventist Church for thirty years. **Apr 5, May 7**

Valerie Knowles Combie, PhD, is a retired professor of English at the College of Liberal Arts and Social Sciences at the University of the Virgin Islands, Saint Croix. After more than fifty years as an educator, Dr. Combie has enjoyed a more relaxed pace since May 2023, working in the garden, reading, and writing, as well as volunteering with Maranatha on projects. **Jan 10, Dec 31**

Kathy Beagles Coneff is retired from editing and teaching Bible-related curriculum. She is the mother of a blended family of three sons and a grandson and granddaughter. She continues to work with the Bible study curriculum for youth Sabbath School with the North American Division. **May 1, Sept 18**

Aminata Coote fell in love with books as a child. She writes Christian contemporary romance novels that point to a God bigger than our failings and who walks with us through our trials. She is also the author of several Bible studies and devotionals for women. She lives in Montego Bay, Jamaica, with her husband and son. **Jan 27, May 31**

Cheri Corder has been invested in women's ministries for many years, including as one of the founders of Women's Ministries in the Upper Columbia Conference and later as the director of several ministries, including Women's Ministries for the Oregon Conference. She has enjoyed speaking at numerous retreats, camp meetings, and churches. In the last five years before retiring, Cheri served as Missionary Care coordinator for Adventist Frontier Missions. **Feb 18, May 5, June 20**

Patricia Cove is a semi-retired elementary teacher. Her husband, George, passed away in 2024 after sixty-five years of marriage. Her current interests include outdoor pursuits, tramping beaches, reading, knitting, and writing stories for this women's devotional book series. She lives in Ontario, Canada. **Mar 23, June 13**

Shana Cyr-Philbert, MD, MSc, is a family practice physician and public health professional in Saint Lucia. Dr. Cyr-Philbert is passionate about changing lives through music and medicine. She loves family and enjoys raising her son, Nate. **Dec 12**

Marilee Serns Dalton, EdD, has had a lifelong commitment to ministry—as pastor's wife, nursing instructor, homeschool mom, and principal and teacher in both Seventh-day Adventist schools and public schools. She is a water skier, marathoner, hiker, and adventurer. Dr. Dalton currently sings with a praise and worship team, teaches a youth

Sabbath School class, and serves in prayer ministry and as a "neighborhood pastor." She finds great joy in spending time with Jesus, her two daughters, and five grandchildren. **June 11**

Leah J. M. Dean is an advisor, speaker, and coach to leaders and organizations across the globe. She is also the best-selling author of the book *Assemble the Tribe*. Through her work, Leah shares strategies to help her clients and audiences work smart, live well, and love people. Leah lives in Bermuda with her husband and two children. **Dec 2**

Ardie Diaz serves as the director of Women's Ministries and Family Ministries in the Northern Luzon Philippine Union Mission of Seventh-day Adventists in Manila, Philippines. She is passionate about training women to become committed leaders in the church. She also cherishes spending time with her grandson, Thirdy. **Feb 8, Nov 7**

Edna Bacate Domingo, PhD, lives with her husband in Grand Terrace, California, USA. A retired nursing professor, she remains engaged in academic consulting for nursing programs. Planning and coordinating medical missions to the Philippines fulfills Dr. Domingo's passion for missions. She enjoys participating in Sabbath School lesson study. Writing and gardening are hobbies that keep her upbeat. Dr. Domingo lives with her husband and loves taking care of three young grandchildren. **Feb 26**

Dagmar Dorn is the Women's Ministries director for the Inter-European Division and lives in Switzerland. She is a nurse-midwife and has worked in different countries. Dagmar enjoys traveling and meeting people. She is impressed over and over again by God's love. **Feb 22, Apr 4**

Aparecida Bonfim Dornelles graduated with a theology degree at the age of sixty-four from UNASP-EC (São Paulo-Brazil), the college she had dreamed of attending since she was young. She likes to get involved with church activities, Bible studies, small groups, reading, and crafts. A widow, she has two daughters and two grandchildren whom she loves very much. **Sept 11**

Joan Dougherty-Mornan enjoys discovering God between the pages of the Bible and through life's experiences and having daylong conversations with Him. She has two daughters, a son, and two grandchildren. She loves caring for her grandchildren and the family that God has blessed her with. Her hobbies are reading, writing, and crocheting. Her most rewarding and enjoyable pastime is living abundantly unto Christ. **Jan 4, Dec 21**

Louise Howlett Driver, a missionary's daughter, pastor's wife, mother of three married sons, and grandmother of four grandkids, lives in Idaho, USA, where she supports her husband, who is still preaching and involved with helping others. She enjoys reading, gardening, and putting puzzles together. She has been writing for this devotional series since 1998 and is blessed each year. **Sept 29**

Pauline A. Dwyer-Kerr holds two doctorates. She is an advanced practice nurse and a professor of nursing. Dr. Kerr is a life member of the Cambridge Honors Who's Who. She has received numerous awards, including one for Childhood Amblyopia Prevention Screening. Dr. Kerr is an ordained elder and resides in Florida, USA. She loves her children and grandchildren and enjoys the outdoors. **Mar 4, Apr 16**

Shylet Chabata Dzvene is a freelance writer and a stay-at-home mum with two wonderful children living in Harare, Zimbabwe. She contributed to the 2023 and 2024 devotional books. Her dream is to use her love of the written word to impact the world for God. **Aug 3**

Alice Emerson serves as the director for the Women's, Family, and Children Ministries Departments in Sri Lanka. She has been a pastor's wife for forty years and has two biological children, two foster children, and nine grandchildren. She loves the Lord and feels really blessed to be a blessing to others. **Aug 21**

Susan Erickson is a Seventh-day Adventist Christian and has been for over forty years. She loves God's creation and spends a lot of time in nature. She looks forward to the soon coming of Jesus, and she seeks to be like Him. **May 20**

Martha J. Feldbush and her husband, Marty, live in Vail, Arizona, USA. She was an educator in Adventist schools for more than twenty years, seven teaching kindergarten. She has worked for twenty-five years, as of this writing, as a dyslexia therapist. She enjoys books, music, needlework, swimming, travel, and dabbling in writing and art. **May 14**

Mona Fellers is a retired paramedic living on the high prairie of Wyoming, USA. She is active in her local church and enjoys leading Bible studies and working with women's ministries. She lives with her husband and has two daughters and two grandsons. **Mar 31, May 24**

Elena Flores lives in Geneva, Illinois, USA, a small suburb near Chicago. She has two wonderful boys, aged eleven and seven. She has worked as a cardiology nurse for the past fifteen years and is currently working toward her master's degree in nursing. She discovered her love for writing while navigating rough waters. God allowed her to discover His infinite love and mercy even in the storms of her life. **Jan 28, Apr 8**

Sharon Follett enjoys walking in the woods with her husband, Ron, teaching music classes and piano lessons, leading adult and children's choirs, and writing new words to songs. **Feb 14, July 10**

Shirley Sain Fordham is a retired educator. She is a wife, mother of three married adults, and grandmother of eight. She enjoys family, friends, strangers, technology, crocheting, scrapbooking, and her West End Seventh-day Adventist Church in Atlanta, Georgia, USA. She will continue to live, love, laugh, and learn until Jesus comes again. **Jan 16, July 4**

Sylvia A. Franklin serves as administrative assistant to the Women's Ministries director of the Pacific Union Conference of Seventh-day Adventists. Event planning, singing, playing games, and writing are among her favorite things to do. **June 26, Nov 15**

Cherryl A. Galley, PhD, rejoices in anticipation of resurrection day! Daily, she strives to reflect Christ's love. Her functions within the church spread across a wide variety of ministries. Dr. Galley retired from her professional career in counseling and collegiate education. She served as a full-time faculty member, a department chairperson, and dean of the School of Arts and Sciences. Some of the things she enjoys are studying the Bible, word games, number puzzles, writing, reading, music, praying with others, and photography. **Jan 13**

Claudette Garbutt-Harding lives in Orlando, Florida, USA, with her husband, Keith. They have been married for more than forty-five years. Now retired, she has a vibrant prayer ministry and encourages others to explore creative ways to pray. Mrs. Harding loves to write for the women's devotional and encourages other women to write. She helps with their editing. She has written an autobiography, *16 to 61 and Beyond: A Teacher's Personal Journey*, and a manual, *Ten Helpful Hints for Principals*. **Sept 22, Dec 30**

Cheri Gatton lives in Idaho, USA. She holds an MA in pastoral ministry from Andrews University and is the pastor of the Parma Seventh-day Adventist Church. A sought-after speaker, Cheri has a special passion for ministry to women, youth, and young adults. She and her husband, Dave, live close to their two married children and are "Gigi" and "Papa" to six precious grandchildren. **Jan 3, Aug 31**

Dawn Goad, a registered nurse, lives in Bisbee, Arizona, USA, five miles from the Mexican border, with her husband, Erick. Both are active in their little church. Dawn is the church treasurer, Cradle Roll and Kindergarten teacher, AV helper, and pianist. She is also the coordinator of Southern Arizona Women's Ministries with her sister Audra. She has three adult children and three wonderful grandsons with whom she loves to spend time. Her goal is to always have Jesus shine through her as she cares for her patients. **Dec 16**

Lela Moore Gooding, PhD, Oakwood University professor emerita of English, was an educator for forty-five years. She thanks God every day for her new job as caregiver and companion to Earl Gooding (Alabama A&M University professor emeritus), the brilliant man she married in 1965. They have five children—a son, a daughter, their spouses, and a goddaughter—six grandchildren and three great-grandchildren. **Sept 13**

Kaysian C. Gordon is a mother, financial advisor, author, speaker, and Bible teacher. She has published two devotionals and a children's book, coauthored with her daughter. She is her church's director of finance and stewardship and is passionate about stewarding God's resources in all areas of our lives. She is also a Sabbath School superintendent and speaks to various women's groups. **Mar 2**

Alexis A. Goring is a passionate writer with a degree in print journalism and an MFA in creative writing. She is an author of inspirational romance fiction stories and devotionals. Alexis loves following Jesus Christ and spending time enjoying delicious food with her loved ones. She's the founder of the *God Is Love* blog, where she teaches people about the God who loves humankind with all His heart. Her first devotional book, *Stories and Songs of Faith: My Journey With God*, was published in April 2020 and is available for purchase on Amazon.com. **Jan 14, Oct 24**

Debra Gough resides in North Augusta, South Carolina, USA. She has been a certified medical coder for more than thirty years. She enjoys her family, which includes one daughter and three grandchildren. She enjoys walking, her church family, teaching her primary class, and visiting neighbors, especially those who have lost their partners. **Nov 20**

Cecelia Grant is a retired medical doctor living in Kingston, Jamaica, and she longs for Christ's second coming. Her hobbies are gardening and listening to good music. Cecelia has a passion for young people, to whom she is always giving advice and encouragement. She has been a contributor to these devotional books since 2010. **Jan 25, June 8**

Jasmine E. Grant is a retiree, mother, and grandmother who resides in New York City, USA. She enjoys sharing the Scriptures and testimonies with people in general, but Jasmine has a special place in her heart for young people. She enjoys teaching them about the Savior and encouraging them to excel in whatever they do. **Mar 24**

Winsome Joy Grant takes delight in appreciating the awesomeness of God and the beauty of nature. Her main goal in writing for these devotionals from New York, USA, is to glorify God. She also hopes to inspire and encourage others to stay the course on this heaven-bound journey. **Apr 12**

Mary Jane Graves is old enough to remember that the "good old days" were not always so good! She is a widow, mother, grandmother, and great-grandmother who lives in North Carolina, USA. **Sept 4, Oct 7**

Tamia A. Griffith hails from the twin-island Republic of Trinidad and Tobago. As a writer, she utilizes her gift of storytelling to inspire and uplift others. Passionate about conveying messages of hope, love, and spiritual growth, Tamia hopes to touch the hearts of readers with her writing. Outside of her literary pursuits, she enjoys experimenting with new recipes in the kitchen and taking long walks in nature. Tamia finds that the beauty and tranquility of nature fuel her creativity. **Aug 17, Dec 15**

Nolwazi Gumbi is from the tiny Kingdom of Eswatini in southern Africa. She is a pediatric occupational therapist by profession and finds fulfillment in making a difference in the lives of children with disabilities. She has previously served as the senior Youth Ministries director of the Eswatini Conference. In her spare time, she enjoys reading, eating out, and swimming. Nolwazi's life vision is to be a blessing to the world and an honor to her Creator, and her mission is to know Him, be known of Him, and make Him known. **Oct 5**

Miranda Hadley is the wife of a pastor/teacher. She is the mom to four children and the grandma to one. She and her husband started an online church service during COVID-19 and continue to broadcast live each Sabbath at 9:00 A.M. Central Time from Texas, USA. **Mar 15, Nov 19**

Marsha Hammond-Brummel is a Title 1 math teacher who lives in Claremont, New Hampshire, USA. On weekends from May to October, she often can be found with her husband, Ken, at the historic Washington, New Hampshire, Seventh-day Adventist Church, telling the stories of the early Adventist pioneers to visitors. **June 4, Aug 9**

Myrna L. Hanna is assistant vice president for Administrative Affairs and Alumni and Donor Relations at Loma Linda University Health. Her favorite things include travel, spending time with family, and encouraging others to make the most of the talents God has given them. **Feb 2, Nov 2**

Mie Hashimoto is serving as a pastoral intern for the Japan Union Conference in the Odawara, Shizuoka, and Fujieda churches in the East Japan Conference of Seventh-day Adventists. She received a General Conference Women's Ministries scholarship in 2022. **Dec. 11**

Bessie Russell Haynes is a retired Seventh-day Adventist teacher who worked as a missionary teacher in South Korea for more than twelve years. She relocated to the

Pacific Northwest in the northern part of Washington, USA, to be near her precious grandchildren, two who live in Vancouver, British Columbia, Canada, and the other two near Seattle, Washington, USA. Traveling, reading, writing, and gardening are her hobbies. She awaits Jesus' soon return! **Apr. 29**

Karen Holford works at the Trans-European Division as the director for Family Ministries, Women's Ministries, and Children's Ministries. She is also a registered family therapist and freelance writer. She is passionate about helping people experience more of God's amazing love for them. She loves walking in forests, writing about God's love, and being with her growing family. **Feb 23**

Dorian Honey is retired and currently lives in beautiful British Columbia with her wonderful husband of forty-five years. Her focus is to live for Jesus, and she prays each day for opportunities to be His hands and feet. She loves walking, growing vegetables and flowers, and spending time in God's Word and with family. **Apr 23, July 24**

Tamyra Horst writes from Bernville, Pennsylvania, USA, where she lives with her husband of more than thirty years, Tim. An author, speaker, and Communication director for the Pennsylvania Conference of Seventh-day Adventists, Tami loves being a mom to her two young adult sons, being a friend to an amazing group of women, enjoying quiet time with a great book and a cup of chai, and sharing adventures with those she loves. **Jan 7**

Charmaine Houston is a health-care professional who lives in Pennsylvania, USA, with her two children. She enjoys reading and running. Recently, she placed first in her age category in a local 5K race. **Apr 30**

C. Marion Hudson earned a BS degree in biology and later an MBA and MSIS. She is a teacher of the Word and looks forward to the time when our minds will be in harmony with God's mind. **Apr 28**

Carolyn Huffstickler is an ESOL teacher in Virginia, USA. She loves tulips, the ocean, and spending time with children. Memories of her mother, who was always up before dawn with her opened Bible, are her inspiration for how to start each day. **Aug 29, Oct 20**

Kathy Hull lives in Maiden, North Carolina, USA, with Johnny, her husband of forty-five years. They have two grown sons, John and Justin. Spending quality time with God, family, and friends is among her favorite activities. **Nov 14, Dec 14**

Shirley C. Iheanacho is retired and lives in Huntsville, Alabama, USA, with Morris, her husband of more than fifty-four years. She is a church elder, writer, speaker, prayer warrior, ministry leader, and philanthropist. Mrs. Iheanacho encourages women to share their stories. More than seventy devotional articles by thirty-nine women have been published. Funds from her book, *God's Incredible Plans for Me: A Memoir of an Amazing Journey*, provide scholarships for needy female students. **Jan 2, Mar 29**

Greta Michelle Joachim-Fox-Dyett is an artist, potter, and teacher at Southern Academy of Seventh-day Adventists and an adjunct lecturer at the University of the West Indies. She lives in Trinidad with her husband, Arnold. Now empty nesters, they are enjoying spending time together while missing their girls. **Aug 22, Nov 1**

Elaine J. Johnson and her husband of nearly sixty years live with their oldest daughter, Kathy, and wonderful son-in-law. She enjoys interacting with her grandchildren and great-grandchildren and attending her home church in Cleveland, Ohio, USA. She enjoys reading, writing, playing games on her iPad, and contributing to these devotional books, which she has done for more than twenty years. **May 3, June 27**

Mary C. D. Johnson is an enthusiastic high school Spanish teacher in California, USA. She travels the world on mission trips whenever she gets a school break. She also enjoys scrapbooking, writing, cooking, playing the piano, and being outdoors. **Jan 22, Nov 3**

Sheila Johnson (deceased) resided in Trinidad and Tobago. She was an avid gardener who also enjoyed worshiping her God, praying intercessory prayers for friends and family, studying the Bible, and sharing her life testimonies to encourage and inspire others. **Sept. 21**

Deidre A. Jones has moved to Connecticut after a lifetime in Virginia, USA, with her husband and their Yorkie, Tuff. She enjoys baking, listening to audiobooks (a great way to elevate chore time), and painting watercolors. Her graphic design business, DeidreJonesDesigns.com, provides resources for churches to empower their volunteers to engage dynamically in meaningful ways. **June 29, Sept 26**

Gerene I. Joseph is married to Elder Sylvester Joseph. They have two adult children, Sylene and Sylvester Jr. She served for six years as the director of Women's and Children's Ministries in the North Caribbean Conference. Presently, Mrs. Joseph is the director of the Education Department for the same conference, headquartered in the US Virgin Islands. She is a published author who enjoys writing poems and playing the piano in her spare time. Mrs. Joseph is also a certified lay preacher and has conducted three evangelistic series. **June 2**

Emma Nangula Kakona is a Christian educator and entrepreneur who has passionately led as the volunteer director for Women's and Children's Ministries in the Namibia South Conference since 2016 and serves on the executive committee of the conference. Currently, she also holds the position of ASI vice president in Business Development at the Southern Africa Union. Her dedication and leadership in multiple church roles underscore her commitment to uplifting and supporting her community through various ministries and organizational responsibilities. **Feb 3, Aug 16**

Priscila Kandane is the Women's Ministries and Children's Ministries director and ministerial spouses coordinator for the Western India Union in Pune, India, where her husband, Pastor Ujwal Kandane, serves as president of the same union. She was called to service as a teacher from 1991 through 2015, when she was appointed as Women's Ministries director and Ministerial Spouses (Shepherdess) coordinator for the Mumbai Metro Section of Western India Union. She later served in these departments in the North Maharashtra Section. She loves to read, listen to music, travel, and teach. **Feb 12, Sept 14**

Anna Karatzidou-Papaioannou was born in Greece, in the district of Macedonia. Her family was one of the first to become Seventh-day Adventists in her county. For the past twenty-seven years, she has lived in the United Kingdom. Anna is an English teacher and an administrator. She established her own private English language school in Greece and ran it for more than ten years. She has been teaching students from all over the world for more than twenty-five years. In administration, she currently serves as a personal assistant for the Women's Ministries Department in the Trans-European Division. At her local church Anna serves as a coordinator for the family worship services and a panelist for the Sabbath School Broadcasting class. She enjoys studying the Bible and meditating on God's Word. **Jan 31, May 17**

Carolyn K. Karlstrom lives in the state of Washington, USA, with her husband, Rick, and her sweet kitten. She is involved in prison ministries, women's ministries, and her church's live-streaming program. Her blog, *Carolyn's Corner*, can be found at CarolynKarlstrom.com. **Aug 19, Nov 29**

Grace A. Keene was born on December 31, 1935. For twenty years she lived in New Rochelle, New York, USA, before moving to Florida. There, she raised her family (and some other people too), whom she still points to the lovely Lord Jesus and His joy and comfort. She now resides in a Tennessee retirement center and remains intensely interested in doing what Jesus asks all of us to do: "Go and tell." **Jan 11**

Sonia Kennedy-Brown lives in Ontario, Canada. She is a retired nurse and fills her time with reading, writing, and witnessing. The motto that guides her life is, "If I can help somebody along life's way, then my living shall not be in vain." Due to her own experience, she does motivational presentations to support those with disabilities. **Aug 18, Oct 15**

Kênia Kopitar is Brazilian but lives in the USA to follow God's purposes for her life. She loves to help people and talk with neighbors. She is the crazy cat lady of her street and has a collection of cat cups her friends have given her through the years. **July 22, Oct 27**

Yana Kosian has two grown-up children, Daria and Roman. She was born in Ukraine, where she lived in the city of Kyiv. She is a lawyer by profession and worked in an international law firm in the litigation department. In 2022, after the invasion of Russian troops, she and her family were in occupied territory, where they took shelter in a basement without food, water, or electricity. With God's intervention, they were rescued. Fleeing death, they found themselves in Germany, where they now live. **July 7, Sept 23**

Betty Kossick (deceased) contributed to this women's devotional book for many years. She worked as a freelance writer of varied genres and as a journalist, author, and poet for both religious and secular publications. In 2006, she published her memoir, *Beyond the Locked Door*. She developed and edited *From Port Vista*, the newsletter for the Florida Living Retirement Community. Much of her work can be found by googling her name. She passed to her rest in February 2022. **Jan. 24, May 6**

Durdica Kukolja lives in Melbourne, Australia. She loves to work with children and has spent many years as a physical education teacher. Durdica is a mother of two and grandmother of six. She loves them all, and they adore her. Durdica is happily married to Mladen Kukolja. **Feb 16**

Mabel Kwei is a retired university and college lecturer. She did missionary work in Africa for many years with her pastor husband and their three children. Mabel now lives in New Jersey, USA. She loves to read a lot, paint, write, and spend time with little children. **Feb 17, Aug 2**

Juliet L. Lucas Languedoc holds a master's degree in educational psychology from the University of the Southern Caribbean. She has authored three books and coauthored one with her husband. She is a certified and commissioned teacher. Juliet currently teaches information technology/computer classes for the elementary, junior, and secondary levels at Saint Thomas-Saint John Seventh-day Adventist School in the United States Virgin Islands, where she previously served as the Bible teacher. Juliet is married to Pastor Jerry Languedoc. She enjoys praying for others, meeting people, singing, witnessing, decorating, crocheting, and sharing the good news. **Feb 4**

Faith Ann Laughlin, EdD, has over four decades of teaching experience. As a teacher, mentor, advocate, and writer, she inspires her students and readers to embrace their God-given potential and live as lifelong learners and faithful disciples. Her life's work reflects her unwavering commitment to faith, family, and education, leaving a lasting impact on all who have the privilege of learning from her. **Jan 9, Mar 17**

Wilma Kirk Lee, LCSW, is married to the love of her life, W. S. Lee. They have shared their lives for almost sixty years. She is mother to Anthony, deceased; Adrienne, married to Carl Jones; and Amber. Wilma is "GoGo" to her three grandsons. She enjoys reading, crocheting, and listening to music. Her favorite color is purple. **Mar 14, June 24**

Loida Gulaja Lehmann spent ten years selling religious books in the Philippines before going to Germany and getting married. She and her husband are active members of the International Seventh-day Adventist Church in Darmstadt, Germany. Both are involved in radio, prison, and laypeople's ministries. Loida's hobbies are traveling, nature walks, writing, and photography. **Feb 5**

Sharon Long was born in Trinidad but lived most of her life in Canada. In 2015, she retired from the government of Alberta after working for thirty-four years in child welfare. She does contract work for the Alberta College of Social Workers and is active at the West Edmonton Seventh-day Adventist Church. She is the mother of four, grandmother of six, and great-grandmother of two. Sharon is passionate about people and is happiest when serving others. Every day above ground is a good day and a new opportunity. **Aug 12, Sept 20**

Rosemary Kasandra Lucien hails from the beautiful island of Saint Lucia. She is presently employed as the bookstore assistant with the Inter-American Division Publishing Association bookstore. Her passion is to serve the Lord as she intercedes on behalf of His people. Her interests are reading, writing, and beach hopping. **Apr 21**

Lynn Mfuru Lukwaro was born and raised in Tanzania. She and her husband, Gureni, live in Sharjah, United Arab Emirates, together with their two beautiful daughters, Eliana-Naghenjwa and Kristen-Sara. They serve the Lord in Sharjah Seventh-day Adventist Church. She enjoys traveling, stories, nature walks, teaching, and reading. **May 12**

Magdalena Alina Lupu has years of experience as a nurse and psychologist. She and her husband, Pastor Doru Lupu, have a daughter. Mrs. Lupu loves helping people, traveling, and reading. She is fulfilled in her new position as a grandmother! Mrs. Lupu serves as the Women's Ministries director of the Moldova Conference in Romania. **Mar 27**

Marcella Lynch taught home economics and authored *Cooking by the Book*. She hosted a cooking show that aired on 3ABN for fifteen years. A member of the General Conference of Seventh-day Adventists Nutrition Council for thirty years, Marcella taught nutrition instructor courses across the USA in churches and at camp meetings and hundreds of plant-based cooking classes. Retired now, Marcella lives with her husband in southern Oregon, USA, and enjoys having their grandchildren nearby. She is active in their church cooking and health outreach programs and loves to can, freeze, and dry produce and fruits on their twenty-seven-acre farm. **June 12, July 16**

Betty Lyngdoh is the director of Youth Ministries, Children's Ministries, and Communication for the Northeast India Union Section in Shillong, India. She also has held the position of director of Women's Ministries at the conference and union level. She is married to Dr. L. F. Lyngdoh, is the mother of three sons, and has three granddaughters. **Jan 19, July 2**

Nancy Mattison Mack is an American born in India to a missionary family. She returned to the USA to attend college. She and her husband, Bill, raised their family in Maryland, USA. When they relocated to India to direct Adventist Child India, a General Conference donor-funded program for educating needy children, she became the third generation of Mattison missionaries who have served India. Sponsoring a child's education is effortless at adventistchildindia.org. **Dec 24**

Lindy Lou S. Magdadaro writes from the Philippines, where she loves to serve the Lord in her local church. **July 8**

Rhona Grace Magpayo is a retired optician who enjoys going on mission trips with her husband, Jun. A photography enthusiast, she is grateful for opportunities to travel the world, capturing sunsets with her iPhone. She is blessed to come home to Maryland or Florida, USA, and to have a family that loves the Lord. **Sept 8**

Anamaria Maier is a Romanian translator and interpreter. She loves to serve God and his children through the gifts He entrusted to her. **July 18, Aug 15**

Mayra Rivera Mann lives in Lawrenceville, Georgia, USA, with her husband and works as the registrar for Atlanta Adventist Academy. She has two grown sons and a stepson. She loves traveling, reading, and scrapbooking. **Dec 18**

Evis Kachana Matali is currently an accounting student in Namibia, Africa. She began writing as a child when she asked her father for a doll, and he told her, "Books must be your friends." Though she hated being told that as a child, she loves that advice now. Though she never received the doll, she received something greater—a love for literature, reading, and writing. Books have been a great blessing to her throughout her life, and she hopes they will be for someone else too. **Dec 10**

Deborah Matshaya is an admitted attorney of the High Court of South Africa. She is a dispute resolution specialist in a private firm. Deborah is currently working toward an MBA. She spends time in church each Sabbath, runs and swims each Sunday morning, and relaxes by listening to music. **Jan 12**

Nicole Mattson currently resides near the beautiful shores of Lake Michigan, USA, with her husband, Terry. Both are avid nature lovers, but Nicole particularly enjoys hiking and exploring national parks. They are smitten with their seven grandchildren and enjoy every minute spent with them. **Aug 27**

Katie McCluskey lives in Idaho, USA, with her husband, Lloyd, and two girls, Elly and Zoe. She enjoys homeschooling her children and working part-time as a registered nurse. Reading is a passion of hers, and she can often be found curled up on the couch with a good book. **July 26, July 27**

Carol McLeod taught for forty-four years in the Pacific Northwest and Hawaii. Now retired, she is the proud mother of two daughters and grandmother of two granddaughters. She loves to read, walk, and stay in touch with good friends. **Sept 3**

Judelia Medard-Santiesteban is from the Caribbean island Saint Lucia. She is a high school teacher of health and family life education and is involved in women's ministries and youth ministries. She has authored two children's books that empower children to speak out against sexual abuse. Most importantly, she is "learning to lean on Jesus." **Feb 27**

Annette Walwyn Michael is a retired English teacher and former assistant professor of English at Oakwood University. She has published two well-received books in the Caribbean. She has also been published in the *Adventist Review* and other periodicals. Married to Reginald, a retired pastor, Annette is mom to three adult daughters and the grandmother of eleven. **May 27, Aug 25**

Sharon (Clark) Mills is a retired educator who enjoys working on Maranatha projects with her husband, James. They live in Crossville, Tennessee, USA. Sharon enjoys traveling, writing, and spending time with friends and family. She looks forward to Christ's soon return. **Jan 17, June 19**

Minenhle Lindelwe Mlilo serves as communication secretary and is the youngest board member at the Krugersdorp North Seventh-day Adventist Church in South Africa. With a background in finance and internal auditing from the University of Pretoria, she passionately serves the Lord through various outreach initiatives. Minenhle advocates for those in need, exemplified by organizing blood drives that have saved over seventy lives. **Aug 28**

Punyo Moni is a teacher at Itanagar Adventist School in Arunachal Pradesh, India. **May 18**

Reva Lachica Moore is a mother of two sons and a grandma of four. A former chemist/medical technologist, God allowed her to retire nine years early so she could work full-time at Adopt a Minister International. This nonprofit, faith-based ministry supports hundreds of unemployed theology graduates in the Philippines and other countries. To learn more, visit a-a-m.org. **Sept. 17, Nov 16**

Alyssa Morauske has been married to her husband for ten years, and together they are raising two children in the beautiful, rainy Pacific Northwest of the USA. With a background in psychology and experience working in the mental health field, she brings a compassionate perspective to her writing, which she views as a calling from God. Inspired by her journey as a mother, including raising a child with special needs, she writes to encourage women to see God's faithfulness in every season of life. When she's not writing, you'll often find her gardening, cooking, and playing outside with her children. **Apr 10, Nov 24**

Lila Farrell Morgan is a widow and writes from a small town in the foothills of Western North Carolina, USA. She loves her four adult children, five grandchildren, and a growing number of great-grandchildren. Reading, contemplating the Creator's handiwork in nature, researching differing topics on the internet, and playing table games are some of her favorite pastimes. She looks for the positive in life and enjoys a good laugh. **May 13, June 17**

Valerie Hamel Morikone writes from Southern Illinois, USA. She lives on a lovely farm that she and her husband, Daniel, now call home after moving from West Virginia, USA, where they worked for the Mountain View Conference. Delighted to be near her son and daughter-in-law, she especially relishes more time with Daniel since they are both retired from full-time work. **Sept 24**

Mie Morita is the departmental director for Women's Ministries, Family Ministries, and Children's Ministries and an announcer for Voice of Prophecy radio in the Japan Union Conference. She loves to evangelize with her pastor husband of twenty-five years and read the Bible with small groups. **Dec 28**

Bonnie Moyers lives with her husband Carl, and Milo, a ragdoll kitty, in Staunton, Virginia, USA. This freelance writer is a mother of two, a grandmother of three, ad a musician for several area churches. **Dec 17**

Esther Synthia Murali is the coordinator of the Ministerial Spouses Association at the South Karnataka Section of Seventh-day Adventists, Mysore, India. She is a physiotherapist by profession, but her passion is ministering with her pastor husband. She has a son, Ted, and enjoys playing guitar, painting, gardening, and photography. **Apr 17**

Vanessa T. Mutambara is a devoted mother and wife, passionate about family and community. She is a Senior Youth Leader trainee, developing skills to make a positive impact. A counselor in the Pathfinder Club at Goodhope Seventh-day Adventist Church in Harare, Zimbabwe, she guides young people in their spiritual journeys. **Apr 19**

Jannett Maurine Myrie, MSN, is a medical missionary who finds great joy and fulfillment in sharing the love of Jesus with everyone. She is the proud mother of Delroy Anthony Jr. Jannett enjoys traveling (especially cruises) and is an avid reader. She makes her home between Florida, USA, and Jamaica. Jannett is ever so thankful to Jesus for loving her unconditionally and blessing her to trust the plans He has for her and her family. **July 9, Oct 22**

Cecilia Nanni is a psychologist who specializes in mediation and conflict resolution, as well as narrative therapy and community therapy. Currently, Cecilia serves as a volunteer coordinator and counselor in Central Asia. **Feb 9, Aug 11**

Nokukhanya Ncube writes from Zimbabwe. **Apr 14, Sept 5**

Natalia Nikolenko is a Ukrainian refugee living in Germany. She loves to help children learn to pray and trust in God. Ever since she was baptized at the age of twenty-eight, she has organized programs and camps for children. God blessed her with many ideas for activities and sketches, and many children attended. Natalia prays that this Christian influence will remain in their hearts even though the war has changed everything. **Oct 18**

Elizabeth Versteegh Odiyar lives in Kelowna, British Columbia, Canada. She has served God in church, in Pathfinders, and on mission trips. She retired from managing the family chimney sweep business after thirty-three years. She is married to Hector, and they have twin sons and a daughter, all of whom are married and serving God. They also have four delightful grandchildren. **Apr 22, Oct 19**

Lynn Ortel has an MA in counseling and is a licensed professional clinical counselor. She feels privileged to have served the church as conference director for Communications, Family Ministries, Women's Ministries, and Children's Ministries. Lynn also served as the conference Ministerial Spouses Association leader, and she currently volunteers in the Arizona Conference as Women's Ministries coordinator. Her personal mission statement is "to live a life of love" (Ephesians 5:1, 2, NCV). Lynn has traveled across the USA and overseas sharing about the God who makes a difference in our lives. She is married to the wonderful Mike Ortel, and their three children have given them six grandchildren. **Jan 15, Nov 12**

Sharon Oster is a retired teacher assistant living in Evans, Colorado, USA, with her retired pastor husband. She enjoys day trips in the nearby Rocky Mountains. Sharon and her husband have three children and nine grandchildren. **Feb 20, June 9, Dec 1**

Hannele Ottschofski lives in southern Germany, where she has been active in many facets of women's ministries. Hannele is passionate about helping women develop their God-given gifts and using them to be the best they can be. She has written several books about women in church and society. **Mar 20, May 4**

Karen Pearson is a speaker, writer, and editor. She served as the Prayer Ministries coordinator at the Idaho Conference of Seventh-day Adventists and as an associate pastor with her husband, Michael. She worked at the Pacific Press® Publishing Association for almost ten years as director of Publicity and Public Relations. Karen previously edited the E. G. White Notes for the Sabbath School Lessons and edited these women's devotional books for several years. Her greatest joy is to share stories of Jesus with others. **Apr 2, June 1, Aug 30, Oct 12**

Premila Pedapudi is the administrative assistant for the Department of Women's Ministries at the General Conference of Seventh-day Adventists in Maryland, USA. She is married to Joseph Kelley and is the mother of a son, Praveen, and twin daughters, Serena and Selena (who are married to Samuel and Ebenesar)—all are a great support to her in her ministry. Her first grandson arrived in July 2019. Premila is passionate about women's ministries and loves to sing, read, teach, and preach. **Nov 26, Dec 8**

Sueli da Silva Pereira lives in Patos de Minas, in the state of Minas Gerais, Brazil, and works in the city hall. She is a Sabbath School teacher and enjoys music and writing for her blog. Sueli is married to Clarindo and has three children: Arthur, Eric, and Samuel. She currently participates in the instrumental worship group of the Central Church of Patos de Minas. **Feb 6, Oct 26**

Diane Pestes has written two books, *Prayer That Moves Mountains* and *Prayer Still Moves Mountains* published by the Pacific Press® Publishing Association. She is an international speaker who resides in Oregon, USA. She is known for her commitment to Christ and loves to recite Scripture in nature and post it on YouTube. She finds exercise relaxing and enjoys the grandeur of nature and traveling with her husband and mother. **Aug 6**

Angèle Peterson lives in Ohio, USA, and as the Holy Spirit impresses, she has contributed to the women's devotional over the years. However, Angèle longs for the day when these books are a thing of the past and we are in heaven. Until then, she continues to serve her local church in Oberlin and helps her sister keep the giving legacy of her family alive as the vice president for the Carter Peterson McMillan Foundation (thecpmfoundation.org). **Jan 30**

Elena Petrescu, PhD in philology, loves to read, travel, and do handwork. She has two children and three grandchildren. She enjoys working in the Women's Mission Department in her local church in Bucharest, Romania, where she leads the weekly women's prayer hour. She also offers free tutoring for students at the Adventist Theological High School. Both she and her pastor husband are retired. **May 30, Oct 3, Dec 6**

Karen M. Phillips writes from eastern Kentucky, USA. She is happily married to her husband, John, and has four children and three grandchildren. She volunteers in human resources for a number of different ministries. She also partners with John in their worldwide ministry, HeReturns. Her passion is proclaiming the Lord's end-time message and being an instrument in saving souls. **May 11, Aug 10**

Shannon J. Pigsley resides with her husband, Brad, in Council Bluffs, Iowa, USA. She has a full-time job but enjoys spending her free time camping, traveling, and doing nature photography. She also enjoys writing devotions for the Council Bluffs Seventh-day Adventist Church website, where she uses some of her photographs of nature. She has been the women's ministry leader at her church for the past six years and enjoys sharing her love for God and the many ways He has touched her life. This submission, "Finish the Race," is dedicated to Pastor Taariq Patel, an inspirational pastor. **Aug 26**

Merle Poirier writes from Silver Spring, Maryland, USA, where she worked for more than twenty years in the Adventist Review office. She is the author of *Renew*, three devotional books (vols. 1, 2, 3) that cover the entire Bible with lessons, particularly for young parents but equally relatable to anyone else. She particularly enjoys studying the Bible to find new and unique applications to familiar stories. **Nov 30**

Beatrice Tauber Prior, PsyD, is a clinical psychologist, author, speaker, and owner of Harborside Wellbeing in North Carolina, USA. Dr. Prior is the best-selling author of *Grandma and Me: A Kid's Guide to Alzheimer's and Dementia*. She considers it an honor to be the mother to her delightful daughter and wonderful son. She cherishes moments spent with family, friends, and loved ones. **Nov 8**

Jessy Quilindo, originally from Seychelles, is currently the honorary Women's Ministries director of the Singapore Conference of Seventh-day Adventists. A clinical nurse by profession, she is studying counseling psychology to better serve the women of her conference. Jessy is married to Steven, her husband of more than thirty years. They have two young adult sons. She enjoys cooking, home decor, and gardening but finds her greatest reward in women's ministries. **June 21**

Mary Ranjan serves as director of Women's and Children's Ministries for Bangalore Metro Conference, India. Before 2023 she served in the South-Central India Union Section for eight years as director of Women's and Children's Ministries. **Jan 5**

Jerlyn Richards is a testament to the Christian adage, "Let go and let God." She is a loving wife and the mother to an energetic and oh-so-full-of-life toddler. She believes that all things do work together for good for those who love the Lord. However, it is in His time and not ours. She lives with her husband on the island of Dominica in the Caribbean. **Feb 7**

Julie Richardson is a wife, mother of four, and grandmother of twelve. She is the first ordained female elder within the Bermuda Conference of Seventh-day Adventists and serves at the Warwick Seventh-day Adventist Church. Her hobbies are reading, walking, gardening, and encouraging others in their walk with God. **Mar 6, July 5**

Jenny Rivera writes from Brisbane, Queensland, Australia, where she works as a wound management stomal therapy specialty registered nurse. She is involved in the Sabbath School department at her church and shares her musical flute talent in two different orchestras. She enjoys traveling, reading, and spending time with family and friends. **June 5, Nov 23**

Taniesha K. Robertson-Brown has always had a deep appreciation for the ever-present beauty in words. As a result, she takes every opportunity she can to share God's goodness through her written work. Taniesha is the author of *Godly Families in an Ungodly World*, and her most recent publication is *When the Spirit Leads*. She is the editor of the English version of the book *Among Saints*. Taniesha has also authored numerous electronic and print devotional publications. She is married to Courtney, and they have two sons, Preston and Prescott. **May 8, June 10**

Avis Mae Rodney writes from Guelph, Ontario, Canada. She is a retired justice of the peace and a retired women's ministries leader for the Guelph Seventh-day Adventist Church. Avis is blessed to be a mother, grandmother, and wife of Leon, her dear friend and husband of more than fifty years. **Nov 25, Dec 29**

Debbie Saul-Chan serves as the director for Family Ministries and Children's Ministries in the Singapore Conference of Seventh-day Adventists. She lives in Singapore with her husband, Mark, and two daughters. She enjoys writing and sharing stories, floral arranging, photography, gardening, hiking, and traveling. She has written a weekly devotional, *I Will Go in Faith*, published in April 2022 by the Ministerial Spouses Association of Southern Asia-Pacific Division. **Jan 20, Nov 4**

Danijela Schubert, DMin (Fuller Theological Seminary), lives in Melbourne, Australia. Originally from Croatia, she has lived, studied, and worked in France, the Philippines, Pakistan, Papua New Guinea, and Australia. Dr. Schubert is happily married to Branimir. Together they have two grown sons. **Feb 25, Sept 10**

Omobonike Adeola Sessou is Women's Ministries and Children's Ministries director at the West-Central Africa Division of Seventh-day Adventists in Abidjan, Côte d'Ivoire. She is married to Pastor Sessou, and they are blessed with four children. Her hobbies include teaching, counseling, making new friends, and visiting with people. **Jan 21, Apr 11**

Minsozi Sibeso-Mweemba is a geologist working for the government of the Republic of Namibia. She is a wife and has a daughter, Joelle Esther. She serves as welfare departmental leader in her local church in Windhoek. She is active in women's ministry in her local conference, where she uses her passion to empower women, especially young women, for service to the underprivileged. She also serves with her friends in a community service ministry called Tabitha Helping Hand. **Oct 14, Dec 26**

Rose Neff Sikora and her husband, Norman, live happily on their hobby farm in the beautiful mountains of North Carolina, USA. She is retired from a forty-five-year career as a registered nurse, and she volunteers at Park Ridge Health. She enjoys walking, writing, and helping others. She has one adult daughter, Julie, and three lovely grandchildren. She desires that her writing will bless others. **Mar 5, June 28**

Christie Simon-Waterman is the mother of two beautiful adult daughters, Christa and Cayla. She has been married to Marlon for twenty-six years and lives in Perry Hall, Maryland, USA, but was born on the beautiful island of Trinidad and Tobago. She attends the Baltimore White Marsh Seventh-day Church. Her mother, Angela, was the person who taught her at a young age that God is love. Currently, she is the president of the Maryland Nurses Association. She loves sharing God's goodness by the way she lives her life and by daily sending out Bible verses to inspire others. Her hobbies include spending time in devotion with God every morning, getting a weekly massage, traveling, and teaching CPR. **May 9, June 18**

Yvonne Curry Smallwood enjoys spending time with God, family, and friends, as well as reading, writing, and crocheting. When she is not writing, you can find her in a craft store purchasing yarn for the many crocheted blankets and afghans she creates and donates to a local hospital and nursing home. Her articles and stories have appeared in several publications. She lives in Maryland, USA. **Jan 23**

Kristina E. Smith writes from Decatur, Georgia, USA. Once again, she is excited to be part of this amazing group of Christian women writers. In 2012, she self-published a book, *Thoughts From God's Favorite Child*, and has been defending that title ever since. Her hobbies include traveling, photography, cooking, reading, writing, and Sunday brunch. **Aug 7, Nov 28**

Melinda Smith is an attorney from Troy, Michigan, USA. She has been involved with Moms in Prayer International for many years. She enjoys walking, Bible journaling, and Bible study. **July 15**

Debra Snyder was born and raised in Massachusetts, USA, but God led her to Nebraska and her husband, Kevin, in 2012. She is the mother of three wonderful children, Jacob, Samantha, and Steven. She is active in her church and enjoys writing devotionals and spiritual poetry. Debra loves connecting with others and sharing what God places on her heart about her life experience and how He has led in her life. To learn more about her poetry or testimony, email her at dlsnyder70@gmail.com. **Oct 28**

Candy Monique Springer-Blackman is from the twin-island Republic of Trinidad and Tobago. She lives in the Republic of Barbados, her husband's home country. They attend the King Street Seventh-day Adventist Church, where Candy serves as Sabbath School superintendent. She is the administrative assistant for the principal of the Barbados Seventh-day Adventist Secondary School. Her passion is décor and design. **Mar 16**

Jill Springer-Cato lives on the lovely twin Island of Trinidad and Tobago with her husband and two young adult sons. She is a music minister who loves listening to local gospel music and is a member of the South Caribbean Conference Music Advisory. She is a church leader who is involved in all aspects of church life. **Oct 2**

Eva M. Starner, PhD, LPC, is an educator and counselor and has worked with families for more than thirty years. She is divorced and has facilitated her church's DivorceCare program (see divorcecare.org) since 2013. Her children are her greatest accomplishment. Dr. Starner has three adult daughters and grandchildren whom she loves and spoils as often as she can while she waits for the soon return of our Lord and Savior, Jesus Christ. **Aug 24, Dec 25**

Galina Stele, DMin, is the director of Women's Ministries at the General Conference of Seventh-day Adventists in Maryland, USA. Previously, she worked as a professor at Zaoksky Theological Seminary, as Ministerial Spouses Association division coordinator, and as director of the Institute of Missiology in the Euro-Asia Division, and then as a research and evaluation manager at the General Conference Office of Archives, Statistics, and Research. She is the wife of Dr. Artur Stele, the mother of a married son, and the happy grandmother of one grandson. Galina was born in Kamchatka but grew up mostly in Kazakhstan in the former United Soviet Socialist Republic. She loves reading, writing, gardening, cooking, and completing puzzles. **Mar 3**

Ardis Dick Stenbakken retired after serving as director of the General Conference Women's Ministries department. She edited these devotional books for seventeen years. Ardis lives in Colorado, USA, with her husband Dick (see BibleFaces.com) in a home with a view of one hundred miles of the Rocky Mountains. She keeps busy with church activities, Bible study, occasional oil painting, and family. Ardis is especially proud of her daughter, Rikki, and son, Erik, their spouses, and the four awesome grandchildren. She is passionate about women's issues and what the Bible says about women. **Mar 8, June 14, July 29**

Shantel Stephens has been a baptized Seventh-day Adventist for more than thirty years. She enjoys Bible journaling and teaching young people about God. She is learning daily to understand how God reveals Himself through life's circumstances. **July 12**

Rita Kay Stevens, a retired medical technologist, lives in Lacey, Washington, USA. She enjoys being involved with women's ministries in her local church. She is blessed to have enjoyed more than fifty years of marriage to Jim, a former church administrator and evangelist. They have two adult sons, a daughter-in law, and two grandchildren. She likes to travel, read, walk, and encourage others. **Mar 19, May 22**

Bianca Timşa Stoicescu is the editor of Radio Voice of Hope. She loves to write children's stories, play sports, read, travel, and socialize with people. **Sept 9**

Jeyarani Sundarsingh is a teacher who has served in Adventist mission schools for thirty-five years, being in charge of senior secondary students. Reading is her primary hobby, and recently, she has ventured into writing. Before retirement, she served as Women's Ministries director and Shepherdess coordinator of the Southeast India Union Section of the Southern Asia Division. She loves to serve the Lord in every possible way and strives to do her humble part to hasten His coming. **Apr 15, Oct 6**

Carolyn Rathbun Sutton, a former editor of these devotional books, lives close to her children in northeast Georgia, USA. Though widowed, she continues volunteering in her local church and as an ambassador for Adventist World Radio. She continues to find immense joy in creative writing, music, and following Jesus. **Apr 25, Sept 6, Oct 21, Dec 5**

Arlene R. Taylor retired from health care after decades of working with Adventist Health facilities. Still living in the Napa Valley of northern California, USA, she devotes her time and energy to brain-function research, writing, and speaking. **Mar 18, July 31**

Karin Tegeman comes from Sweden but lives in Switzerland with her husband. She is a social media manager with a master's degree in psychology. Passionate about faith and design, she creates inspiring Christian stationery. She is actively involved in the Inter-European Division Women's Ministries Department. She enjoys hiking and exploring the mountains in her spare time. **July 25, Dec 4**

Rose Joseph Thomas, PhD, is the associate director of Elementary Education for the Southern Union of Seventh-day Adventists. She lives in the USA and is married to her best friend, Walden. Rose has two adult children, Samuel Joseph and Crystal Rose. She has three happy and fun-loving grandchildren, Adrian, Gianna, and Aaliyah. Rose loves to read, cook, and spend time with family. **July 3, Sept 15**

Sharon M. Thomas is a retired public school teacher. She still enjoys working part-time. Other interests include reading, card making, quilting, bicycling, walking, playing piano, and being with family. **Sept 28**

Stella Thomas enjoys retired life by being involved in outreach ministries. She is blessed to live near her four wonderful grandchildren in Maryland, USA. **Mar 30, Nov 13**

Magdalena Toma is a pastor's wife. She and her husband live in Romania and have been working in the field for over twenty-nine years. They have three children. **May 19, Aug 23, Sept 27**

Lillian Torres is the associate Evangelism and Church Regeneration director for the Pennsylvania Conference. **Mar 13, Sept 7**

Nadia Trossero is the Education superintendent for the Pennsylvania Conference. **May 15, Nov. 5**

Ann Trout and her husband, Steve, enjoy spending time with their two adult children and their spouses and especially with their grandchildren. Ann teaches at a local community college and has published two devotional books. **May 26, Sept 16**

Sibongile Tshabalala is a passionate communicator, weaving words that inspire and uplift. With a bachelor's degree in journalism and communications, she masterfully uses media to empower women on their faith journeys. Her heart for mission work, both in her community and internationally, has deepened her belief in the transformative power of faith and service. Sibongile is dedicated to guiding young women to embrace their identity in Christ and encouraging them to pursue their divine calling with unwavering purpose and passion. **May 10, Sept 1**

Donna L. Tucker, a data analyst, is an active member and elder at Hillcrest Seventh-day Adventist Church in Nashville, Tennessee, USA. She has two adult sons and enjoys spending time with her two grandchildren. She loves to travel with her husband and has started baking outside of her home as a side business. She loves the Bible and has a passion for teaching Sabbath School. **June 7**

Rebecca Turner loves seeing how biblical characters and their stories are tied together, finding hidden gems of insight, and then sharing her discoveries. She retired in 2025 with more than thirty-five years of service at the Seventh-day Adventist General Conference. While working in Women's Ministries, she was blessed by friendships gained and inspiration received from the authors published in this book series. **Apr 1, July 19, Dec 22**

Ekele P. Ukegbu-Nwankwo is a Nigerian-born mother of four and a board-certified chaplain with a doctor of ministry in health care chaplaincy (Andrews University) and a doctor of naturopathy (International Institute of Original Medicine in Virginia, USA). She is a licensed life and health financial professional. She is trained in the counseling of singles, groups, and families. Her passion is to empower others for holistic, sustainable life transformation through the power of the Holy Spirit. Her published book, *Simple Solutions: A Trip Into Sustainable Well-Care*, is available on amazon.com. She lives in Columbus, Ohio, USA. **June 15**

Olga Valdivia is a published author and a passionate gardener who lives among the trees and birds surrounding a little white house located in Idaho, USA. This is where she lives and makes a living with her husband. **Mar 11, Apr 24**

Desrene L. Vernon is a communication practitioner. She has taught communication courses at public and private universities, including Andrews University and Washington Adventist University. She enjoys traveling, public speaking, reading the Bible, and playing Bible Bowl, Scrabble, and Words With Friends. **Apr 27, July 17**

Krupa Victor is Women's Ministries director at the Southern Asia Division of the Seventh-day Adventist General Conference. She lives with her pastor husband in Hosur, India. Mrs. Victor has served as director of Women's Ministries, Children's Ministries, and Family Ministries and as the Ministerial Spouses Association coordinator at administrative levels of the church (sections, unions, and divisions) for thirty years. **Apr 20**

Cecilia Voinea loves everything, including prayer, study, books, reading, translating, singing, sewing, cooking, creating, inventing, walking, gardening, helping people, taking care of small children, and traveling. She is grateful for the beautiful life God has given her. **Nov 22**

Faye Wadlington currently lives in Florida, USA, and loves to provide music therapy to those in hospice centers and nursing homes. Every fall, she picks apples and enjoys the season. She is eagerly waiting to go home with Jesus and wants nothing more than to meet you there. **Jan 29**

Barbara J. Walker is an ordained elder at her home church in Jackson, Mississippi, USA. She is the director of the South Central Conference Women's Ministries for Mississippi. She has served as director of the Morning Manna Prayer Ministries in the same conference since November 2012. **Dec 13**

Gyl Bateman Walker lives in Niles, Michigan, USA, and has three grown sons. She retired from working as a behavioral medicine nurse at a local hospital. Gyl enjoys pursuing her hobbies, being active in the local community and her church, and helping her sons at their local store. **Oct 17, Nov 11**

Lyn Welk-Sandy lives in Adelaide, South Australia. She has worked as a grief counselor and spent many years as a pipe organist. Lyn loves church music, choir work, and playing hand chimes. She enjoys nature, photography, serving where needed, and caravanning around the outback in Australia with her husband, Keith. Lyn is a mother of four, grandmother of nine, and great-grandmother of seven. **Feb 19, July 11**

Domaz Wellington lives in Mequon, Wisconsin, USA. She is a wife, mother, and grandmother. Domaz has been a professor in the area of human services and general education at Milwaukee Area Technical College for nearly twenty-five years. With the guidance of the Holy Spirit, she recently launched her private practice, Journey Within Christian Counseling, LLC, as a licensed professional counselor and marriage and family therapist in training. Domaz has served as a women's ministries leader, Sabbath School teacher, and in other capacities at Sharon Seventh-day Adventist Church. She and her husband enjoy serving God, serving the community, biking, listening to audiobooks, gardening, exercising, and traveling. **Aug 14**

Gail Wettstein is the mother of three adult children and a couple of adored in-law kids and wife to an amazing husband. She began texting her thoughts and wishes to them each morning to say "I love you" and to help them in their life journey. When they all encouraged her to write a book, she compromised and began her blog, *familytexts* (familytexts.wordpress.com). **Feb 13, June 23**

Avonda White-Krause is a wife, mother, grandmother, and great-grandmother living in Southwest Michigan, USA. She loves her family and friends, attending church, reading, NASCAR racing, computers, crocheting, and gardening. She taught special education for thirty-three years and is now retired. **Aug 1, Dec 20**

Jazmin Wildman and her husband, Carlyle, pastor the Allentown and Easton churches in the Pennsylvania Conference, USA. **Apr 18, Oct 1**

Julie Williams serves as a chaplain in Pennsylvania, USA. She holds a PhD in counseling psychology. Dr. Williams is a new author for the devotional book series. **Feb 1, Aug 13**

LaKeisha Williams, PhD, is an experienced educator and children's advocate. She enjoys traveling, singing, and writing in her spare time. Her husband, Dr. Toussaint Williams, is the executive secretary for the South Central Conference. They reside in Nashville, Tennessee, USA. **Feb 28, June 30**

Judith Woodruff Williamson is a retired dental assistant residing in Loveland, Colorado, USA, with her husband, Wes. She has a married son living in Alaska and a married daughter and two grandchildren living in Germany, whom she enjoys traveling to visit. Judith is also a porcelain artist who teaches painting classes. She volunteers at her church and loves her garden. **May 21**

Cyndi Woods is a mom of two and has been the wife of a wonderful, God-fearing man for over twenty years. She is a blogger and writer and has written articles for The Disability Network for over a year. Her heart is in ministry and leading others to know Jesus. She is also blind. Visit her on her *Clear Vision Ministry* blog at CyndiWoods.com. **Apr 6, July 1**

Gayle Cochran Wright resides in Cody, Wyoming, USA, with her husband, Ken, and cat, Fiona. When she's not working in customer service, she enjoys hiking, paddle boarding, gardening, and baking. As an amateur photographer, she loves to capture the local mountain scenery and amazing wildlife. She creates calendars and greeting cards as a way to share the surrounding beauty with others. **Apr 9, Oct 25**

Siew Ghiang Yan lives in Singapore. She's been helping to care for her mother for many years. **Oct 13**

Farzana Yaqub serves as the Children's Ministries director in the Pakistan Union, where her husband serves as treasurer. They previously served as missionaries in South Sudan. Farzana loves to train children how to become friends with Jesus. She counts it an honor to serve in God's vineyard. **Aug 20**

Tatyana Zvereva is a professional massage therapist and is married to a retired pastor. She served as the head of the music department in her church in Ukraine. When there was no one to play, she started playing the piano. Later, at the age of forty-eight, Tatyana went to music school, where she learned to play and arrange music for choirs and soloists. She loves to sing. They now live in Germany after fleeing Ukraine. **Nov 9, Nov 18**